Bent . . . Not . . . Broken

Bent . . . Not . . . Broken

A Story of Survival

J. C. KING

Archway Publishing books may be ordered through booksellers or by contacting:

Archway Publishing
1663 Liberty Drive
Bloomington, IN 47403
www.archwaypublishing.com
1 (888) 242-5904

ISBN: 978-1-4808-6161-9 (sc)
ISBN: 978-1-4808-6162-6 (e)

Library of Congress Control Number: 2018904256

Print information available on the last page.

Archway Publishing rev. date: 04/16/2018

CONTENTS

THE STORY STARTS

The year was 1976. I awoke with a start. My body was drenched in sweat. My head felt like it was on fire, as if somebody was sticking a hot poker into my skull. *Damn. The same nightmares. Will they never stop?* I asked myself.

I sat up and swung my legs off the bed. I lit a Lucky Strike, blew a large smoke ring, and blew a small one through it. Smiling, I remembered the first time I smoked. I was nine, and my friends dared me to take that first drag. I did. Coughing and hacking, I said, "*Yea, that was good.*"

Opening the nightstand drawer, I saw the gun. For several moments, I just stared at it as I had done so many times in the past. I picked it up and unlocked the trigger lock. I opened the chamber. It was fully loaded with six rounds of .38 caliber bullets. More than I needed. I closed the chamber and put the barrel in my mouth. I was just starting to put pressure on the trigger when my eyes misted over. Tears rolled down my cheeks and fell to the floor. My head felt like it was going to explode. I took the gun barrel out of my mouth. My mind screamed, *why did you do this to me?* Many times, I had asked myself that question, but I still did not know the answer. More than once, I had asked God to save me. *As a man, a husband, and a father, have I really done my best, or has it all just been make believe?*

I lay down, my legs dangling off the bed, the Lucky hanging loosely from my lips. The gun, still clutched in my hand, lay on my chest. My eyes closed, and my thoughts wandered back to the beginning. It seemed like so many lifetimes ago. *Haven't I been through rough times before? Haven't I survived?* But I knew that this time, I would need all my strength to make it through to the end. I drifted back into a deep and troubled sleep.

CHAPTER 1

The Beginning

It all began in a room that was dark except for the one lightbulb hanging precariously from the ceiling on an old, frayed cord. The shadows around the room loomed large and seemed to be alive with the slight back-and-forth movements of the light as they danced on the walls.

There was only one door leading to the hallway, and it was hanging crookedly on its hinges. The white paint was chipped and peeling, and there were deep marks in the wood where it had been punched and kicked many times. There were only two windows in the room. The first one was behind a rusty metal sink, which was filled with dirty dishes. The other window was over the radiator I was tied to.

On a previous occasion, I had scraped some of the scum off the bottom pane of glass. Looking through it, I could not see the street below or the sky above. All I saw was a brick building with some type of lit sign close to the window. I saw pigeons on the windowsill. Every time I tapped on the window trying to gain their attention, they just flew away.

At night, I heard them cooing to each other. I imagined they were cooing to me, telling me all about their day. I would coo back, and in my imagination, *they always answered me*. Because the adults in the apartment rarely spoke to me, except in anger and because there were no other kids, I spent many nights cooing to those pigeons while the adults would look at me like I was crazy, laugh, and shake their heads. No one knew I was building a relationship with animals that would carry me through into adulthood.

I saw dozens of roaches clambering in the garbage on the floor stacked against the wall. There seemed to be more and more of them as the garbage pile grew daily. My eyes burned and itched because the air was hot, sticky, and filled with a smoky haze. I saw them sitting at the table—two men and two women. One woman had long, curly, light hair and looked young and skinny. She had a cigarette dangling from her bright-red lips. Occasionally, she would look at me and put her fingers to her mouth and say hush to me. I saw one of her hands resting high up on the leg of the man sitting at her side.

Occasionally, he would press her hand hard against his crotch. She would smile and take another sip from her beer as she squeezed down. They were playing cards. A radio was playing jitterbug music loudly in the background. All four were talking at the same time, almost drowning out the music with their cursing. My ears were ringing, and I didn't know how they could understand each other.

The pains in my stomach reminded me of how hungry I was. I had not eaten since sometime very early that morning. The previous night, the same four had left a piece of pizza lying on the edge of the table, and that morning, I was able to reach it. Eating it hurt me because my lips were still swollen from the night before when the other woman had caught me trying to grab some leftover food on a small plate and had slapped me full in the mouth. Afterward, she gave me a small piece of bread crust with some green stuff on it. I did not know what it was, but I did not care. I ate it quickly before she changed her mind.

On a previous day while I was alone in the apartment, they had left an ashtray filled with cigarette butts and burned wooden matches on the edge of the table. I had tried eating butts before but did not like the taste of the tobacco, but because I was so hungry, I had sucked the heads off the matches. To my amazement, I found that I liked the sulfur taste, but it made my belly hurt. I had also found a beer bottle sitting on the radiator with a little beer still inside. Drinking it, I felt a cigarette butt slide down my throat. By that time, I was used to them, so I kept drinking.

Sitting on a blanket on the floor in nothing but an old pair of soiled underwear, I saw the rope tied to my ankle. It wasn't real tight, and I had tried many times to untie it, but I was never able to do so. The other end was tied to that radiator I had come to hate.

I was lying on that old blanket watching them play cards while holding that empty beer bottle I had been playing with. I was just about to fall asleep when one of the women cursed. I heard a dish hit the floor with a crash. Looking over I saw half of a sandwich lying among the broken pieces between me and the table. Nobody was paying any attention to it. Instead of standing up, I started inching forward on all fours. At that moment, I saw a flash of gray and heard the gnashing of teeth. I saw the biggest rat I had ever seen just inches from my face and standing over that sandwich. His bloodshot, dark-red, dead-looking eyes stared at me. His large, yellow-stained teeth were chattering so fast that they were just a blur. Every hair was bristling as its body shook uncontrollably. He was just daring me.

I grabbed that beer bottle, swung it hard, knocking the rat across the room, and reached for that sandwich. One of the males hit me in the face with the back of his hand and knocked me onto my dirty blanket. He picked up the sandwich, took a bite, laughed, and kept on playing cards. That was not my first or last run-in with rats or backhands. That is the only memory I have of my birth mother.

CHAPTER 2

First Lesson

Later that night, the four stopped playing cards. Each couple headed to separate bedrooms. Just as they were about to enter them, one woman stopped and walked to the table. She picked up something wrapped in newspaper and an open beer bottle with a little inside. She walked over to me, looked down, and said, "Here you go, kid. Enjoy it." She dropped the paper-wrapped item onto my blanket and handed me the beer. I set the beer down on my blanket and quickly unwrapped the paper. I found a ham bone with a little meat and fat still on it. The smell of that ham bone was as intoxicating to me as a bottle of wine is to an alcoholic.

Once before, I had seen rats chewing on bones in the garbage, so I knew what to do with that one. I chewed on it for the next two hours. When I couldn't get any more meat off, I sucked on the fat trying to get every ounce of juice I could. I drank some of the beer.

When I had to pee, I walked as far as that rope would let me and peed on as many of those roaches as I could, as they scurried away.

For years, the smell of that ham stayed with me and became my meat of choice.

The next morning, I was awake when one couple came out of a bedroom. The man was fully dressed, but the woman was wearing only panties and a bra. They were arguing and yelling at each other. They were drinking beer. The woman finished hers and grabbed another that was sitting on the table from the night before.

As she threw her head back to gulp it down, she fell over backward and landed on top of me. Uncontrollable laughter racked her body. She looked directly into my eyes and said, "God! You stink, kid."

The man was looking at her lying there with her legs spread wide. He said, "You look like the drunken whore you are!"

With an unintelligible growl, she kicked out with her bare foot and caught him right in the nuts. Moaning, he bent over grabbing himself and said, "To hell with you, bitch." He walked out the door and slammed it so hard that chips of paint fell to the floor.

She was still lying on top of me. Looking at me she said, "To hell with you too, kid." She got to her knees and wobbled over to the table. She used it to help herself up to her feet. She was still holding onto that beer.

The other couple came out of the second bedroom and tried to comfort her, but she would have none of it. Still holding the beer, she staggered back into her bedroom slamming the door behind her. She screamed out some muffled curses. I heard a dull thud and the breaking of glass against the door.

Shaking their heads, the other couple went back into their bedroom. They left their door slightly ajar. I could not see into the room, but I heard moaning, groaning, slapping, and squeaking sounds. Afterward, the male started snoring with that peculiar noise I had heard him make in the past. I heard a thudding punch. The female yelled, "Hey, asshole! How about me?" as his snoring turned to a grunt. As young as I was, about five or six, I knew they were playing a game, but I did not know what it was. I watched the rats and roaches while waiting for whatever was coming next.

For the rest of the day, I sat on the blanket with my back against the wall trying to think of what I had done wrong. I kept my legs drawn up tight against my chest. My chin rested on my knees. My biggest fear was that the rats would return and bite my toes off. I watched both doors hoping somebody would remember me.

That evening, the three of them left the apartment. The man was the last to leave. He opened a beer and put it and half a sandwich on the windowsill over the radiator. Looking down at me, he said, "Good luck, kid," and walked out the door. He turned the one light off, plunging the room into darkness. I never saw any of them again.

I hungrily ate the sandwich even though it tasted as if the bread had soaked up several bottles of beer. I was thirsty, but I knew the beer would make me pee again, and the room and my blanket already smelled like my underwear, so I waited alone, hungry, and cold.

In the darkness, I hugged my knees. A small shaft of blinking red, white, and blue light coming from that sign next door streamed its way in through one of those dirty windows. I watched rats and roaches battle for scraps in the garbage in their struggle for life.

That long night alone in the darkness, I learned my first lesson—no matter what life threw at me, I could survive.

CHAPTER 3

Those Same Old Feelings

The next morning, a woman and a man came into the apartment, took me away, and placed me in foster care. My treatment in the foster home was not much better than what I had experienced where I had been living. The front door of the house was solid wood, old, and painted bright red. The living room was filled with old, dusty, and raggedy furniture. The couch looked as if it had been used for jumping on. The back of it was sagging, and the four cushions were different colors and sizes. The stuffing was coming out through tears.

Two ripped, overstuffed chairs were well worn. Bare wood showed through the arms. An old, brown, round-top radio about as tall as me was blaring music. The wood floor was dull and scarred as if somebody had dragged something heavy over it many times. There were two windows with old, torn curtains that were closed; only a small amount of light came through the dingy glass. An old lamp sat on a three-legged table, but it was off. The room was eerie in the semidarkness.

The woman and man left me alone with my foster parents, who instructed me to call them Mr. Gibson and Miss Agnes. They sat in the two overstuffed chairs and made me sit on the floor in front of them while they went over the house rules. There were so many that I just kept nodding and saying, "Okay."

The most important rule was that I was never allowed to go into the kitchen or their bedroom. I already knew there were other kids in the house because they had told me about them when I had first come in, so I figured I would do whatever they did—follow their lead so to speak.

After they finished telling me the rules, they told me to go to my room. They pointed to it down a hallway. I walked in that direction and passed a small kitchen. The table was covered with dirty dishes. I saw two chairs and one small window. The glass was painted a dark color. Hardly any light shined through. The floor tiles were so dirty that I couldn't tell what color they really were. Most of them were cracked and chipped. There was one small lightbulb on the ceiling giving off a dull glow. The sink and cabinets appeared to be some type of a white metal with rust showing through. There was another stack of dishes with food stuck to them piled high in the sink. A white stove looked like it was made of the same metal the sink was. It had several white knobs on the front. A slight smell of gas tickled my nose.

I had been told that there was only one bathroom and that every morning after breakfast, each kid would have a turn but not until after our foster parents were finished with it. If during the daytime I needed to use it, I had to request permission first. On the way to my room, I peeked into the bathroom. The sink was hanging on the wall with only one faucet that had a continuous drip to it, leaving a green stain around the drain. The toilet bowl had a brown ring around it. It looked as if everybody in the neighborhood had been using it.

The seat was cracked in two places and stained badly. The first time I sat on it, I got such a pinch on my butt that it drew blood. When I showed it to my foster parents, they whipped me with a big, wide leather strap that hung on a nail in a hall closet and sent me to bed with no supper. I told them that I hadn't broken it, but they did not believe me.

Whenever I used the toilet after that, I never sat on the seat. I always raised it and sat directly on the toilet, which was always wet and cold and had hairs stuck to it. There was no tissue; we used sheets of newspapers that were stacked up on the floor beside it. They had told me that I could tear off only one small piece for wiping. The paper was stiff and tore very easily when wet. It was hard to flush, and if my foster parents heard me flushing more than once, they would yell or sometimes come in and swat me in the back of my head saying, "I have to pay for that water, you little bastard!"

If I got anything on my hands, I could wash them in the sink, but there was no soap and only cold water. The ink from the paper left black marks on my hands and butt, so most of the time, I did not wipe. There was an old, four-legged cast iron tub piled high with junk. I never saw it used the entire time I was there.

My foster parents were older than the two couples I had been living with. Both had long, unruly, gray hair and smelled like my blanket and underwear in my former home. They spent every day sitting in the living room in those chairs talking, arguing, and yelling sometimes at each other and other times at the blaring radio, which was kept on all day and night.

Mr. Gibson chain-smoked cigarettes, and Miss Agnes always smoked nasty cigars. Whenever I had to walk into the smoky room, I coughed profusely. Every two days, some kid delivered beer to them, which they drank morning to night. Mr. Gibson was so tall and heavy that when he was sitting in the chair, the cushion sank almost to the floor. He looked weird because his knees were up as high as his shoulders. When she was sitting in her chair, Miss Agnes kept her fat legs spread so far apart that the stench wafting from her was putrid. Whenever either one of them wanted to get up, we kids were called to help them.

Mr. Gibson's voice was low, gravelly. He was always coughing and spitting into a rag he kept shoved next to the chair's cushion. When he raised his voice, my ears vibrated and hurt. He always had his hands down inside his pants front and back scratching himself.

When Miss Agnes spoke, it sounded as if she were hissing her words as her tongue would stick out between her missing front teeth. What teeth she did have were stained yellow and rotten. She always looked and acted mad, and her hair was sticking out sideways so much that she reminded me of that big rat standing over the dropped sandwich that night.

She always wore the same old, thin dress that hung to her ankles. There were several holes in it, and one day while I was helping her out of the chair, one of her breasts popped out. It looked like a large, overcooked egg with a broken yoke. Her dark nipple was covered with hair. Looking at me, she gave out a girlish giggle and asked, "You like that, kid?" I shook my head no and walked briskly away.

Both were very strict. If we did not obey them, we got a whipping on our bare bottoms with that big, leather strap and were sent to bed with no supper. We ate only twice a day, so I tried very hard to behave. But for one reason or another, it seemed I ended up getting whippings constantly.

I had been told that there were two bedrooms, but I was never allowed to go into theirs. The door was always closed. I had to hold my breath when I walked past it. The smell coming from under the door made my nose burn and tingle.

Beside me, there were three older boys and one younger girl in the home. We all shared the second bedroom. The older boys were very demanding of the girl and me. They got to do everything first. Mr. Gibson or Miss Agnes always brought us our food, and we kids could eat only in our bedroom. At meal time, there was hardly enough food to go around. The older boys would eat first and leave the young girl and me scraps.

Usually at breakfast, all we got was soupy oatmeal with lots of lumps. After a time, though, I came to like those lumps because they gave me something to chew. Most of the time, it was cold and bitter tasting, and what little I did get usually had a fly or two in it. It was also gritty tasting; I never figured out why.

For supper, we usually got leftovers from our foster parents' dinner. They would scrape all their food together into one pan. Sometimes, they gave us only one or two forks or spoons, and at other times, they gave us no utensils depending on how much beer they had drunk that day. By the time we got it, the food was cold. That did not matter to me because I was so hungry all the time.

Sometimes, if Mr. Gibson and Miss Agnes fell asleep in their chairs, the older boys would steal food from the kitchen and eat their fill. They would hide the leftovers in our bedroom for later. Only once did I try to steal some of the hidden food. The three of them shoved me down and peed all over me.

It was summertime, and because of the heat in the apartment, the food would spoil quickly. On occasion just for fun, they forced me to eat spoiled food. One time, I threw up on one of the older kids when they were forcing me to eat some bad-smelling mashed potatoes that were covered with black stuff. That night, he tied me to my bed with some shirts and left me all night. When I told him I had to pee, he laughed and said, "Piss in your shorts!" Having done that many times in the past and having no other option, I did.

Our bedroom was small and did not have a dresser. There was one small closet, and all our clothes were bunched up on the floor. It did not matter because we almost never changed clothes. I had only one pair of shorts and no underwear; the one pair I had had been thrown away when I arrived. I had two short-sleeved shirts but no shoes.

The mattresses on the three beds were ripped; stuffing was coming out of them. There were no pillows; each bed had one old blanket. The one, small, dirty window had been nailed shut. Those same old feelings stayed with me. I thought everything was my fault, but I could not think of what I had done wrong.

CHAPTER 4

The Need

I was the youngest of the boys; the girl was younger than me. Rachel was a pretty, dark-haired girl who always looked at me with very big, sad eyes. She never smiled. She hardly ever spoke to anybody.

Because there were only three beds in our room, I slept with Rachael. Every night when we went to bed, she would hold my hand while falling to sleep. The next two older boys, Ron and John, slept in the second bed. The oldest boy was a mean, big, fat, redheaded kid named Paul. I guessed he was about thirteen. He slept in the remaining bed by himself.

Sometimes to punish me for whatever reason only he knew, Paul would sit on me until I thought I would die. It was hot, and I could hardly breathe. About every other night, he would slip into my bed and lie down between Rachael and me. He would push one hand inside my shorts and the other inside Rachael's panties. His hand was always sweaty as he roughly manipulated my penis. The first night he did that, I yelled for him to stop. He covered my mouth tightly and said, "Shut up. If you tell anybody, they won't believe you, and then I'll sit on you until you're dead." After he left, I held Rachael's hand as she cried herself to sleep. I believed him. After that first night, I never complained.

At times, the other two boys would take Rachael into the one closet we had for long periods of time. I did not know what they were doing to her, but I think in my heart I did. On those occasions, she would come out of the closet, walk to our bed with her head hanging down low, and just sit. I would always hold her hand. She never said anything; she just stared at the floor.

The two boys would laugh and whisper to each other looking and pointing. Sometimes, one would slap me on the head. I know now that during my early days, I started to develop a need to help others even if it meant I would be subject to physical abuse. There were not any places to hide, so Rachael's and my lives were controlled by these older boys.

CHAPTER 5

A Promise

Our foster parents' bedroom was next to ours, and some nights, we heard a lot of noise coming through the thin wall. It sounded like they were jumping on their bed screaming and growling at each other. Ron and John laughed and snickered. I saw Paul with his hands inside his pants; he had a strange look.

Sometimes in the morning, Paul would stay in the bathroom so long that I had to pee in our closet. Once, Miss Agnes opened the door to the bathroom and yelled, "Oh my God!" She walked in slamming the door behind her. They did not come out for a very long time. When Paul did come out, he had a sheepish look. He lay on his bed with his back to us and stayed there all morning, not even bothering to eat breakfast.

After that, occasionally, Miss Agnes would come into our bedroom and tell Paul to come with her. They would walk into the bathroom and spend a long time there. He always came out and went directly to his bed without saying anything.

Once, we heard him sniffling and crying. The other two boys started laughing and making fun of him. Though Paul was mean to me, I started to feel sorry for him. I made a promise to myself that I would never let anybody see or hear me cry.

CHAPTER 6

Hurt the Ones I Love

Other than our bedroom, the only place we could go was the backyard and then only with permission. It had a tall wood fence with barbwire along the top. Our foster parents had three big angry dogs they kept in the yard. Even though we were allowed there, I never went out there alone.

Every time somebody came to the house, they made all of us go into the backyard and stay there until the people left. It was a mess—nothing but dirt, rubbish, all kinds of old junk, and dog shit everywhere. On one occasion, Paul made the other boys hold me while he forced shit into my mouth. He tried to make me swallow it as he held his fat hand over it. Luckily for me, Mr. Gibson called us into the house, and I was able to spit it out. That is not a taste you easily forget.

Once, he picked me up and threw me into the middle of those dogs, which always barked and growled at us. He laughed as he did so. They bit me several times. He told our foster parents that I had been tormenting the dogs and that they had just been protecting themselves. I told them what had really happened, but they did not believe me and gave me a bare-bottom whipping with that strap. I was sent to bed with no supper. Nothing was said or done about the bites.

A few days later, I snuck out a large piece of newspaper from the bathroom, and when all of us went into the backyard, I wrapped some fresh dog shit in it and brought it into our bedroom. I kept it hidden in my shorts until the next morning. When Paul went into the bathroom, I smeared it all over the frame of his bed. Many times, after that, he would ask, "Who keeps farting? Whoever it is, stop it. You stink!" I told only Rachael what I had done, and for the first time, she gave me a huge smile and a little hug. He never found the reason for the smell. I felt good about what I had done.

As time passed, I started withdrawing into a black hole that had no bottom. For many years, I was shy, soft spoken and most often did not rely on anybody except myself. I spent many hours just watching people and their behavior. I hardly ever cried; I kept everything inside. I was learning at an early age not to trust anybody and was forming attitudes.

I was in foster care for about a year. It was a traumatic time; I received many beatings and was abused. Nobody ever believed me when I told the truth, so lying became second nature.

One day, a woman showed up and took me away. I left there with the clothes I had been wearing—a well-worn pair of shorts, a threadbare, short-sleeved shirt, no shoes, and no underwear. The woman was holding a baby. Nothing was said to me, so I never asked any questions. We rode for many days. I silently looked out the bus window wondering what was next.

My early days altered my life and caused me to hurt the ones I loved the most. That knowledge haunts me to this day and makes me weep.

CHAPTER 7

Love and Respect

I felt a terrible pain. I opened my eyes and realized the Lucky had burned down to a nub and was searing my lips. I quickly put it out in the overflowing ashtray on my nightstand. I put the trigger lock back on my gun, put it in the drawer, and headed downstairs to the bathroom.

I saw our dog, Smokey, lying by the front door. He wagged his tail as I walked past. I glanced at the clock. It was 2:45 p.m. My kids were late, and I was worried. I took a quick shower, dressed, made a cup of coffee, and sat at the table to wait. Smokey walked over and rested his chin on my leg. He looked up at me with his big, sad, brown eyes and gave out a soft whine. I patted his head and said, "Don't worry boy. They will be home soon." He too knew they were late.

The thermometer outside the window read twenty-two degrees. It was snowing again. I realized why they were late coming home from school, but that made me only more anxious. My wife was working the day shift at a hospital. Times were hard, and we needed the extra income. I watched the kids while she worked.

Just as I was finishing my coffee, I saw the school bus stop at the end of our driveway. Smokey started barking; he had heard it too. I opened the door, and he ran as fast as he could to meet the bus. I laughed watching his short legs trying to carry him swiftly over the packed snow that had turned to ice. He reminded me of the coyote chasing the roadrunner; only Smokey was slip-sliding all the way down the walkway.

I saw my two girls get off the bus just as he reached them, jumped up, and licked their faces still barking with excitement. The girls rubbed his head and ears. They looked so damned cute in their winter coats and white hats pulled down over their ears and tied under their chins.

My oldest, walked up the cleared driveway toward the walkway with Smokey right on her heels. My youngest, headed across the front yard struggling to walk in the waist-deep snow.

I smiled and thought of how she took life just as I had done when I was her age, as if it were an adventure. Her sister waited on the front steps for her. As they entered the house with Smokey happily beside them, they asked me to drive them to their girlfriend's. I knew it was a couple of miles away. I asked, "Do you girls have any homework?" As one, they said, "No Dad, I did it in school." I knew they were lying. They just wanted to leave before their mother got home. They knew that would not fly with her.

Laughing, I told them to go change and I would warm up the car. They ran upstairs looking at each other laughing and giggling as if they had gotten away with something. I smiled and headed out to the car.

A few minutes later, the girls came out of the house running toward me—no hats. I saw their long, blond hair flowing behind them. They were laughing and happy. I took a deep breath and thought; *God, if you're real, please make sure I do the right thing for my kids. I want them to remember all the good times too.*

They got into the car. I listened as they talked to each other laughing and giggling. I thought about; all the new beginnings they would experience in their lives, and I hoped they would make it through unscathed. I vowed to always treat my wife and kids with the love and respect they deserved. Little did I know how difficult that would be.

It was now the spring of 1948. It was like waking from a long sleep. I opened my eyes. I was lying on a bed. The air was hot and sticky. The room was bright; sunlight was streaming through an open window. I was wearing a pair of clean shorts but nothing else.

I got up and walked into the next room, the kitchen. I saw a pretty, dark-haired woman. She was short; she was not much taller than me. She smiled and asked, "Are you hungry, son?" Not saying anything, I sat at the table and saw the most food I had ever seen. I said, "Wes's eat." I looked at the woman and asked, "Are you my Mama?" She smiled. "Yes, son, I am."

That was my first memory of grits, eggs, and homemade biscuits. The grits were hot and had lots of lumps. The eggs were on top of them, runny and gooey, and they were covered in what she called country gravy, which was thick and greasy and had lots of meat in it. The eggs were small. Mama said they were from bantam chickens. I had no idea what a bantam chicken or even what an egg was, but I didn't care. The biscuits were light, fluffy, and very big. Mama spread homemade butter and blackberry jelly on them for me. I ate and ate until my little belly was filled almost to bursting.

After I had eaten and drunk a big glass of raw, cold milk, I asked Mama where we were. She told me Mayville, Louisiana. She said we were living with my aunt Josie and her husband, my uncle Buck.

While she was cleaning up the breakfast dishes, I explored the house. I saw a large, freestanding metal sink with no running water in the kitchen. A metal bucket sat to the side of the sink. Mama was using water from it to wash the dishes. Next to the sink was a big box with a lid. I opened the lid and saw a huge block of ice with some food sitting on a shelf on top of it. On another shelf, I saw some milk in a jar. Mama said it was called an icebox. She said that once a week, an iceman delivered another block of ice. She chipped off a small piece for me. I sucked on the ice chip as I continued to explore.

Two open-shelved cabinets on the kitchen wall contained all kinds of boxes, bags, and cartons of food. I walked down a short hallway and came across two small but clean bedrooms each with a bed covered with white spreads. Next to the beds were nightstands with lamps.

I looked in the small closet and saw a pair of clean shorts and a clean, simple, black dress hanging neatly. I spotted a pair of black, short-heeled shoes in the middle of the floor. Lying on the nightstand in the bedroom in which I had awoken was a book.

An old but clean couch, with no rips, sat in the front parlor as did two cushioned chairs with a shiny wooden table and lamp between them. I saw another room through two open windows. I walked out the door and discovered that the other room was in fact a porch that had been recently painted gray; I could smell the freshness.

The walls of the porch were wood, only about as high as my chest, and painted white. It had not been recently painted, but the paint was not chipped or cracked. The porch was screened in from the wood almost all the way up to the top, where more wood came down to meet the screening.

I saw a white fan hanging from the ceiling; I felt a slight breeze from the slowly turning blades. There was no noise. I remembered seeing a fan my foster parents had had. It was gray and sat on a table next to them in the living room. It made a loud whapping sound as it turned from side to side. They had it for only a short time when it started making more noises, and it was moving very slowly only to one side. Mr. Gibson had picked it up, walked into the bathroom, and threw it into the tub with all the other junk, and that is where it stayed.

I had never seen screening before. The only open window I had encountered did not have any screen. I tried pushing my finger through it, and when I could not, I thought, *what a strange-looking window. I wonder how you open it.*

I saw my first porch swing. It looked well used but in very good shape. The chains holding it up were shiny. I jumped onto the swing, but my feet could not reach the floor. I got off, pushed it hard, and jumped back on. I loved it. For a few minutes, I just sat in the swing and enjoyed the back-and-forth sensation.

I sat in one of two white rocking chairs and started rocking back and forth hard. Pretty soon,

I had it rocking so hard that I almost fell off the front. At one point, the back of the chair hit the wall and made a loud bang. I jumped off and ran to the swing looking for a place to hide. I thought for sure Mama would come out and hit me, but to my surprise, she hollered from the kitchen, "Be careful, son."

The yard was fenced in and had a wooden front gate but no barbwire. A walkway led up to the front steps. A tall tree beside the front steps and the walkway had some type of round and green items lying on the ground underneath it. I picked one up. I had never smelled or seen anything like it. I bit into it and found it to be hard and very bitter; it made me pucker up.

Later, I asked Mama what it was, and she said, "That's a persimmon. If you eat it before it ripens, it'll be bitter and will make your mouth pucker up." I did not tell her I had already tried to eat it; I was still trying to spit the bitter residue out of my mouth.

Beside the front gate was a green bush with small, orange-colored fruit hanging from the limbs. I bit into one and found it to be slightly sour, but the peel was kind of sweet; I liked it. I picked and ate a handful. Later, I asked Mama about them also, and she said, "They're cumquats. When they're ripe, you can eat the whole thing peel and all." Again, she did not ask, so I did not tell her I had already eaten some.

On the side of the house were three big trees with small, dark-colored items hanging from the branches. I climbed up into one of the trees and tasted one. It peeled easily. It was soft and tasted very good. I ate several, skin and all. Mama later told me, "They're called figs. You should pick them only when they turn a dark color. That means they're ripe, and you can eat the peel and the inside." As before, I did not tell her I had already eaten some. If she did not ask me something specific, I never volunteered any information about what I was doing or had done.

Behind the house was a small, rock-lined pool. Water was running continuously into it from an old iron pipe coming out of the ground. Mama said, "It's called an artesian well. That's where we draw water for drinking, bathing, cooking, and cleaning." I cupped my hands and drank some. It was very cool and had a metal taste from that iron pipe. I liked the taste.

There were a couple of fish in the pool. I caught one, but it struck me with its sharp fin on its back. I dropped it fast and asked Mama about the fish. She said, "They're catfish. We keep them in the well to keep the pool clean. They eat stuff off the bottom and sides." Again, I did not tell her I had caught one or that it had stuck me.

I had not seen a bathroom; when I asked her about it, she said, "If you have to go, there's an outhouse way out back in the barnyard." She explained that they didn't have an indoor bathroom or running water and that the outhouse was a small building with a door and a seat with two holes so two people could use it at a time. She said, "The poop goes into a pit under the outhouse." I had never seen or heard of one before, so I decided to see it the first chance I got.

Later that afternoon, I met Aunt Josie and Uncle Buck. She was a small, dark-haired woman and looked a lot like Mama. She smiled, laughed, and cackled a lot. She showered me with a hundred wet kisses and left bright-red lipstick all over my face. She was very nice but smelled overwhelmingly of sweet perfume.

Uncle Buck was a short, skinny, dark-haired man. His clothes hung on him as if they were two times too large. He also laughed a lot, and he smelled like beer. He patted me on the head and said, "Welcome, young Johnny." He gave me a hug, and his slight beard stuck into my cheeks.

I asked, "Is that my name?" He said, "It is."

I liked my aunt and uncle, but with all the kissing and hugging, I did not trust them. Afterward, I ran into the bedroom where I had been sleeping and hid under the bed, fearing one of them would come in, drag me out, and beat me or whip my bare bottom for some unknown reason. I lay there for a couple of hours; nobody came looking for me. Eventually, Mama called me out of the bedroom for supper. Again, I saw the most food I had ever seen. I sat and said, "Wes's eat."

Years later, relatives told me that as I was growing up there, every time I walked past a table, I would say, "Wes's eat." Mama, Aunt Josie, and Uncle Buck all laughed at me as we began to eat.

After that initial meeting, I did not see a lot of Uncle Buck. Mostly, I saw Mama and Aunt Josie. Every time Uncle Buck came into the house, he would grab Mama and start hugging and kissing her and dancing around the front parlor with her. She would laugh and giggle like a young girl. She reminded me of that time Miss Agnes giggled when her breast popped out.

Whenever my uncle hugged and gave me wet kisses, he smelled of alcohol. I always tried to stay away from him. I was distrustful of him even though he was always nice to me.

My world was changing fast. There were not many rules, and I spent most days by myself. I spoke only with Mama and Aunt Josie. When other people would stop by, I would go someplace and hide. Except for my cousin Drew. I really liked him.

CHAPTER 8

Rules and Consequences

I had only two rules. The first was that at bedtime, Mama would make me sit on our bed and she would read to me from the book on the table beside the bed. She called it a Bible, and when she finished, I had to kneel and say prayers. I didn't know what they were, so she taught me the Hail Mary and the Our Father.

The other rule was that on Sunday, she and I would walk about five miles to church. On the way, we had to cross a bridge over a small river. Whenever we did, I would always run ahead of her, so I could get right down to the riverbank to look for gators, snakes, turtles, and anything else that was around. She always made sure I had a clean shirt and shorts even though I did not have any shoes. She would yell at me because she was afraid I would dirty them before we got to church.

There was an iron cattle guard across the road right in front of the bridge. I could usually find a nice snake there, and I was always catching one and poking it at her. I would laugh when she would run away. She was short and had very short legs, but boy, could Mama run fast even though she was barefoot too. She had only one pair of shoes, which she wore on Sunday, but she carried them to church. She said she did not want to scuff them up.

At church, she would sit on the front steps and put them on. In church, she made sure I sat quietly, and if I didn't, she would pinch me hard on my bare leg. I always saw other kids, but I was very distrustful of them and never spoke to them.

One Sunday when we were at church, a little girl behind us started talking to me, but I ignored her. Mama grabbed me by the ear and pulled me out of the pew and right out of the church. Once outside, she said, "Don't talk with little girls. They're dirty and nasty."

She said that I should not be talking at all in church and that God was mad at me. I told her I wasn't talking, only the girl was. She didn't believe me. She pulled down my shorts right on the front steps and whipped me.

Every Sunday on the way home, we usually stopped at a drugstore in downtown Mayville and I would get a 5¢ ice cream cone. I always got three scoops: chocolate, vanilla, and strawberry. But on that day, she told me all the way home how bad I had been, and that God would punish me. I did not get ice cream that day. I learned that even telling the truth sometimes had bad consequences.

CHAPTER 9

Curious

As the days passed, I eventually wandered into the barnyard. I was amazed and curious. I saw some gray stuff hanging from trees. I didn't know what it was. I tasted some; it was dry, stringy, and bitter. I asked Mama what it was, and she told me that it was moss, that it grew wild all over the south. She said folks used it for bedding and stuffing for pillows and other things.

I saw animals I had never seen before—chickens big and small of many different colors. There were geese, ducks, two cows—one brown and one black and white—a red horse, turkeys, cats, and a big, mean white rooster. He attacked me the first time he saw me. He was almost as tall as I was. He had huge dewclaws that looked like small knives. I wasn't prepared for his attack, and he laid me open with them. I learned very quickly to stay away from him. He had been around a long time and was very smart. He stalked me whenever I ventured into his domain, and he laid me open on many other occasions.

The old, rambling barn that was half falling was filled with many smells. Some of them were nice while others were very pungent. I saw chickens laying eggs in nests. At first, I was very curious and just watched them sitting there clucking. At one point, I went over and raised the ass end of one, so I could see where the egg was coming from. Shoving my small hand in, I tried to see if I could pull one out. After another one got up and left, I walked over and saw a couple of eggs in the nest. Remembering how good tasting the grits and eggs were and having seen Mama crack them open, I cracked one open and sucked the yoke out. It was raw and did not taste the same as what Mama had cooked for me, but it did not taste bad, so I ate it. I ate the second one also. There was no one there to stop me.

I saw other eggs in nests, so I started gathering them and throwing them at the outside of the barn. I liked the way they stuck and then dribbled down. The hens would peck and try to stop me, but I learned quickly they were no match for me. Except for that old, white rooster, I was top dog in the barnyard, and I loved it. I was the biggest there, and I could do whatever I wanted.

Mama never came outside, and Aunt Josie only rarely, and that was to milk the cow or gather eggs. To keep her out of the barnyard, I started gathering them for her. At one point, she told me to slow down on them because we could not eat them that fast. I did, but she didn't know how much fun I was having with them. By then, I was throwing them at the animals.

One day, I saw a large cat holding a kitten in its mouth. I thought it was trying to kill or eat the kitten, so I threw an egg at it. The egg hit the cat and broke all over its side. It dropped the small one and started licking the egg off. I ran over and stomped on it, and it started flopping around on the barn floor, blood oozing from its nose. I stomped it again, and it quit moving. The kitten ran away before I could catch it. I was sure I had saved it from a horrible death. Of course, years later, I learned that that was how mother cats moved their young.

Behind the barn, I saw two very large pigs in a small, fenced-in area. They were lying in black mud; my nose stung from the stench. It smelled like the backyard at my foster parent's house, only worse.

Some small pigs were inside the enclosure, and more were running around and rooting in the dirt outside. I was able to catch one of the outside ones. I picked it up by the hind legs, and it squealed so loudly that the other small ones ran back into the pen and the large ones got up and starting grunting, snorting, and butting the fence with their snouts toward me. I punched the piglet several times and threw it into the pen. It ran over to one of the large pigs, which smelled it and rubbed it with its snout.

All afternoon, I wandered around the barnyard tormenting the animals in one way or another. I caught several baby chicks, placed them in an old bucket, and put a piece of wood over the top. I sat on it. After a while, I saw that they were dead, and I just left them in the bucket.

I walked farther out back to where the cows and horse were grazing. The horse came right over to me and started nibbling on my hand. Her lips were very soft and hairy. When she stuck her tongue out, I hit it with my fist and laughed when she snorted and ran off.

At dusk, Mama called me in for supper. I thought for sure I would get a whipping for my bad treatment of the animals, but to my surprise, she told me to eat. She never asked me what I had been doing, so I did not tell her. It was a new world for me, and I felt I was in charge and could do whatever I wanted with no consequences. I was letting my anger manage my life. I was also hearing voices that were telling me to do these things. I started talking back to them.

I wandered around the barnyard every day. I found the outhouse Mama had talked about. It had two holes just as Mama had said. It smelled awful.

One day as I was sitting on one of the holes, I saw that there was no paper but that there was a catalog with page missing. I had not liked using newspaper before, so I did not want to use pages from that book. I threw it into one of the holes.

One day, I went into the barn and saw a large black-and-white animal. I thought it was a big, fluffy cat. It was holding an egg between its paws and lapping the yoke out. I was so mad that I ran at him yelling and throwing an egg I picked up on the way. Of course, I missed, and he ran under a wall and out into the backyard into a woodpile. I hunted him for about an hour, but he never came out.

I told Mama what I had seen. She told me to be careful because it was not a cat. She said, "He's a wood pussy, and if you mess with him, he'll spray you with awful-smelling stuff from his ass." She said that if I got sprayed, it would take a long time for the stink to wear off and I would not be able to come inside the house until it did.

A few days later while hunting for it, I stepped over some wood and stepped right on its back. I had a piece of wood in my hand. He squealed, and I hit it hard before it could spray me. It never ate any of my eggs again.

CHAPTER 10

Eating Crawfish

Every day, I ventured farther into the swamp behind the house. One day, I came upon this slow-running, muddy, and foul-smelling ditch that reminded me of the outhouse smell. I saw frogs, minnows, and large, round, black things with short tails swimming around. I grabbed a couple and ate them. I found them to be juicy but bitter. When I got home, I asked Mama what they were. She said they were tadpoles and would turn into frogs later. She told me to be careful around them because snakes, lamprey eels, and crawfish ate them, and they would bite me too. She also said we could eat crawfish; she explained what they were and how to catch them.

The next day, I asked Mama for a piece of bacon. By then, I had started carrying a small knife I had slipped out of the kitchen and kept hidden under the house. I did not know if I could find the same spot or not, but I did.

Years later, I realized I had an uncanny way of finding my way around. It did not matter if I was in a deep swamp or a strange city; it seemed I had built-in GPS.

At the ditch, I cut a small sapling, tied a thin vine to the end, and tied the piece of bacon to the vine. I had never seen a crawfish, but Mama had told me all about them. I was excited because this was something else I could eat.

I flipped the bacon into the water, and it floated. I did not know what to expect, so I just sat and waited. After a couple of hours, nothing had happened, so I pulled the bacon in, ate it, and went home. I told Mama all about my crawfishing and that I had not gotten even a bite. She laughed and said, "You need to keep the bait on the bottom in the mud."

The next day, I got another piece of bacon and headed into the swamp. On the way, I stepped on something sharp. I sat and saw that it was a rusty old nail on a board. It had gone through my foot and was sticking out by my big toe. There was not a lot of pain, but it just looked funny, and there was a little blood coming out by the nail hole. When I pulled it out, it felt as if the inside of my foot was coming out with the nail. I kind of liked the sensation.

I threw that board far away, so I would not step on it again. I wondered if crawfish would like blood, so I rubbed some on my bacon. I got to that smelly crawfish hole and wondered how to make the bacon sink to the bottom. Mud was clinging to my feet and between my toes, so I thought, *Why not the bacon*? I balled it up and covered it in mud, and the mud held the bacon on the bottom.

After a while, I started pulling the bacon in every few minutes. One time, I noticed that a small part on one end was bare of mud and it looked as if something had been gnawing on it. The next time I pulled it in, I had my first look at a crawfish.

Through trial and error, I learned to use just enough mud to make the bacon sink but leave some exposed. I learned how to very slowly bring them in close to the bank and grab them before they escaped. After I had four or five in my pocket, I caught a big, fat one. He looked enormous to me, about an inch and a half long with two big claws. Remembering Mama had said that they were good eating, I snapped its head off, sucked the juice out, and ate the tail, shell and all. Not much to the claws, though. I snapped them in two and sucked out what juice there was. When I got home, I told Mama all about my crawfishing. I never did tell her I was eating them raw; she never asked.

After a few days, my foot was hurting, and it was getting bigger. I noticed a red line starting at my foot and running up my leg ending just under my shorts. I thought I should tell Mama. When I showed her, oh how she cried and prayed to Jesus, Mary, and Joseph to save me. She asked them to please don't let me die. She was carrying on so much that I totally forgot the pain. I said, "Mama, I'll be okay. I'm sure those people you are praying too heard you and will come and save me. I won't die like that wood pussy did when I hit it on the head after I stepped on it out back in the woodpile."

Mama stopped crying, laughed at my wood pussy story, and started whistling. She made me soak my foot in boiling-hot saltwater. That hurt worse than the nail pain, but the red line started disappearing. The next morning, my foot felt better, and that red line was gone. She told me that Jesus, Mary, and Joseph had come in the night and helped me, so I wouldn't die. I was sure proud of Mama. She knew just whom to call on for help. She sure called on them many times for me in my life. I believe I needed all the help I could get.

I started going deep into the swamp every day. Some days, I would see wild pigs and cows. One day, I tried to catch a piglet, but those big pigs would have none of that. I had to climb a tree to get away from them. They kept me treed until after dark. The cows ran as soon as they saw me. When I asked Mama about the animals running wild, she told me that people let them roam free in the countryside and once a year they would go out, catch them, and put their mark on the babies so everybody would know who owned which. Sometimes, they would catch, kill, and eat them. I asked her, "If I caught one, could we eat it?" She said, "No, because it would belong to somebody else even though it might not have a mark on it yet. That would be stealing." She warned me to stay away from them. She said that they were very protective of their young and that the old ones had long, sharp teeth called tusks. She said, "They don't eat meat, but they could cut you up bad and kill you."

One day just to see if those pigs would really kill me, I caught a cat in the barn, cut its throat with my knife, and found those pigs. I threw that cat right in the middle of them. There was a lot of squealing and grunting, and they ate him quickly. I realized they would eat meat. I decided to stay away from them.

One day, I came upon this old, muddy canal about a mile back through the swamp. When I asked Mama about it, she said, "Be careful because it's very deep and you don't know how to swim." She said that the alligators there could grab me, pull me into the water, and drown me. Then they would eat me. Even though I had not seen one, I told Mama, "I'm not afraid of any old alligator." Mama just laughed and said, "I know you aren't."

CHAPTER 11

A Lesson Learned

It took me a few days before I saw my first gator. I was sitting on the bank of the canal and watched as it took one about two hours to stalk, catch, and eat a bird that was walking around in the water eating frogs and small fish. That gator grabbed that bird by its body and pulled it underwater. After a few minutes, the gator came back up and flipped that bird around until the head was going down its throat first. It looked funny to me because that bird had a very long neck and real long legs. The feet were sticking out of his mouth after the rest of the bird was out of sight.

I learned a lesson about patience from that gator and have used that lesson throughout my life. Many times, when I felt like giving up on something, I would think about what it took that day for the gator to catch that bird, and I continued with what I was doing. I have always been grateful to that gator for the lesson.

I returned one day just as it was eating a big fish. I told Mama about the gator eating the fish and asked how it could have seen it because the water was so muddy. She told me it was probably a catfish because they were all over the canal and sometimes swam on top of the water. I asked her if they were good eating, and she said, "The best along with hushpuppies."

The next day, not having a hook as Mama said I needed, I fashioned one out of a rusty nail. Going out to that stinking ditch, I caught a big crawfish. I went to the muddy canal, cut a vine, and tied one end to the bent nail and the other to a low-hanging tree branch. I jammed the crawfish onto the nail and dropped it in the muddy water. I left it there figuring I would come back the next day and check it.

That afternoon, I was coming in from setting that line not thinking of anything except telling Mama what I had done. The rooster ambushed me as I entered the backyard. Boy, what a bloody mess.

A few days later, I was coming from that old swamp again and saw my cousin Drew waiting for me washing his hands, which were bloody, at the well. "Hey, little man, let's go in and get supper."

I went in and asked Mama what was for supper. She was happy. "Chicken," she said. "That old rooster won't bother you anymore."

My cousin was just standing there smiling. Normally, we did not eat roosters, but that was the best chicken and dumplings I ever ate.

The next morning, I was up early. It was warm even though the sun was not up. I put on my shorts—no shirt or shoes—and quietly slipped out the back door into the dark shadows. I wanted to check that line. I had also seen a large snake coiled up lying in the tall weeds at the top of the canal. I figured if I returned as the sun was coming up, I could catch it while it was still sleeping.

I arrived just as the sun was breaking over the treetops but did not see that snake. As I quietly searched through the tall weeds, I saw my vine moving fast back and forth. Something was on it. I shinnied down the muddy bank, grabbed the line, and pulled it in. A big, long snake had the bottom half of my catfish in its mouth. I grabbed the snake behind its head and pulled it off my catfish. I looked in his mouth and did not see fangs, just rows of teeth, so I knew it was not poisonous. Mama had told me that poisonous snakes had fangs.

I held on tight to that snake. I did not want to waste that fish, so I unhooked it, took it to the top of the bank, and hid it in some weeds so gators would not find it. That's when I saw another large snake, the same one I had seen the previous day. I put the one I already had around my neck, grabbed the new one behind its head, and checked its mouth. I didn't see any fangs, so I wrapped it around my arm and headed home, deciding to take the catfish with me.

When I walked in the back door with one snake around my neck, the other around my arm, and the catfish in my hand, Mama ran out the front door yelling, screaming, and carrying a big butcher knife. I had never seen her run so fast. In no time, she was down that dirt road onto the bridge over that old muddy canal yelling, "Get them damned snakes out of the house." Those snakes and I smelled of the canal mud. I never could understand how the canal mud and the outhouse mud could smell alike; they were about a mile apart. Years later, I realized that the ditch I was catching crawfish in ran right past the outhouse over to the canal.

I wanted to skin and eat those snakes, but Mama said no. She cooked me some grits and eggs but not before I took those snakes out back and turned them loose by the barn. That night we ate the catfish. Mama rolled it in yellow cornmeal and fried it in lard along with some homemade hushpuppies in an old iron skillet. Mama was right; catfish and hushpuppies were the best eating.

After that day, occasionally, I would catch one, play with it for a while, and put it back under the barn. One day, I caught a baby chick and fed it to one of the snakes. I sat there for two hours as it ate it. Sometimes I would run over a baby chick with an old wheel barrel.

My Aunt Josie had an old brown cow. Sometimes, I would watch while she milked it sitting on a three-legged stool. I sure liked fresh milk. One day, I planned to get some of that milk. I went up to the cow and fed her some tall grass I had just pulled from the front yard. She really liked it. For several days, I kept feeding her that grass. Pretty soon, I saw her looking over the fence at me whenever I was in the barnyard, and I swear she was wagging her tail and waiting.

One day when nobody was watching, I took an extra big handful of that grass, climbed over that fence, and laid the grass on the ground in front of her. As she started to eat it, I slipped between her rear legs, grabbed one of her teats, and started sucking. It must have startled her. She jumped forward and kicked me in the head. I was knocked to the ground. She raised her tail and shit all over me. I could not believe it. I just lay there watching as she ran off. I thought, *I really wanted some of her milk*.

CHAPTER 12

First Meeting

In 1976, I was working the midnight-to-eight shift patrolling the south end of Sandy Town. It was raining hard. My partner and I had just gotten coffee. We parked at the top of Brant City, a section of Sandy Town. A car pulled up beside the cruiser with the driver's window down. I rolled down my window. The driver said, "Officer, I'm almost out of gas. Could you follow me home to make sure I get there?" My partner, an old-timer, yelled, "We don't run a taxi service you know!"

I had been in the department for only a couple of years, but I told my partner, "We are tonight." I turned back to the driver and said, "Sure, mister. We'll follow you." He said thanks and started driving toward the Green Harbor section of town.

I rolled up my window and started following him. My partner told me in no uncertain terms how angry he was. He said, "You better learn that people will use you as much as they can and give nothing in return." I said, "That's life. I'll deal with it when I need to."

We followed the driver home. I pulled up behind him in his driveway, and he walked over to the cruiser and thanked me. I told him he had a brake light out and should get it fixed. He thanked me again and said he would.

As we drove off, my partner said, "You should have written him a ticket." I replied, "You're a cop. You have a ticket book. Why didn't you write the ticket?"

He put his head against the headrest and closed his eyes. I continued patrolling the area.

About a week later, I was patrolling in the same area but with a different partner. I spotted the same car, and the taillight was still out. Putting my blues on, I pulled him over. I got out and told him that was my second warning about his taillight. He apologized. He was obviously embarrassed when he told me he had lost his job and did not have the money to fix it. It was about 2:00 a.m. We talked for about fifteen minutes on the side of the road. I asked what he was doing out so late. He said he had been visiting a sick friend. I was skeptical, but I kept talking to him. It didn't take long before I began to like him.

At the end of our conversation, I told him, "Tomorrow, I'm coming over to you house, and you and I can look at that light, okay?"

"You know how to do that?"

"How hard can it be?"

So, it was agreed.

The next day, I drove over to his house. He was waiting for me. We took the bulb out, and I drove him to an auto store. I bought him a new bulb. We went back and put it in his car. We checked it out and found that it worked. He was very grateful.

I met his live-in girlfriend. She thanked me for not having written him a ticket the night before. I learned that they had a mutual friend who was dying of cancer and that they were trying to spend as much time as possible with him. She said that she too had recently lost her job. I spent about two hours just talking with them, and I went away feeling good.

Having ridden and having talked with the old-timers in the department, I knew they had seen a lot more than I had, but I thought that their judgments were at times from another era. Times had changed, and they should change with them. Laughing to myself, I thought, *Hell will freeze over before that happens*.

The driver and I became fast friends. I came to know him as Lucky. He got to know my family, and they thought he was nice and very funny. They loved to listen to him talk. They said he sounded just like a duck if one could talk.

One day after he left my house, my wife said, "I'm glad Lucky's your friend. He really likes you." Sitting in my recliner, I put my head back and reflected on another first meeting so many years ago and how that one had turned out so differently.

One morning in the summer of 1949, I was watching Mama cook breakfast. I saw she was very happy. She was whistling the same tune she always whistled. It must have been the only one she knew. I asked her why she was so happy, and she said, "Your daddy's coming to visit."

Nobody had ever mentioned him, so I did not even know I had a daddy. I watched as Mama started making the biggest breakfast I had ever seen her cook. She made a tall pile of hotcakes. I slipped one off the top, and Mama just laughed and said, "Now don't you fill up before your daddy gets here because he loves to eat."

A short time later, a large man came in through the front door. He looked bigger than any man I had ever seen, even Mr. Gibson. I asked, "Are you my daddy?" He stopped and just stared at me for a few moments. His eyes got glassy and weird looking. He hit me on the side of my head with the back of his hand. "Don't ask stupid questions." He knocked me to the floor and continued walking into the kitchen where Mama was. He never said another word. Memories of long ago also involving backhands came rushing up in me.

In a few minutes, he and Mama walked out of the kitchen, his arm around her, and into the bedroom where Mama and I slept. He slammed the door shut. Still on the floor where I had landed, I sat up, placed my back against the wall, drew my knees up against my chest, cradled my hurting head in my hands, and rested my chin on my knees. I heard loud noises coming from the bedroom. Mama was giggling as she did when she and Uncle Buck were hugging, kissing, and dancing around the room. I heard my daddy say, "Try harder. Try harder."

Right after that, aunt Josie came and took me onto the front porch. We sat in those rocking chairs with me rocking hard. I asked her about my daddy, but she kept saying "hush now, Johnny. Don't talk!" My first meeting with my father was less than I had expected.

I did not see Mama or my daddy again that day. Later, aunt Josie went into her bedroom and shut her door. That night, without supper, I slept on the front porch in the swing.

The next morning, I was up early. Running into the kitchen, I saw Mama cooking grits and eggs. She was whistling. I asked her where my daddy was. "Gone," she said.

After that, we saw him only occasionally. Whenever he was around, he did not talk to me much; he just kept hitting me. One time, I asked him, "Where do you live?" He said, "I told you, don't ask so many goddamn questions!" He picked me up, threw me onto the couch, and walked away. I could not figure out why he had done that. Again, I did not know what I had done wrong, but I never cried.

I started killing more animals again, mostly the baby chicks because there were so many of them and easy to catch. Sometimes, I would twist their heads off and watch as they flopped around on the ground, blood spurting out of their necks. Other times, I would tie their legs together, throw them into the outhouse, and watch as they would be slowly sucked all the way down into the shit.

Sometimes, I would catch frogs, cut their legs off, throw them back into the water, and watch them drown. After a while, I snuck large kitchen matches out of the house. I would make a small cage of branches and twigs, put chicks and whatever else I could catch in it, and burn them to death.

Remembering how I had liked to suck the heads off burned matches, I started again. I still liked the taste. One time, I caught a feral kitten, tied a piece of string around its neck, and hanged him from a tree limb. I sat emotionless and watched that cat slowly die twisting and clawing at its neck. I was angry but did not know why. Most of the time, I saw only Mama and Aunt Josie and occasionally my cousin Drew. He was always soft spoken and very nice, and I liked it when he was around. He would take me riding in his truck; I enjoyed those times.

Nobody ever asked me what I was doing or where I had been, so I never told them anything. I started cooking and eating things I caught. I continued to spend all my free time in the swamp by myself. I enjoyed being deep in that black hole; it was becoming very comfortable and enjoyable, but most of all, it felt safe.

CHAPTER 13

First Friend

One day, I decided to go in a different direction than I had gone before. After walking for what seemed a couple of miles, I came upon a boy sitting on the bank of a pond. He was fishing with a cane pole, and he had a couple of nice fish lying on the bank beside him. He was bigger and a little older than me. Memories from my past with Paul welled up in me. I crawled into some bushes, sat, and watched him. I was ready to run if I had to. He caught a couple more, nice fish, packed up all his gear, picked up the fish, and headed off.

The next day, I cut a nice sapling, tied a vine to it, and tied that rusty nail to the other end. By that time, I could catch as many crawfish as I wanted by hand. All I had to do was grasp leaves, weeds, and mud on the bottom and throw them on the bank. I spread them out and found lots of crawfish hiding in the mixture. I caught a pocketful and headed over to that pond.

I sat in the bushes and waited for a while. Not seeing anybody, I walked to the edge and hooked one of those crawfish, and flipped it into the cool, clear water. I sat and waited for a bite. I wasn't sitting too long before I heard someone say, "Hello." Startled, I dropped my pole, jumped to my feet, and started to run away. I saw it was the same boy from the day before. I thought I was in for a beating for fishing in his spot just as Paul would have done if he had caught me in his spot. He said, "Wait! I won't hurt you."

I am not sure what it was, but something in his voice stopped me from running. I turned to face this new threat. I looked at him; he was grinning. He sat at the edge of the pond and said, "Let's catch some fish." He unraveled his line and cast it. That cane pole made a loud *whap* as it hit the water. Not really understanding this behavior and feeling a little curious, I walked back and sat about ten feet from him. As I was adjusting my crawfish on the nail, he looked at it and laughed. He asked, "Don't you even have a real hook?" I replied, "I've caught lots of fish on this old nail!" Lying still came easy to me.

He laughed and started making small talk. Mostly, it was him talking and me listening, not saying anything. After about an hour, he had caught four nice fish. I had had several bites but had caught none. He got up and looked at me. I jumped to my feet almost falling over backward as I started backing away, not saying anything. He smiled and said, "Hey, how about we meet here tomorrow and catch some more fish?" I stared at him saying nothing. He walked off leaving all four of his fish where they lay.

As soon as he was out of sight, I grabbed those fish, made a stringer out of a slender branch I cut, and headed home. I arrived just before dark and told Mama and Aunt Josie all about how I had caught the fish in that muddy old canal and how I had to keep fighting off a big old gator. I told them how I made mud balls and threw them at him to let him know I meant business. I said, "That last one hit him right in the eye, and he went underwater and never came back. I don't think that old gator will be messing with me again."

Mama and Aunt Josie laughed and said, "I bet he won't." Mama told me to clean the fish and she would cook them for supper. I cleaned the fish, and Mama fried them in lard and made some of her great hushpuppies. We had a great meal with a big glass of warm milk. Mama usually gave me warm milk with a little honey at bedtime. She said, "It will help you to sleep." To this day, I still drink that warm milk and honey.

The next morning, I was up before daylight. I went to the muddy creek behind the outhouse and caught a handful of crawfish, stuck them in my pockets, and headed to the pond. I waited for a couple hours, but the boy never showed up. That time, I had brought more crawfish and had lots of bites but caught only one nice, fat fish.

Every day for a week after that first meeting, I went back to that pond. One day, just when I was about to give up, the boy came back. He sat near me and started talking about how his mother had been in bed sick all week and his father was working on their farm every day. He had not wanted to leave her alone. He brought me a beautiful cane pole with line, bobber, and a real hook. I did not know what to say. I just smiled and nodded. He did the same thing. He was becoming my first friend.

We talked for hours mostly about fishing and the swamp. I told him about Mama and Aunt Josie. He did not know either. Nobody had ever just sat and talked to me like that, not even Mama. He said he lived on a farm with lots of animals including some milk cows. He said his mother and father sold milk, eggs, and fresh vegetables that they grew. He said they also grew sugarcane. I asked him what that was, and he explained it was a stalk that grew like corn and they made cane syrup and sugar from it. They also grew corn to feed the cows. He said his name was Ray, and he invited me to his house, which was way through the swamp and on the other side of a creek. I told him I would think about it and would let him know the next day.

I still had doubts. That night, I talked to Mama about Ray and his family. She told me she did not know them very well but from what she knew, they were a nice, God-fearing family.

The next day, I met Ray at the pond. We fished for a while, and then he showed me how to get to his house. I went there; it was big and had a huge kitchen with running water. His father was a big man with a deep voice. He shook hands with me saying he was glad to meet me. I was very impressed. His mother was a big woman also, but she had a high, shrill voice. Both were very nice.

Ray took me all around their farm and showed me a mule with which they plowed their fields. Late that afternoon, his mother fixed supper and asked me to eat with them. We ate fried chicken, creamed corn, corn bread, and collard greens. It was delicious. By the time I got home, it was dark, and Mama and Aunt Josie were just going to bed. They never asked me where I had been or what I had been doing. Mama read the Bible to me, and after saying my prayers, I told her goodnight and crawled into bed. Within moments, I was sound asleep.

Ray and I started spending a lot of time together. I started helping around their farm, and I could tell his father really appreciated my help. I was starting to feel good about myself. Many days, I would eat breakfast, lunch, and dinner at their house. The food was simple but hot and good. In the morning, his mother would get up early and bake biscuits. Afterward, she would gather eggs, make grits, and fry bacon. Even today, whenever I smell bacon frying, my memory shoots back to those happy days long ago.

At lunch, there was usually some kind of vegetable soup with fresh, homemade bread. Sometimes, Ray and I would take his father's rifle out into the woods and shoot squirrels and rabbits. I learned very quickly how to skin both. His mother would make chicken and dumplings, only sometimes, there would be other meats instead of chicken. Supper was the best. After supper was over, we'd sop leftover biscuits in cane syrup mixed with homemade butter.

One day, Ray asked me if I had ever ridden a mule. I told him I'd never ridden one and in fact had never seen one before then. That day, we got on Jasper the mule and headed into the swamp with his father's rifle. It was rough going, but that old mule just plodded along as if it were nothing; he seemed to know the way.

After a while, John told me he was taking me to a secret place that only he knew about. About an hour into the swamp on old Jasper, we came upon a mound and a group of large rocks piled together. In the middle was a small cave. The opening was tiny, and we almost had to crawl to get in. Going inside, Ray lit a small fire in the middle with wood that was neatly piled in a sort of pit. As the fire got bigger, he sat on a rock and invited me to do the same. He asked me, "What do you think?" I told him it was awesome and asked, "How did you find this place?"

He said that one day while he was squirrel hunting, he shot a deer, which ran off. He followed the blood trail to the rocks, where he found the deer dead. He said that he saw the small opening. Exploring farther, he found the cave. Inside, he said, "I saw something I had never seen before." He got up and walked to the back telling me to follow him. He brought a lit stick from the fire and showed me drawings on the wall. It showed stick people killing all sorts of animals; I could not even imagine what some of the animals were.

He said he had asked around and learned that hundreds of years ago, people lived in the swamp and made homes in caves and made drawings of their lives. He had found stones chipped into arrowheads and spearheads. He said he had never told or showed that place to anybody and begged me to do the same. I promised, but he said, "A promise is not enough."

I asked him what else I could do to make him believe I would keep my promise. He told me how in the old days, for two people to become close and completely trust each other, they had to become blood brothers. He said each one would cut himself and they would mix their blood together. They would then know everything about the other, and nothing or nobody could ever break that blood bond. Not really understanding but by then completely trusting Ray, I told him "Okay." We made small cuts on our thumbs and mixed our blood.

Leaving the cave that day, I felt very old and wise. Over the past seventy-plus years, I have kept my promise to Ray and have never spoken of that cave to anybody until this writing.

With all the animals Ray had on his farm, he also had an old, one-eyed cat that stood about a foot high. He called him Bob because he had a short, bobbed tail. He had one ear that was only about half regular size and looked as if something had been chewing on it. The other ear was missing, and hair had grown over his ear hole. Ray said he had just shown up at the back door one day with a dead rabbit in his mouth and had never left.

Sometimes, he would follow us into the swamp when we would go rabbit and squirrel hunting. After skinning and cleaning them, we would feed Bob the guts. One day, Ray and I were sitting on his back porch when we saw that old cat coming from the swamp. To our astonishment, he was herding a family of live rabbits. He brought them right up to the porch, looked at us, and started meowing. We burst out laughing. We gathered the Mama rabbit and her babies and took them back into the swamp, where we turned them loose. I was learning from Ray about kindness toward animals. After that, I would go out of my way to hunt and find wild animals. When I caught them, I loved to play with them and sometimes raise the babies until I set them free.

I admired a lamp in Ray's living room. Ray told me that he had made it. I couldn't believe it. He told me how when he was younger, his father had taken him way back in the swamp and they cut a cypress knee, a part of the tree growing up out of the swamp water. They brought it home, dried it, and made the lamp. I asked if he would help me to make one for my Mama. He did, and I made the most beautiful lamp in the whole world. I kept that lamp until moving in 2002.

Mama and I lived with Aunt Josie and Uncle Buck for about a year. I did not even know we were leaving. One morning, Mama packed her and my clothes in an old, scarred suitcase that she put a small chain with a small lock around, and we left. It seemed Mama and I walked on dirt roads for hours. I did not get to say goodbye to Ray or his family, and I never saw them again, but I have never forgotten him and the kindness he showed a small, unknown white boy he had met in the swamp.

CHAPTER 14

Turtle Soup

Mama and I moved in with my aunt Bees, my uncle Lew, and my cousin Jimmy Joe. Aunt Bees was Mama's sister. She was a large woman who seemed to be cooking all the time. She made the best pies and biscuits I had ever eaten, but of course I never told Mama that. She was a genuinely warm and loving woman, and I immediately liked her.

Uncle Lew was a big man, bigger than my daddy. When he spoke, it was soft but meaningful; you knew exactly what he meant. We saw my father only about two or three times a year. If I knew ahead of time he was coming, I would go into the swamp or stay right beside Uncle Lew. My father would still hit me for no apparent reason. I never understood why he hit me, but he never hit me when Uncle Lew was around. I still would not cry, but I never told anybody either. Without Ray around, I again became quiet and withdrawn.

Their house was clean and neat just like Aunt Josie's had been. There was a kitchen with running water from a well. There was a dining room filled with a big table, lots of chairs, and a cabinet that held all the dishes. The front parlor was filled with soft chairs and a big couch. I loved to climb up on the couch and jump over to the chairs. There were two tables with lamps on them. There were three bedrooms. The room Mama and I slept in had a large bed with four big posts on it. Sometimes, I would climb them and swing around on them, just like you see monkeys do.

There was a night table with a lamp and Mama's Bible, which she continued to read to me at night. There was also a dresser with many drawers and a small closet. Sometimes, I would hide in the closet when my father came. There was also a regular closet with a door. There was a bathroom with a tub. When we needed hot water, we would heat it on the stove.

Their yard was fenced. Out back were a few farm animals—a couple of cows, caves, a horse, a mule, chickens, and some ducks and geese. My uncle and cousin were very friendly and warm hearted, and I spent as much time as possible with them. My cousin even took me to downtown Mayville to the Tchefuncte River to go fishing a few times. He showed me how to make a bobber out of a lily pad bulb. He also showed me where the big gators were and told me to be very careful around them.

He had a punching bag nailed onto the top of a fence post in the side yard; he would punch it every day. I could not reach it, so I would climb up on the fence and punch it while hanging onto the post. He would laugh then pick me up, so I could punch it as he did.

Uncle Lew would take me hunting for snapping turtles in the swamp way out back. He had this long pole with a sharp hook on the end. He would reach into the mud, hook a turtle, and pull it out. He let me try it a few times. The turtles were too big for me, but he always helped. He would praise me when we got one out. Back home, he showed me how to cut the turtle out of its shell. We would make a fire in the backyard and make snapping turtle soup right in its shell. He would just laugh when I would try it and make a face. He would ask, "You like it, Johnny?" I would never say no to him, but it was terrible.

I loved Uncle Lew and my cousin Grant Jo. My cousin had a sister, Laura, who did not live with them, but I met her a few times. She was always nice to me, and I liked her too.

Right off the dirt road coming into Aunt Bees house was a great crawfish hole. There were times when I would catch ten or twelve. One day, Uncle Lew said that if I would catch and bring some crawfish home, we could cook and eat them. Nobody had ever told me to cook crawfish because I had never asked. After that, I started bringing them home. Uncle Lew and I built that fire right in the backyard, and we boiled those crawfish in a turtle shell.

When there was no rain, it would dry up, and I would walk way back in the swamp to the creek that fed the hole to catch crawfish. That was where I first saw wild hogs. Remembering my experience with hogs, I was very careful. They were mean. They treed me a couple of times when I was messing with the little ones, which squealed when I grabbed them. One time when I was back there, I sharpened a stick with that same old knife from Aunt Josie's to try and kill one, but I couldn't get close enough without them charging me.

Whenever my father came around, I stayed away from him; hate and fear were in my heart. Uncle Lew and my cousin had jobs, so whenever they were not around, I spent time in the swamp by myself as I had done before. I was very comfortable in those surroundings.

One morning, Grant Jo told me he had joined the army and was leaving. I asked him if I could go with him. When he said no, I cried so hard that he hugged me. He kept talking and talking to me, but I couldn't stop crying. He picked me up and let me punch that old punching bag. I finally stopped crying, but I stayed beside him all that day.

That night, I cried myself to sleep. The next morning, I watched him leave. I did not see him again until 1975. When I returned married and with two daughters, he was old, fat, and almost bald. That night just before I fell asleep, tears rolled down my cheeks as I remembered those lost times so long ago.

Not long after Grant Jo left for the army, Mama told me that Uncle Lew was in the hospital. I kept asking and asking for her to take me to see him, but she always refused. I never saw Uncle Lew again.

A short time after that, we moved again. Many years later, Mama told me he had died a few years later from cancer.

CHAPTER 15

The Ghost

One day, I met Jason, a young boy who lived next door, and we became friends. While crawfishing one day in my favorite crawfish hole, I told him about some of my fishing experiences. Later that day, he asked me if I wanted to go fishing the next day. I told him yes. He said there was a graveyard at the edge of the swamp behind his house where we could dig up some worms. We planned to meet at his house right after daylight the next morning.

The next day just after daybreak, I walked to his house with my old cane pole. He came out to meet me. He grabbed his cane pole, and we headed to the graveyard. There, he pointed out one spot, next to a grave stone, saying he had dug there in the past and had dug some big, fat worms. He walked into the bushes and came back with an old, broken-handled shovel. It did not take us long to fill our can with the biggest earthworms I had ever seen. We walked five miles to the Tchefuncte River in downtown Mayville to fish.

Day after day, Jason and I dug for worms in that old graveyard. One day, Jason and I were standing in our backyard talking about digging for worms and going fishing. Mama, who was hanging clothes near us, said, "You boys need to stop digging for worms in that old graveyard!" I replied, "But Mama, that's where we get the big, fat ones." Mama never said anything else. Shortly after that, we left for our favorite worm hole.

We had just started digging when we heard frightening, ghostly noises coming from behind us. Looking back, we saw a huge ghost behind a headstone two rows over from where we were digging. It seemed to be hanging in midair. It terrified us so badly that we could not move. As our bodies trembled in fear, pee ran down our legs and onto our bare feet.

The ghost started coming our way. After what seemed an eternity, we ran all the way home still peeing in our pants. I could not find Mama, so I told Aunt Bees about what we had seen. She laughed and told us that the ghost of an old Creole fisherman protected the graveyard and that we should never dig for worms there. Jason and I never dug there again. Later that afternoon, I told Mama about the ghost. She repeated the story Aunt Bees had told me and said, "If he catches you, he'll take both of you to hell."

Many years later, Mama had a good laugh when she told me and my wife that on that day, she had climbed the fence in the backyard, run through the swamp, and reached the graveyard before we did. She hid behind a gravestone, and when we got there, she came out with a sheet over her head making all those scary, ghostly noises.

After telling us that story, occasionally, I saw Mama smiling at nothing. I thought just maybe she was thinking of the day she made two barefooted kids pee in their pants.

CHAPTER 16

Old Haunts

Late one night in 1977 while I was working the midnight-to-eight shift, I was riding alone in the cruiser. About two in the morning, I was dispatched to a domestic 911 call. As I arrived, another one-man cruiser pulled in behind me. We went to the door and were met by a woman screaming and yelling at us to lock up her boyfriend. She was so upset that I could hardly understand what she was saying.

The boyfriend was standing about two feet from her. We separated the couple, and I took the woman to the kitchen to take her statement. She said that she had worked the four-to midnight shift at a hospital and had gotten home about one that morning. She said her boyfriend watched her six-year-old son while she was at work. She said she was in the process of buying the house and would sometimes work overtime because she needed the money. Her boyfriend was disabled and was on Social Security Disability.

That night when she got home, she went to check on her son and found him lying on his bed crying. She said she hugged him and asked him what was wrong. At first, he kept telling her nothing was wrong. After repeatedly asking him, her son finally said that her boyfriend had hurt him. She got angry. "How did he hurt you?" After she repeatedly asked him, he finally told her that her boyfriend had played with his penis and had hurt him. He said that the boyfriend told him, "You better not say anything to your mother or I'll hurt you really bad." She asked him how long that had been going on, and he said, "A long time. I'm sorry, Mama."

She said she had awakened her boyfriend and asked him about it. She could tell he had been drinking. He denied it. They argued, and he hit her. He said, "Yeah, I did it to the little bastard. He wouldn't shut up tonight, and he kept crying and asking for you."

With the mother present, I asked the young boy, "Did somebody hurt you tonight?" He said yes, that his mother's boyfriend had bitten his penis. I arrested the boyfriend and advised the mother to take her son directly to the hospital to get him checked out and then come to the station to make a full, signed statement. She said she would.

As I was transporting the boyfriend to the station, he was acting and talking as if it were no big deal. He said, "I don't know why she's making such a big deal about this. She told me that one time, she had had sex with a sixteen-year-old boy, so what's the difference?" I looked at him in my rearview mirror and with disgust asked, "Do you have any idea how long that child will remember this?" He replied, "Bullshit. He's a kid. He'll forget it by tomorrow, and when she buys that house, they'll forget this ever happened just as I've forgotten things in my life."

I jammed on the brakes. Because he was handcuffed from behind, he went flying forward and hit the wire cage between the front and rear seats. He screamed in pain. I turned and saw red lines crisscrossing his face. I said, "Sorry about the waffle face. A black dog ran out in front of me, and I had to put the brakes on fast." That old black dog has helped many policemen across this land over the years.

After that, he never spoke again. For the remainder of the ride back to the station, my thoughts returned to those times so many years ago. I knew that he was wrong and that some old haunts are never forgotten.

In the summer of 1949 shortly after Uncle Lew went into the hospital, my father showed up. Mama packed that same old suitcase. We got into his car and left. My father drove us to another house, dropped us off, and left shortly after that. It was a month or more before I saw him again.

We moved in with my Aunt Rosie and Uncle Ed. They lived in a small house in downtown Mayville. Betty Ann was their daughter. By then, I was six going on seven. Their house was very small. It had a kitchen and living room area, two small bedrooms, and an outhouse. Mama slept on an old couch in the living room, and I slept in one of the bedrooms with Betty Ann. I think she was about thirteen.

Every night, Mama would come in and spread a blanket over us. After she left, Betty Ann would put her hand inside my shorts. During those long nights, she pulled, sucked, kissed, and bit my penis and made me do similar things to her female parts and breasts. My thoughts would return to Paul. It seemed so long ago that he had threatened me and had done to me what she was doing. Just as Paul did, she would always say, "If you tell anybody, they won't believe you, and then I'll bite your penis off." For emphasis, she would bite my penis real hard. As with Paul, I believed her, and I never told anyone.

Eventually, my penis was hurting, and my right testicle was so sore to the touch. Mama noticed my pain. When she asked me what was wrong, I told her only that my penis hurt. She took me several times to see my cousin Drew, who was not a doctor. While examining me, he asked if anybody was doing anything to my penis. I always told him no. Mama asked me pointedly if Betty Ann had been hurting my penis. I told her no, as well and very emphatically.

We lived with my Aunt Rosie and Uncle Ed for only a short time. After a while, my penis stopped hurting, but my right testicle continued to hurt for years. I pushed the abuse further and further down each night along with everything else I was experiencing. It seemed to fit nicely into that black hole. I never spoke of any abuse until shortly before I wrote this book and then only after a lot of begging by my wife, to talk to her.

CHAPTER 17

Our Own Home

One day, my cousin Drew showed up driving his old Ford pickup. Mama packed that same old suitcase, and we got into the truck with me riding in the back as I usually did.

Our next move was into an old, metal-roofed house that had a fence around the whole property with a large gate at the driveway. Just like all the other houses in the area, we had a metal cattle guard in front of the gate. Years later, I learned that it was our own home my father had bought from my cousin. The house was twelve feet wide and twenty feet long.

The outside was just rough boards for the walls. It had a front and rear door. One window was in the kitchen, and another was in the bedroom. There were no inside walls, just rough-cut two-by-fours that were the back of the outside walls. There was no attic, just walls that went all the way to the roof.

In the kitchen was an old wood stove and a small table with two chairs. Next to it was a very small room with nothing in it. On the other side of that room was a bedroom with only one bed and nothing else but an old coffee grinder nailed to the wall. Sometimes, I would stand on Mama's bed and play with that old grinder. Mama would just laugh and ask, "What are you grinding up now?" I would say, "All kinds of critters."

Off the bedroom was a lean-to room where I slept on an old army cot. There were no sheets or pillow, just an old wool blanket. My mattress was made of burlap stuffed with moss; it smelled bad. I saw right through the cracks of the boards on the walls and floor into the yard and underneath the house. It had no running water or electricity. Our neighbor, Miss Joyce, had a well in her backyard with a hand pump. Mama would send me over to pump a bucket of water and drag it back to the house for cooking, bathing, and cleaning. We had an outhouse with only one hole.

We had very large trees in the yard. I found brown nuts on the ground and saw green ones on the trees. One day, I cracked one open and tried eating it. To my surprise, it was very good. I asked Mama what they were, and she told me they were pecans. After that, I started exploring the property. Way out back of the house, I found thick brush with no way through it. By then, I knew my cousin Drew lived on the other side of our property. Every day, I would cut a small path through the thick brush with the same old knife until I reached the back of his property. One day, I noticed some berries hanging from a tree by the fence I climbed to get into my cousin's yard. I stood on the fence post and started eating them. They did not taste too bad, just kind of sour. I kept eating and eating. Pretty soon, I felt dizzy and fell off the fence post into a blackberry briar patch. As I landed, I heard a familiar rattling sound. It was a big rattlesnake. Still feeling woozy, I saw him coiled about three feet from my head. I knew from having watched them while living with Aunt Josie that they could strike quickly.

Under her old barn were several rattlesnakes, and once, I watched as one struck a chick, killed it, and ate it whole. I rolled quickly to my right just as the snake struck; it missed my head and recoiled quickly; it prepared for another strike. I jumped up, climbed the fence, and ran to my cousin's back door. Entering, I saw my cousin and his new wife just sitting down to eat. Forgetting about the snake, I looked at the food and said, "Wes's eat." My cousin laughed and said, "Sit down, little man, and let's eat."

My cousin was always good and kind to me. He was like the father I should have had. He was gentle; he spoke quietly and always treated me like a son. He called me little man. He had an old, blue Ford pickup, and he would take me everywhere with him. He owned some property and cows far away on Brewster Road, also known as Bootlegger Road. Whenever he went out to his farm, he would take me. He always let me ride in the back of his pickup. He would drive slowly along the dirt roads; I saw snakes in the ditches slithering away as we passed.

Whenever we went to his farm to milk and feed the cows, one of his neighbors would come over bringing an old, ugly, reddish-brown dog with one blue and one brown eye. I was always amazed at how easily that dog would herd those cows right up to the barn for my cousin. His owner told me that he was a good cow dog but was an even better hog dog. He said he hunted raccoons at night with the dog. I asked him what the dog's name was, and he said, "Hootie."

My cousin's cows were all inside a fenced area. Cousin Drew would never let me go inside that area because there was a bad bull in there. On one occasion, I was standing just outside the fence when suddenly something very rough went up my neck and onto my head. Not knowing or caring what it was, I was over that fence in a second. Once on the other side, I turned and saw an old black-and-white cow just standing there chewing her cud. I realized she had licked me. My cousin yelled, "Little man, get out of there!" Everything had happened so quickly that I had forgotten about that bull. Turning I saw him charging me as fast as he could. By that time, he was almost on top of me; I raced to the fence. My cousin was running our way yelling at the bull, which was snorting and grunting right behind me.

Out of nowhere, that dog latched onto the bull's nose. He went down almost at my feet. The bull got up, and the dog stood between me and him. My cousin arrived and chased the bull off. I hugged the dog so hard that he started choking. My cousin asked, "Are you all right, little man?" I told him I was. I asked, "Did you see what that dog did?" He said, "I sure did," and he gave the dog a hug. I told him that a cow had licked me, and I had jumped the fence in fright. He laughed and had me climb the fence as he went back to feeding and milking the cows.

Every time we went to the farm after that, the dog would stay with me. Most of our time was spent in the woods looking for anything we could catch. On one occasion while we were at the farm, the neighbor asked me if I wanted that ugly, old dog. I jumped at the chance. I asked my cousin if I could have him. He said yes, and we took Hootie home with us. The two of us rode in the back of that old truck. I named him Red because of his reddish color. I hugged him while riding back to my cousin's house, and he just kept lapping my face.

CHAPTER 18

Red

Red and I were inseparable. Mama even let him sleep with me. We tracked all kinds of wild animals through the swamp. One day, we saw my neighbor's cat. He looked and acted wild as he hunted birds. Red treed him quickly, so I threw sticks at him trying to get him to come down, but he never did.

Onward we trekked. We came upon a hen with a bunch of chicks. When I tried to catch one, she pecked me. Red growled at her, grabbed her by the back, and flipped her in the air. He rounded the hen and her chicks up, and we played with them for an hour. Sometimes, I would throw one away, and Red would get it and bring it back to me. When we started, there were lots of chicks. I noticed that Red would lie down, hold one between his paws, and lick and lick it. Then it just disappeared. By the time we left, there were not as many chicks. I never saw him eat any, but I suspected he had.

Mama and I had chickens running around our yard. One day as I was gathering eggs, I saw Red crack open an egg and suck the yoke out just as I had done. I smiled and kept gathering eggs. Once while fishing in a swampy pond, I hooked something big. I thought it would pull me into the water. I yelled to Red, "Get it, boy!" Quicker than I could say it again, he was in the water and about two feet deep trying to catch what I had on my line. Eventually, he came up with a long, thick-bodied lamprey eel. It was so funny to see him trying to keep a hold of that eel. I finally went into the water myself, and we tried to catch it, but it was so slippery that we could not hold onto it. We finally got tired and let it go.

Another time, we came across a sow and a couple of piglets. When I tried to catch one, she treed me, so Red was on her like a bullet. I remembered what his previous owner had said about him being a good hog dog. I yelled, "Get her, Red!" She finally ran off, and Red came back and barked at me in the tree. I climbed down, and he licked and licked my face. I hugged him hard. I felt he had saved my life. I loved Red.

Day after day, Red and I trekked through that swamp trying to catch anything we could. Ray Paul, and old man who lived next door to my cousin, had a large catfish pond in his backyard.

Sometimes, my cousin would take me over there, and we would catch a few catfish. Of course, I always brought Red with me. We would skin the fish, and his new wife would fry them in an old iron skillet. My cousin always told me to be careful not to let Red in the pond because there was a three-foot gator in it. He said nobody knew where it had come from; it had just shown up one day. He told me if that gator caught me or Red, it would grab us and do what he called the death roll; it would drown then eat us. I told him that I wasn't afraid of an old gator but that I would be careful.

Without his knowledge, Red and I use to sneak through the swamp behind our houses and go over to that pond alone. The pond was muddy around the edges but not very deep. Red and I harassed that gator unmercifully. We tried to catch him, but he would stay in the middle in the deep water. I never let Red go way out there.

Other times when my cousin would take us over to the pond, the gator would see us coming and go underwater reappearing way out in the deep water in the middle or on the other end of the pond, being careful to stay far away from us. Red would run around the pond barking at him. My cousin never could figure out why that old gator acted afraid and would hide every time my cousin brought Red and me around. It wasn't until 2013 that I told him how we had harassed that gator, and after all those years, Cousin Drew shook his head and laughed.

Years ago, one of my other cousins bought that property, moved the gator, and filled in the pond. The gator grew very large at a shipyard where my cousin Drew worked for over fifty years. My cousin said he stayed around, and he would feed him every day.

Red had one blue and one green eye; both looked fake or glassy. I would hold his head tightly and look deep into his eyes trying to figure out why they looked so weird. Red would only look back and lap my face. I laughed, and we headed into the swamp to find some animal to catch. He had a lot of white and a reddish color to him. I remember he must have weighed over fifty pounds.

I had Red for only a short time. My father showed up one day; the next morning, he tied a rope around Red's neck and took him away. Later, I found out he had given him to a man who lived down the road. He had a fenced-in yard and a few other dogs. Whenever I walked past his house, I always heard the man yelling and beating his dogs, which would be barking, yelping, and whining. It gave me the chills; I just wanted my dog back. My father never said why I couldn't keep Red.

Much later, I happily learned that Red was a Catahoula leopard dog, and I believe Red was just a cur. They were a very old breed and believed to be a mix of Indian and French dogs. It is believed that the Indians bred Beauceron dogs and red wolves to create the Catahoula breed. Indians used them for hunting game; they were also bred for hog and cattle herding. The breed is recognized by the United Kennel Club and the American Kennel Club as a herding dog breed. In 1979, Governor Edwin Edwards signed a bill making the Catahoula the official state dog of Louisiana. This information makes me smile and so very proud that Red had such a rich history.

CHAPTER 19

Scooter Won't Hunt

Down the dirt road from our house was a small store called Iona's. This country store carried a little bit of everything that people in the area needed. It was very rare that Mama would give me a penny for some bubble gum or a piece of candy. Many times, after playing in Ione's feed stock room, she would give me a soda pop and a piece of penny candy or gum of my choice. I usually chose bubble gum or a chocolate Black Tar Baby candy. Looking back on those days, I remember Ione as a warmhearted black woman who treated a young white boy with respect and love. There was, never any black/white relationship incidents.

On days that I didn't go to Ione's store, I would head over to my favorite telephone pole. Out of the few that were around, there was one that had black tar oozing from it that I chewed on. It didn't taste like the Tar Baby or bubble gum Ione gave me, but I had nothing else.

One day while retrieving a big wad of tar from the pole, Mr. Wilson, who lived in the big white house next to the pole, shouted out to me, "Hey Johnny, you want to go for a walk with Scooter and Me?" "Yes Mr. Wilson," I said. I often climbed Mr. Wilson's fence to play with Scooter, one of his old black-and-tan coon hounds. Somehow, Mr. Wilson always knew when I was there. He would come out onto his front porch and holler, "Johnny, you come out from under that damn porch and quit playing with Scooter." I always came out sad and saying, "I'm sorry, Mr. Wilson, but he's so friendly, and I just love him." "I know Johnny, but I've told you that you can't play with a hunting dog. It ruins them."

I liked Mr. Wilson, but I liked his wife more. She would give me homemade cookies and a big glass of raw milk. I relished those days. I always snuck a piece of cookie out to give to Scooter, on my way home.

I waited by the front gate, and in a few minutes, Mr. Wilson came out carrying his shotgun. He called to Scooter, who was under the porch. I knew coon hunters hunted at night with their hounds, but thinking I was finally getting to go coon hunting with him, I didn't give the daylight trip a second thought. As Scooter passed through the gate, I spat out my tar ball. He jumped up on me, his paws hanging over my shoulders, almost knocking me to the ground as he lapped the black dribble from my lips. Both of us were so happy to be together.

Next to Mr. Wilson's house was a dirt road leading into the swamp. I knew it was where Mr. Wilson, Scooter, and his son, Josh, hunted coons and sometimes fox. Mr. Wilson walked down the dirt road, his gun slung over his shoulder, with me and Scooter right beside him. At one point, he looked down and said, "Johnny, today, you're going to learn a very valuable lesson."

We walked to the edge of the swamp, and Mr. Wilson called Scooter over. He said, "Sit, Scooter." He did as he was told, and Mr. Wilson turned and started walking away calling me with him. Walking beside him, I looked up, smiled, and said, "He minds good, Mr. Wilson." He stopped, reached down, and tousled my hair. "Yes, he does, Johnny, but Scooter won't hunt." He raised his shotgun. *Kaboom!* He shot Scooter right between the eyes.

I never spoke with Mr. Wilson again even though I would sneak over to grab a tar ball occasionally from that telephone pole. For many years, I carried the burden of Scooter's death with me believing that my love for him had caused Mr. Wilson to shoot him. Love became an emotion I feared even though I sought it out desperately, even from a dog.

CHAPTER 20

Hooey Stick

I had no grandparents, so my cousin Drew's new wife said I could call her parents Maw Maw and Paw Paw. We would visit them quite a bit. They lived on the other side of my cousin's farm way out in the woods. On the dirt road leading to their house was a small bridge over a muddy creek. Sometimes, I would go crawfishing off that bridge.

One day, I hooked something very heavy and could not pull it out. I went to the house to get my cousin to help me. We pulled the biggest snapping turtle out of that creek I had ever seen. I asked him if he had ever made snapping turtle soup. He said, "No, little man, I haven't." I was just as happy he hadn't, so we turned it loose.

Maw Maw and Paw Paw had several old, rambling, half-falling-down barns and sheds. I used to explore their dirty attics and jump down into the hay piles on the ground floor. Once when I did that, something stuck me in my butt. It didn't hurt too badly, but I saw it was an old, broken-handled pitchfork. I threw it to the side and continued jumping a few more times. Then I kept on exploring. I went in a room and saw a large rattlesnake trying to eat a small chicken. I sat and watched. After what seemed like hours, the snake finished and slithered away through a hole in the wall.

There were so many tools in that old barn; I had no idea what some were used for. Most of them were worn and covered with spiderwebs. They looked like they had not been used in years. On some occasions, I was lucky enough to catch rat snakes, and I would play with them for hours. I wanted to bring one home, but Maw Maw and my cousin's new wife would not let me. And they said that my Mama would not want them at my house.

Sometimes, I would make a makeshift rat trap and catch one. I would tie it to something and put it where I knew the snakes hung out. Pretty soon, one would come out and eat the rat.

One time, I caught a baby rabbit and tied it to a piece of metal behind the barn near a hole under the floor. I sat there for a half hour before I saw a huge rattlesnake, bigger than the last one, come out. It coiled. Its dead eyes watched that rabbit twisting, jumping, and trying to escape. Its first strike missed, but its next one did not. It took only moments for that little rabbit to die. I sat and watched fascinated as the rattler ate that baby rabbit. I thought it looked kind of funny to see his little feet and small white tail go down his throat last.

One day, I went to the back pasture with Paw Paw to get his horse. It was the biggest horse I had ever seen. At that time, I still did not own shoes; he pointedly told me to be very careful to not let the horse step on my foot. I was so thrilled to be around this beautiful animal that as we were walking back to his barn, my hand resting on his leg, I got too close, and sure enough, he stepped on my foot. By the time we got back to the house, I was bawling. No matter what he, Maw Maw, or my cousin and his wife said, I kept crying.

Paw Paw took me onto his front porch. We sat in an old rocking chair, me on his lap, and he started whittling on a piece of wood. He said he was making me a toy and asked if I knew what a hooey stick was. When I said no, he started explaining it to me as he continued to whittle. I stopped crying and got very interested in the hooey stick. We sat on that porch all afternoon while Paw Paw whittled. He finished it, showed me how it worked, and gave it to me saying I could keep it. I loved that hooey stick and kept it for years. I hid it from my father. I remember how Paw Paw would sit on that porch and play his fiddle. I sure liked to listen to his music.

Many years later, I made a hooey stick for each one of my four kids. In the 1980s, I mentioned a hooey stick to a kid where I was working. After much discussion, I made him one. He really didn't want it, so I kept it. I showed it to several friends and said I wanted to sell the idea to a toy company. Soon after, a friend showed me an ad in a magazine; a company was looking for new inventions. I didn't consider the hooey stick to be an invention, but I contacted them by phone and explained my idea of wanting to sell it to a toy company. They told me they would help me accomplish that and sent me a folder asking for information and a drawing of the toy. At first, I was reluctant to give them all the information, but they were very convincing, and I gave them more information with a drawing. I told them there was a cute story that went with the toy.

After a couple of weeks of not hearing from them, I called. The person I had been speaking with said, "You said you didn't want to give us all the information, so I sent your package to be filed in the basement." I told him that I had given them more information and had been waiting to hear from them. He said, "I'll have to go to the basement and dig out your file. That will take me awhile." He assured me he would contact me soon. He never did. After one month of calling many times, he never answered the phone, and I never heard from the company again.

A few months later, the same friend who had given me the information about the company told me he had seen hooey sticks being sold in a store in a nearby town. I drove to the store and asked the manager about the hooey stick. He became very excited; he said, "It's the hottest-selling toy in the store." He showed it to me, and I bought one. I opened the package, which said it was a Whip-o-will or Hooey Stick. I asked him to show me how it worked. He did, and I realized he did not know everything about how it worked. I pulled my original out of my jacket pocket and asked, "Would you like to see an original?" I showed him how it really worked, and he was amazed.

I left the store that day torn between being mad and sad. I came to realize that my life was on an upward path. I smiled. I knew that was another of life's many lessons.

CHAPTER 21

Jake

During the rest of that summer, I continued exploring our land and the swampy area. One time, I came upon an older boy who was crawfishing. At first, I thought was just one of the black kids who lived in the area. He had a peculiar accent, and when I asked him, "Are you a black boy?" he said, "No, I'm a Cajun." I didn't know what that was, so I did not ask anything else, and we started talking about crawfishing. He showed me his bucket filled with them.

After that day, he and I met a few times in the swamp to crawfish. We talked about fishing, snapping turtle soup, gators, and all kinds of animals. He told me sometimes he trapped gators and muskrats and sold their hides and meat. I asked, "Who do you live with?" He said, "With my Mama." I smiled and said, "I live with my Mama too." He told me his name was Bray.

I found many animals in the area including many types and colors of snakes. I also found some small, gray animals. They looked like small pigs with a rat-looking tail and long, sharp claws. I tried many times to catch one but never did. They always escaped into holes in the ground. I described them to my cousin, and he told me they were armadillos. He also told me to be careful around them because they had big teeth and long, sharp claws for digging.

Many years later, I told my wife how I still wanted one for a pet, and I think she said something like, "You'll have a snowball's chance in hell of bringing one into our home!" About that time, I found out that the Louisiana armadillo carried leprosy.

Another time while exploring a particularly thick area, I found a nest of kittens. I grabbed one, stuck it in the pocket of my shorts, and headed home. I showed Mama what I had caught. She just laughed and said it would die in a few days. She said I should take it back to the nest. I said, "Oh no, Mama. I want to keep and raise it." She said, "Okay, but don't forget what I said. Never let it go outside by itself at night because there's an old tomcat around who will certainly kill it."

Our neighbor had a nanny goat, and I asked her for a little milk. I watched as she milked that goat, but when I tried to, I could not get the goat to keep its leg on my shoulder.

I kept the kitten with me every day and tied him to my bed at night so none of my pet snakes would eat him and so that tomcat would not kill him. One night just as I was about to go to bed, I was standing in Mama's bedroom holding my kitten. He started twisting and turning trying to get down. He scratched me, and I finally let him go. He climbed the wall and went out through a small opening by the roof. I had not known that hole was there, and I could not understand how the kitten would have known.

I went outside quickly and looked everywhere for him. After about an hour or so, I went back in and told Mama I couldn't find him. She said, "He won't make it through the night. That tomcat will get him." I went to bed and lay there for what seemed hours. I heard a howl. I knew it was that tomcat because I had heard it before. I jumped up and ran outside but did not see anything. I returned to bed and tossed and turned all night.

The next morning, I found my kitten. He was as stiff as a board. I picked him up and tried to make him stand several times. I saw blood on his neck and knew he was dead. When I showed him to Mama, she said, "Yep, he cut his throat." I buried my kitten under one of the pecan trees and went searching for the tomcat.

One morning, Aunt Rosie and her daughter, Betty Ann, arrived at our house. Mama told me that Betty Ann would be staying with us for a time because Uncle Ed had to go to the hospital in New Orleans for an operation and that Aunt Rosie would be staying with relatives in New Orleans. I never said a word; I just walked away and stayed in the swamp until it got very dark.

When I returned, I told Mama I was not hungry and went straight to bed. It was not long before Betty Ann came in and got under the blanket with me. That was another long, painful night of my youth.

The next morning when I went outside, she followed me as I walked into the swamp. She pushed me down into the mud and again told me if I ever told anybody, she would do very bad things to me. She followed me around all day.

I had heard a bird making a unique whistle. I could not whistle, so I improvised. I asked Mama later what kind of a bird it was, and she told me it was a bobwhite. After that, every time I heard one, I would answer by making a sound I thought was like its call. I always thought the bird was answering me.

I started making the same sound. Betty Ann asked what I was doing. She just laughed when I told her I was whistling. She whistled loudly and said, "That's how you whistle." I asked her if she would teach me to whistle. She said she would, if I promised not to tell anybody what she was doing to me at night. My penis was hurting again, and my right testicle seemed to be hanging lower.

She continued to abuse me at night, but she kept her word and taught me to whistle. I kept my promise; I never complained or told anybody. She used two fingers to whistle. I never got the hang of whistling that way, but I did learn with no fingers. She stayed with us for about a month, and I never saw her again until many years later.

One day, I was in the outhouse whistling to a bird and listening to its answer. Suddenly, a snake slithered right up from the hole between my legs. Luckily for him, I realized I knew him. It was just an old king snake I had named Jake; I played with him occasionally. I picked him up. "Where have you been, Jake? I haven't seen you lately."

I wrapped him around my neck, pulled up my shorts, and spent the rest of the day playing with him. Sometimes, I would sneak him into my bed and talk to and pet him. While falling to sleep, I would usually wrap him either around my neck or my arm hoping he would stay there through the night, but most times when I woke up, he was gone. I figured he had slithered out of one of the many cracks in the walls or floor.

CHAPTER 22

Hate in My Young Heart

About 3:00 a.m. one cold winter night in 1978, my partner and I received a radio call from the station to respond to a house in the Brant City section of Sandy Town. The caller, a young child, was crying saying that her father was beating up her mother badly.

We got there and heard yelling and screaming. "Police! We're coming in." We entered, and I saw a woman on the floor and a male standing over her yelling at her while holding her by the neck. The woman was bleeding from her face and neck. I immediately put him under arrest. My partner returned to the cruiser to retrieve a first-aid kit. Upon his return, I asked him to take the handcuffed man to the cruiser while I took a statement from the wife. I helped the woman into a chair. Her cuts were not severe, but I bandaged her up and advised her I would call for the ambulance to take her to the hospital to get checked out if she wished. She declined. Her seven-year-old daughter was standing beside her.

In her statement, she said that her husband had a bad temper. About an hour earlier, he had gotten angry that their daughter had left her homework scattered all over a table. He had awaked the daughter and told her, "Clean up this goddamn mess!" His yelling had also awakened her, and they started arguing. It progressed from there, and he started beating her.

The daughter confirmed everything her mother had said. She said, "He's like this all the time. He's just angry. I hate him so much. I wish he would die." I looked at her with sadness in my heart and said, "Honey, your father is sick, and he needs help." That was not what the young girl wanted to hear. She again said, "I hate him," and she began to cry.

We took the man to the station. After he was booked, I wrote my report including everything the wife and daughter had stated. When I got to the part of the young girl saying how much she hated her father and wished he would die, I stopped and thought about it. For a few minutes, I started remembering how so many years ago, I also had hate in my young heart.

I turned seven in the fall of 1950. I started seeing my father regularly; it seemed he was always there. I still did not like him. He did not talk to me very much, but when he did, he was always hard on me and would tell me how bad I was. I could never do anything right in his opinion. He was still always hitting me, usually backhands to the head. One time when he came home, he started clearing the land out behind the outhouse with a scythe. He gave me a hand sickle and told me to cut an especially thick area of weeds. He had started a fire and was burning everything including dead weeds and brush. Having never used or even seen a hand sickle before, I watched him as he was using the scythe. I started hacking at everything he told me to. He started screaming that I wasn't doing it right. He took the sickle from me and hit me hard in the back with the handle, knocking me down. I just lay on the ground waiting for the next blow. After seeing what it did to weeds and brush, I was scared. I thought he might cut my head off like he would a chickens'.

Some man who was helping him yelled, "Hey, the fire's getting away." He stopped, looked at me, and said, "Now see what you've done!" He ran to the fire and started beating it back. He called me over and pointed at one part of the fire and yelled, "Beat that fire back with a piece of brush!"

I tried to pull up a small bush growing beside the fire, but the roots were too strong for me. Because I was taking too long for him, he grabbed me by the neck, picked me up, and threw me toward the fire. He screamed, "The next time I tell you to do something, you goddamn better do it quickly!" I landed a foot or so from the fire, got up, and grabbed a piece of wood to beat the fire with.

Late that night as the fire started dying down and was under control, my father told me we were going inside. As we got through the door, he grabbed me by the neck from behind, picked me up, and carried me into my room. He threw me on the cot, and my head hit the metal at the top. I bounced off and fell between the cot and the wall. I slowly crawled back onto the cot, and my father hit me. "The next time I tell you to clear the brush, goddamn it, you better do it right!" Nothing was said about supper.

Whenever my father was home, he slept with Mama. My bed was in the lean-to room next to theirs. There was no door, just a doorway. We always went to bed at sundown, and I would lie in my bed and hear him yelling at Mama, "Do it harder! Try harder!" Once, I snuck to the doorway and peeked into their bedroom. I saw my father with his back to me standing naked next to the bed. Mama was sitting on the bed facing my father. He was holding her head with his hands and pushing and pulling her so hard I thought he was hurting her because she was making weird noises and so was he. I had no idea what they were doing, but I was remembering some of the things my cousin Betty Ann had done to me, and I thought how his penis would hurt in the morning.

One day, Mama just left, and I was staying with my cousin Drew. Nobody told me where she was. It didn't matter to me because I loved being around him. A few days later, he told me that Mama was in the hospital in Bogalusa and that she had had a baby girl. My cousin took me to see her. I walked up to her bed and saw Mama nursing the baby. I looked at the baby and said, "I don't want her. Take her back." Mama looked sad, but my cousin just laughed and said, "Now little man, that's your sister." I had been the only kid in our family, and I did not want another one around.

Again, I had feelings I did not understand. My father was hitting me; I thought I must have done something terribly wrong, but I did not know what it was. At this point, the only animals we had were chickens that ran around in the yard. We had a couple of very active roosters, so we always had a couple of dozen chicks. As I had done in the past, I started torturing and killing them. Somebody gave me an old, crooked-barreled BB gun. The BBs cost a nickel a pack, and we could not afford them. Instead, I would light and chew the burned heads off some kitchen matches. I would drop the sticks into the BB gun barrel and shoot the chicks. I watched them walking around with matchsticks sticking out of them, and I felt no emotion. In those days, I lived with a feeling of dread all the time but didn't know why.

At times, our neighbor's goat would ambush me and butt me hard. One time, he hit me so hard that he knocked me to the ground and kept on butting me until I thought I was a goner. I told Mama, and the next day, she came out with me. When he butted me, Mama grabbed his little tail, pulled him up in the air, and rubbed a turpentine-soaked rag on his ass. That goat jumped a fence. I think it is still running.

In my room, I saw outside through the cracks in the walls and the floor. When it got dark, we went to bed. When it got light, we got up. At night, I would curl myself into a fetal position under the wool blanket with just my mouth and nose sticking out and scoot as far up to the top of the bed as I could. Every night, big rats would crawl over me and run around the room. As I had in the past, I worried that they would eat my toes off. When I complained to Mama, she would tell me to hush because they wouldn't eat my toes off.

My father heard me complaining one time. That night at dark, he picked me up by the scruff of my neck, carried me into my room, threw me onto the cot, and took my blanket. I covered my head with my arm but still got a backhand to my face. I heard him mumble something about me never amounting to anything if I couldn't fight off some rats.

That night, with no blanket to protect me, the rats were all over me and my bed. I slept in a fetal position, kept my eyes closed, and hoped they would not eat my toes off. For many years going forward, I slept in a fetal position, and I still do to this day.

The next day, my father was gone, and Mama and I walked downtown to buy a big rat trap. That night, I lay under the blanket waiting for those rats to run all over me and my cot. After what seem forever, I heard a loud *snap*. It seemed it took a couple of hours for that rat to die.

The noises it made that night are still in my head. As soon as it was light out, I ran in to tell Mama. When we checked the trap, we saw a huge rat caught by its long nose up near the eyes that showed blood red. It looked weird with the trap clamped down and dried blood all around its head. Its eyes had bugged out of its head. I saw that it had a lot of extended nipples and there were about a dozen babies around it. I asked Mama, "What should we do with the babies?" She told me to grab a handful and come outside. Once outside, she showed me how to throw them against a pecan tree. They made a loud popping noise, like popcorn, when they hit the tree. I thought that was the most fun I had ever had.

We did catch more big rats. I always looked for babies, but only a couple of times did we catch a Mama rat with babies, but there were more fun-filled times with those popcorn sounds I loved.

CHAPTER 23

My First Love

A young girl my age, named Carol, lived next door with her mother, father, and a sister. She had long blonde hair and was my first love. We spent many hours together. Sometimes, we would walk to the end of her property and see the yard of the old man my father had given my dog Red to. He had quite a few, and we often heard him beating them. On one occasion, Red came to the gate, saw Carol and me, and started whining and wagging his tail. The old man came out and hollered, "Get out of here you goddamn kids!" He started beating Red. Carol and I ran and never went back. We did not want to see Red get beaten anymore.

One day, we talked Carol's mother into letting us sell snow cones. Her father went to an icehouse and bought a block of ice. Her mother gave us bottles of mixes to make the snow cones. Of course, nobody bought any, so Carol and I ate them all. That night, I was throwing up green and red but mostly purple—my favorite—bile all night.

Their five acres were fenced and were next to our five acres. They had two horses. We would climb up on a fence post to mount one and ride. The weather was so hot that it would just plod along. I kept trying to get it to move faster, but it wouldn't. I got off, found a pointed stick, got on, and jabbed the horse. It jumped, bucked, and ran right at a fence. We had no saddle, so I was holding onto its mane. It stopped short of the fence, and I flew into the barbwire on top of the fence. Carol was laughing hard; I got real mad at her. Hanging from that fence, I just looked her, and for a whole minute or two I wanted to hit her. Then I laughed too, and the tension was broken. Boy did I love that girl.

Carol and I would hang out at Ione's store. One of her rooms held sacks and sacks of animal feed. We would play for hours in that room jumping from pile to pile. When we were finished playing, as before, Ione would give us a bottle of soda.

Ione's house was next door, and she had an artesian well in her backyard. In the pool that was fed by the well were about a dozen goldfish. Many times, Carol and I tried to catch them. We never did, but every time Ione caught us, she would yell, "Leave my goldfish alone you kids."

The store had a lot of penny candy, and occasionally, she would give us some. It also had a back room with a lot of old stuff on shelves. We loved to look around that room. Ione and her family were black, but they treated Carol and me as if we were members of her own family. She and her family were always so nice to us, and we always treated them with respect. Whenever my father was around, he forbad me to go to her store. He would say, "Stay out of that goddamn nigger's store."

It was Carol who introduced me to childhood sex without abuse. Mama would take a bath in our old washtub. She would have me bring a few buckets of water from the well next door. She would heat water and bathe in my room. One day, Carol wanted to go to my house, and I told her Mama was taking a bath. She convinced me we should go peek at her. We saw right into the room through the cracks. Carol kept whispering about different parts of Mama's body to me and giggling.

At one point, we thought Mama had heard us, so we ran off to her house. Her parents had an old barn with many rooms. The roof was metal, and it was not used much. One time, Carol, her sister, and I climbed on top of the roof and started sliding off into some bushes. The first few times went okay, but after her sister broke her arm, we never did that again.

On that day, after peaking at Mama, Carol and I ran to the barn and went into one room we used as a playhouse. Carol convinced me that boys and girls could show each other where they peed. Remembering my experience, I did not want to, and I told her no. But she kept on and on. Carol was the love of my life, so I was eventually convinced.

The first time, we just showed each other. After a few times but still remembering my experiences, we started touching each other and exploring each other's bodies. That time, I felt no pain. Carol was getting more and more brazen. Every time we were together, all she wanted to do was go to the playhouse and play doctor.

One day while in the playhouse, I was naked lying on my back and Carol was naked standing next to me. She was pretending to operate on my penis. Her mother called out for us to come get some lunch. Carol yelled back that we did not want anything. The next thing we knew, her mother walked in on us. There was a lot of screaming and crying, and her mother sent me home. After that, I could be with Carol only on a very limited basis.

Years later, family members including cousins and aunts told me that they all thought Carol and I would get married one day. But after moving away, I never saw her again until many years later and only once in another town.

CHAPTER 24

Abuse by Two

I had an old, red wagon somebody had given me. It had only the two back wheels. I used to drag it around with my BB gun and shoot matchsticks at everything. One day, I lay down in the wagon with my BB gun and fell asleep. I awoke with a start and saw an old black-and-tan bloodhound I recognized as belonging to one of the black families down the road. Its head was under my shorts; it was sucking on my penis. I jumped up. As he was running away, I took aim and shot him with my crooked-barreled BB gun. That was the shot of a lifetime. The matchstick stuck right in his asshole. I never saw that dog again at my house.

Occasionally, I would hang out with Bobby Joe, a boy my age who lived down the street. He had a big arbor in his backyard loaded with muscadines—small, green, sweet-and-sour grapes that we loved. He also had a nice creek out behind his house with small fish, crawfish, snakes, and an ornery old gator. Sometimes, we would really torment that gator until he went underwater and swam upstream away from us. We would wait for what seemed like hours for him to surface, and when he did not come up, we would get in the water and catch some of the other critters.

Behind that creek was a big swampy area that we loved to explore. Sometimes, we would climb the moss-covered trees there, and we could see all the way to the edge of town. We even started talking about building a fort in one special tree we really liked.

My friend had an older brother named Mike, who had a friend named Carl. I did not like either one because they were always pushing me around and making fun of how skinny I was. They laughed saying things like they would like to pull my shorts off and suck me. My friend warned me to stay away from them. He did not say why, just, "Stay away from them."

One day when my father was home, he grabbed me by the throat, picked me up, and asked me if I had been hanging around Mike, Jason's brother. I told him no, but he did not believe me. He backhanded me hard and told me, "I'm not going to tell you again. Stay away from Jason and his brother." He never said why, and of course I didn't ask.

A few days later, my father was gone; I went to see Jason. I knocked at the back door, and Mike answered. He said Jason was not there but to come in. When I said, "No, I'll come back," he came out of the door with his friend following close behind. He grabbed my arms and told his friend to grab my legs. I started yelling, screaming, kicking, and trying to get away, but they were big and powerful. I would guess they were seventeen or eighteen. Mike put one hand over my mouth, and they started carrying me to the swamp. I bit his hand, and he punched me in the face. I wasn't knocked out but, I was dazed for a few moments. I continued to struggle. They started running while carrying me.

Near the swamp, Mike told Carl to pull my shorts off. He did. Mike took me by both legs and raised me high enough, so he could put his mouth completely over my penis and scrotum. He started sucking, kissing, licking, and biting me as they carried me into the swamp. They took me to an area where the ground was overgrown with green moss and was only slightly wet but spongy. I knew the area, so I knew exactly where we were. I was so exhausted by then that I could hardly fight.

Mike was still holding his hand over my mouth as they laid me on the moss face-down. Carl knelt behind me, picked my hips up, and tried to enter my anus with his penis. Mike was sitting down in front of me as he held my head with one hand. He held my hands behind my back with the other hand and forced my mouth over his erect penis.

I had no idea what all that was about; I only knew what they were doing was bad. Within a minute or two, Mike ejaculated into my mouth while Carl had entered my anus a little, and it was hurting badly. I was screaming for them to stop, while spitting and gagging. Mike lay back on the moss with a big sigh. I kicked hard and landed a foot right on Carl's scrotum. He yelled out in pain. I scrambled to my feet and ran continuing to spit out his semen as best I could.

I ran back towards the house, picking up my shorts and ran across the street to Albert's house. He was a young black kid I knew and played with but, only when my father was not around. His mother was sitting on her front porch snapping beans. Crying and sobbing, I ran up onto the porch. She stood and quickly took me in the house. She grabbed a dish towel, wet it, and swabbed at my anus to stop the bleeding. She cleaned blood off my legs, penis, and scrotum. She told me to put my shorts back on.

Sitting in her old rocking chair, she held me tight in her lap. After covering me with a blanket, she rocked me in her warm and loving arms all the while humming to me. As my crying started to subside, I saw Albert standing beside us. He had tears in his eyes as he held my hand. I remember how a great calmness came over me as her warm love flowed into my body. I reached out and took Albert's other hand in mine and closed my eyes.

I never spoke to or saw my friend Jason, his brother, Mike, or his friend, Carl, again. I have never spoken of this incident until recently. During the writing of this book, I told my wife of the abuse by two, and we cried together during my telling.

CHAPTER 25

The Pool

When I was six, I had my own special place to go fishing all alone. It was about half a mile back into the swamp on the other side of the dirt road in front of our house.

I awoke one warm, bright, summer day. Somehow, I knew that day would be the day. Right after breakfast, I told Mama, "Today is the day I'll catch me one even if I have to get into the water and catch it by hand!" Mama laughed and said, "Don't forget about those snapping turtles. When they bite, they won't let go until thunder and lightning."

I had my red wiggler worms in one pocket of my shorts. I grabbed my cane pole and headed barefoot into the swamp. The pole had to be long because the fish I was after hid in the shallow water among the weeds and lily pads, but when they became scared, they would swim to the deeper water way out in the middle.

I reached the pool and saw them. I was always amazed at how beautiful they were. The water was so clear that I saw to the bottom. I stood for a moment and watched them. Their rainbow colors shining in the bright sunlight looked like fireworks. I saw their clean bodies so sleek and slender moving through the water with such grace, barely a ripple, and their bright eyes sparkling. I thought I never wanted to leave that place.

Pulling a wiggler out of my pocket, I noticed it had a ring around its head; it was already wiggling trying to get away. Unraveling the line from my pole, I jammed a homemade hook fashioned from a safety pin through the ring and back through a second time. When leaving Aunt Josie's house my other cane pole was left behind. On previous occasions, they sometimes got off my hook easily, but that time, I had kinked the tip of the pin hoping it would hold them.

I knew these fish liked the big fat ones, so after hooking the worm, I shook the pole hard several times. That wiggler looked mad, but it stayed on, and the pin shone brightly in the sunlight. I cast my line out, and the pole made a loud *whap* when it hit the water. To my amazement, it did not scare the fish. I had an old cork for a bobber, and I had it set about four inches up from the wiggler just to make sure I saw it.

After a few minutes, a big, fat fish hit my bait and started to run. My pole was lying on top of the water, and by the time I picked it up and tried to set the hook, he was gone taking my wiggler with him. The fish stopped and stared at me. I saw bubbles. I just knew it was laughing at me. I smiled and kept on fishing through the morning and into the afternoon with the same results.

Along about suppertime, I got an idea. I entered the water and felt cool mud oozing between my toes. I waded in up to my knees. The pool was only about a foot deep; it was fed by a small creek. When I got up to my waist, I wasn't sure how deep I would sink into the mud, but I kept on going. I started gathering branches, weeds, lily pads, and whatever else I could and made a trap. I walked around the pool using a limb to herd fish toward my trap. I was surprised to see that a few had entered. I started moving toward the entrance. The mud and water were getting deeper, so I could not move very fast. I stepped on something very sharp. I felt it cut deeply into the bottom of my foot. Ignoring the pain, I continued slowly toward the entrance of my trap.

I saw about a dozen or, so fish trapped inside. I stood there enjoying the moment. They started darting in all directions, some even jumping over the barricade. I was in awe wondering why after all that time they were afraid of me. I turned and saw something that made my blood run cold and my hands tingle with anger. A water moccasin was swimming straight at me with its mouth wide open showing its long, needle-like fangs. It was hissing loudly, and its eyes were bright and sparkled like fire. I knew he must have been mad at me for taking his food.

I tried to get out of the pool, but the mud was slowing me down; I could barely move. I knew that black demon was venomous. I had seen one bite, kill, and eat a fish in another creek. Afterward, I played with him for a while. Every time he would go underwater trying to get away from me, he would pop right back up to the surface. But this one looked angry. Mama had told me about one of her uncles who had been bitten on the ankle by a water moccasin and eventually lost his entire leg.

The snake got close and struck, but I had taken one of the branches, and using it for leverage, I hurled it as far as I could. In doing so, I fell headfirst into the water right into the middle of the school of fish and went under. I popped up gasping for air. I saw that the snake was coming back fast and was headed for my face. Just as he opened his mouth to strike, a panicked fish swam right in. As he bit down, I grabbed him right behind the head and started squeezing. I kept squeezing and twisting until his head popped off. I threw it into the swamp and left his body in the pool. I thought, *He's eaten a lot of them. Now, the fish can eat him.*

I got out of the pool and headed home. I saw Mama in the backyard cooking some crawfish my cousin Drew had dropped off. She saw me limping and asked what had happened. "Nothing," I said. "I just stepped on something." She pointed and asked, "What you got in them shorts?" I said, "Just some red wigglers." I reached into my pocket to show her, and amazement flooded my face. I pulled out the most beautiful fish in the world. In all the excitement, it must have swum right into my pocket. Showing it to Mama, I said, "Look! I caught one just like I told you I would!" She said, "Clean it, and I'll fry it. It will taste good with these crawfish." Looking at the fish, I told Mama, "I can't eat it." She laughed and said, "Go turn him loose then." I took him to a nearby creek and released him. I am not sure if he lived because he sank to the bottom.

That night, I dreamed of swimming with those fish, of seeing their bright eyes gleaming, their rainbow bodies shining brightly in the moonlight as they glided effortlessly through the crystal-clear water. Every time I looked at them, they would make bubbles as they laughed with me. I never returned to the pool. I had caught one, and that was all I ever wanted.

For years after that incident, the bottom of my left foot hurt. I never did go to a doctor about it. After it healed over, a lump appeared, and it started itching. Sometimes, it itched so much that I would scratch it until it bled. It would still itch. It took many years for the lump to go away and the itching to stop.

CHAPTER 26

Damn Lamprey Eel

Another time back in that old swamp, I was hauling in a big, fat crawfish when something grabbed it and took off almost pulling my pole out of my hands. I sat in the mud and fought that devil for what seemed an eternity. When I was finally able to drag it onto the creek bank, I saw it was a weird snake. After spitting out bits of my crawfish, it started slithering back to the water. I realized it was a lamprey eel; Red and I had once tried to catch one. I knew Red would be proud of me, so I tried to pick it up. It was so slippery that it slipped right out of my hands just as before. Having nothing else, I took off my shorts, wrapped it up, picked up my pole, and headed home naked but carrying that eel.

When I walked in the back door, Mama asked, "What you got in them shorts?" When the eel hit the floor, Mama screamed, ran into the bedroom with a big knife, and yelled, "Get that damn lamprey eel out of this house and put your shorts on!" I said, "I thought you said it was good eating." She said, "Take it out back and skin it first."

Out back, I tried and tried, but it was just too slippery. Finally, I drove its head onto an old nail in one of our pecan trees. Mama cooked it in her special white flour gravy she called country gravy. I did not particularly like the eel, but I loved her country gravy over biscuits.

I never brought home another one, but I had learned an easy way to skin one. In the years following, I nailed and skinned squirrels, rabbits, and catfish easily with just a pocketknife, pliers, and a nail.

CHAPTER 27

School

In the fall of 1950, I was seven and ready to start school. My first experience was in a parochial school. One day while I was playing in a woodpile trying to catch the wood pussy, Mama called me in and said, "Johnny, I have a surprise for you." At the time, we were visiting the home of two people known to me as Aunt Flo and Mr. James. Mr. James was missing one leg, and I used to love walking around on his porch with his crutches pretending I was missing a leg. It made him laugh as he sat in his old rocking chair sipping moonshine.

We were on the porch. Mama made me sit down as she brought out a pair of black shoes. Looking at them I noticed they had holes in the soles. I laughed and poked my fingers through. I asked Mama about the holes. She said, "Don't worry. I'll put some paper over them." She put some cut-up newspaper inside the shoes to cover the holes. I knew what shoes were; I had just never owned or worn any. I put them on. They felt strange. I walked around on the porch stomping, just as Clydesdales horses do. Mama said, "Now don't you go out into that old swamp with those shoes on." Of course, I did, and I lost the right one. She was mad, but she replaced it. The new one was not only different looking, it was brown and had a hole in the sole.

Mama walked me to school on the first day. It was about five miles away and behind the church we attended. The last thing she said was, "Johnny, stay away from those little girls. They're dirty and nasty!"

I looked around the room; the other kids were staring at me, and I didn't like that. I didn't know what to do, so I let out a loud whistle. Everybody laughed. The nun came over to me, grabbed me by my ear, and pulled me out of my seat. She told me to go to the office and tell them what I had done.

I left the room, but instead of going to the office, I ran toward home. I caught up with Mama in a short time but kept myself hidden from her until we got home. I walked into the house saying, "Mama I don't like that old school." She grabbed me by my ear and marched me right back. I again left, but that time, I stayed in the swamp until dark.

After the first day, I did stay. The schoolhouse was small. It had three rooms with three rows in each room. In the one room, the first row was first grade, the second row was second grade, and third row was third grade. Each room was the same. The highest grade was the ninth. I was in the first grade. Because it was a Catholic school, we were taught by nuns, who were strict and stern. During that time, Mama started telling me every time I did bad things that she would take me to Covington, Louisiana, and give me to the brothers. She told me they hung bad boys in a closet and beat them with a big leather belt. I remember thinking how funny Mama was; I did not believe her.

Many years later, I talked to Mama about those times, and we laughed. I asked her about the brothers she had mentioned. She told me that their school was a seminary where young men were sent to study to become priests. We laughed a little bit more.

After a time, I found that school was not so bad especially since I had no choice in the matter. Lunch was simple and cost a nickel. Dessert was always the same—one teaspoon of peanut butter and one of jelly. Mix them up, and I had dessert.

The kids played marbles at recess. They were not allowed to bring marbles into class, so they would hide them around the schoolyard. I didn't have any marbles and could not afford to buy any, so I would watch where the other kids would hide theirs and steal a few from each one until I had a stash of my own.

As it turned out, I was a great player, and I won a lot. One boy had a beautiful leather bag with a drawstring that I loved. One day, I watched where he hid his bag. After everybody went inside, I took the bag and went to class. I got a whack on my knuckles for being late.

During class that afternoon, I couldn't keep my hands out of my pocket. I took the bag out and opened it to look at those beautiful marbles. Of course, they spilled out all over the floor. Everyone realized I had stolen the kid's bag of marbles. The nuns whipped me and used a ruler across my knuckles. But by age seven, I had learned to hold my feelings inside, so it wasn't that bad. I still did not cry. I think it infuriated the nuns just as it did my father.

We also played tops. The object was to spin your top on top of another spinning top. If you could, you would win that top. I sharpened mine one day on a stone, spun it, and cracked another kid's top. After a couple like that, the other kids wouldn't let me play with them anymore. I was still winning marbles though. I know some kids tried to find my marbles, but I hid them way up under the church. It was a real dark and spooky place, so nobody else ever went under there.

My cousin Drew spoke with the priest, and I started being an altar boy for Mass on Sundays.

There were four of us at each Mass. I was too young to learn the Latin, so when the other altar boys would say it, I would just say, "Blah, blah, blah," and everybody in the congregation would laugh because they heard me.

We sat during the gospel. My cousin always sat in the first row. After the gospel, the priest and other altar boys would resume Mass, but I would be sound asleep. My cousin always woke me up with "*Pssst!* Johnny! Little man, wake up!" and the congregation would laugh. I would run back to join the other altar boys to once again only say, "Blah, blah, blah."

Somebody had given me an old red bike that I rode to school. It was very rusty, and it did not have a chain guard. The handlebars were bent. It had no fenders, and when it would rain, dirt and grime from the roadway would come up and cover the front of me. I would get to school, and the nuns would say, "Go home, change clothes, and come back when you're cleaned up." Of course, I left school and never came back that day. I learned to play hooky in first grade.

We had a dress code, so for the first time in my life, I had to wear long pants and underwear. One day on my way to school, my pant leg got caught in the chain. Lying on the ground on top of the bike, I could not free my pant leg. I saw a shadow. I looked up and saw the biggest black man I had ever seen. He said, "White boy!" laughed, and reached for me. His reaching for me scared me to death. I immediately thought of the day Mike and his friend had reached for me and carried me into the swamp. I screamed, yelled, and kicked at him while punching as hard as I could. He continued to laugh. He picked me up by the nape and spun the bike's pedal, which freed my pant leg. Still laughing he picked the bike and me up. Getting back on I could still hear him laughing as I sped away.

One day, I was crawfishing with Albert, the little black boy whose Mama had rocked me to sleep after I was raped by Mike and Carl. We were in a ditch in front of Albert's house after a night of hard rain and the crawfish were so abundant they were just about crawling into our pockets. We were having so much fun I did not notice my father walking towards us. Suddenly Alberts Mama called him saying, "Albert, come here now." As he ran upon the porch I turned and seeing my father started to run upon the porch myself, but my father caught me. He had walked down from our house, and finding me, he grabbed me by the throat, picked me up, and started backhanding me while saying, "I don't ever want to catch you playing with niggers. Do you hear me, plowboy?" With his hand around my throat, all I could do was nod. He threw me down, and I landed in the creek. He turned to Albert, who had a terrified look on his face, standing beside his Mama. Before he could speak she said, "What don't you leave that poor boy alone?" My father said some terrible words about "Black bitches and their offspring." She took Albert and went inside. I healed, but I have never forgotten that day. The hatred and venom in my father's voice was something I could never understand or believe in.

One day as I was biking to school, I saw a snake trying to get out of my path. It slithered into a ditch. I jumped off my bike and followed it. I was in my glory. The water it was in was only a couple of inches deep, and the snake could not hide underneath. I squatted, and it reared its head back to strike. I did not know what kind of snake it was, but I knew that strike mode. As it struck, I dodged and laughingly said, "Oh snake, you'll never bite me!" It reared its head for a second strike. Its mouth was wide open, and it was hissing. I saw inside its mouth—it was as white as cotton. I had never seen one like that before, but my cousin Drew had warned me about that type of snake: "There's a snake known as a cottonmouth. It's mean, and if it bites you, you'll die. So be careful, little man."

Still laughing, I grabbed a twig and shoved it into its mouth. It bit down, and I saw venom coming out of its fangs. I wondered how long it would be before that snake would be able to eat anything. I stayed for an hour to play with it. I think it must have used all its venom up biting that twig. Oh yes, I played hooky that day. I found Albert, and we went crawfishing, knowing my father was not home.

Late one night while I was sleeping, Mama came running into my room from her bedroom screaming. She took my sister and me into the kitchen and pushed a table against the door. We crawled under the table. I hear a terrible roaring noise. The door was banging like crazy. The wind was howling, and Mama was praying to Jesus, Mary, and Joseph.

Afterward, the floor where I was sitting, and my shorts were soaked in blood that had come under the door from outside. I never did find out where the blood had come from. In the morning Mama wouldn't let me go outside for a long time. When I finally was able to go out I saw blood all over the door and steps.

Walking around the yard, I saw old pecan trees down. For a while, I had fun climbing on those trees. The next day in school, the kids made fun of me when I told them about the blood on my shorts. The nuns overheard them and made everybody bow their heads and say Hail Mary's and Our Fathers. After that, I went further down into that black hole I kept hidden from everybody and promised myself I would never tell them anything else. I never did. I was keeping more feelings shoved way down deep.

Mama told me I would grow up to be big and tall. I told her I did not want to. My father was very big, mean, and tall to me, as were Mike and Carl. I was frightened of them. I kept telling her I never wanted to be big and tall, and after a while for some reason, Mama made me wear a red dress around the house for about a week. I don't know why she made me wear it. I suspect now it was just to shut me up.

CHAPTER 28

Paw

I knew my cousin Drew's father as Paw. He had the ugliest feet I had ever seen. He never wore shoes except on Sundays for church. I used to poke at his feet and laugh. Sometimes, I would hold my nose and say, "Pew you," and he would laugh.

One day, my father drove Paw to Baton Rouge, and he asked my father to let me go with them. Paw had bought a Model T, and my father towed it home for him with his car. When we got back to Drew's house, I started to get into the T, but my father grabbed me by the neck, picked me up, and backhanded me saying, "I never want to catch you in that goddamn car!" He never told me why, just not to get in it. Of course, he did not do that in front of my cousin or Paw.

His threats did not stop me. Whenever my father was not around, I would meet Paw through the swamp on another dirt road. I was too little to reach the pedals, so he would let me sit on his lap and steer the car. We would go down the dirt roads with both doors flapping at about thirty miles per hour. Sometimes, I stayed on the road, and other times, I drove into a ditch. It didn't matter to Paw; he would gently steer the car out of the ditch. We always had fun and a lot of laughs. I loved Paw.

CHAPTER 29

My First Swimming Lesson

I was working the midnight-to-eight shift in the summer of 1978 patrolling the south end of Sandy Town. During such patrols, I came across all kinds of lakes and ponds. I had grown up fishing and was always on the lookout for good spots.

Late one summer night, my partner and I received a radio call about a fire in the woods off an old railroad bed. I knew the area; kids liked to party there. We used our blue lights and headed for it fast. We saw about a dozen kids partying. Most of the kids I knew by sight, and some I knew by name. The fire was well contained by the rocks they had piled up to make a fire pit. Some of the boys and girls were drinking beer. My partner wanted to start making arrests. I took him aside and said, "Look, I know most of these kids, and they're not bad. They're never in trouble, and there is really no place for them to go in town. They're out here partying and not hurting anybody."

It took a lot of talking, but my partner finally agreed to let the kids go. I told the kids that we would have to take their beer and that they had to leave. Most of them knew me, but some knew my partner and his reputation. They left immediately.

I saw a boy I knew walking up from a nearby lake. He was carrying a fishing pole and a couple of good-sized largemouth bass. He started looking around for his friends. I talked to him just as the fire department arrived to put out the fire. My partner yelled, "Hey, Gator, looks as if he likes to fish too." During that period of my life the nickname of Gator was sell established throughout the town. The boy told me that the lake was filled with many kinds of fish and that night or day fishing was great. I explained the situation to him, and he left.

At the time, I owned a twelve-foot aluminum boat. One morning, while off duty, I put my boat in the water near where the kids had been partying. About a half hour afterward, a cruiser flashed its blue lights at me as he drove past. About a half hour later, I saw another cruiser pull up. The lieutenant in charge of the midnight-to-eight shift got out and said, "I can't believe you're fishing with a cane pole." I replied, "Yep. I've been using one all my life."

He asked, "Having any luck?" I pulled a stringer from the water with a nice bass, perch, and a sunfish attached. I had caught more, but I always turned loose what I did not want to eat. I just loved to fish.

He asked, "What are you using for bait?"

"Dough balls."

"I've never heard of using dough balls."

I took some out of a plastic bag and showed him. He looked at me, smiled, and shook his head. He was amazed when I told him I had used them ever since I was a boy growing up in Louisiana. He said, "I guess I learned something new today. Hey, if you don't want to eat all those fish, don't forget about me."

After he left, I pondered our talk. My eyes misted over and my mind clouded as I remembered all the times I had not told him about. Especially the one about when I had gone fishing with my father and wound up having my first swimming lesson.

Paw worked as a nighttime security guard in a shipyard on the Tchefuncte River in Mayville. Occasionally, my father would take me fishing at night on one of the old piers while Paw was working. We fished for catfish, and we always caught them using dough balls. This was my most favorite thing to do because Paw had an old, one-eyed dog that would chase flashlight beams. Sometimes, my father would throw a nickel to him, and the dog would catch it in midair and keep it in his cheek like a chipmunk does.

My father started taking me fishing every time he was around. Sometimes, we went at night, and other times, we went during the day at the shipyard or somewhere else on the river. A bridge crossed a creek that ran under the dirt road leading down to the lighthouse on Lakeshore Road and emptied into the river. In the day, we used worms and dough balls as bait.

One day while fishing in the creek, the water was very clear, and we saw the fish, but they were not biting. We tried worms, some big, black-and-yellow grasshoppers, and dough balls, but nothing worked. My father walked over to his car, opened the trunk, took out a .22 caliber, lever-action Marlin rifle, and shot several fish. He sent me into the creek to retrieve them. We took them home and cleaned them in the backyard, and Mama cooked them.

Whenever we were going catfishing, Mama always made us a big dough ball, and then we used smaller dough balls on hand lines to fish off a pier. In the daytime, we saw big gators lying on the riverbanks soaking up the sun. At night, we saw them in the water; their eyes would shine brightly in the moonlight or when Paw would shine his flashlight on them. On one occasion, we saw some animal go into the water and start to swim across the river. In a matter of moments, a big gator grabbed the animal and dragged it underwater with hardly a fight.

When he was fishing, my father was always in a good mood even though he treated me harshly at times. He was always coaching me quietly and gently. It was obvious to me that he knew a lot about fishing, and I was eager to learn and to please him. When we fished during the day, we always went very early in the morning, usually before the sun was up, so we could be wherever we would be fishing at first light. He always said that was the best time to catch fish because they were hungry at daybreak. On a few occasions while we were night fishing at the shipyard, my father asked me if I knew how to swim. I told him that I had not learned yet, but that Grant Jo said he would teach me one day. Of course, he was away in the Army now and my father new it.

One night, he asked me again about swimming. I just told him not yet. I was scared to death he was going to tell me to swim in the river. He explained the difference between swimming in saltwater and freshwater. He said that he had been swimming all over the world and that it was easier to swim in saltwater because the salt helped you to stay afloat. He said it was very difficult to swim in freshwater because there was no salt in it and the freshwater would pull you down. He became very quiet, and in a few minutes, he got up. I thought he was going to pee off the pier. That night was very dark because it was cloudy. He grabbed me by the nape of my neck with one hand and grabbed my shorts with the other. He threw me into the river. The water was about ten feet below the pier. As I was falling, I heard him yell, "Learn to swim, plowboy."

I hit the dark water and went under. My thoughts were on the gators nearby. Somehow, I made it back to the surface and flapped my arms. I started to swim toward a tugboat tied to the pier about twenty feet away. I reached it and climbed up some old tires tied to the boat's hull. He said, "Good thing you learned to swim because them gators were coming for you." I climbed out of the water and ran to hide. I stayed hidden while he walked around yelling, "Get your plowboy ass in the car!" He eventually drove off, and I spent the rest of the night with Paw.

The next morning, Paw dropped me off at my cousin's house. I walked home through the path out back. Upon arrival, I found my father had left. All Mama said was, "Are you hungry?"

I never trusted my father again. There were many times afterward that I thought about that night and believed he had been hoping I would drown or the gators would get me. I always wondered what I had done wrong that had made him hate me so much.

CHAPTER 30

The Pirogue

One cold winter day in late 1978, I was on patrol in the Brant City section of Sandy Town. Dispatch called about a medical emergency at a friend's house on Ocean Street. I put on my blue lights and went there. I saw an ambulance pulling up. Running inside, I found my friend, a retired Sandy Town policeman named Mr. Simmons, slumped over in his overstuffed chair. I asked, "Are you, all right?" His response was slow and slurred. The left side of his mouth was drooping, and he could not raise his left arm. I suspected he had had a stroke. I knew he had heart and other medical issues. Tears filled my eyes. I knew I was witnessing my friend's final descent. After the ambulance had taken him to the hospital, I stayed with his wife for an hour to help her calm down. Afterward, I drove to the police station to inform the on-duty officers of his condition.

At home, I told my wife and kids about his condition. All were sad. He was in the process of retiring just as I was joining the force in 1974. Because of my passion for boats, my family had become close friends with him and his wife. At the time, he had a twenty-four-foot wooden boat he kept moored in the South River in the Hum Rock section of Sandy Town. Not able to enjoy the boat himself, he asked me if I would like to buy it. I told him I would. An amount was agreed upon, and I became the owner of the *Se-Tag*. I kept the same name in honor of our friendship. When I told him about the name, I saw happiness in his eyes and heard the heart felt thank you in his voice.

Late that afternoon, my wife and I drove to the hospital to visit him. He was on monitors and IVs. He was in good spirits but was very weak. His speech was still not back to normal. My wife and I stayed until visiting hours were over. There were tears in his eyes as we were leaving, and I gave him a hug and a kiss on the forehead saying, "I'll be back tomorrow to see you." I gave his wife a hug and whispered, "If you need anything or if his condition changes, please call, okay?" She nodded and said, "I will."

My wife and I got home, and I told our kids about his condition and that it did not look good. Early evening that night, the phone rang. I looked at my wife and shook my head. After talking for a few minutes, I hung up, turned to my wife, and said, "He's gone." My kids and us started to cry. Over the past few years, we had become close to him.

After talking for a few minutes, I grabbed a pint of blackberry brandy and told my wife I would be back shortly. I walked out into the cold night air to the edge of our property. I looked at *Se-Tag* stanchioned beside the driveway. I had had the boat trailered there for the winter over the past three years. Smiling, I made a toast: "This one's for you. I will treasure your friendship forever." I took a long pull on the bottle of brandy. I climbed in the old boat and sat in the captain's chair. Looking around the boat, I said, "You're old and need a lot of work, but my family and I have already had lots of fun on you, and we'll do so again." I took another long pull of brandy, leaned back, and disregarding the cold creeping into my bones, I let my thoughts return to another time and place long ago and a ride on another old wooden boat.

One day, my father came home and woke me at 5:00 a.m. "Get up. I'm going to show you something very special today." I was scared, and told him I did not want to go, but he said, "You're going." He dragged me out of my bed. He drove to downtown Mayville and parked off the road near the creek where he had shot the fish. Getting out of the car, he took the rifle out of the trunk and walked to the riverbank with me following slowly behind. Going through a lot of brush, my mind racing, we reached the river. He pointed to an old wooden boat tied to a tree. He told me that the boat was a pirogue. He said that when he was a kid, it belonged to him and his best friend Jo Jo. "We used it for fishing, catching muskrats, and sometimes gators. We sold the skins and the meat."

We got into the boat, and he started paddling; at least I thought he was paddling. He said he was sculling, and he showed me how to do it. After a few minutes, he told me to try it. I tried, but the paddle kept slipping out of the notch in the back of the boat. He became very angry and started hitting me with the barrel of his rifle. I tried again with the same result. Again, he hit me saying, "Goddamn it! You can't ever do anything right, and you'll never amount to anything, plowboy."

Eventually, he sculled us down river toward Lake Pontchartrain. Just before reaching the lake, we came to a canal. He sculled into it for about half a mile. We started to smell a terrible stench, and he told me that the smell was coming from a gator's nest. He said the nest had been there ever since he was a kid and maybe even longer. He said he and Jo Jo used to catch baby gators there and sell them.

As we approached the nest right on the bank of the canal, I saw a big gator watching us with mouth wide open and hissing loudly. He said, "She has eggs in that nest. If we come back in a week or so, we can catch some babies." He continued sculling.

Not far from that nest, we came to an open area, and I saw the most gators I had ever seen.

Most of them were about three feet long. He said these stayed in this old rice paddy because if they went into the river, the big gators would eat them.

As we entered the area, they came right up to the boat. My father raised his rifle and shot one in its head. He handed the gun to me and said, "Shoot that one," pointing at another gator. I aimed and pulled the trigger. The shot completely missed the gator. He grabbed the rifle and shot the second gator. He hit me so hard with the barrel of the rifle that I went flying out of the boat into the water. I stood and tried to run for what looked like solid ground. The water was shallow, only about two or three feet deep. The mud was pulling me down just as it had that day in the pool. The area was only about ten feet away. As I walked that way, I looked behind me and saw several gators following closely.

I reached the spot and found that it was not dry but marshy and covered in green scum. As I stepped into the gooey mess, several snakes slithered away. My father yelled, "Get back into the goddamn boat or I'll leave you here." I yelled, "I want to walk back to the car." My father said, "You can't. It's too far, too swampy, and there's no dry land." He sculled over to where I was and said, "Get in the goddamn boat, plowboy!" I got in, and with pure disgust in his voice, he said, "You're never going to amount to anything, plowboy! You can't do a goddamn thing right!" He sculled back to the gators he had shot and made me help drag them into the boat.

He covered the gators with an old tarp already in the pirogue. While sculling back to the car, my father talked the whole way telling me what a good-for-nothing kid I was and how I would never amount to anything. I stared at the bottom of the boat not saying anything. I wasn't listening; my thoughts were on Red and how he would have made short work of one of those gators if they had tried to eat me. Red and I had trekked through the muddiest mud and swampiest swamp chasing whatever we could catch. He was my best friend in the whole world, and I missed him badly. Everything he was saying was shoved down deep, where nobody would ever see it.

We loaded those gators into the trunk and drove home. He stopped at the gate. Without looking at me, he said, "Get out, plowboy." I was not moving fast enough for him; he looked at me and again said, "I said get out, plowboy!" He said something I did not understand: "You look just like an old nigger pulling a plow." Many times, he had called me plowboy, but I had never heard those words before, and I did not know what they meant. By then, I knew he hated blacks. With these new words ringing in my ears, I then knew why he hated me so much: I was a nigger. I got out, and he drove off with the gators in the trunk. I climbed over the gate and ran and ran until I came to a special place Red and I would sometimes go. Lying down and chewing on a piece of grass, I closed my eyes and pictured Red and me running through the swamps. I cried myself to sleep.

Later that evening, Mama and I were sitting on the back steps when my father drove up. He walked to us, looked at me, and said, "Go to bed, plowboy!" Head hanging down, I walked inside, shutting the door behind me. For a moment, I listened and heard him say to Mama, "I got some good money for those gators." I never saw those gators again, and nobody ever said anything about them. I figured he had sold them as he had said he had done as a kid.

A couple of weeks later, I was with Drew in his backyard. The question was rambling around in my head. Finally, I asked, "Drew, am I a nigger?" He stopped, looked down at me and said, "Why no, little man. You're a white boy. Why do you ask?" I shrugged. "I don't know." Nothing else was said. I still couldn't figure out what I had done wrong to cause my father to hate me.

One day after I started school in the fall, my father showed up. Mama started packing the old suitcase. I asked, "Mama, where are we going?" She put her fingers to her mouth and said, "Hush now, Johnny." My father heard me and very harshly said, "Go get into the back seat of the car, plowboy."

He came out carrying the suitcase and placed it in the trunk. Mama was carrying my sister, and she put her in the back seat with me. She got in the front seat, and my father drove off. As we drove past my cousin's house, I wanted to cry, but instead, I said, "I don't want to leave." My father reached around the front seat and backhanded me. "Shut the hell up, plowboy!" Nobody had said anything to me, but I knew we were leaving Louisiana. My whole world was being taken away from me. I was so sad that I started to cry inside, not letting my father hear me.

CHAPTER 31

Leaving Louisiana

We moved to Green Springs, Florida. My father had been stationed there in the navy for several years. He drove all day and into the night stopping only for gas.

When we got to Florida, my father stopped in front of the weirdest looking place I had ever seen. It was white and covered in metal, and it had two windows and one door. My father opened the door. It was basically three rooms—two small bedrooms and a kitchen/living room combination with a small table, two chairs, and a couch. There was a very small bathroom with a metal shower. There was a small porch with no railings at the front. We were living in half of a Quonset hut. Another family lived in the other half.

The beatings from my father became a daily routine for one reason or another. I became known, in the neighborhood as the kid who was always in trouble and who would not pay attention to anybody. I started getting blamed for many bad things. I was withdrawing further and further into that black mass of my tortured mind. I wouldn't talk to anybody; everybody just started ignoring me, and I ignored them.

The neighbors must have spoken to my mother and father, because one time, my father asked me, "What's wrong with you? Are you stupid? Goddamn it! You're never going to amount to anything, plowboy!" When I did not answer, he beat me and sent me to bed with no supper. Something I was starting to notice was that I got a lot of whippings and beatings but that my sister did not. It was becoming a fact of life for me that whether I did something bad or not, I got blamed for it. Sometimes, my sister would do something bad, but I got the blame. Other times, I would do bad things and when asked about them would just say I had not. What was the difference? It did not matter—good or bad, I got blamed. It was easy to lie whether I needed to or not. I had no feelings of remorse or guilt.

I found a hiding place from my father; it was an old drainage line that was a little taller than me. Unknown to me then, it started in the naval base, ran through the area where we lived, and ended up draining into the St. Johns River a couple of miles from us. Whenever I knew my father was coming home, I would hide there. The lid was very heavy, but it was pushed to the side, so I could get in. One day while I was down there, somebody pushed the lid into place. I was trapped. For what seemed miles and hours, I walked and crawled before I found a way out where it emptied into the river. I never hid in there again. I believed it was my father who had put that lid on because on another occasion, he had seen me going into the drain. The next day, he asked, "Why were you going into the drain yesterday?" I said, "I was chasing a rabbit, and he was a big one, Daddy." I knew he would like that story because on some occasions, he and I went rabbit hunting. He would shoot a rabbit, and we took it home, skinned it, and ate it. My sister did not want to eat rabbit, so he never made her. I liked rabbit, so I ate all of mine and asked for my sister's share. Mama did not eat rabbit either. She said, "Rabbit is heathen food."

My sister and I shared a bed in one bedroom. One day, a stray cat showed up at our front door. My father was not home, so I started playing with him in the bedroom. Just before I knew my father would arrive home, I put the cat outside. A little while later, I heard my father's car pull up. In a few minutes, my father walked in holding the cat and saying, "Look what I found." I asked, "Can I keep him?" To my surprise, he simply handed him to me and walked off. I played with that cat every day.

One day, my father came in the house yelling for me. I tried to get out the door, but he was blocking it. I was holding the cat hoping he would not hit me. He grabbed it out of my hands and swung it around by its tail. He threw the cat down. It ran off. I saw that my father had broken its tail. He started hitting me with his belt and buckle telling me something he had heard on the base earlier that day that I had done. He said I was seen by the trucks and was inside them. Even though I had spent the day playing with the cat and had not gone near the base, I said, "I'm sorry. I just wanted to see inside the trucks." I knew it did not matter.

After that day, we named the cat Muepps because whenever he wanted to go outside, he pushed the screen door open with his paw and as he ran out, his bent tail always got caught in the slamming door and he would yelp "*Muepp*." One day, I could not find him. I looked everywhere. I checked under my bed and found a hole in the covering underneath; Muepps was inside. The bed was just a wood frame with a very thin mattress, and sometimes, I would crawl inside the frame, holding Muepps tight, and hide from my father. He never found me there.

Once while I was outside of our unit, the woman who lived in the next unit behind ours came running outside, saw me, and said, "There's a big snake in my house! I'm going to call the shore patrol!" I told her I would catch it for her. She asked, "Aren't you afraid of snakes?" "Nope," I replied. "I've caught plenty of old snakes." She told me it was by her stove.

I went in and saw a rattlesnake coiled up right where she had said it was. Using two of her pots, I approached the snake. His tail was really moving, and his rattles were loud. I could tell he was mad as hell. Getting close but just out of his reach, I let him strike several times. The last time, he hit one pot a little slower, and I used the other one to trap him. I grasped him right behind his head. I looked in his mouth and saw long, needle-like fangs. I had seen what rattlers could do. I was sure glad he had not bitten me. I took the snake outside; the rest of his body was dragging on the ground behind me. A couple of neighbors were watching as I walked out carrying that snake. I couldn't understand why they were so scared. I told them, "Don't worry, he was just looking for something to eat. I'll take care of him." I carried the snake across the road and turned him loose in the thick brush, where I knew there were lots of rabbits.

A few months later, a big machine showed up in our neighborhood. I ran over to see what was going on. The machine was tearing down that same Quonset hut. A lot of people were standing around watching. I asked the woman who lived there, "Why are they tearing down your house?" She told me that a little while after I had caught that snake for her, she had found another in the same place. She said she had reported it to the shore patrol and somebody had come to remove it. She forgot to tell them about the one I had caught for her. Later, when she remembered about that, she told the shore patrol about it.

They decided to dig up the flooring. We watched all day as they dug. Once they had everything out, they found a big nest of rattlesnakes. To me, it looked like a hundred, but it was probably a dozen or so. It did not matter. I was happy to see them. I loved snakes, crawfish, lamprey eels, and all wild animals.

That night, my father came home with news of how the navy had probably saved that woman and her family from horrible deaths. Looking at me, he said someone had caught a rattlesnake before that but had never reported it to the shore patrol. Continuing to stare at me, he asked, "Do you know anything about that?" Very easily, I told him, "Nope." He replied, "I better not find out it was you!" He never found out.

One day, I came upon a young black boy playing in a ditch. I asked, "What are you doing?" He said, "I'm catching tadpoles." I said, "I used to catch and eat them." He asked, "Do they taste good?" I lied. "Yes." He caught one, and I told him to eat the whole thing in one bite. I laughed when he spit it out and said, "They have a bitter taste." I said, "Yeah, but you get used to it."

I noticed he had something sticking out of his ear. I asked him what it was, and he said, "Leaves." When I asked why he put leaves in his ears, he said, "My daddy hits me a lot, and it helps." I asked, "What do you mean?" He replied, "The hits don't hurt as much." He told me he put leaves in his nose to help with pain and bleeding.

I started putting leaves in my nose and ears. One day while my dad was hitting me, a leaf popped out of my ear. My father picked it up and asked, "Why do you put leaves in your ears?" With my head hanging low, I said, "I don't know" and shrugged. He really started yelling at me, and the beating got worse.

Sometimes, I put too many leaves in my nose and ears. When that happened, I had leaves sticking out. When Mama saw them, she immediately took me to the base infirmary to have my ears and nose washed out. I stopped putting leaves in my nose and ears because I did not like the washing out by the doctor. They used long tongs to reach inside my nose and ears to pull the leaves out. They then pushed a metal tube in and used cold water to flush out all the residue.

One time, instead of leaves, I put pencil erasers in my ears. Because of the color, Mama could not see them when she checked my ears. The erasers stayed in my ears so long that I developed an infection. Mama took me back to the base infirmary. The doctor had a hard time getting the erasers out. Afterward, he again washed out my ears and gave me a shot in the butt for the infection. When he stuck the needle in, I yelled, "That hurts!" and jumped off the table. I ran with the needle and syringe hanging out of my butt. The doctor had pulled my shorts down to give me the shot, and as I ran, they fell to my ankles. I kicked them off in the hallway. Nurses and corpsmen were chasing me around the building, but they never caught me. I ducked under a stairway and pulled the needle out.

After hiding for a while, I walked naked back to the emergency room. Mama, my father, and the doctor were waiting for me. My father did not say a word, but when we got home, I got another beating with his belt.

The black boy and I became friends, but we knew we had to keep our friendship secret. We would meet in a secret place in the nearby woods. I told him how my father would beat me and tell me he was sure that one day, niggers were going to kill us white folks. I also told him how my father kept a loaded rifle and shotgun beside his bed. My friend said his father had told him that one day, whitey would hang all black people, and that he kept a loaded handgun under his mattress.

One day, my father came home unexpectedly and caught me playing with the black boy. He got out of the car, picked him up, and threw him into the ditch we were playing in saying, "Get out of here, you goddamn nigger!" He started beating me. That time, he used his fist not only on my head but also in my stomach. He screamed, "I told you I never want to catch you with a nigger!" He picked me up and threw me into the back seat of his car. When we arrived home, he again picked me up, carried me inside, and threw me on the bed saying, "You keep your goddamn ass in that bed!" I lay in bed crying until the next day after he left for work. Mama came in asking, "Are you hungry?" I said no. I got up and ran out to the woods. I found the young black boy there. We hid all day. Neither of us wanted to talk about the incident from the day before. After that, we drifted apart, and I never saw him again.

Another time, Mama gave me some items to take to a friend on the other side of our Quonset housing area. She said, "You better come right back, or I'll call the shore patrol." On the way back, I was walking by a white picket fence. A pretty girl named Betty Sue was hanging onto the gate. She had long, light-brown, banana curls, and she was wearing a puffed-out pink dress. She asked me if I wanted to come to her tea party. She reminded me of my first love, Carol, so of course I said yes.

We sat at a child's table with four chairs. She had two dolls sitting in chairs. She told me to sit in the chair across from her. She talked to the two dolls as if they were our children; she referred to me as Daddy. "Look, Mary Beth and Sarah, Daddy's home from work."

Remembering my experiences with Carol, I didn't want any part of being a daddy. I was about ready to bolt when her mother brought us tea in a small, flowered teapot and some cookies. On the table were four tiny teacups with saucers that matched the teapot. One set was in front of each of us, and one set in front of each doll. She poured tea into all four cups. She continued to talk to the dolls and me as if we were a family.

After drinking a cup of tea and wolfing down half a dozen cookies, I grabbed the teapot and gulped down half the tea. She got mad and made faces at me. "That's not how a daddy drinks tea in front of his children." I had heard enough. I got up and said, "I better go home." As I ran out of the yard, I heard her crying and telling Mary Beth and Sarah, "Daddy's leaving us." Years later, I wondered, *could she have lived through that experience with her own father?*

On the way home, I saw a shore patrol truck. He stopped and called me by name over to his loud speaker. Instead of going over to the truck, I ran home. Mama was real mad and yelled at me. I was out front when my father got home. He started beating me. A neighbor finally came over and made him stop.

I was becoming more withdrawn. When people would ask me something and I did not answer fast enough for my father, he would tell them I was deaf and stupid. But it was just that I did not want to talk to anybody. I was talking to myself more and more. Sometimes, people would hear me and shake their heads. Every day I was angry, and I hated my father more and more.

One day, my father said to Mama, my sister, and me, "Tomorrow, we're going to pick blueberries." The next morning, he woke us up early. We walked to the field next to the road coming into the Quonset area. My father found a bush that was loaded with berries. As he picked some, he heard a rattling. Looking under the bush, he saw a big rattlesnake. He called me over and said, "Kill that goddamn rattlesnake!" I saw the rattler coiled and ready to strike. Smiling, I picked up two sticks, and using them as I had used the pots, I tired that snake out. Trapping him under one stick, I picked him up. Instead of killing the snake, I walked back to where we had already picked blueberries. I turned him loose under another bush that was not a blueberry, but I couldn't resist using the stick to open his mouth just to see those fangs as he spurted venom.

By then, my father was already onto another big bush. I thought he had never noticed. He called me over. For a moment, he just stared, but then he backhanded me and knocked me to the ground. I spilled all my blueberries. He yelled, "When I tell you to do something, goddamn it, plowboy, do what I say! Now pick up those goddamn blueberries." I had argued with myself about killing that snake. I believe I won the argument and wanted to save it. I loved all snakes.

Fishing continued to be the only times when my father was gentle and would teach me things, and I eagerly looked forward to those days. One afternoon, he let me know we were going fishing the next morning. He told me to dig up some worms. I excitedly raced to a special location I knew where I could dig for some. Wanting to impress my father, I made sure I took only the big, fat ones. I filled my can and walked home proud of my selection of worms.

I put them on the Quonset huts porch. Inside, I saw my father and sister sitting at the table eating and talking. Mama was standing at the stove cooking. With a happy grin on my face, I blurted out, "Daddy, I dug us some good worms, and I left them right on the front porch" as I walked to him. My father stopped talking and motioned me over. With a huge smile still on my face, I approached. He grabbed me by the neck and pulled me to within an inch of his face, which had turned into a twisted demon's face. Unable to speak, I tried to get away, but his grip was like a vice. In a slow and deliberate voice, he said, "Don't you ever interrupt me when I'm talking to your sister, do you understand?" Not being able to answer, I just nodded as fear coursed through my body.

With a mere flick of his huge arm, he tossed me across the room and said, "Go to bed now!" I walked into my bedroom and found Muepps lying on it. I was crying, and my father must have heard me because he yelled, "Stop that goddamn crying or I'll come in there and give you something to cry about!" I grabbed Muepps and buried my face in his thick, soft fur. My sobs continued, but they were muffled.

Mama came in and asked, "Are you hungry?" I had stopped crying but was still holding Muepps tightly. I shook my head. Mama left. I pulled Muepps close to my ear. Listening to his soft and gentle purring, I fell asleep.

Early the next morning, my father woke me by shaking me hard and saying, "Get up! It's time to go fishing!" I am not sure if I said out loud, "I don't want to go" or if I only thought it. The next thing I knew, my father threw a glass of water in my face and yelled, "I said get up, goddamn it!" He yanked me out of bed. I landed on the floor and saw him bending over to kiss my sleeping sister.

Shortly after that, we left our house carrying cane poles and the can of worms. I was lagging not wanting to go because I was still feeling the fearful effects of the night before. Daylight was just breaking as we walked through some heavy woods and came to a tall wire fence with one strand of barbwire on top. We saw cattle grazing a long way off. We climbed over the fence and continued walking. After a few minutes, we heard and saw cattle running in our direction. My father told me to run and pointed in a direction that was more toward the running cattle. He ran in the opposite direction.

Dropping my cane pole and can of worms, I started running as fast as I could in the direction my father had told me to. Looking back, I saw they were chasing only me because my father was in the clear on the other side of the fence. Just before they reached me, I was able to climb over thinking I was safe. As the cattle reached the fence running at full speed, one bull leaped and almost cleared the top but got hung up on the barbwire. I stood shocked as he bellowed and fell to the ground on my side. Scrambling to his feet, he started toward me, but I was next to an old oak tree with some low-hanging branches and was climbing as fast as I could. The bull snorted, pawed the ground, and butted the tree several times. He kept up his snorting and pawing, but after about ten minutes, he tired of it and left.

I waited until he was out of sight before I climbed down. My father came walking up. I started to say how close we had come to getting trampled when he hit me full in the mouth with a backhand that knocked me to the ground. "Goddamn it! Can't you do anything right? You shouldn't have worn that red shirt. Everybody knows Brahman bulls are attracted to red. Now see what you've done? You messed up our fishing trip!"

With my head bowed, I walked behind him home staying on the outside of the fence. I felt terrible because I had ruined the day. I wanted to apologize, but I was afraid to talk. Before that day, I had never heard of a Brahman bull much less seen one.

We lived about a mile from St. Johns River. Without any warning, my father woke me up early one morning before the sun was up saying, "Get up! We're going fishing!" That time, I got up immediately, remembering that glass of cold water in my face. We walked to a fish camp where you could launch boats or rent them and buy live bait. My father bought a couple of dozen shiners. We put them in a large jar with a large mouth. My job was to swirl the water in the jar every few minutes to get fresh oxygen into it. On previous trips when one or two would die, I always got a beating and a "Goddamn it! Can't you even do this right? Jesus Christ! You'll never amount to anything!" That time, I made sure I kept my hand in the jar all the time. My father rented a small wooden rowboat. As he was rowing out in the river, he yelled, "Goddamn it! Try to keep those shiners alive this time!"

After a few minutes, he anchored the boat in the middle of a large patch of lily pads. My father had an old fishing rod and reel. I had only a hand line. He hooked shiner after shiner but kept on losing them and cursing loudly every time. Sometimes, a fish would take them, and other times, they just got off the hook. My father would let me use only some old wooden lures he had. I tied one to my line and tossed it. That one was green and white with some red on the belly, and it had three sets of treble hooks on it. It kind of resembled a largemouth bass, and it was my favorite.

It landed on top of a large lily pad about ten feet from the boat. Having fished many times like that, I knew just what to do. I let it sit there for a few moments before quickly pulling it off. It made a small splash as it hit the water. Almost immediately, something hit that lure and started a run. It took all my line's slack, but I had tied the end to my wrist. It was running back and forth, and I yelled to my father, "Daddy! I got a bass!"

He turned to look at me, and that bass broke water and jumped about two feet into the air. It was shaking its head hard trying to dislodge the lure, but I saw that it had swallowed two of the three treble hooks; only one set was out of his mouth. As my father got to his feet, he angrily shouted, "Goddamn it! You're going to lose him!" He started my way.

Seeing him coming, I grabbed the line and pulled hard to set the hooks. I started pulling hard trying to bring the bass to the boat, but he was strong, and all I could do was hold onto the line. My father reached me and screamed, "Give me the line!" I said, "No." He got madder and tried to take it, but I wouldn't let him. I moved to the farthest point of the bow and held my hand over the side of the boat. He finally gave up and sat, letting me fight this monster fish. The fish was strong. I had never caught one that big. My hands began to bleed, and time after time, he almost pulled me overboard, but I hung on for dear life not wanting to face my father's wrath if I lost it.

I am not sure how long it took me to boat that fish, but when I finally got him next to it, my father reached down, grabbed it by the gills, and brought it aboard. I looked at my father with the biggest grin I think I had ever made. He too was grinning. He made a stringer from another piece of line and put the bass back in the water after tying it off on the side of the boat. We fished for a little while more until my father lost all the shiners, and then we headed into the fish camp. He had caught one small bass, which he also put onto the homemade stringer.

At the fish camp, he had them weigh my bass—twelve pounds and a few ounces. All the fishermen congratulated my father and asking him what he had used for bait. He was all smiles telling them he was using shiners, but never once did he tell them I had caught the fish.

Walking all the way home, my father carried my fish and I carried his. We carried them by putting our hands down their mouths with our fingers sticking out through the gills. I forgot about the fish camp, and I couldn't keep my eyes off that bass. I was so proud of it and couldn't wait until we got home so I could tell Mama and my sister all about it. My father never said a word.

At home, my father told me to take his fish and go in. He walked to our neighbors carrying my fish. I stood in the door long enough to hear one neighbor say, "My God, That's a big bass!" He laughed and said, "He was hard to bring in." As they talked, I tried to tell Mama about my fish, but she took my fathers from me and said, "Be quiet and go to your bedroom."

In my bedroom, I saw my sister playing with Muepps. I lay down, curled up with my knees drawn up to my chest, and went to sleep. Nothing was ever said about my bass, and I never saw it again.

On another occasion, he again woke me before daylight with the usual, "Get up! We're going fishing!" That time, he drove deep into the woods. He parked on the side of the road, and we dug for some worms. I had a new cane pole he had bought me, and he had brought an old bamboo fly rod in a metal case. Carrying them and the can of worms, we walked a long way back into the woods. Eventually, we came to a small lake and started fishing by some lily pads. We started catching brim, perch and goggle-eye, small pan fish I had caught many times in Louisiana. He was very helpful teaching me the proper way to fish, what hooks to use, and how to keep the bait looking alive. Back home, after he and I cleaned the fish, Mama rolled them in flour and fried them in lard in her old, cast iron skillet. She also made hushpuppies. I cherish those memories.

I believe we lived in Green Spring for about one year and during that time, I have no memory of attending any school.

CHAPTER 32

Shots Fired

One quiet Sunday morning in October, I was patrolling the south end of Sandy Town on the day shift when all cruisers received a radio call about a female who had been assaulted in the business center by a male subject who had a handgun. A detailed description was given of the male and the car he had driven away in. I called dispatch saying that I knew a male and his car living in the town next to us that matched both descriptions. Dispatch radioed back saying they would notify the police department in that town.

The suspect's direction of travel was unknown. I drove toward the business center thinking that if the incident had just happened, I might find him closer to the center. As I drove through the beach area, I saw a car parked next to a seawall. The car was far enough away from me that I couldn't see what it looked like. I approached the car from the rear. When I got within fifty feet, I saw it was not the one I was looking for. I drove out.

As I was approaching the main road, I saw a slow-moving car coming toward me. I immediately knew it was not the car I was looking for. My eyes were moving constantly left and right looking for the suspect's car. As the car coming toward me neared, I glanced to my left just as the male driver was next to me. His window was down, as was mine. I saw a male passenger in the front seat looking at me with a smile and pointing a large, black, semiautomatic handgun at me.

I immediately lay down on the seat and spun the steering wheel as I hit the gas. The cruiser spun around behind the car, which was still moving. Sitting up, I flipped on the blue lights and siren. The car had moved about a hundred feet, but it stopped, and I pulled within twenty feet of it. All of that had taken a mere two minutes. I stopped and shut off the siren but kept the blue lights on.

I grabbed the radio. "I have a man pointing a gun at me!" The male with the handgun opened his door, exited the car, and faced me holding the handgun, but he pointed it to the sky. I exited my cruiser. Gun drawn and pointed at the suspect while staying behind my cruiser door, I told him, "Drop the gun or I'll shoot you!" He laughed and took a step toward me still holding the handgun pointed at the sky. I heard dispatch calling repeatedly asking me where I was. I could not answer.

I again said, "Drop the gun or I'll shoot you!" I saw about five or so teenage boys on a front porch about twenty-five feet away. These kids were hooting and hollering, "Shoot the pig! Shoot him!" over and over. The subject looked at the kids, laughed, and took another step toward me, still pointing the gun up. He was standing beside his car, and with each step, he neared the trunk. I said, "Put the gun on the trunk or I'll shoot you!"

I heard the captain who was in charge that day speaking on the radio to dispatch. He told them he had passed my location a short time earlier. I heard him give dispatch my location, and he told them he would back me up.

Within moments, the captain arrived. As he exited his cruiser with gun drawn, the subject took another step toward me. He was next to the trunk still holding the handgun pointed up. The kids were still yelling, "Shoot the pig!" This time the Captain yelled, "Drop the gun!"

The subject, still laughing, started lowering the handgun. I did not know if he was going to shoot me or lay the gun on the trunk. I yelled, "Lay the gun on the trunk or I'll shoot you!" Smiling, he placed the gun on the trunk. I yelled, "Back up and place your hands behind your head!" The subject complied with my order still smiling.

After he backed up, I ran over to him while the captain kept him, and the driver covered. I picked up the handgun. With total amazement in my voice, I told the captain, "It's a goddamn plastic toy gun!" The captain asked, "Are you shitting me?" He walked up to the subject and said angrily, "Are you fucking crazy? This officer is one of the best shots in the department. I was the third best, with the Captain of course being the best. He could have killed you!" The subject simply shrugged.

The captain told me to bring the subject to the station as he went over to talk to the driver. I put handcuffs on him and put him in the rear seat of the cruiser. As I was getting into the front seat, I saw the kids on the porch still hooting and hollering. I recognized them as locals who called themselves the badass crew. I laughed and said, "Have a good day, kids." They yelled, "Fuck you, pig!" and a few other choice retorts. I had arrested all of them one Christmas Eve night. They were throwing snowballs at cars, but some of them were also throwing rocks, and they had broken several car windows. They hated me.

As I arrived at the station and took the subject out of the cruiser, the captain arrived. I took the handcuffs off, and the captain took the subject into another room to speak with him in private. About five minutes later, he came back with the subject. He looked at me shaking his head and said, "He did this whole thing as a Halloween prank!"

I looked at the subject. "You did this as a Halloween prank?"

"Yeah. I didn't think it was a big deal."

"You kidding me? If you'd brought the barrel of your gun down, I would have shot you dead. Do you realize that?"

"I do now," he replied without much conviction.

The captain and I spoke with him at length. After getting all his information—he was twenty-four, from New Hampshire, staying with his friend who'd been the driver—he was released.

A few nights later, I was patrolling with a partner on the midnight-to-eight shift. It was a cold, rainy, windy night. Of course, he wanted to know everything that had transpired in the gun situation. After telling him the story, he asked, "Why didn't you shoot him?"

"Because he never brought the gun down to bear on me."

"Bullshit. I would've shot him the minute he got out of his car."

I looked at him. "Well, I didn't, and I'm glad I didn't."

"You'd have been covered. You should have shot him."

I didn't answer.

A little later, I pulled into an empty parking lot. I turned off the headlights off but left the parking lights on. My partner was sound asleep. The stiff wind was making the cruiser rock back and forth. I rolled my window down halfway. The cold night air felt refreshing, and the cold rain pelting my face felt like little needles. I opened a deck of Lucky Strikes and lit one. Putting my head back on the headrest, I took a long drag, sucking the smoke deep into my lungs. As I blew it out through my nose, I let my thoughts wander.

I replayed the gun incident in my head just as it had happened. In the end, I still thought I'd done the right thing not shooting the kid. I wondered if he knew how lucky he was that it had been me and not some other officer. My thoughts returned to another time and another place long ago. I remembered it as if it had happened the previous day.

It was in the middle of the night. My sister and I were sleeping when Mama came into our bedroom and woke us up. "Hurry and get dressed."

I dressed and went into the kitchen/living room area of the Quonset hut. I saw Mama with that same old suitcase packed and sitting by the front door. My father was very angry about something. He was cursing loudly and holding a small black handgun. He checked to make sure it was loaded. I saw his rifle, his shotgun, and another gun with a large clip in it all leaning against the door. What he said made a chill run through my body. In an angry and harsh voice, he said, "Them goddamn niggers are running wild, and we have to drive right through them. I'm going to be ready!"

I always hated it when he talked about black people in that manner; I never understood why he did. He told us all to get into the car. I picked up Muepps intending to take him with us. My father tore the cat from my arms, opened the door, and threw him out into the cold, rainy night, saying, "We aren't taking no goddamn cat!"

The cold air hit me when I stepped out. The rain felt like needles jabbing me in the face. I couldn't even see the car. The wind was making howling noises and blowing so hard that it almost knocked me over.

My father carried the guns. Mama, carrying the suitcase, my sister, and I followed him. He threw the suitcase into the trunk and told my sister and me to get into the back seat. Mama got into the front seat. As we got in, he handed me the rifle and said, "Hold this. You might need it!" He got into the driver's seat and put the pistol, the shotgun, and the new gun on the seat between him and Mama. We drove off. Though he said nothing about where we were going, I knew in my heart we were leaving Florida for good. Except for some fishing trips, I had a lot of bad memories there, and I wasn't unhappy about leaving.

My father drove through the night while rain pelted the windows and the wind blew hard pushing the car all over the road. Raindrops started coming through my window and splashing me, but I didn't say anything. When the drops splashed on my sister, she yelled at me to close the window. Without asking anything, my father reached behind and backhanded me in the face. "Close the goddamn window, plowboy, and keep the gun away from the rain in case you need it!"

I tasted blood. The window wasn't open. The rubber around it was old and cracked, and it leaked. I knew it would not change anything anyway, so I said, "Okay, I did." I positioned myself and made sure the water wouldn't splash on my sister.

The next day, we were on a dirt road, and my father stopped and got us some sandwiches as he was gassing up. I got my first Nu-Grape soda. I loved it. The rain had stopped, and he continued driving. Sometime during that night, my sister and I had fallen asleep. We were awakened by Mama screaming loudly. Sitting up, I saw that my father was driving very slowly. There were black people all over the road and on the hood of the car. Some of them were running beside us and pounding on the car and windows. All I heard was Mama praying to Jesus, Mary, and Joseph and the blacks yelling and screaming. My father was cursing loudly, "Goddamn niggers!" He yelled, "Johnny, keep that goddamn rifle ready!"

He rolled his window down. He picked up his handgun, rested it on the door, and started shooting—*bang, bang, bang*. Mama and my sister were crying loudly. Sitting up as high as I could, I put the barrel of the rifle against my window when I saw a black face pressed against it. Shaking badly and in a scared voice, I yelled, "Okay, I'm ready, Daddy." I saw bullets from my father's gun hitting some people; others fell away from the car. My father sped up and kept firing the handgun at them until it was empty.

When we were clear, he turned to me and with the most demonic eyes I had ever seen, he said for the first of many times, "Don't ever let niggers take your mother and sister alive. They'll rape and kill them!"

I was eight. I knew why I was holding the rifle and what was expected of me—to protect Mama and my sister at all costs. My father continued driving until we reached his next duty station with no more incidents.

CHAPTER 33

Ocean View Amusement Park

My father had been transferred to Virginia. He was stationed aboard a ship and started going to sea a lot, leaving us alone. We moved into an apartment in Ocean View right on the ocean, and I loved it. We lived on the third floor. The apartment had a living room, kitchen with a small table and two chairs, two small bedrooms, and a small bathroom.

As before, my sister and I slept in the same bedroom. My sister hated getting sand all over her, so I started hanging around on the beach by myself. I loved to fish, but I did not have any fishing gear. I had left my cane pole in Florida. Sometimes walking along the beach, I saw small fish swimming close to shore. I would try to catch them, but I never did.

Sometimes, I saw blue crabs swimming along, and occasionally, I would catch one. I always brought it home, and Mama would boil it for me. I was still a skinny kid, and sometimes, I wandered onto other beach areas where there were older kids who would push me around or beat me up. It did not really bother me because beatings had become a part of my life; I was used to them. When I just stood there staring while talking to myself but not running, they called me names, but I did not care. I always came away thinking, *They, only think they're hurting me.* I shoved all those feelings further down deep.

I started going to a school about a mile away; I walked to it every day. I had lost a year of school and was placed back in first grade. School held no interest for me. I quickly became the new kid who was stupid. I did not get along with any of my classmates, I didn't listen to any of my teachers, and I didn't care what anybody thought of me. I never talked to them anyway. I was a loner; whenever possible, I stayed by myself. There was a hill with lots of woods in the sand dunes behind the school. Whenever I could, I would go there and watch the other kids and the teachers.

A few times, I just skipped school and walked to the Ocean View Amusement Park. I had never seen anything like it. Because I was such a scrawny, skinny, towheaded kid, I was able to sneak onto many rides. My favorite place to go was the house containing animals, which included snakes. There was a jar with the head of a big rattlesnake in it; a rabbit was in its mouth. Every time I went to that exhibit, I would stand in front of that snake and just stare at it for a long time. One day, an attendant asked, "Why do you always come here and stare at that snake?" I told him it was all wrong. He asked me what I meant. I pointed to the snake and said, "The head of the rabbit is sticking out of the rattlesnake's mouth." He laughed and said, "Yeah, that's how they caught and killed him."

I said, "Snakes always eat rabbits headfirst. That rabbit's head shouldn't be sticking out of the snake's mouth. His hind feet should."

"Kid, how do you know so much about snakes?"

I told him where I had come from and talked about my experiences with snakes, gators, and other animals. He seemed amazed at my stories. After that, every time I was in the exhibit, he would ask me to repeat stories for other people.

One day, I went back and saw that the exhibit was closed. I talked to the attendant and learned a large python had escaped and gone under the building. I said I would go under after it. He laughed. "No, son. They're bringing in a professional."

The python was eventually caught and returned to the exhibit. They never did change that rabbit in the rattler's mouth though.

In class, I was so disruptive that they would often send me out to sit on some bench or chair. Pretty soon, I learned just what to do to get out of class. No matter where I was, if I saw bigger kids bullying smaller kids, I always stood up to the bullies. Sometimes, a fight would break out and I would get beaten up. When the adults asked what had happened, I wouldn't say anything. One of the kids would point at me and of course, most of the time, I was punished for starting the fight. I really did not care what people thought. I was slipping deeper and deeper into that black hole. In my mind, I was right and all of them were wrong.

CHAPTER 34

Secret Places

On the first floor of our apartment building was a pretty, dark-haired woman named Jane. When I think back on her now, she was probably in her late twenties or early thirties; back then, I thought of her as a girl, not a woman. She was always calling me honey and saying, "What a handsome young man you are, Johnny."

One day, my father had just returned from sea and told me to get something from her. Her husband was in the navy too, but he was at sea. Not knocking, I opened the door and went in calling her name. I walked down a hall and saw her standing in her bathroom totally naked and just looking at me. I stared back at her mesmerized. I didn't know if I should run or ask her for the item my father had sent me there for. I did neither.

She motioned me into the bathroom. In a daze and before I knew it, I was going in. She shut the door behind me and locked it. She asked me if I was afraid. I was not able to speak; I was staring at her breasts with large, extended nipples. I shook my head. I liked her because she was always so nice to me. She sometimes gave me cookies and milk or made me a sandwich. I loved the way she spoke to me—always in a loving way.

Sometimes, she rubbed my back and shoulders. Other times, she would run her fingers through my hair and say, "What beautiful hair you have, Johnny," and she would kiss me full on the lips. I loved the attention. I thought she was the most beautiful girl I had ever seen.

She sat on the toilet and slowly undressed me. I never said a word, nor did I try to leave. For the next fifteen to twenty minutes, she talked to me in a gentle voice as she touched me. She had me touch her and told me about her body and mine. She said, "When you grow up to be a big boy, you can put your penis in my vagina, and I'll teach you how to make love."

Of course, everything she was telling me was beyond my understanding, but I came away liking the way she had let me touch her.

When I left, I had forgotten to ask for what it was I had gone there for. I had been there for quite a while, and when I got back, my father was furious. I told him she had been on the phone and I had had to wait. I said she did not have what he had wanted. He backhanded me and said, "You should have asked another neighbor!"

That night, I started having my first dreams about girls and all their secret places.

One day, my father came home with a bag of funny-looking shells. He opened one. He said it was an oyster, and he ate it. He opened another and scraped its shell out. He put it on his hand and told me to eat it. It looked like a big ball of snot. I said, "No I don't want to." He grabbed the back of my head and put his hand over my mouth to force me to eat it.

As soon as it hit my stomach, I put my hand over my mouth and threw it up into my hand. My father was so mad that he again grabbed the back of my head, held my hands, and forced the oyster back into my mouth. He held my hand over my mouth with his, so I could not spit it out and made me swallow it again.

After a few moments, he let go of my hand. Wrenching and gagging, I threw it up all over him. He hit me so hard that I flew across the room. He looked at me with disgust. "You'll never amount to anything, plowboy." He ate the rest of the raw oysters.

Even though today I eat fried oysters, and love them, I have never eaten a raw one again.

CHAPTER 35

KKK

We lived in that apartment for only a few months. In all, I would say I attended school for only about a week.

One day, my father came home and told Mama to pack the suitcase. He drove us away, and we never looked back. We moved into a small house. It had two bedrooms, a living room, kitchen, and a tiny bathroom. There were woods all around us. Our closest neighbor was about half a mile away. I felt at home.

Two months later, my father shipped out to sea again. As I had done in the past, I went into the woods by myself looking for anything new. I started building lean-tos and spending a lot of time in them. I would build snares to catch rabbits; I would skin them, build a fire, and cook them. A couple of times, I snuck my father's rifle out and started shooting it. I found out I was a good shot. I could then shoot rabbits and squirrels; I didn't need snares. As always, Mama never asked me where I had been or what I had been doing. I never told her even though sometimes I would be gone for a day or two.

Sometimes when my father was home, he held meetings with men I never knew. Mama, my sister, and I always had to stay in our bedroom during these meetings. I started hearing words like Ku Klux Klan. I asked Mama what that was, and she said, "Hush now, don't talk."

When they used those words, they would always say, "Goddamn niggers. We need to kill them all!" I could never understand why all of them, my father included, hated blacks so much. On several occasions, I asked Mama about that when my father was not around, but she would always say, "I don't want to talk about it." I had had two black friends in my past and had never found anything to hate them for.

Sometimes at night, my father took his rifle and shotgun and met others in front of the house. He would leave and not come back for several days. Mama always acted very scared during those times; she would keep the doors and windows shut and locked. She made my sister and me stay inside the whole time. Again, I would ask, but she wouldn't talk about it. I was just glad he was gone.

When my father returned, he was always very angry and would beat on me again and again telling me while holding his rifle or shotgun for emphasis and jabbing it at me saying, "Never let goddamn niggers take your mother or sister alive!" I knew what he meant and would say, "Okay, Daddy, I won't." He would then repeat it and say, "You better not!"

We lived in that house for about a year or so. During that period, I did not attend any school.

CHAPTER 36

Delmar Trailer Park

My father came home one day and told Mama to pack everything up. We again got into the car and drove off.

My father had bought a trailer that was eight feet wide and thirty-two feet long. We moved into the Del Mar Trailer Park in Morgan Creek, Virginia. The trailer had a living room with a couch and chair. The kitchen had a sink, refrigerator, four cabinets, and a stove.

My sister and I slept in bunk beds that were part of the hallway leading to the rear. The bathroom had a toilet, a small sink that hung on the wall, and a metal shower. There was a small bedroom next to the bathroom in the rear with a door opening to the outside. The bathroom door was used when opened as the bedroom door. The lot the trailer was sitting on was twenty-five feet wide by fifty feet long.

The day after we moved in, my father drove into the woods across the street to cut down pine trees. Somebody had given him an old, six-foot, crosscut saw. It had large teeth and handles on both ends. He took me with him to cut the pines down. He was a grown man, but I was still just a child; I was neither big nor strong enough to use the saw. Time after time, he tried to use the saw with me on one end. The result was the same as if a 300-pound man and a 30-pound child tried to use a seesaw. After the third try, he was so mad that he hit me with one end of the saw. The blow knocked me to the ground, and as I lay there, he hit me again with the saw handle. He yelled at me, "You can't do a goddamn thing, can you, plowboy?" For the first time I was crying so hard, in front of him, that I couldn't answer. I could only shake my head no. He dropped the saw and got a smaller bucksaw and an axe from the trunk of his car.

My father used the bucksaw, and in a short time, he had enough pine trees cut down to make fence posts. I used the heavy axe to cut limbs off the trees. I wasn't big enough to keep up with my father, and when he finished cutting down the last tree, he came over to me. I was so scared that I backed away. He hit me on the arm with the axe handle saying, "Don't you ever run from me again!" That statement reminded me of the time I had run from him while at Paw's shipyard during my first swimming lesson. It stopped me in my tracks.

We peeled the bark off the pine trees, cut them into six-foot posts, and brought them home sticking out the car windows and trunk. It was getting dark. At home, he told me, "Go in and take a shower, and use only cold water. It'll do you good." I was doing as I was told when he came in after a few minutes. He pulled open the shower curtain and made me turn around, bend over, and wash my ankles and feet. He reached under me saying, "Make sure you wash these too" as he cupped and manipulated my testicles.

Having finished my shower, I put on the same pair of shorts I had been wearing that day and walked to the kitchen. The trailer had no table that we could eat at, so my sister and Mama were sitting on the couch holding plates of food and eating. My father was sitting in the one chair also eating. It was strange to see him eating; he rarely ate with us. For the first time, I noticed how he ate. He held his plate in his right hand with his arm around it as if he were protecting his food. He held his fork in his left hand as if it were a shovel, and he did look as if he were shoveling the food into his mouth as fast as he could and swallowing it without chewing. Many years later, I learned that prisoners in jail ate that way. To this day, I have never found out anything about his having been in jail.

As I walked into the living room, he looked up long enough to say, "Go to bed. The next time, plowboy, you better do it right!" I turned around and walked to my bunk. I heard him telling Mama and my sister, "That goddamn kid can't do anything right. He'll never amount to anything, and he's stupid. I had to cut those pine trees by myself today!" I heard my sister laugh, but I never heard Mama say anything. I was tired, sore, and hungry. Burying my head in my pillow, I cried myself to sleep.

The next day, we dug holes around the trailer and put the posts in them. He showed me how to put in a little sand and water, tamp it down, and repeat the process until the holes were filled and the posts were in solid. We nailed wire fencing to the posts. We made a gate out of the same posts and wire. That day was uneventful with only a few mentions of "Goddamn it, plowboy!"

Within a week, my father shipped out overseas.

The first summer in Morgan Creek, I spent most of my time alone fishing and exploring the nearby woods. There was a large bay of saltwater with which I'd had no experience. There was also a small area of saltwater just off the larger bay. Where the two met was a creek-like area I called the Point.

During that first year, we had a big storm. When it was over, I found an old board that had blown up from the storm. It was two inches thick, six inches wide, and ten feet long. It floated, and I started using it as a boat. I found an old cane pole that I knew just what to do with. I would dig for worms, paddle out on the board into the bay, and fish. To my surprise, I wasn't catching any fish.

During low tide, I saw a lot of minnows in the shallow water at the Point. Using my T-shirt, I would catch a few, put them in a glass jar, and use them for bait. Remembering the shiners from my past, I made sure I kept swishing the water around. I started catching fish with those minnows. After a while, I got tired of the board and started fishing at high tide from the shore. I always caught fish with minnows in the weeds.

One day, I cast my line out, laid my cane pole down, and walked away. A few minutes later, I came back and could not see my pole. Looking all over, I finally saw the pole a short way out in the bay. It was being pulled farther out. Having no fear because my father had told me how saltwater would hold me up, I jumped in and swam after it. I managed to grab it, but I had to clamp it between my teeth while swimming back to shore.

Reaching shore, I pulled a fish in. It was the biggest I had caught yet, about fifteen inches long. I showed the fish to a neighbor and asked him what it was. He told me it was a puppy drum. I was told they looked just like drum fish because they had a black dot just behind the gills. I didn't know anything about either one, but I sure liked eating them. Sometimes, Mama would cook them for me, but when she didn't want to, I would scale and gut a fish, stick a branch through it, and hold it over a fire.

Not many kids lived in the park, and I did not get along with those who did, so I just avoided them. I trapped or shot a lot of rabbits and squirrels but not much else. As before, I would skin and cook them over a small fire. I was very disappointed because I found only a few of my favorites—snakes.

When those fleets of ships would leave, not many men would be around. My father was away for most of that first summer and many more after that. Mama still never asked, so I never said anything about where I was going or what I was doing. I had only myself to answer to. I was alone, but I was doing well. As before, when my father came home, he would disappear for days with his guns. I stopped asking Mama where he was. As in the past, I was just happy he was gone.

CHAPTER 37

Cold

The great blizzard of 1978 hit the Northeast in February. I happened to be off that day. Some lost electricity for about three days, and others lost it for longer than that. Our neighbors across the street moved in with us because we had a coal stove to heat our house. We put all our refrigerator items in the snow outside the back door.

At the time, we had four children and our neighbors had two. There was nothing we could do, so my wife, our neighbors, and I sat at the kitchen table, played cards by candlelight, and drank.

Our older girls kept the younger kids busy in the family room playing games. The snow was piling up. By the next morning, it was halfway up our front door. It took my neighbor and me four to five hours to clear a small walkway and a path to the street in our driveway. I knew I should have been at work, but I had no way of getting to or even contacting the police department. The roads were impassible.

Not long after we cleared a path to the street, a four-wheeled cruiser showed up and an officer came to the front door saying, "They need you at the station now!"

It took me only a few minutes to get in uniform, and I rode with the cruiser to the station. After arriving, I was told I would be at a security checkpoint at the entrance to the Brant City section of Sandy Town. I was told it was imperative that I got there quickly because looting was already a problem there. I was taken from the station by cruiser to my post.

Upon arrival, I found that I was stationed with a Massachusetts state policeman and a Massachusetts national guardsman. On the first day, a cruiser brought us sandwiches and coffee twice. Both days were cold, but the trooper had a pint of blackberry brandy under his seat. The temperature was below freezing, and it continued to snow. We sat in the trooper's cruiser with the heater on until somebody approached us. We took turns getting out. Many people were trying to get into the area, but we had orders because of the looting not to let anybody in whether they lived there or not.

The second day arrived, and snow, wind, and the cold prevailed. More national guardsmen arrived, and they patrolled on foot in Brant City proper. That morning, a girl I knew only by sight and reputation approached our station and solicited all three of us for sex. The state trooper and I turned her down, but the guardsman did not. He and she walked out of sight. We never saw him again. A cruiser again brought us food and coffee. Both were cold, and the blackberry brandy was gone.

On the third day, our station was moved about a mile farther out. For the duration of the storm, the trooper and I stayed on security check. When we first arrived at that station that morning, an older male approached us on foot. The trooper and I got out of the cruiser. The male walked up, looked around, and pulled a large Mason jar out from under his heavy coat. He smiled. "I know what it's like being out here in the cold. I made some homemade brandy. Would you boys like some?" He handed the jar to me. I looked at the trooper, and he looked at the man and said, "Yes, thank you." The man walked off, and the trooper and I smiled as we got back into the cruiser. Twice that day, we again received cold food and coffee, but at least we had brandy.

Late that night, the trooper received a radio call from his dispatcher telling him to leave. He apologized because he knew I would have to stand outside in the cold all night. It was still cold and snowing, and the wind was blowing hard, but I had the brandy to sip through the night.

When the blizzard was over, and life returned to a reasonable, the state troopers and the national guardsmen left. A rumor was circulating around town that about fifteen guardsmen who had been stationed in Brant City had come down with different sexually transmitted diseases

The next morning, a cruiser showed up saying my station was being closed. Getting in, he dropped me off at the police station. For the first time, I ate hot food and drank hot coffee. I was so cold that my hands and feet were numb. Sitting there, my thoughts returned to another time and another place so long ago.

I started school again in the fall. I had been out of school for two years. I was now nine years old. Because I had no school records I was placed in the second grade in a public school. The school was like all the others. I could not adjust to the class, and I did not want to. In class, I was disruptive and would not listen to anybody. I know the teachers tried, but I just did not care about anything they had to say.

That winter, I was cold. Growing up in the deep south, I had never seen snow or cold weather as we were experiencing. I was constantly sick with a cold, and at one point, I caught the flu and was bedridden for a week. Mama called it "That goddamn Asiatic flu." I was so sick that I could not even walk to the bathroom by myself; Mama had to help me. Anything I ate just came right back up. My father came home during that time. Every time I coughed, sneezed, or showed any signs of being sick, he would give me two tablespoons of kerosene. After I complained about the taste, he started putting a pinch of sugar in it, but that did nothing for the taste.

I knew it would not do any good for me to complain except get me another backhand, so I said nothing and kept taking the kerosene. It did not take long before I started trying to do whatever I could not to sneeze or cough. On one occasion, he caught me holding my nose, so I would not sneeze. He backhanded me so hard that he literally knocked the snot out of me.

The week I was down with the flu, he woke me up every morning around five or five thirty before he left for work to give me my dose. I can't remember ever being as sick as I was that week.

I still wore the shoes with holes in the soles that were covered with newspaper. I had only two pair of socks with holes in the toes of both, two pair of cuffed, long pants, and two long-sleeved shirts. For a jacket, Mama told me to put my second long-sleeved shirt over the first one and button it all the way up. The school bus picked us up in front of the park, so it wasn't too far to walk—about half a mile—but I was so cold that winter that sometimes, I would sit down in the snow by myself on the way home from school and cry. The other kids walking by stared at me, laughed, made fun of me, and called me names like swamp boy because they knew I had come from Louisiana.

I spent the entire first winter in the trailer when not at school except when my father was around. During those times, I would go off into the woods, make a small fire, and sit close to it trying to keep warm.

We heated our trailer with kerosene from a large glass jug dumped upside down on top of the heater. Whenever we needed more, I was given the task of getting it refilled. Even when my father was home, and he had his car, I was told to take the gallon jug and walk down to a gas station that would hand-pump the kerosene into it. Directly in front of the park was a four-lane divided road. The gas station was on the other side of the road. One day, having no real experience with a double-lane road and coming back with a full jug of kerosene, I was so cold and not paying attention. After crossing the median strip, I stepped out in front of an oncoming truck. To this day, I can still hear the air horn on that truck and see the driver in the windshield. He had pure panic on his face as the trailer started skidding sideways. I saw the trailer skid over the median and an oncoming car hit it. I left as fast as I could. I never said a word to Mama or my father.

One other time coming home with the kerosene, I slipped on ice and fell. I broke the glass jug and cut my hand. When I got home, my father was so mad that he gave me a hard whipping with his belt and sent me to bed with no supper. It didn't really matter because I was sick and had not eaten in a day or two anyway. After that whipping, all I wanted was to go to bed. Lying in that bunk crying, all I could think about was how much I missed Louisiana and my cousin Drew. As I was falling asleep, I said out loud in a crying voice, "I want to go home."

My father heard me and raced into the room. He hit me with his fists saying, "Goddamn it, stop your goddamn crying, plowboy, or I'll give you something to cry about." Luckily for me, I was under my blanket, which was a heavy, woolen navy blanket.

That winter was the worst I had ever spent in my young life. I don't believe I was ever as cold since then.

CHAPTER 38

Making New Friends

In early spring, big bulldozers showed up and started clearing the wooded land next to us. Every day when I came home from school and the workers left for the day, I played on all their equipment. I would sit on them and pretend I was driving. Eventually after being around so often, a couple of workers let me ride with them while they were bulldozing when their boss was not around. Those were thrilling days; they reminded me of the times I rode with Paw in his Model T.

With all the heavy equipment, it did not take long for roads and lots to be cleared. Within a short time, the whole area was filled with trailers. A bath and washhouse were built right in the middle of them. I could shower only every two or three days, and they were what my father called "navy showers"—only cold water even in the winter. That meant I would get into the shower, turn the water on, wet myself down, and turn the water off. I would soap down, turn the water on, rinse myself, and get out as fast as I could. Whenever possible and even in the middle of the day, I would shower in the bathhouse. I wasn't there to bathe. Sometimes, I would stand in the hot water for an hour or more just to warm up.

Very slowly, I started making friends with some new kids who had moved in. I was nine, going on ten, at the time. I met Jay, Rob, and Tim, who were all twelve. We made another friend, Harry, who was fourteen. Except for Tim, their fathers were chiefs in the navy; Tim did not have a father, just his mother. Even though in the past I had had difficulty making friends, the five of us became close quickly. Remembering those times, I believe that because I told them about my life in Louisiana, instead of making fun of me, they always wanted to hear more.

My friends all smoked. I really wanted and needed friends, so I let them talk me into smoking. I will never forget the first time. It was at night, and we were at the Point. One of them lit a Marlboro and handed it to me. I was hesitant and just held it for several minutes. I kept looking at the cigarette and then at them. Getting impatient, they started saying, "Chicken, chicken, chicken!" By the time I was nine, I had tangled with gators, snakes, wild hogs, and more. I had fought with a damned lamprey eel. Nobody was going to call me chicken for not doing something. I put it to my lips, took a big drag, and pulled that smoke deep into my lungs. I thought my chest would explode. I started coughing so bad that one of my friends, being so helpful, started whacking me on the back as they all asked, "How was it? You like it?" Still coughing, I said, "Yeah, it was good." Just like that, my smoking days started. They did not end until twenty-five years later.

My friends all smoked Marlboros, but I chose Lucky Strikes. Whenever we were walking around, and we saw a Lucky Strike pack on the ground, the first one who saw it would step on it, hit the closest person, and say, "Lucky Strike and no strike back!"

I loved being a part of something. We all had Zippo lighters that we had stolen from stores. When I got my first lighter, they showed me how to break it in as they said. I repeatedly opened and closed the lid until it was loose. I did the same with the wheel that activated the flint. Then I would use two fingers to open the lid, and *snap*, use thumb and middle finger in a loud snapping motion near the wheel, and *zap*, the lighter would light. It would happen so fast that other people would shake their heads and ask, "Wow! How'd you do that?" We never told anybody our secret.

Eventually, the lid and wheel would get so loose that we had to replace the lighter. We hid our cigarettes, lighters, and anything else we wanted to safeguard, including our bathing suits, in the attic of the old bathhouse.

The five of us were the coolest nine-, twelve-, and fourteen-year-olds in our area. We were together every day in the summer of 1952 because my father had gone to sea and Mama never bothered asking me where I was going, what I was doing, or where I had been. Since I had four friends to hang out with, other kids never made fun of me anymore.

At that time, everyone was talking about flying saucers. People described them as upside-down, saucer-shaped, metallic-looking craft, and nobody knew what or where they were from. Every night, we heard jets flying. One night, I heard a loud explosion, and the next day, everybody was talking about how a jet had shot down a flying saucer.

My father came home late that summer. One day, he, Mama, my sister, and I were getting out of our car at the same time as our neighbors were. Somebody yelled, "Hey look! There's one of those flying saucers!" All of us looked and saw a metallic, saucer-shaped craft flying overhead. It wasn't up very high, and we saw it clearly. It was not flying fast, and it was headed toward the Morgan Creek Naval Base. Everybody saw it was nothing like any airplane we had ever seen before, and it looked like what people had described as a flying saucer.

We watched it fly over the base and out of sight. My father said, "Forget you ever saw it, and never talk about it! Do all of you understand?" Nothing else was ever said about the incident. I have never spoken of it until recently as I was writing this book. I told my wife, kids, and a few others about the incident, all of whom I hoped wouldn't think I was crazy!

In the fall, my friends and I started going to the same school. That year, I met a chubby, blond girl; I fell madly in love with her. In those days right after lunch, the teacher would make us lie on the floor and take a nap on blankets kept in the room. She and I would lie next to each other, talk, giggle, and hold hands. One day to impress her, I lay on my back with my mouth open wiggling my tongue. I captured a fly and ate it. She giggled and squeezed my hand hard. I knew she was impressed.

We ate lunch together. When we went outside at recess, the other kids would play games but not us. I would take her aside and tell her about all the animals I had caught and seen in Florida and Louisiana. On some occasions we would lie in the grass, looking for four leaf glovers. Sometimes right after a rain, I would take her to find earthworms. I would wrap them in a piece of notebook paper and keep them in my pocket until I got home that night. I would wrap them up in an old T-shirt I had found or had stolen. I then put them way in the back of my underwear drawer, so Mama would not find them. Sometimes, I used them for catching minnows to fish with.

In class, I sat behind her, and she would pass me notes. She wrote in one, "I like you. Do you like me?" There was a yes or a no box to be checked. I checked yes and passed it back to her. The teacher must have seen us because she walked over and took the note. Calling me to the front of the room, she read the note aloud in a sarcastic voice. She made a face and said, "Aren't you the lover boy!" I did not know what she meant, but I didn't like what she said. I didn't care what she said about me, but then she started talking to my friend. "I can't believe you like such a bad and stupid boy like Johnny." That really made me mad, and I yelled, "Stop talking about her!" In years past, I would have never said anything. Hanging around with my new friends had changed me a little, but not where my father was concerned.

For punishment, she drew a circle on the blackboard with chalk and made me put my nose in it. She said, "Stand there until I tell you to sit down!" I was even madder that she tore the note up as the entire class laughed. I licked the circle off the board. When some of the kids saw me doing it and laughed, she looked at me angrily. She made me stand with my nose to the blackboard with no circle. I was not allowed to go to lunch or recess. She stayed in the room during both to make sure I did not take my nose off. At the end of the day, just to show her who was the real boss, I licked some of her writing off the blackboard. She was so mad that she yelled, "Get out of my classroom now!"

The next day as soon as I entered the room, she called me to her desk. She handed me a paper hat that was tall and came to a point. She told the class, "This is a dunce hat, and because Johnny is dumb, he'll wear it all day!" She pointed to the blackboard; that time, she had drawn a circle but had filled it in completely with chalk. I put the hat on, walked to the blackboard, and licked the entire circle off. I stared at her. All the kids were laughing. She slapped me in the face, took the hat, and told me to sit in the hallway. She followed me into the hall and made sure I sat. She walked away down the hall towards the office.

As soon as she was out of sight, I walked back into the room, sat behind my friend, and started talking with her. My teacher returned shortly with the principal, who made me follow him to the office, where he paddled me. I looked at him with no emotion. He told me to sit on the bench in the outer office. I sat there for the whole day with nobody talking to me. At the last bell as I was leaving to catch the bus, he came out of his office and said, "In the morning, you report directly to this office!"

The next morning, I reported to his office. The principal placed me in a different classroom. I saw the girl only occasionally because our class took different times for lunch and recess.

I wasn't sure there was a God, but Mama always prayed to Jesus, Mary, and Joseph so often that I started praying to them at night. I begged them to have her family move into our trailer park. The following year, my prayers were answered, but she would have nothing to do with me. Once again, my heart was broken.

School that year was still nothing but a nuisance. I never paid attention, and I was disruptive all the time. Some days, I was so bad that the teacher would send me to the principal, who would made me sit on that same bench all day long doing nothing.

One day, the teacher told us she had to go to the office and would be back in a little while. Of course, right after she left, the class exploded. I had made three paper airplanes during class, and I threw them out a window and watched them fly down from the third floor.

I saw a big kid, who was a real bully, putting large tacks on pupils' chairs. I followed him and picked them up. He put one on the teacher's chair. I did not like our teacher, but I picked that one up too. I put all the tacks in my desk.

When the teacher returned, she sat and screamed. She jumped up crying and ran out of the room. A little while later, she came back with the principal.

The class was very quiet. He asked, "Who put the tack in the teacher's chair?" The bully jumped to his feet, pointed at me, and said, "Johnny did it!" I said, "I did not!" I said that the bully had. I told them that I had taken one off her seat and that he must have seen me do that and put another one on it.

The principal walked to my desk, lifted the top, and found the tacks I had put there. I again explained to him what had happened and how after picking them all up, I had put them in my desk, so the kid would not have them.

The principal and teacher left the room without saying anything; they took the tacks with them. All the kids started pointing at and talking about me. The kid who had started the mess threw a lead pencil at me that stuck right into my leg through my pants. I pulled it out, but the lead broke off and stayed in my thigh.

About half an hour later, the teacher returned, and class resumed. I sat head down not paying attention to her. About an hour after that, there was a commotion at the door. Looking up I saw Mama and my father standing there. The class became deathly quiet. The teacher looked at me with a hateful stare. I slid down in my seat trying to hide; just the top of my white hair was above the desk. I heard my father stomping into the room. My body went limp, and I started to cry as the kids around me stared. He picked me up by the throat and started backhanding me so badly that blood from my nose and lips went flying and landed on nearby students, who scrambled out of their chairs.

Some of my classmates started crying, and others ran out the door. The teacher started crying and yelling for my father to stop. I continued crying hysterically and kept saying, "It wasn't me, Daddy! I didn't do it!" He threw me into my desk so hard that I broke a slat in the backrest. I was not crying from pain but because once again I was being blamed for something I had not done. I believed my father and others would never believe me about anything.

After my mother and father left, the teacher sent me to the office by myself. The assistant principal sent me to the nurse's office. While she was working on me, she shook her head and said, "You need to stop this bad behavior." By then, I had stopped crying. I said, "Okay." I knew it would do no good to tell her the truth.

The assistant principal made me sit on that bench for the rest of the day. On the way home that afternoon, I walked with my friends taking as much time as I could, before going home. As I walked into the trailer, my father grabbed me by the neck with one hand and my ass with the other and carried me to his bedroom. His belt was lying on the bed. I was crying and saying, "I didn't do it, Daddy! I didn't do it!"

He stripped me naked and threw me onto his bed. He started whipping me. I crawled to the other side and fell into the space between the bed and wall. I was trapped. He walked around the bed and continued to whip me. The buckle was leaving marks. While he was beating me, the cotton balls the nurse had put in my nose to stop the bleeding came flying out. He became even more furious. "Are you doing weird stuff again with your friends?" I never had a chance to explain.

Afterward, he carried me to my bunk bed and threw me into it. I pulled my legs up into a fetal position and cried myself to sleep wishing I would die. I had so much hate for my father that I wanted him dead also. I had so many bruises, and I was so sore that I could not go back to school.

The school year was within a few weeks of being over, and after that incident, I never attended that public school again.

That summer, my father did not go to sea, so he was always around. When he was gone sometimes for days with his guns, I would sneak off with my friends.

I had told them what had happened at the public school and who had really put that tack on the teacher's chair. The only consolation I had was that two of my friends beat that kid up badly. They were suspended for a week, but they said they didn't care because that was what friends did for each other. That taught me to always back friends up. Never be a rat.

Mama never said a word to me or my father. I spent the summer, on my fathers' command, raking our yard over and over, with an old, broken-handled, iron rake.

CHAPTER 39

Sister Nun Gun

In the fall, I turned ten. I was placed in the third grade. My sister and I were enrolled in a parochial school near the Ocean View Amusement Park. My four friends were still going to the public school. My sister and I rode a city bus every day to and from school. I had to wear long, blue pants, a long-sleeved, light-blue shirt, a blue tie, and a blue, baseball-type hat. My sister wore a blue skirt and a white blouse.

The nuns at the Catholic school were very strict. They paddled our butts or hit our knuckles with their rulers at the drop of a hat. They had these little clickers they used that sounded like a cricket chirping every time they wanted our attention. We had one nun we called Sister Gun. Whenever she caught me doing something wrong, she hit my knuckles with a bigger-than-normal ruler, and I would taunt her, "Nun Gun, Nun Gun, blah, blah, blah." It drove her so crazy that on one occasion, she cried out, "Goddamn it! Stop saying that!" That got the rest of the class laughing.

One day, I raised my hand and said I had to go to the bathroom. As I walked down the hall, I saw Sister Superior walking toward me and staring at me. She always looked mad. She was walking with a purpose. I wondered if she was looking for me. I did spend more time in her office than any other kids did. Stopping me she asked, "Johnny, does your mother always sign your papers?"

Every time we failed a test or quiz, we had to have a parent sign it and bring it back the next day. With a straight face, I said, "Yes Sister Superior, she signs all my papers."

She held up the paper I had turned in that morning, pointed to the signature, and asked, "Why did she sign it Miss?"

I shrugged and said, "I don't know. I guess because she forgot." I kept walking to the bathroom. I had been signing my mother's name all year, and that was my first mistake. I never heard anything else about signatures for the rest of the year.

I was in third grade, but I was so disruptive that they put me back in second grade. After a week, I was still so bad that they gave up and put me back in third grade. I believed they just wanted me to finish school and leave as quickly as possible.

There was a lot of talk and whispers among the kids about sex between the nuns and the priests. Some of the kids said they had seen nuns and priests going into bathrooms together and locking the doors.

We had a fifteen-year-old boy in our class who was very slow talking. The other kids made fun of him, but I did not. For some reason, I spent time with him at recess and found I liked him. Thinking back about him today, I would say it was probably because his name was John, the same as the friend I had made in Louisiana. He was quiet and soft spoken. He said he enjoyed fishing, and he told me about some of his fishing trips. Of course, I loved to talk about Louisiana, and I told him about my fishing excursions there.

We spent many hours together during recess. One day, he did not show up for school. After a couple of days of not seeing him, I asked other kids if they knew why he was not in school. The kids told me that Sister Superior had caught him and a nun in an empty classroom having sex during recess. We never saw him again, and I was saddened that he left because he was the only friend I had in that school.

At recess, the boys picked sides and played keep-away with a tennis ball. One day while I was walking by, not playing keep-away, with my own ball that I was bouncing, a black dog that had been running around chasing the other kids' ball bit me on the hand just as I caught my ball; that drew blood. I went to the nurse, who stopped the bleeding and bandaged the bite.

The next day, Mama and I walked to the sick bay at the Morgan Creek Naval Base. I told everybody that the dog had just been trying to get my ball, that it had not bit me on purpose, but because the dog was never found, they gave me a rabies shot in my stomach, around my navel, and said I had to get a total of twenty-one.

Every morning before school, Mama took me to the base, and I got a shot. After I had received thirteen shots, the wound turned red, swelled up, and itched badly. The doctor said I had become allergic to the shots and stopped giving me them.

I still did not want to play keep-away with the other kids, so I started sitting on the ground in front of the gym throwing the ball against the door. Every day at recess, I just sat and threw that ball by myself. I had no interest in anybody or anything the kids were doing.

Once as recess was starting, I was walking toward the gym. I noticed some kids playing marbles, which interested me. I watched them for a while. As had been the case in Louisiana, nobody could bring marbles into the classroom. I didn't have any marbles or money to buy any, so I watched where the other kids hid theirs just as I had done in Louisiana. I had wised up enough to steal just a few from each hiding spot so nobody would miss any.

I played every day at recess, and I always won. I started using a steely, and I won a lot of marbles with it. After a while, the kids would not play with me if I was using it, so I had to use plain marbles, but I still won. By that time, cat's-eye marbles were popular. I started using a large one called a boulder and was winning big. Again, the kids quit playing with me if I used it, so again, I started using a regular marble and still won. I started taking them home and keeping them in shopping bags. I tried to keep them hidden from my father, but he found them. Instead of taking them and whipping me, he told me to keep winning them. I had finally done something right, as my mind swirled.

One day, he came home with a slingshot. He said, "Bring some of those marbles and come with me." I put a couple of dozen into a container and followed him into the woods remaining in our park. As we walked, he talked about how he and his best friend growing up had used them to kill birds, rabbits, and anything else they could with a slingshot and stones. He asked me, "Do you know what this is?" All smiles and thinking I finally would tell him something I knew to be true, I said, "It's a slingshot, Daddy." Without warning, he backhanded me and knocked me about three feet into the brush. He came charging in, grabbed me by the arms, and raised me above his head. He shook me harshly. "Goddamn it, plowboy, you don't know anything, and you never will. This is called a nigger shooter. Do you understand?" I was crying and said, "Yes, Daddy, I understand." He shook me again and asked, "What's it called?" I replied, "It's a nigger shooter, Daddy, used for shooting niggers." My response must have agreed with him because he put me down and said, "Okay then."

He taught me how to use it; he said, "I'll make you a smaller one just in case any niggers try coming around."

That event on my life's path has haunted me more than most others. My father did make me one, but I never practiced with it unless he was there. The next time he went to sea, I burned it.

CHAPTER 40

Happy Dreams

One day, Sister Superior sent a notice to all the classes that she needed a crossing guard. They were there when I got off the city bus in the morning and got on in the afternoon. Sometimes, I would watch them for so long that I would miss a bus and would have to catch a later one.

I loved the idea of standing in the middle of the street with the power to stop cars, so kids would be safe crossing the street. My greatest attraction was having the crisscross white belt with a badge pinned to it. I talked to my friends about how I would love to be a crossing guard. They thought it was foolish, but I told them I did not care because one day I would be one. They laughed. "You? A crossing guard?" That'll never happen." But their negativity did not bother me one bit. I knew what I wanted.

At recess that day, I spoke to Sister Superior. "I'd like to be a crossing guard." She stared at me for a few minutes before saying, "No. As long as I'm Sister Superior in this school, you'll never be a crossing guard! The guards are kids who are honest, very well behaved, and trustworthy, which you are not!" I stared at her and said, "Okay."

The next day, I did what I knew best. I went back in the office requesting to be a guard. Every day for a week, I was in her office. She told me that the position had been filled by a girl. I did not care; I continued to pester her until after two more weeks, she had had enough of me and told me not to ask her again. I still didn't care. Every day, I would go to her office and ask. Finally, one day, she agreed to let me try it for a week. She said, "If I get one bad report on you, and I know I will, I'll pull you off so fast you won't know what hit you!" I smiled and promised her I would be good—meaning my behavior—and I would do a good job. She said, "Huh. We'll see."

One of the best parts of the guard position was that I arrived half an hour early to go on duty, but I got out of school half an hour early to fill my post. For a solid week, I was the best student in the whole damn school during school hours. After that week, I did not wait for Sister Superior to approach me; I went to her office to see her. She was shocked that I was there, but she said she had gotten only good reports on my actions as a crossing guard. "Keep it up, Johnny."

For the first time in a long time, I had something I loved doing, and I enjoyed the respect kids showed me as a crossing guard. I said, "Thank you, Sister Superior. I'll try harder."

At the end of the school year, Sister Superior said, "I don't believe it, but you've done a great job, Johnny. Do you want to be a crossing guard next year?" I happily told her yes. That night when I went to bed, my dreams were about being a crossing guard and working my way up until all the crossing guards were under my command. I would tell them were to go and what to do. Every night, I had happy dreams of one day riding in a police car still wearing a badge and arresting people for bad things they had done. Little did I know what was to follow.

CHAPTER 41

Crossing Guard

In the spring, my father returned from a deployment. The first night he was home, as usual, he made my sister and me leave the trailer, and he locked the doors. Only he and Mama were inside. We were never allowed back inside until he called us.

Sometimes, my sister would go into his car and fall asleep in the back seat. I just hung out with my friends until they had to go in. I would sit in his car in the front seat and pretend I was driving. My sister would wake up, laugh, and say, "You'll never drive a car. You're too stupid, Daddy said."

About midnight, my father came out yelling for us. He told my sister to go to bed. He was holding my crossing guard belt and badge. He said, "I hear you were a crossing guard at school this year."

"Yes, Daddy, Sister Superior said I did a good job too, and she asked me to be a crossing guard next year."

He started beating me with that belt. "You'll never do a good job at anything, plowboy, and you goddamn sure aren't going to be no goddamn crossing guard!" He did not stop until that white belt turned red with my blood. He made me throw the belt with the badge pinned on it into the garbage can.

I cried myself to sleep. He heard me and said, "Don't make me come in there! Stop your goddamn crying, plowboy!" I shoved my head deep into my pillow as I cried myself to sleep.

The next morning, he slept in, but I got up early. I retrieved the belt and badge, stole somebody's newspaper to wrap them in, and hid it in a drainpipe in the woods that had not been used in years. I wanted to be the best crossing guard ever but putting that belt and badge in that pipe was the hardest thing I had ever done. My sprit was low, but I shouted, "I'll try harder, Daddy! One day, you'll be proud of me!" That mantra has served me well throughout life.

In the fall, I told Sister Superior that I couldn't be a school crossing guard again. I made the excuse that my father did not like me coming home that late every afternoon after school. She asked me where the belt and badge were, and I told her my father said he would mail it back to the school.

I reverted to my same old self that school year; my behavior became worse. I was angry all the time. I became more withdrawn and quiet. I was still staying by myself except for hanging out with my friends at home and playing marbles, my obsession.

CHAPTER 42

The Accident

My father was home for about six months. In early 1953, he bought a new Oldsmobile. The day he bought it, he and Mama picked up my sister and me at school. I got in and wanting to stay as far away from him as possible, I sat behind Mama and just stared out the window. My sister was excited about the car, and she sat forward in her seat talking to my father over his shoulder.

He had driven only a few blocks when a car rammed us right where I was sitting. The impact turned our car completely around and pushed us on the curb on the opposite side of the street. My father was so mad that he beat the steering wheel so hard that it bent. He saw the other car still up against ours right where I was sitting. He screamed at me, "Goddamn it! You should have told me that car was coming so I could've gotten out of the way!"

It was a long reach, but he started backhanding me back and forth and making me bleed. After a few minutes, all four of us got out of the car. The other driver, a black man, walked over and said, "I'm sorry. I was test-driving the car and the brakes went out." My father glared at the man and started backhanding me and again said, "You should have told me the car was coming!"

The other driver said, "Hey, it's not his fault. I lost my brakes." My father started yelling and cursing. He said, "Niggers back home got hung for doing bad things to white folks!" My father was on such a tirade that I thought he would attack the poor man. The man looked at Mama, my sister, and me and said, "I'm sorry" and left the area at a run. He never came back even when the police showed up.

My father knew the two policemen. He kept up his language even to them. "Goddamn niggers don't know how to drive, and they shouldn't own cars!" The car was not drivable, so the police called the Morgan Creek Naval Base, and a navy car was sent to pick us up.

During that time, my father was on shore patrol duty. He and a policeman patrolled the

Ocean View area, where my school was. He wore his CPO navy uniform with a shore patrol armband.

One night, he came home late and brought a pizza. He woke Mama and my sister up, and the three of them sat in the living room eating it. I was still awake, but I did not let them know that. After they had gone to bed, I waited until I heard him snoring. I snuck into the living room and ate the last piece. That pizza was the only food I ever remember him bringing home.

CHAPTER 43

Locked Up

One night after he had gotten home late again, he was in bed with Mama, and I heard him telling her how they had found a car with an officer and a whore in the front seat and a sailor and a whore in the back seat. He described in detail what they had been doing. I heard him say, "Try harder, goddamn it!" I had heard him say the same thing to Mama in the past. Mama replied, "I am trying!" He replied, "You're not doing it right. Goddamn it, try harder!"

After that night, if I was still awake when he came home, I would put my pillow over my head until I fell asleep.

One afternoon, my friends and I walked to the Ocean View Amusement Park. We liked watching the roller-coaster going around one curve because the rear wheels always came off the tracks. We always thought we would one day see all the cars flying. As we were standing there, a police cruiser pulled up with a policeman driving and my father riding shotgun. The policeman was one of the two who had responded to our car accident.

My father got out of the car. He was wearing his CPO uniform with the Shore Patrol band. He grabbed my arm and asked, "What the hell are you doing here? I told you never to come to this goddamn place!" I looked at my friends and then at him and said, "We're going to the movies." He shoved me into the rear of the cruiser. He looked at my three friends and said, "Get the hell out of here and go home!"

My friends ran off in the direction of the movie house. The policeman drove to a nearby police station. When we arrived, my father dragged me into the station and down a long, narrow stairway into the basement. From what I remember, there were three cells with at least one person in each. He opened the door of the last one, which had one person in it, and threw me in. He slammed the door shut. "This is where bad kids belong!" He locked the cell door, nodded to the old drunk in the cell, and left.

There was only one metal bunk, and the drunk was on it. That night as I slept on the floor, which was covered in old vomit, piss, and many other vile bodily fluids, the drunk woke me up. He said, "Keep your goddamn mouth shut, kid," as he forced me onto the bunk. For my entire life, I had been beaten down, subdued, and completely dominated by my father to the point that I had no dander in me. As that dirty, nasty, foul-smelling drunk was pulling my pants off, somehow, my young mind revolted. He knelt in front of me and took my penis in his mouth. I kicked him in the nuts. He yelled and fell back. Quick as a cat, I started kicking him all over his body. He made so much noise that somebody from upstairs yelled, "Goddamn it! Keep it quiet down there!" I thought my father had yelled that. I stopped when the old drunk started whimpering. Blood covered his body.

My father never returned for me that night, and I slept on that metal bunk. The next morning, the drunk was turned loose, but the officer said my father would be back for me. About midmorning, he did return. By then, I was the only one downstairs. He was in his CPO uniform. He opened the cell door, entered, and started backhanding me. "I never want to catch you down her again, and I hope you learned a lesson last night about how kids are treated in jail. Now get your ass home, and you better be there when I get home!"

I ran out of the station; some officers laughed as I left. When I got home, Mama never asked me anything, but she made me grits and eggs after I had taken a cold shower. I stayed in the trailer for the rest of the day, but he did not come home until very late that night.

Today as I write this story, I know he did not want me in the area because of women. One of my friends had told me that he had seen my father with a woman going into the tunnel of love. On another day, he had seen my father with a young girl. He said she looked like a teenager, and he had had his arm around her. Over the years, Mama always talked about "Daddy and his whores."

CHAPTER 44

The Little Morgan Creek Gang

While my father was home, he made me stay in the yard and rake it. The yard had very little grass; it was mostly dirt with no leaves to rake.

After a month, he deployed again. Mama still never asked about me and my activities, and I never told her anything. My friends and I wanted to join a gang called the Morgan Creek Gang. We were too young to join, so we formed our own gang, the Little Morgan Creek Gang. We wore white T-shirts with our cigarette packs rolled up in the sleeves. We grew our hair long and combed it in back into a DA, a duck's ass. Mama would always tell me when my father was coming home so I would get a haircut before he did. When he would deploy, I would let my hair grow.

My father returned sometime after the first of the following year. I had been so bad that Mama had not told me he was coming home. When he came in and saw my hair, he borrowed some hair clippers. He started at my neck; he cut my hair to about halfway on the top of my head and stopped. He left it like that and made me wear it until it all grew back out, and I got regular haircut.

My gang all understood my situation and never made fun of me, but one day, an older kid did. Our oldest member, Harry, beat the kid until he cried. He then made him apologize to me. By then, I knew my father would go to sea for about six months, be back for a couple of months, and again leave for another six months. From then on when I knew it was getting close to the six months, I got a haircut.

My gang and I had taps on our shoes. My friends put them only on the heels of their shoes, but I put them on the heels and toes. When my father found out, he took my shoes off and beat me with them with the taps. I had tap marks on my body and was proud of them; I showed them to my gang. Afterward, he took the taps off and threw them in the garbage. Of course, as soon as he left for work, I retrieved them.

Once, I stole somebody's shoes, put the taps on them, and kept them hidden in the old washhouse. I wore them only when I was away from home. Once a year, my father bought Mama, my sister, and me a pair of shoes. They always had holes in the soles, so we put newspaper over the holes.

Nobody messed with our gang. We thought it was because we were tough. In truth, it was probably because everybody was afraid of the Morgan Creek Gang, and we lived in their territory. We turned to petty crime. There wasn't anything we couldn't or wouldn't steal. Hubcaps were big items in those days especially baby moons, spinners, and full moons. Some older kids who had cars would take cabinet handles, drill holes in their moon hubcaps, and screw the handles onto them to make their own spinners. They would look cool especially at night if they put lights under the fenders that shined on the spinners as they drove around.

Lisa, a young woman in our neighborhood, would give us money, drugs, cigarettes, and sex for whatever we stole. Sometimes, we would wait until we had several pairs of hubcaps, and then we would change the hardware around so even the owners would not know which one theirs was.

Bringing her these always meant we would get sex or at the least a quick blow job if she was too busy. Whenever my friends had normal sex with her, they loved to talk about it. They would tell me, "She likes to fuck in a rocking chair."

I tried not to go inside her house, but on some occasions, my friends made me. Many times, she asked me, "When are you going to fuck me, Johnny?" I always said, "I don't want to," and I would leave as fast as I could. She would laugh as I left. All my friends would tease me saying, "You'll have to do it sometime." By then, three of my friends were fourteen and the oldest was sixteen. I was still only eleven, so I had not yet experienced that wonderful part of puberty.

Except for the beatings when my father was home, I had some good times. We did a lot of bad things. Once, we threw a fourteen-year-old boy into a cage with two large dogs. He had been stealing hubcaps in our neighborhood. It was terrible. We never got caught for that, and we never saw him in our area again. At times, we would steal a car for a joyride and return it, but only after putting gas in it.

Out in front of the trailer park was an old bar. Right behind it were four small cabins that patrons of the bar and working girls would use. The cabins had one bedroom with a bed, a nightstand with a lamp, and a closet. There was a small bathroom with toilet, wall sink, and shower. The small living room had only a couch.

We had Jimmied a rear window of one cabin and fixed it, so we could come and go without being noticed. Inside the closet was an entrance to the attic. We nailed some boards onto the wall and used them as a ladder. We used the attic as a clubhouse for smoking and drinking beer we would steal from the bar or our fathers. One time, our oldest gang member brought some pot. The first time we smoked it, we ended up laughing so loud that a neighbor heard us. He came to the cabin looking, but never found us.

Sometimes when we were in the attic, a bar patron and a girl would come in to use the bed. We had small holes in the ceiling, and we watched as they had sex. My friends still made fun of me because I had never had sex. They would say they were going to pay one of these girls to have sex with me. I always told them no way would I have sex there because I knew they would be watching. I never told them about the sexual abuse I had suffered.

Several kids from Ocean View came into our neighborhood and started using one of the vacant cabins as a clubhouse. One night, we waited until they all were inside and set it on fire. As they were running out, we let them know we had set the fire. They never came back. That cabin did not burn to the ground, but it was never used again. It was now all ours.

We stole so much candy and other junk food and cigarettes from a store run by an old couple that it was a wonder they did not go out of business. We turned in coke bottles and received 2¢. When the thirty-two-ounce bottles came out, we got 3¢ for them. They would stack cases of bottles outside their back door. Two of us would pick up a case or two, go inside, and get the money. They would bring the cases back outside, and two more would bring them right back in. They knew it, but they were afraid of us. It was our neighborhood. If there was any messing around, it was our gang doing the messing.

One day, we started making what we called zip guns. We packed match heads in the connecting end of a bicycle spoke. We then packed paper over the match heads. We would light the end with our Zippos and *bang!* it would shoot the paper wads. One day, I melted down some old lead sinkers I had and replaced the paper with lead. We started shooting at everything—cats, dogs, and lights just to name a few targets.

One day, one of the gang members suggested we rob the old couple. I was against the idea from the beginning and told them so, but the other four decided to do it anyway. Of course, I finally relented; it was my gang. What else could I do? We entered the store with zip guns and Zippos at the ready. Our T-shirts pulled up high were our masks. Harry, the oldest, said, "Give us all your money and some penny candy!" The old man laughed. "I know you kids. Is this a joke?" Tim held his lighter too close to the end of the spoke, and the zip gun went off. The shot broke a glass jar on a shelf behind the counter. The pieces fell and knocked over items on a glass case below. One of those items fell over and shattered the glass top, which in turn broke penny-candy jars in the case. The old woman screamed as she jumped backward knocking other items off a shelf along the wall behind her. The old man tried to catch some items but slipped and fell. He hit his head and almost knocked himself out. As he lay on the floor moaning, the woman screamed, "Get out of here! Leave us alone!" We ran off after grabbing handfuls of penny candy laughing our asses off.

It was months before we went back into the store again. When we did go back in, the old man never said anything to us but always gave us funny looks. After that, we never tried to rob anybody again. We used our zip guns only to scare kids coming into our neighborhood. Most of the time, we would pull them out, show the kids, and they would leave for good.

Once, we placed one of my father's .22 caliber rifle bullets on a pine tree and shot it with a zip gun. Something—we were never sure what it was—came back and grazed Jay's forehead. It was either the lead from the bullet or the brass casing. Either way, we never did that again.

A gatepost in my front yard had a hole in the top. One day, I took one of my father's shotgun shells, placed it in the hole, and was about to shoot it with my zip gun. At the last minute, remembering what had happened with the bullet, I took a nail and hammer and hit it. The whole post exploded. My gang helped me replace the post. When my father came back from overseas, Mama told him somebody had hit it with a car and I had replaced it.

I smiled and asked, "Did I do good, Daddy?"

With one of his special looks, he backhanded me and said, "The gate's hanging crooked." He sat with my sister and gave her a trinket he had brought back for her.

CHAPTER 45

Making Money

My dream in those days was to make money, run away and return to Louisiana. My two best friends, Jay and Rob, said they would go with me. We ran away twice. The first time, we skipped school and hopped on a train. Jay and Rob got on all right, but when I tried, one foot slipped, and I was dragged for a couple of miles hanging by one leg. Somehow railroad dicks saw us. The train stopped, and they started chasing us but never caught us. We hid in the woods and went home two days later.

The next time, we again skipped school, but that time with three other kids and my gang. Two truant officers saw us. They got out of their cruiser and tried to talk to us, but we ran away. All along the bay on the opposite side of our trailer park, people used the sand as a beach. We ran toward the end of the bay, and as we approached it, a different cruiser stopped at the edge of the beach. Two big, fat truant officers got out and yelled, "Get over here, you little fucking bastards!"

People all over the beach were laughing their asses off watching those two fat officers chasing us. Sometimes, we only walked and taunted them. One fell in the sand, and it took his partner and a man on the beach to get him up.

It was low tide, and we crossed the bay in the mud. We almost lost one of the kids in that mud. The tide was coming in, and he sank so deep that he could not get out. It took all of us digging as fast as we could to save him from drowning.

We hid in the woods all night. The next day, the three other kids went home. My gang and I stayed away for two more days. My sister had gone home that first day and asked Mama why I had not been in school. When I got home, all Mama kept asking was, "What girls did you have with you?" She never asked anything else. I kept telling her that there were no girls. She kept telling me as she always did, "Stay away from girls. They're dirty and nasty!"

I always had one scheme or another to make money to run away. As I had in the past, I collected worms after a hard rain. I decided to sell them for a penny each as fish bait. I kept them in my pocket during school and took them home that afternoon. Mama had an old, hand-wringing washing machine on the ground right outside the kitchen window. I had noticed that every time she washed clothes, worms would come up from the ground in the soapy water. I started gathering them up as well. I nailed a sign on the gatepost that read, "Worms 1¢." I would give an extra worm to anyone who bought ten. I kept them wrapped in that notebook paper in the rear of my underwear drawer.

One day when I got home, Mama told me people had been there asking about fish bait. She had told them that she didn't know anything about it. She asked me about them; Mama couldn't read my sign. I just told her I was selling them, and I kept them outside and under the trailer. So far, I had made about $2. I kept that hidden in the woods in that drainpipe along with my belt and badge, which I intended to take with me.

One day, Mama found the worms in my drawer. She was screaming mad; she boiled both pair of my underwear and both T-shirts. She said she was going to tell my father, but of course, she never did. After that, I kept them in a box outside and did well until the weather turned cold and they froze. I believe that by that time, I had made about $3.

One day, I spent 10¢ on a toy Indian. If you filled the bottom of the toy with water and squeezed the bulb, his skirt rose, and water shot out of his rubber penis. I thought it was great, and I showed it to everybody. Of course, Mama found out and wanted to see it. When I showed her how it worked, she screamed, "God will punish you. You are a heathen and are going to hell!" She was talking more like my father than herself. "I'm not going to let you keep a heathen nigger toy!" She grabbed it and cut it up into a million pieces. "God will punish you for having that terrible nigger toy!" I was taken aback by her words because it was rare I ever heard her talk about blacks that way. I did not answer her, and I never brought another one home. I did steal one and kept it hidden in that old drainpipe.

My next venture was snakes and turtles. I would catch them at the Azalea Gardens, about ten miles from home. It was a large area filled with many small lakes and ponds and of course hundreds of azalea bushes. I would go into the water when I saw turtles sunning on logs and swim underwater right up to the log, reach up, and grab a turtle. I always carried an old burlap sack with me to put them in. The water snakes were harder to catch, so I usually caught many more turtles than snakes. I had a lot of fun catching them because there were always people walking around. Sometimes, they stopped and watched me. I was always trying to sell whatever I caught. A couple of times, I was able to sell a small, green-striped turtle for 50¢.

I never could sell any of the snakes, though, even when I showed people how nice they were to handle. I thought I could sell some to pet shops. I came home one day with a sack full. Mama asked, "What you got in that sack?" "Nothing," I replied. "Empty it out now!" she said. I had made a small cage of some wire I had found. It was about five feet across but only about a foot high, sitting on the ground. When I emptied those snakes and turtles into that cage, she ran into the trailer. The whole neighborhood heard her. The turtles were trying to get out of the wire cage, and the snakes were getting out quickly. I tried to catch them, but they slithered in different directions. One neighbor heard Mama's screams and came running out. "Johnny, what are you up to now?" She saw snakes headed toward her trailer and yelled, "Johnny! I'm going to kill you!" I eventually caught most of the snakes, six of them. The rest disappeared under different trailers.

It had taken me all day to catch that load, and I wasn't happy when I had to turn them loose in the woods. I kept one snake because I had it sold to my friend Scooter for 50¢. I brought it over to him. He was happy to get it and paid me.

About a week later, he asked me if I could catch another snake for him. I said, "Sure I can. What happened to yours?" He said, "I lost it."

That night, everybody in the neighborhood heard screaming and yelling. The next day, Scooter told me, "I don't need another snake. Mine crawled inside my sister's nightgown last night while she was sleeping, and my mother said she would kill me if I ever brought another one into the trailer." He was sad. But I was sadder because I had lost a sale.

I had also kept one of the turtles. I cut a hole in the edge of his shell, with one of Mamas kitchen knives, tied a string through it, and took him to where kids were swimming. I let the turtle swim around and then dragged him back to shore showing the kids. One kid really liked it, got 50¢ from his mother, and bought the turtle. Later, I heard the kid had been playing with the turtle on the street; a car had come along and squished it.

But by then, I was on to other ideas. I had about $4 in my runaway kitty. My next venture was pigeons. One of our neighbors had a large cage of about a dozen and a half. I started helping him feed them, clean the cages, and take care of them. He said he sold the young pigeons to people who ate them. Within a few months, he was transferred someplace. Before he left, he asked me if I would like to have them. I was seeing dollar signs. "Sure, I'll keep them!"

He had bought a lot of pigeon food and left it all with me. They were really no trouble because they never left the cage. I only had to scoop up poop and throw it in the woods. I started going around the park collecting old and stale bread from people. I crumbled it up and had all the food I needed. I was waiting for the Mamas to have babies; I would be rolling in money.

One day after some babies were born, Mama yelled, "Johnny, come quick! Your damn pigeons are eating each other!" Going out to the coop, I saw her beating my pigeons with her broom. "Mama, they're not eating each other. That's how Mama pigeons feed their babies." Mama left cursing, "Goddamn filthy birds."

I named my favorite pigeon Billie Coo. I would walk into the cage and call her, and she would come right to me. I could walk around the neighborhood with her on my shoulder; she would never fly away. I loved Billie Coo. My father was at sea when I first got them. When he did come back, things changed fast. The first day, I wanted to show him my beautiful pigeons, and I told him how I could make money selling the babies. He walked to the cage and made me open the door and shoo them out. I told him they had never been outside and would not know how to come back. He hit me so hard that I fell against the chicken wire and put a hole in it. He repeated, "I said to put them out, plowboy. Now goddamn it, do it!"

I opened the door and shooed them all out, including Billie Coo. Some of the babies flew away, but others didn't. Most of the adults stayed in the nearby trees. A few, including Billie Coo, stayed on top on the cage. I watched them while my father went back into our trailer. In a couple of hours, he came out and told me to call them back. I called, and Billie Coo came right to me. I called, "*Coo coo coo*," and a few of the other came, but the rest stayed in the trees.

My father walked back into the trailer and came out with his rifle. I begged him not to shoot them. He hit me with the barrel of the rifle and shot all those that were in the trees. He made me pick up and clean all of them—pulling out feathers and guts.

That night, he made us, meaning he and I, eat all those pigeons. I did not want to, so he hit me across the mouth and knocked me to the floor. "You'll eat every goddamn thing your mother puts on your plate whether you like it or not!"

The next day, he did it all over again. That time, Billie Coo did not come right down. He shot her as she sat on top of the cage cooing at me.

That night, I was dying inside as we ate Billie Coo and the others. I kept staring at my father. I wanted him dead. I wanted to shoot him. The next day, he slept in and I went out early while the sun was starting to come up and let all the others out. When they just flew into nearby trees, I threw rocks at them to chase them away. That morning when he left, he never looked at them. That afternoon when he came home, I told him somebody must have opened the gate and let them out. I still had only $4 in my runaway kitty.

My next venture was roots. One time, my father had made some root beer from extract using a pitcher of water, three or four lemons, and five or six cups of sugar. My father told me it was made from a sassafras tree root. I started hunting in the woods for that tree. Sure enough, I dug up one root, smelled it, and chewed on it. It tasted like root beer to me. Again, I saw dollar signs. I figured that if I could gather a lot of them, I could make enough that I would be able to take my friends Jay and Rob with me. Maybe we could ride a bus to Louisiana instead of hitchhiking.

I dug what roots I could and cut them off that tree. On the way home, I walked by a neighbor's trailer and noticed that the trees in her yard looked just like the one with the root I had chewed on. Occasionally, I would babysit her two-year-old son, so I knew her well.

One day while I was babysitting him, he tried to eat my small turtle. He was choking on it, and I used some kitchen tongs she had to retrieve my turtle. I was so mad I took him outside, sat him on the ground, and let him eat all the Japanese beetles he wanted. That night, he became so sick that they had to take him to the base infirmary. They never did figure out how he had eaten those beetles as he threw up legs and shells.

Anyway, I went in and told her about my plan to sell the roots, and sure enough, she gave me permission to dig them up if I did not make a big mess. I promised I wouldn't. She left to go shopping. When she came back, shit hit the fan. I had dug about a hundred holes, some a foot deep. There was dirt and roots everywhere, and I was nowhere to be found.

The next day, she showed my father what I had done. He called me over to her house and beat me with one of those long roots. She came out and made him stop, telling him to just have me fill in the holes. None of those roots tasted like root beer anyway. So, went that venture. I still had only $4.

CHAPTER 46

An Old Outboard Motor

For one reason or another, I was getting beaten almost every time my father was around. There were times I deserved it, but not every time. I was always getting grounded to our yard and blamed for things I did not do. I had to continue raking the yard, dirt and all.

Once when I was grounded, he came home with an old outboard motor. He nailed a board to a tree, attached the motor to it, and tried to start it. He pulled on the cord over and over. I was still raking when Mama called me inside and told me to go to the store for some items. When I came outside to go, he asked me, "Where the hell are you going?" I said, "I'm going to the store for Mama." He didn't say anything; he just kept pulling that cord, so I left.

When I came back with a bag of groceries, he called me over. He punched me in the head, which knocked me to the ground, and he kicked me in the stomach. "I bought this goddamn motor for you, plowboy! The least you could do is help me get it started!" I got up and started pulling the cord. He picked the groceries up and walked into the house.

Sometime after dark—it seemed like hours had passed—I was still pulling on that old motor. He called me in and told me to go to bed. Nothing was said about supper. We did not have a boat, and the next day, he took that motor to work. Nothing else was ever said, and I never saw the motor again.

CHAPTER 47

Lawn Broom

One time when I was raking the dirt, my father came home with a type of rake I had never seen before. Today, we call it a lawn broom. He handed it to me and said, "Rake the yard with this, plowboy!" He went into the trailer as I started raking the same way I did with the old iron rake. He must have stood just inside watching me because within a couple of minutes, he came roaring out so mad that he broke the spring that held the screen door closed. He grabbed the lawn broom from my hands and started beating me with it. "That's not how you rake with it!" He beat me so hard that *crack!* the handle broke. That made him even madder, and the beating got worse. I felt a crunch, and my nose felt like it was on fire—flat and mashed against my face. He had broken my nose.

Later that week while my father was at work, Mama took me to the base infirmary. She told the doctor I had fallen. The doctor said, "Yeah, a lot of kids are falling down these days." The doctor twisted and pulled on my nose until he thought it was back in the right place. He said if I ever broke it again, I would need surgery. I was black and blue under my eyes for a long time. I always told people that I had broken my nose playing baseball. I said that I was at bat when one friend stood behind me with a bat saying, "Johnny, if you miss, I'll hit it." I said that I missed and that he had swung, breaking my nose. Until this writing, I always thought that sounded like a good story to tell instead of the truth, which I had kept hidden, way down deep, with all other truths.

Once, Mama took me to see the base doctor because I was having a lot of pain in my stomach. I had to get undressed except for my underwear, and he saw a lot of bruises and black and blue marks. I always saw the same doctor, and he said, "The kid falls down a lot, huh?" Mama did not answer him. He asked Mama, "You know what's wrong with him, don't you?" She said, "No, what?" He said, "Nothing. He's just trying to get out of going to school." She got furious with him. She never said anything about the beatings or stomach kicking. He finally said, "Okay, okay–he has what we call a nervous stomach." He gave her some medicine for me. He never did any tests and did not give me much of an examination other than just poking me in the stomach. Mama must have believed him because she tried to make me take that awful medicine. For many years, I had trouble with my nervous stomach. I guess that diagnosis was the answer. Of course, I was forgetting about the kerosene.

CHAPTER 48

Broken Hand

One night, my father called my sister and me into his bedroom. He told me to open the bathroom door to close off the bedroom. He made us take our clothes off except for our underwear and told us to get on the bed with him. He made us lie side by side next to him. He started tickling us all over. Occasionally, he would reach inside my underwear and feel my genitals. He did the same thing to my sister.

That tickling continued every night. Every time, he would put his hand inside my underwear and feel my genitals. One night, I happened to kick out, and my foot caught his wrist. He screamed in pain, and I said, "I'm sorry, Daddy." He started beating me with his other hand yelling, "Goddamn it! Now look what you've done!" My sister climbed off the bed. He stopped hitting me and told my sister, "Get your ass back on the bed!" He got off the bed and yelled to Mama, "I need to go to the infirmary because he broke my wrist. This is the twelfth time since I started boxing!"

Mama helped him get dressed. As he was leaving, he said to my sister and me, "Stay on the bed until I return!" He left. While he was gone, I told Mama, "I didn't do it on purpose." She replied, "I know. He used to box in the navy and broke it eleven times before."

Mama lay on the bed with my sister and me until my father returned about an hour or two later. He had a cast on his wrist. Mama went back into the kitchen area opening the bathroom door as she left. My father lay on the bed with my sister and me and continued tickling us. Once again, occasionally, he would feel our genitals.

The tickling continued each night throughout the summer. My father shipped out overseas just before my twelfth birthday.

CHAPTER 49

Burning Fire

It was a bright and sunny day. I was patrolling the beach area of Sandy Town on the police department's Harley-Davidson motorcycle. Many people were at the beaches, and some were just walking on the roads around the beach. I was feeling great. Most of the people in the area knew me, and I would smile, wave, and stop and talk with them. Sometimes, I had to write parking tickets mostly for out-of-towners.

Once, I wrote a ticket for a beautiful, new Caddy. About an hour later, I was riding through the same area just as the owner and his wife were returning to the car. The gentleman grabbed the ticket from under his windshield and flagged me down. I stopped, shut the motor off, and asked, "May I help you, sir?" Without looking at the ticket, he replied, "Yeah, I got this fucking ticket. What's it for?" I replied, "Sir, you're parked next to a fire hydrant." His wife yelled, "There aren't any goddamn parking spaces. What are we supposed to do?" Just as I was about to answer her, the owner flipped open his wallet, showed a badge, and said in a loud voice, "Look, I'm a Boston cop. Can't you take care of this?"

I had run into Boston cops before, and they were a little humble about tickets asking but not really, if you know what I mean. At the right time and place, tickets can be taken care of. That was not one of those times, nor was he one of those cops. Before I could answer, he tore up the ticket and threw it on the ground next to my bike. I picked up the radio mike and called the station. "I have a problem. Can you send backup my way?" I made sure the owner heard me.

I got off the bike, approached him, and stated, "Sir, may I have your license and registration?" He looked a little befuddled. "What? What for?" I stepped closer. With my eyes piercing his, I repeated my request. A few people had stopped and were listening and watching us. Cursing loudly, the man looked around and went into his car for the paperwork.

Taking his information back to the bike, I wrote him a citation for littering. When I handed it to him, he looked at it, and his face turned beet-red. "You fuckin' small-town cops aren't worth anything. I'm going to your police station and file a complaint with your chief!" I said, "Yes sir, you do that. Have a great day," as I smiled. He was so mad that he yelled at his wife, "Get in the fuckin' car, now!" He sped away spitting sand and gravel everywhere including on me and my bike.

Some of the onlookers came over. "Johnny, if you need a witness, I'll speak up for you." I thanked them. "What cops like that need to realize is that they too are citizens. Just because they carry a badge doesn't mean they're above the law." As everyone left, some of the property owners thanked me and said, "He should never have parked next to that hydrant."

About an hour later, I received a radio call asking me to come to the station. When I got there, the desk officer told me a man and woman were in the lobby waiting to see me. I walked into the lobby and saw them. She was holding a baby. I asked, "May I help you?" The woman asked, "Are you the juvenile officer?" I stated, "I am. How may I help you?" She said, "We need to talk with you." I said, "Okay, let's go upstairs to my office."

In my office, I asked them to sit. "How may I help you?" The man had his hands folded in his lap and was staring at the floor. The woman said, "I think my baby is being sexually abused, and I know who's doing it." She gave me the name and address of a couple who babysit for them.

I asked, "Have you taken your baby to see a doctor or to the hospital?"

She said, "I take her only to our pediatrician, but he hasn't said anything."

"What makes you believe she's being abused?"

She glanced at the male, who was still staring at the floor. "My baby's vagina and anus are red, swollen, and raw looking. Every time I touch either one, she cries. I have to keep a lot of baby powder or salve on her or she'll cry."

I told her that she needed to take her baby immediately to the hospital and get her examined. I assured her I would start my investigation immediately. I took all the pertinent information and asked her if she would call the pediatrician and give him her verbal okay to speak with me about the baby and the situation. She said she would call him and take the baby to the hospital that afternoon.

About a year earlier, the chief had appointed me the juvenile officer. I received permission to attend a seminar on sexual abuse against young children offered by the DA's office. At that time, we had a female officer who was qualified, but I was the only male officer in our department qualified to investigate sexual crimes against children.

Walking downstairs I gave the chief the details I had. He advised me to get the results from the hospital as soon as possible. I agreed. I said I would speak with the baby's doctor for any information to stop this abuse quickly. He agreed and instructed me to investigate the allegations as I saw fit. As I was leaving his office, he asked, "By the way, did you write a parking and a littering ticket to a Boston cop?" I said, "Yes sir I did." He looked at me and said, "Good job. Keep it up."

I made an appointment with the doctor, and the next day, I went there. After confirming with him that the woman had given him her permission to speak with me, I told him about the allegations and asked him if she had told him anything about them. He said no. I asked him if he had ever seen any indication of any type of abuse, sexual or any other type. He said, "Yes I did."

That surprised me. "What did you see? What did you think?"

"I noticed that the baby's vagina was red and puffy and that she would cry when it was touched. After about two weeks, I started noticing that the baby's anus was also red, puffy, and sore to the touch."

"What did you suspect?"

"Sexual abuse."

I asked him if he had told the mother and father or advised the local police of his suspicions.

"No, I didn't."

"You know you have a legal and moral obligation to report it, right?"

His response floored me. "The reason I didn't say anything is because my wife and I go out socially with the mother and father."

I told him I would make a full report on everything he had told me. I looked him straight in the eye and said, "If there is a God, I hope he'll have no mercy on your soul. May you burn in hell."

As I walked out, I heard him sobbing. I knew that what I had said was unprofessional and that he might file a complaint against me, but I had to say something.

I drove to the babysitters' house. I knew the couple casually from around town, and I knew they had two children. My gut was telling me that they were not involved in these allegations, but I also knew that you never knew what people were capable of. I had a job to do, and I would do it to the best of my ability, and that included interviewing the couple.

I explained to them that I was investigating allegations about the baby being sexually abused. They asked if they were suspected. I advised them that the investigation was just underway, and I was interviewing those who knew or took care of the baby. I spent about an hour interviewing the couple and ended up with the feeling that they had had nothing to do with the allegations of abuse.

I returned to the station and reported to the chief about the case. He asked if I had heard from the parents or the hospital. "Not yet," I said.

Three days later, I still had not heard from the hospital or the parents, so I called the parents. The mother answered the phone; I asked, "Have you taken the baby to the hospital to get her checked out?"

"No, I haven't," she said. "Did you talk to the couple who babysit?"

"Can you and your husband come to the station, so we can discuss this matter further?"

"Yes, but it will be in about an hour. I need to feed and change the baby."

"Okay. I'll see you then."

I updated the chief, who asked, "What do you think?"

I told him what I suspected. He said, "Okay, but be careful." I knew what he meant.

About an hour and a half later, the wife, husband, and baby came in. I ushered them into my office. I sat at my desk and looked directly at the husband. "I believe we need to go over the allegations again."

The husband had his hands clenched. He was looking down. "I need help!" he said and started crying.

His wife did not look at him but at me. "If you want to speak with us again, first talk with our lawyer!" She rose and told her husband, "Let's go!" as she stomped out of my office.

I informed the chief about my meeting and updated my report. I closed my office door, sat, and closed my eyes. I let my thoughts wander. I hoped that little girl would not remember, but I was afraid she would. My eyes filled with tears. Painful memories returned. I remembered a long time ago when my own life had taken such a drastic turn, and how I had wished that the burning fires of hell had found him. I wished him dead.

That fall, I turned twelve and was in fifth grade when my father returned from sea. About a week later, he came home one night with a twelve-gauge, single-shot, JC Higgins shotgun and a box of buckshot. He told me, "This shotgun is yours. Keep it loaded beside your bed at all times!" He kept his loaded guns beside his bed and his pistol under his pillow. When he went to sea, Mama would move only his pistol to a cabinet in the bedroom.

As he had told me many times, he said, "You will protect your mother and sister when the niggers overrun us, and you'll kill as many as you can. Always keep back at least two rounds of buckshot!" I knew he meant for me to shoot my mother and sister, so they would not be taken alive. I did not want the gun, and I looked at him with pure hatred in my heart. He must have seen it in my eyes because he backhanded me hard. "Are you listening to me, plowboy?" Still staring at him but wishing he were dead and burning in hell, I answered, "Yes, Daddy, I understand you." He backhanded me again. "You have now become a man, and you will address me as sir and you will address your mother as ma'am! You will always show respect to your mother, sister, and all women, is that understood?" I replied, "Yes sir." He told me to bring the gun and shells outside.

Standing in the front yard, trailers near us on both sides and all around us, he told me, "Load the gun and shoot it!" I had shot his .22 rifle many times but not his shotgun. I loaded the gun, raised it into the air, and pulled the trigger. Nothing happened. He backhanded me hard, and I fell over backward. He said, "You have to cock the goddamn gun first!" I got up and cocked the gun. I put the stock about six inches from my shoulder and pulled the trigger. The recoil knocked me down, and my shoulder felt as if it were on fire. I was on my back. He grabbed the gun from my hands and hit me square in the face with the stock. Blood spurted from my lips. He grabbed me by the neck, jerked me to my feet, and said, "Do it again, but hold the stock against your shoulder goddamn it!"

I was crying hard; my tears were mixing with my blood. Our neighbor, whose trailer was about twenty-five feet away, walked over to see why we were shooting. She was very pregnant. The gun was loaded and cocked, and I was standing there holding it pointed straight ahead as she walked up. Not really noticing her, I slowly started swinging the gun barrel toward my father, the hate in me reaching all the way to my shaking hands. My father punched me in the chest and knocked me down again. As I fell, I inadvertently pulled the trigger. God only knows why that shot went wide and into the ground near her legs. She yelled, screamed, and ran to her trailer. My father took the gun, hit me with the stock again, and said, "Get inside!" as he followed. He took the shotgun into his bedroom.

A short time later, the shore patrol showed up, and my father went outside to speak with them. He left with them but was back in about an hour. He never took me outside again to shoot the gun, but he made sure I always kept it loaded beside my bunk bed.

After that, I did take it out by myself sometimes when he was not around. I would shoot it and pretend I was shooting him. I was becoming angrier and angrier.

Later that night, my father told me to take a shower. I went into the shower and picked up the

Ivory soap, the only kind Mama used, and scrubbed the dried blood off my face and hands. The shower stall was small, but it did have a curtain, which I had closed. As I was scrubbing, the bathroom door opened. My father jerked the curtain back and said, "Turn around, bend over, and wash your feet!" I did as he told me to, and as I bent over, I saw that he too was naked and had an erection. He put one hand on my back to hold me in a bent-over position. With the other hand, he reached under me and started roughly manipulating my penis and scrotum. I tried to stand up. "Stop it!" I yelled. With the hand that was on my back and with great force, he grabbed the back of my neck and pushed my head back down hard saying, "You're now a man, and you need to be treated like a man!" I heard him spitting, and with one finger, two fingers, and finally three fingers, he invaded my rectum. He was twisting, turning, opening and closing his fingers, and pushing them in and out hard. The pain was almost unbearable. He entered my anus with his penis and started humping me. I felt his ball sack slapping against my ass as he started moaning, groaning, and almost growling. Long-suppressed memories of the day I was sexually abused by my friend's brother Mike and his friend Carl in Mayville came back.

I tried to get away, but his hands were on my neck and shoulder. He was holding me down hard, and my neck felt like it was in a vice. I had not let him see me cry very often before, but I was crying and saying, "Stop it! Stop it! That hurts!" as I struggled to get away. But my strength was no match for his, and the shower was small. I started hitting the walls of the shower hoping Mama would hear and come in to see what was wrong. He punched my head. "Keep still, plowboy, and take it like a man!" Felling like he peed inside me, he pulled out of my anus, and he was gone, closing the bathroom door quietly behind him.

I collapsed on the blood-covered shower floor. My anus felt on fire. It hurt just as it had so long ago. Blood continued flowing onto the shower floor. I stayed in the bathroom for a long time until the bleeding had subsided. I rinsed off and stepped out of the shower. I saw an opened jar of Vaseline on the sink. I recognized it because Mama had used it on my lips in the past to stop the bleeding. I stuck my fingers in the jar and smeared some all over my anus. I put a big ball of toilet paper over it. I put on my underwear and opened the door.

The trailer was in total darkness. My father was in his bed, which was only about two feet from the door. I saw the whites of his eyes as he looked at me. Mama was on the other side of him with her back to us. Turning off the bathroom light, head down, I quietly walked to my bunk. I got in, covered up, and cried myself to sleep wondering what I had done to deserve that.

For some time after that, I was in such a depression that I skipped school almost every day. I threatened my sister into keeping quiet about it. When I did return to school, nobody, including Sister Superior, asked me anything. It was as if they did not really care and felt that they had been better off without me. All they wanted was for me to finish the year and get out. I withdrew into myself as I had never done before. All I wanted was to die. When my friends came around, most of the time, Mama told them I was busy and could not come out. When not at school, I stayed in bed a lot. My father and Mama never said a word to me during that time.

One night about two weeks later, I was sitting on the couch. My sister was beside me, and Mama was making dinner. My sister was trying to engage me in conversation about something she was doing. I would have none of it as I just sat and stared at the floor. I did not want to talk to anybody about anything.

My father came through the door just as my mother was filling our plates. I looked at him with pure hate in my eyes. Mama said, "Supper's ready, kids." My sister jumped up and started toward the plates. I looked at Mama and said, "I'm not hungry, ma'am." My father backhanded me so hard that he knocked me off the couch. "I told you you'll eat everything your mother puts on your plate, plowboy!" He pulled his leg back to kick me. I said, "Yes sir, I'll eat."

My lip was bleeding, but I didn't care. I wolfed down everything on my plate using just my fingers. I felt hurt and beaten down. All I wanted was to curl up on the couch and die. I was still wondering, *What, did I do wrong?*

Right after dinner, my father said, "Go take a shower!" Fear gripped me. He must have seen it because he said, "Now, plowboy!" Head down, I walked to the bathroom. I heard him telling my sister, "I have to teach that boy what it means to be a man." My sister giggled.

Reaching the bathroom, I opened the door. When I did so, I remembered that they could not see the bathroom from the living room. *I'm not waiting. I'm running away right now.* I opened the back door and stepped into the cool night air. As I turned to shut the door quietly, something hit me in the back hard enough to knock me against the trailer and to the ground. I looked up. My father was standing over me, and he asked with a snarl, "Where the hell are you going, plowboy?" He picked me up and threw me into the bedroom. Stepping inside, he quietly closed the outside door behind him. He ordered me to take my clothes off, and he started taking his off. As he took off his boxers, I saw he had an erection. My whole world fell apart. I knew I would never escape him.

That time, I did not fight him as he bent me over the bed. When he finished, he slapped me on the butt and in a cheerful voice said, "Now that's taking it like a man, plowboy!"

After that, he raped me about once a week, sometimes twice. I was ashamed. I never told anybody. I became so withdrawn that even the nuns were surprised that I wasn't trouble any more. I did not care about anything or anybody. I just wanted to die. In class, I just sat quietly, head down, saying nothing. When somebody asked me a question, I would look at whoever it was with a blank stare and say nothing. Though I didn't know what I had done wrong, I was blaming myself for whatever it was.

One night when my father was home, I waited until the wee hours of the morning. In the darkness, I took my loaded shotgun and walked up to his bed. There was a lot of hate in me but not an ounce of fear. I raised the gun and aimed at his head. Out of the darkness, he said, "Go ahead, plowboy! pull the goddamn trigger!" I was so startled that I did pull the trigger. The only problem was I had forgotten to cock the gun. He laughed at me. "You can't do any goddamn thing right and you never will, plowboy!" Totally dejected, head down, I walked back to my bunk. I put my gun beside my bunk bed and crawled into bed, once again, crying myself to sleep. Surprisingly, nothing was ever said about that night.

As time passed and the abuse continued, it became a normal part of my young life. Deep down, I knew I must have done something wrong, but I couldn't figure out what. Besides, there was nothing I could do about it. I adjusted my life to fit my circumstances. I shoved it way down deep and hoped it would stay there. I didn't think about it. I became more withdrawn, and I put an invisible shield up so nobody could get close to me. I wasn't letting anybody in no matter what.

On the outside, I went back to being as normal as I could, but I had this deep, gut-grinding anger inside that would not leave. Even with everything that was going on in my life, I knew something else was trying to come out; I just did not know what it was. My life was in turmoil, and I blamed myself. As time passed, I kept pushing experiences like that down deep. I had no one to talk to, no one I could trust. I continued with my life such as it was.

One day, my friends and I saw two kids fishing out in the bay in a small boat. That night, we went to their house to steal the boat, but one of the kids caught us. I turned on that kid and beat him so badly that I left him lying in a pool of his own blood. My friends had to stop me.

We did steal that boat. As it turned out, it was a steel, cement-mixing tub with handles on both ends. It was about four feet wide, six feet long, and about twelve inches high. We kept it hidden deep in the woods beyond the Point. One day, a friend and I took it out to the mouth of the bay by the jetties to go fishing; it would hold only two kids. Ships and ferries came through there. He was afraid their wakes would sink us. I said, "Don't worry. I can swim." I tied a rope around my wrist and to a handle of the boat. Sure enough, a navy ship came by and the wake sunk us. The only reason I did not die that day was because I carried a knife on a piece of rope around my waist when fishing.

That night as I was going to sleep, my last thoughts were *Why did I have to have that knife with me? I know it is a mortal sin to kill yourself, but God wouldn't mind if I died some other way, would he?*

Though I still had some religion in me, we never went to any church as a family. Sometimes during school, the nuns would take us to Mass. Most times, I would hide and not go, but when I did, I never paid attention in Mass either.

One day, I saw a paper matchbook with a picture of a pretty bird lying among the small candles you lit. I waited until nobody was in the church and went back in. I tore the cover off the matchbook and took it home. After that, I would check occasionally and take all the new pictures. Word spread around the school that somebody was stealing God's matchbook covers. I laughed and kept stealing them. I stole many that year and never got caught.

I remember giving up on God. I thought, *if he won't help me, screw him!* I now know my anger was coming out sideways, but at the time, I was happy to do something. If I could not battle my father, at least I was getting even with God, if there was one.

CHAPTER 50

Donnie and Me

Donnie was a young boy who lived a few trailers down from us. Whenever I was around, he always hung out with me no matter what I was doing. He was a great kid, and I knew he looked up to me, so I was very respectful to him. I never cursed, smoked, or did anything bad around him. I also would not let anybody else, even my gang, do any bad things to Donnie.

One day, an unknown boy a little older than me was walking by as Donnie and I were sitting on his tricycle next to the fence in front of his trailer. Donnie loved it when I gave him rides; he would hang onto me with his arms around my waist. Sometimes, I would ride it down the steep hills in our neighborhood by the water.

The unknown kid started cursing and calling me a dumb asshole for hanging out with a little kid. Before I knew what was happening, Donnie jumped off that tricycle, ran over to the kid, and wrapped his legs and arms around the kid's leg. Donnie bit the kid hard on his leg and drew blood. The kid yelled and screamed trying to dislodge him. I was just sitting on the bike mouth wide open in disbelief. Donnie had never shown any hostility toward anybody.

I ran over and got Donnie loose from the boy's leg. He ran off fast. As he ran, Donnie yelled, "You leave my Johnny alone." I yelled at the kid, "Don't ever come back here or I'll sic Donnie on you!" I did not know what to say to Donnie, so I just hugged him. He looked at me and said, "I love you, Johnny." I had never heard anybody say, "I love you, Johnny." I started crying like a baby as Donnie stood up and hugged me hard.

Later, I told Mama about the incident. She looked at me with a strange look on her face and said, "I wub you, Johnny." I did not believe her, and for years, right up to her death, whenever she would say, "I wub you, Johnny" I never believed her. I never heard my father or sister say, "I love you, Johnny." Years later, when people would say, "I love you," I never believed them. That shield stayed up as strong as ever. Many times, I wondered if I would ever find love.

One day, Donnie kept pestering me to take him fishing. The night before had been another bad time with my father in the shower, and I did not want to go. Eventually, I put him in a washtub, gave him my fishing pole, and pushed him into the bay. I did not intend for the tub to go way out, but a slight wind came up quickly. Before I knew it, he was out in the middle of the bay. Except for swimming, which was too far for me, I had no way of getting him back in.

When his mother came home, she was yelling and screaming mad. She called the shore patrol, and they sent somebody in a motorboat to get him. She did not speak to me for a few days, but for some reason, she did not tell my father.

CHAPTER 51

Pennies from Hell

My father shipped out overseas again. Donnie's mother was the only one we knew who had a TV. She was nice, and on occasion, my friends and I would go over to her trailer and watch *Howdy Doody* or other kids' shows. She always gave us popsicles and other treats.

One day when she and her husband were not home, I broke in and stole a jar of pennies she kept on a shelf. Jenny was a girl I really liked, but because I was too shy, I hardly ever spoke to her. I just watched her from a far. She was fifteen, and she had large breasts that mesmerized me. Whenever she babysat in the area, she would have boys come over, some of them my friends, and they would massage her breasts. She told them that her mother also did that every night and that was what had made them so large.

After stealing that jar of pennies, I started leaving a couple of comic books and pennies by her door, knock, and run away. One day, a neighbor's daughter saw the pennies in my pocket and asked me where I had gotten them. I told her some lie and tried to give her some, but she would not take any. After that, nobody said anything to me about the pennies, and I continued to give them to Jenny until they were gone.

It was now 1956, I had just turned thirteen and my father returned from sea. The night after he returned, he told me to come with him. He took me out into the woods carrying a long piece of rope. Going deep into the woods, he stopped under a tall oak tree with a low-hanging limb. He knotted one end of the rope, coiled it up, and threw it over the limb. He turned to me and said, "Come here!" I walked over to him looking at the rope and then at him. I had no idea what he had planned for me, but I was scared and shaking. He tied one end of the rope around my neck. He said, "When I was growing up, we took niggers we caught stealing or doing other bad things out into the woods and hung them!" I looked at the rope and started crying.

He asked me, "Why did you steal that money?"

I told him about the girl. I said, "I gave most of it to her." To my amazement, he did not beat me. He explained why it was bad to steal and what could happen to me if somebody caught me. Still holding that rope, he pulled on it, tightening it around my neck for emphasis. He said, "Stay away from girls. They're nothing but trouble. There are only two kinds of girls in the world. One, you can't do enough for, and the other, you can't do anything right for."

Before walking back home, he raped me, in the woods. Combined with the rape, I remember those pennies from hell as a great lesson learned.

Shortly after that, my father was transferred to the Morgan Creek Naval Base. We lived only about two miles from the base, so he was home every night and a lot of days too. He never shipped out again. I had to work odd jobs to pay back all the money and apologize to the woman. He grounded me for the entire summer to the yard except when I was working for somebody to earn the money.

Every morning, he got up at five thirty to go to work, and he would wake me before he left. It was the way he woke me up that I remember most. Every morning, he would throw a glass of cold water in my face and yell, "Get up, plowboy!" I was immediately sent out to rake the yard. Mama would make me grits and eggs after he had left.

CHAPTER 52

Fuzzy

One hot day while I was raking, my lips puffed out and bloody, my nose also bleeding, my father left for work. He walked by and hit me on the side of the head. He said, "You better not leave this yard, plowboy!" My father said he had weekend duty and would be home Monday, and I had better have raked the entire yard.

Occasionally, one or two friends would walk by to say they were going swimming at the bridge. I only nodded and kept raking. About an hour later, a girl I knew walked by. She walked over to the fence and said, "I'm going swimming. Do you want to go?"

I knew I would get a real beating if he came home, but I also knew he had duty. I decided to go. I told her I had to stop at the old washhouse to get a bathing suit. We then walked to the bridge. For a couple of hours, we jumped and swam with our friends.

After a while, she and I went under the bridge to rest. She asked me if my father had beaten me again. I turned away and denied it. She took my hand and said, "I saw your lips and nose. Your ear looks like a red lollipop." I couldn't hold back. I told her everything, including the sexual abuse. I also told her I had never told anybody else about it, and I begged her, "Please don't tell anybody." She said, "I won't say a word."

I told her I was trying to make money to run away. "I wish I had never been born, and I wish I were dead." She squeezed my hand harder and said, "It's okay. I'm here now, and I understand." She told me she also was being sexually abused by her stepdad. She told me how she was coping with the abuse. "I keep it to myself pushed down real deep inside. I've never spoken to anybody about it." She said that after seeing me occasionally, she thought I also might have been sexually abused. We promised not to tell anybody about each other. I had never had a conversation with her or anybody else like her before. She was nothing like Mama or my father had said.

After hugging, we went back onto the bridge. As I was standing on the railing, I looked up and saw a navy car coming toward us. Fearing the worst, I dove. As my head was about to hit the water, I heard kids yelling and screaming. I saw a motorboat coming full speed at me. I hit the water and saw the propeller pass within a few inches of my feet. I swam down until my head hit the muddy bottom. I wanted to stay there and die. I stayed so long that I barely made it to the surface.

Reaching the surface, I was afraid my father had been in the navy car, had seen me, and was standing on the bridge. Without looking, I swam as fast as I could toward a beach a hundred yards away. There was a pier on the beach, and at the end were some posts in the water. I reached for a post, but my hand slipped. By pure reflex, my left hand shot out to the side, and when I felt something, I grabbed it by pure reflex. Turning my head, I saw that I had grabbed a dark-headed girl I knew by sight right in the crotch. She was the girlfriend of the leader of the Morgan Creek Gang, and her reputation was well known to all of us kids. It was said that she liked to fight and that she carried a big knife. She smiled and said, "You can let go of my pussy now, Johnny!"

Totally embarrassed, I let go quickly and swam away. I reached shore. She followed me, and I told her, "I'm sorry. It was an accident." She believed me or did not care—I did not know which. She grabbed my arm and started asking me all kinds of sexual questions. When she asked, "I've heard you've never had sex with a girl. Is that true?" I yanked my arm from her grasp and turned to walk away. She grabbed my bathing suit and yanked it down hard. She ripped it completely off me except for a small piece around my leg. She dropped it to the sand, pointed at my genitals, and laughed. The beach was filled with women and young kids. Out loud, she asked, "Why do you have only fuzz on your cock?"

Embarrassed and deathly afraid of her, I picked up my suit, covered myself with it, and ran. She chased me laughing, asking over and over, "Why do you only have fuzz on your cock?"

I ran all the way back to the old washhouse covering myself with my torn bathing suit. I put my clothes on and waited for my friends. When they arrived, they were laughing and horsing around. One said, "Hey! That girl wants to know why you have only a little fuzz on your cock." I stared down in embarrassment and said, "I don't know!"

Nothing else was said. The kids started talking about a party that night at the old burned cabin we hung out in near the bridge. They also told me that my father had not been in that navy car. I hung out with my friends. Later, we went to a store and stole a bunch of junk food and some sodas. I got my favorite, Nu-Grape.

We reached the party after dark. A big fire was going, and we started talking to other kids we knew. There was a lot of beer and marijuana being passed around. I was still in a funky mood as my friends tried to get me to relax. I didn't feel like drinking beer, but I did take a hit from a joint twice. I was just starting to mellow out when I saw the girl from the beach walking toward me. I was terrified of her. I ran into the house to hide. Going from room to room, I saw boys and girls making love on blankets, on torn mattresses, or on the bare floor. It was a two-story house, and I ran to the top floor. I found the end room empty except for an old mattress. Shutting the door, I figured I was safe. But my fears were realized.

The door opened. She stood there breathing hard and said, "There you are, fuzzy. I've been looking for you!"

Looking around, I didn't see any escape. I said, "I've been hanging around with my friends, and we're going home now."

"No, you're not," she said as she shut the door behind her. There were three windows in the room, and one was directly behind me. I turned and tried to open the window, but she was on me like a cat. "Where do you think you're going, Fuzzy?"

During the time I spent with her, my mind and spirit were like broken dreams. I lay there letting her do whatever she wanted to and doing to her what she told me to do. For many years after, my mind wiped that and other instances out, shoving it down deep. I now realize that even though that experience was rape by an older, experienced girl, it reinforced a valuable lesson already learned—survival.

When she finished with me, she got up, dressed, and headed to the door. Turning, she said, "This time was for fun, Johnny. Next time, I'm going to cut you! And if you tell anybody about this, I'll tell my boyfriend you raped me, and he'll kill you!"

Word had it that he had killed a boy during a gang fight, so I believed her. After she left, I pulled my Nu-Grape soda bottle out of my ass, got dressed, and went home. Every orifice including my mouth and tongue were so sore that I went straight to bed. Mama never asked me where I had been. I never saw that girl again.

A year later, I learned that she had been killed in a gang fight at age eighteen. When I heard the news, I said to the boy telling me, "I hope she's in hell," but I did not explain why I said that. Later that night before falling asleep, I thought of some of the things she had said to me that night. One thing she had said over and over was, "I love you." I didn't understand why she said that, and of course I did not believe her.

Today as I write this story, I understand why whenever a girl would say those words to me, I would never believe her—even Mama. Lying in my bunk thinking about it, I asked myself out loud, "What if she thought she did?" From the lower bunk, my sister asked, "Who did what?" I replied, "Nobody. Go to sleep!" But she would not leave it alone and kept asking. Eventually, I asked her, "Do think the girl who just died loved anybody?" She replied, "That girl? I don't think she ever liked anybody." As I was falling asleep, I said to myself, *Sad*.

The next morning, I was out early raking the yard. It was a good thing because my father came home just before noon. He never found out I had left the yard.

On the other side of the bay was a muddy ditch that emptied into the bay. In the past at night, a bunch of us, boys and girls, would choose sides and have match fights. We took large, wooden kitchen matches, the same type I sucked the heads off as a child, lit them, and threw them at each other over the ditch. It was lots of fun.

That summer, I did not get to go, but one night, I walked a short distance from my yard when my father was not there and watched them. It was awesome—kind of like watching rockets being fired at each other.

At times, my friends would stop by while I was raking, and my father was not home and fill me in on the match-fight news. One night, a match landed in one girl's long hair. It burned almost all of it off and left her with a bad burn. All the parents got really pissed. The match fights stopped.

CHAPTER 53

Lyle

A kid named Lyle lived in our neighborhood. Everybody knew he was different. Sometimes, he got away from his mother and would wander the neighborhood. Most kids in the area teased him and made fun of him, but when anybody approached him, he would scream unintelligibly and run away awkwardly. Sometimes, he would walk up to a tree or trailer and beat his head against it. It was sad seeing him like that. For some reason I still can't understand, he would allow me to take him to his home. His mother was always so thankful and would offer me cookies or ice cream as a thank you. I always refused. "No ma'am but thank you."

One time, I was raking in my yard and Lyle came by. He saw me and walked over to the fence. He started talking and pointing down the street from where he had just come, but his words were unintelligible. I stood there befuddled. I had never heard him speak. My heart went out to him. I felt so ashamed for all the times other kids, including my friends, had been so mean to poor Lyle. All I could think of to do was give him a hug. I walked over to the fence, and as I started to hug him, he screamed and ran off awkwardly down the street in the direction he had come. He had not gone very far before I saw an older boy I didn't know walk out from behind a trailer and start teasing him by poking his arms and chest. Lyle ran over to a trailer and started beating his head against it. The kid followed and continued to tease Lyle.

The owner of the trailer came out yelling at the kid to stop teasing Lyle. The kid started yelling obscenities at the owner and gave him the finger. I dropped my rake, jumped over our fence, and ran down the street to where they were. I hit the kid hard, knocking him to the ground. I said, "I'm a member of the Little Morgan Creek Gang, and I'll have them come after you if you ever mess with Lyle again." The kid immediately ran off. I think now that maybe the kid was probably more scared of the adult yelling at him than he was of me, but maybe not.

The owner thanked me and said, "That was a wonderful thing you did for a kid who's a retard, you know." I asked, "What do you mean by retard?" He explained Lyle's condition to me. I made sure word got around that the Little Morgan Creek Gang did not want anybody messing with Lyle. I also told my gang about the incident and explained Lyle's condition to them. It makes me feel good now knowing that even with all the bad things going on in my life then, I still had some good in me.

The next day, I found out that the kid had been trying to break into the trailer he had walked out from behind. I smiled knowing that Lyle must have seen him trying to pry open the back door and that was what he had been trying to tell me. I thought, *Maybe Lyle's condition is not as bad as everybody thinks.* I made sure his mother knew what a good thing he had done.

CHAPTER 54

Lance

A boy named Lance lived right behind me. Attached to his trailer's back door was a small four-season room his father had built. In the winter, I would go to Lance's house and play Monopoly. Whenever his father was away at sea and I was at his house, there were times his mother had a male friend come over. Whenever he came, his mother made us go into the attached room and stay until her friend left. The master bedroom was just inside the back door, and there were times we would hear noises coming from that room. We would look at each other, laugh, shrug, and continue our game.

Rita was a pretty redhead in our neighborhood. One warm day, Lance's mother and father had gone shopping, and we were sitting on his patio smoking, drinking his father's beer, and talking. Without telling me anything, Lance yelled to Rita as she was walking by, "Hey Rita, come here a minute." She too smoked, and she asked Lance for a cigarette. He said, "I'll give you a pack and some candy if you'll show us under your panties." At first, she said no, but he pulled out some cigarettes from a pack of Marlboros and some candy from a bag.

She stood there; we could tell she was thinking it over. Finally, she said, "Okay."

Lance told me to help him pull the patio furniture close together but leave room for the three of us between the trailer and the room. Lance and I sat, and Rita stood in front of us with her back to the room. She pulled her dress up showing her panties. Lance said, "Hey! You have to take your panties off!" With a big sigh, she pulled them off and raised her dress again. It was like nothing I had ever seen; I couldn't even talk. I had never seen so much red hair covering a girl's private parts before. Lance was making all kinds of typical young-boy noises. In a few moments, Rita dropped her dress, asked for her rewards, grabbed them, and left. She forgot about her panties. Lance kept them.

Lance's yard backed up to ours. A couple of days later, I was in my yard raking when he walked over to the fence and told me Rita was coming by in a few minutes. He invited me over to see her. I did not really believe she would come back, but my father was not home, so I jumped the fence and went over.

She showed up. Seeing me, she said she did not want to do it again, but Lance offered her more candy and cigarettes. She finally said, "Okay." The three of us went into the fort area Lance had ready. Lance and I sat as before, and she stood in front of us. She pulled up her dress and showed us again. That time, she had no panties on. My mind was racing seeing all the red hair again.

About once a week, Rita would come over, and each time, Lance gave her candy and cigarettes. On each occasion, Lance enticed her closer to us. One day as we were looking at her, she was only a few inches from our faces. She allowed Lance to touch her red hair. He stroked it, wet his index finger, and poked it inside her. She giggled and ran off. I was amazed she had allowed him to touch her.

After that, I never went back. Sometimes when I was walking by his house, I saw the two of them in his little fort. On one occasion, I saw her coming out of the little room. He and I never spoke about those incidents. I have never talked about those times until this writing.

A few years later, after we had left Morgan Creek, Mama received a letter from somebody who still lived there giving her all the news. Mama could not read, so my sister read it for her. The person wrote about Lance's father coming home one day and finding Lance's mother in bed with a man. He had shot and killed them. I asked Mama, "What happened to Lance?" She said, "I don't know." For a while after that, Mama walked around talking to herself. She kept calling Lance's mother "That whore."

In the letter, the person also wrote about my two friends, Jay and Rob, and how they had run away. After about three weeks, they returned home tired, dirty, and starving. They admitted having hitchhiked to Florida looking for me. That night, I lay in my bunk and cried thinking of how much I missed them. I knew how much they must have been missing me. Mama would never tell me who had written the letter. I don't know why, but she never told my father about the letter.

CHAPTER 55

Book of Knowledge

In the fall, I returned to the Catholic school. I was thirteen, and the school had promoted me to sixth grade even though I had not passed any tests. I sat in the back of the class, was quiet, and never spoke to anybody. At recess, I would play marbles, but a lot of times, other kids for reasons unknown to me, would not play with me. At those times, I went back to sitting in front of the gym and throwing that tennis ball. If a test was given, I would print my name on it and pass it forward with nothing else on it. Nobody was saying anything to me, and I never asked anybody any questions.

It was a long and cold winter. My father hadn't shipped out; he was home every night except when he said he had duty, which sometimes lasted for several days. My life was pure hell then. Sometimes late at night because I had not been able to fall asleep, I would put my pillow over my head and cry until I was exhausted and could sleep.

Mama called me to get up and get dressed for school usually around five or five thirty in the morning. If didn't get up fast enough for my father, he would throw that glass of cold water in my face and yell, "When you hear your mother calling, you better get your goddamn ass out of bed, plowboy!" It wasn't long before he took over waking me up. On occasion, he would throw the water in my face without waking me first. That continued through high school.

One day, a salesman came to our trailer. Apparently, Mama and my father knew he was coming, because my father made my sister and me sit on the floor while the man spoke with my parents. He was selling Kirby vacuum cleaners. He showed them how it worked and showed them that it had a secret coin bank in the handle. He told them that if they bought the vacuum cleaner, included in the price was a set of *Book of Knowledge Encyclopedia Britannica*. He went on and on about how this set was so important for the growth, development, and education of children.

For emphasis, he pointed to my sister and me and said, "Those kids will be able to use these books for the rest of their lives. There isn't anything they can't look up and learn about using this set." My father bought the Kirby.

It took about a week for the vacuum and books to arrive. I wasn't interested in them at all. The first day, my father was at work, and my mother used the vacuum. I didn't like it because I thought it was way too loud as she dragged it around the trailer. That afternoon when my father came home, he opened the box and made me sit on the couch. He handed me volume 1 and said, "I want you to read the first chapter out loud!"

My father sat in the chair listening as I struggled through it. Mama and my sister went to the back bedroom and opened the bathroom door to shut themselves off from us. I could not pronounce most of the words, and if I tried too long on one, he would backhand me and say, "Move on!"

By the end of the first chapter, my nose was bleeding, my lips were puffed so badly I could hardly talk, and I was crying. When I finished the chapter, he took the book from me and flipped through pages of that chapter. He stopped on a random page and asked me a question about something on it. Of course, I had no idea what the answer was, so he backhanded me. He flipped to another page, then another, then another, all with the same result. At the end, he grabbed me by the throat, picked me up, looked me straight in the eyes, and said, "You'll learn, plowboy, or I'll beat it into you!" He then sent me to bed.

A short time later as I was lying in bed crying, I heard him tell Mama while they were eating supper, "That goddamn kid is so stupid. I don't think he'll ever learn anything!" I did not hear Mama say anything, but I heard my sister say, "He can't even read."

Every night, my father would make me sit down, read a chapter, and ask me questions. When I couldn't answer a question, he would beat me, made me read it again, and ask me about it again. One night, he hit me so hard that I flew across the room into the wall and cracked the paneling. He told me to take a shower. Because the sexual abuse was ongoing, I knew what would follow. I walked into the bedroom and took off my clothes. Within a few minutes, my father came in, opened the bathroom door, and got undressed. I turned around, bent over the bed, and waited. When he was finished with me, I got dressed and went outside using the back door. I walked into some nearby woods, sat, drew my knees under my chin, and cried. I did not know what else to do.

I finally got the nerve to tell my best friend, Jay. He was so angry. He cursed and cursed my father and wanted to go over and kill him. He told me that he would get one of his father's guns and that I could get my shotgun and we could "Shoot him!" We made many plans about how we would do it. We talked about hanging him as he had threatened to do to me, of shooting him, of one night the gang—myself included—jumping him and beating him to death. I told him that my father had said he had been a boxer and that I did not think that would work. Of course, we never did anything.

My father always called me a plowboy. He said many times, "You look like an old nigger pulling a plow when you walk!" I never understood what that meant. He always told me and others that I was stupid and would never amount to anything. No matter how hard I tried, I could never do anything right for him. The readings with the encyclopedia, the beatings, and the sexual abuse continued. By then, I was starting to pull away even from my gang. Only Jay knew the whole truth, but I was pulling away even from him. All I wanted was to die.

Many years later, Mama gave me those books. "Johnny, you can teach your kids just as Daddy taught you." I took them home and burned them, volume by volume. It was not a cure at all, but I cried as I watched that part of my life, go up in smoke.

CHAPTER 56

Moving

Late one cold, winter night when I was on the midnight-to-eight shift, my partner and I went to a coffee shop to help start the long night ahead. We drove to the beach area of Sandy Town. I rolled down my window and lit up a Lucky Strike. The headlights were on in the cruiser. A car drove past us at a high rate of speed. The tires were squealing as the car went around the sharp curve. The car's headlights were not on. It turned onto a side street still going very fast. My partner put the cruiser in gear, and I put on the blue lights. We chased after the car.

It took about a mile before we caught up with it. I radioed the station our location but could not give them a plate number at that time. After about a half mile, the car was still not stopping. After another mile or so, still traveling at a high rate of speed, it reached the Brant City section of Sandy Town and headed west toward the next town. I radioed the station of our new position and told them the driver was headed toward Lux bury. The station radioed back saying they had contacted them and they were sending a cruiser in our direction.

The driver was going about a hundred at that point and weaving all over the road as he entered the Harbor section of Sandy Town. He slammed on his brakes. His tires screamed, and he started fishtailing, causing smoke to fill the road. He made a sharp left onto a dirt driveway and pulled into a garage.

We pulled up directly behind the car with our blues still on. The driver exited his door and started toward the cruiser unsteady on his feet. His arms were raised, and his fists were clenched. He shouted, "I'm home! I'm safe here! You can't arrest me!" My partner and I exited. The three of us met by the hood of the cruiser. We smelled alcohol on his breath. He growled and attacked us. We fought him, and we fell to the ground. I grabbed the subject around the waist, and my partner had him around the neck. He reached around me and pulled my revolver from my holster. I let go of him, grabbed the hand that was holding my gun, and yelled to my partner, "He has my gun!" My partner yelled, "He has mine too!"

It took every bit of our strength to get our guns away from him and subdue him. My partner yelled, "I have the cuffs on one of his hands!" I yelled, "No! You have me cuffed!" Sometimes in such situations, it was hard to know who you were cuffing as you rolled around on the ground.

We eventually cuffed him and put him in the rear seat of the cruiser. Because my partner and I were out of breath and shaking badly, my partner was having a hard time getting his cuffs off my wrist. He just could not get that small key into that small hole. The Lux bury cruiser showed up, blues on. They looked at us; we were dishelmed and dirty from rolling around in the dirt and trying to get those damned cuffs off. They had a good laugh at our expense.

The perpetrator started kicking, and he bent the cruiser door out. He also kicked the glass out of the window. We needed more officers to help us get him out of the cruiser back at the station, and at the time, he was so combative that we could not book him.

I later found out he had been celebrating his birthday at a club with alcohol and heroin. I learned he worked at a store outside Sandy Town. I had heard rumors about that store. I knew people who knew about these rumors and knew a lot about those kinds of people, loan sharks. They told me about this store, and they knew the guy we had arrested. He was a leg breaker for them. They said he was an ex-steel worker and had a very bad reputation as a collector for the loan sharks. They said he had done hard time, used heroin, and hated cops.

I told them about his yelling, "I'm in my home! I'm safe! You can't arrest me!" They laughed and said, "Yeah, he probably got confused because of the alcohol and drugs and thought he was still in jail. Because of his status in jail, nobody ever bothered him. To him, jail was home, a place where he felt safe."

A couple of nights later, I was riding with a different partner, who asked me about the incident. I told him. He said, "I guess he wasn't safe in his own home, huh?" I replied "Nope."

A short time later, I parked the cruiser in the same lot and was smoking and sipping coffee. I put my head back on the headrest and reflected on my past. I remembered things as if they had happened just the day before. I had the right to feel safe in my home, but the only place I ever felt safe when I was young, was in the woods.

In early spring, my father drove to the Pentagon in Washington, DC, three times with Mama, my sister, and me. He parked on top of a hill and left the three of us in the car for hours as he went inside. Each time, he was wearing his CPO navy uniform. It was hot, and we had no water or shade. He never said a word to us about why he was there.

On the last occasion after leaving the Pentagon, he drove to downtown Washington, parked, and took us to see monuments. At each monument, he would tell me, "Read what it says!" As in the past, I had trouble reading, but even in front of other people, he would backhand me when I could not pronounce some of the words. We would then walk away several feet, and he would ask me what was written on the other monument. By then, I was so shaken that I couldn't answer any questions. He was disgusted; he took us back to the car. Once inside, he leaned over the front seat and beat me so badly that blood was flowing. That time, even my sister was crying. He told me how stupid I was and that I would never amount to anything other than a plowboy. He really got mad because I had peed in my shorts and it had gotten on his car seat. When my sister saw the pee, she laughed at me. Mama said nothing; she just looked straight ahead. He drove back to Morgan Creek.

When we got home, he said he was being transferred to Maple Wood, Florida. He went on and on about the wild animals such as bears, panthers, and snakes. He told me many times that if I left the house, they would kill me. I thought, *I don't care. Let them eat me.* He told me about large bobcats bigger than dogs and how they would kill and eat me. He told me how they had been known to come into a house through an open window at night and kill and eat kids. Every day, it was one story after another about some wild animal. If I believed him, we were moving into darkest Africa and would be lucky to survive. I couldn't wait to get there because I knew I would feel safe in the woods.

When I told my gang we were moving, they were upset. Two of them wanted to go with me. Of course, we knew that they could not. After moving, I never saw any of them again. One day, I told Greg, another kid I knew, that we were moving to Maple Wood, Florida. He said, "No you're not. You heard me say that my father was getting transferred there." I assured him that we were moving there.

While working at the Morgan Creek Naval Base, my father had some of the guys working for him make lifters and a set of coil springs for his car. The day we moved, he drove the car home from the base, and the car's rear looked as if it were ten feet in the air. He backed up to the trailer, jacked it up, and hooked it to the car. In just a few minutes, we left Morgan Creek forever. As we were leaving Del Mar Trailer Park, everyone in my gang was standing on the side of the road not waving goodbye, but I saw their sad faces.

My father pulled the trailer to Florida. It took him days because he took backroads. On the way, we had a few problems. Once late at night, he got lost during a heavy rainstorm, and while turning around, he got stuck in the mud. He made me get out and watch his tires as he tried to get out. He wanted to know if they were spinning. When I banged on his window and told him they were, he yelled, "Get in the goddamn car!" I was soaking wet and covered in mud. He backhanded me and yelled, "You're getting mud all over the goddamn seat!" He waited an hour until the rain stopped. He told us to stay in the car as he went looking for somebody to tow us out. He was gone about four hours. It was just starting to get daylight when he returned with a farmer driving a big tractor. All he said was, "The farmer had to finish watching his goddamn wrestling!"

Another night, a deer ran out in front of him, and when he jammed on the brakes, the car and trailer jackknifed across the road. It took forever to get straightened out again because it was a small road with ditches on both sides.

One time during the day, we were high up in some mountains. Looking out of the rear window, I saw all the way down the side to the bottom. The houses and cars looked like ants. He was driving so close to the edge that Mama was screaming for Jesus, Mary, and Joseph to save us. I kept looking down and praying to God that we would fall off and die. My sister heard me and said, "Daddy, Johnny's praying to die." My father reached over the seat and backhanded me, saying, "Keep your goddamn mouth shut! Can't you see I'm driving!" I said, "Yes sir." I continued to pray that God would make him run off the road, but only under my breath.

CHAPTER 57

The Door

We arrived in Maple Wood. My father parked the trailer on an empty lot near Al's House of Pizza and drove straight through to Mayville, Louisiana. There, he dropped Mama, my sister, and me off at my cousin Drew's house. I was so happy to see him and to be back in Louisiana, but on the outside, I was very quiet and shy. As Mama sat and talked with him and his wife and my sister talked with his girls, I went out and headed to the woods. I stayed in the woods for a long time walking around and seeing some new sights until my cousin yelled, "Little man? It's supper time." I ignored him and supper.

Just before dark, I walked back and went into the house; Mama told me there was some red beans and rice for dinner. I told her I wasn't hungry. In the front parlor were a couch and several overstuffed chairs. I went in, lay on the couch, and fell asleep.

I am not sure if my father returned that night or the next morning. But early the next morning as usual—about five or five thirty—he roughly woke me up and said, "Get in the car, plowboy!" As I went out the back door, I saw my cousin leaving for work in his old truck. When I saw him wave, I wanted to get into the truck with him. Instead, head down, I walked to my father's car and got in the back seat. I sat on the passenger's side to be far away from him.

A few minutes later, he came out and told me to get in the front seat. My heart dropped. I started shaking. I got into the front seat and slowly shut the door. He looked at me and said, "We're going to Aunt Beth's house. I need you to go up into the attic to retrieve an item."

I remembered my Aunt Beth and Uncle George from years before. I nodded and looked out the window. He hit me knocking my head into the door with a bang and asked, "Did you hear me, plowboy?" Without crying, I turned, looked him straight in the eye, and said, "Yes sir!"

At that time in my life, I would shake uncontrollably at times, but I felt absolutely nothing for that man except for one thing—something I could not explain. He had taken away everything I was, had, or would be as a kid.

After driving away from my cousin's house, he headed down dirt roads deep into the woods. We crossed a bridge, and I looked at the muddy water in the canal. I wished I could slide down the bank as I had done so many years before, enter that muddy water, and let the gators get me. He yelled, "Your goddamn door isn't closed. Open it and then close it!" As I opened the door, he made a sharp left. The door swung wide open. I put both hands and arms through the open window and held on. If my window had not been open, I have no doubt that I would have fallen out of the car. After going through the turn, he swung hard right and the door swung closed with me still hanging on. He yelled, "What are you, stupid? You never open a car door while driving through a turn!"

He hit me with his fist. Feeling trapped, for the first time ever, I revolted. I opened the door. The car was coming to a stop but still moving. I jumped out, hit the ground, and rolled. I got to my feet and ran. I saw my Uncle George's and Aunt Beth's house in the distance. I ran as fast as I could toward it.

I saw my uncle in the yard walking to his barn. I ran over to him. Looking down at me, he asked, "What happened to you? Why do you have blood on your face and dirt all over you?" I saw my father—tires squealing and throwing up dirt—pulling into the driveway. I ran into the barn only a few feet away. My father drove right up to him and got out. I heard him ask, "Have you seen Johnny?" My uncle said, "Yes. He's in the barn. What happened to him? He's all bloody and dirty."

My father said, "That stupid kid opened the car door as I was driving down the road. He banged his face on the door and fell out."

They talked for a few minutes, and I was called out. We walked into the house. I made sure I walked on the other side of my uncle.

Aunt Beth washed the blood off my face. After drinking coffee, my father and uncle walked outside and were gone for about an hour. I stayed inside talking with my female cousin. She and my sister were close, and she asked me many questions about her.

When my father returned, he told me to get in the car. A few minutes later, he came out, got in the car, and said, "Don't you ever run from me again. You hear me, plowboy?" I looked at him and said, "Yes sir." Just to make sure I understood him, he backhanded me across the face. I don't know why we went there. He never sent me into the attic to retrieve anything. Maybe he had planned on my falling out of the car and then running over me.

He drove back to my cousin's house. His wife was making breakfast. My father again left. Right after eating, I headed for the woods. I climbed the fence in the backyard, found that special spot where Red and I used to hang out, sat, drew my knees up to my chin, and cried. I prayed to God that I would just die. Eventually, I lay down and slept there all day dreaming of Red and me and how we used to roam those woods.

I returned to the house just before dark. My cousin was home from work, and my father came in a few minutes later. He announced to everybody that in the morning we were going to New Orleans to see my aunt Leslie. I did not know who that was, and I had no interest in going. Later, when my father wasn't in earshot, I asked Mama, "Can I stay here tomorrow?" She just shook her head and said, "Hush now."

CHAPTER 58

News

I woke up the next morning to Mama's whistling and humming. I got off the couch and walked into the kitchen. She was cooking breakfast. My father was at the table drinking coffee. As I walked in, he turned and stared at me. With head down, I walked to Mama and asked, "Ma'am, what's for breakfast?" She said, "Grits, eggs and bacon." I sat at the table with my hands in my lap and stared at the floor. In a few minutes, my sister came out and sat next to my father. They started talking about the trip.

After breakfast, we got into the car and left. My father said, "You better be on your best behavior today, plowboy!" Nothing else was said during that trip.

We arrived in New Orleans and stopped at an apartment, where I was introduced to Aunt Mattie and Uncle Drake. I had never met them before. I learned that she was my father's twin. Her apartment was like the one we had lived in for a short time in Ocean View. It was wide and very long. It had a formal living room that looked as if it were never used. The next room was a second living room with a stairway going upstairs to two bedrooms and a full bathroom. The next room was a dining room with a large dining table and six chairs. I saw two more chairs in the corners and a large hutch filled with many dishes.

I had never seen such a big table. I asked, "How many kids do you have?" Everybody laughed. My father was not there. As he usually did when arriving someplace, he left after about ten minutes. I was amazed at all the dishes in the hutch. The next room was the kitchen—small but very clean. A bathroom was off the kitchen.

As Mama and my aunt and uncle were talking, I walked into the backyard, which was small and fenced in. No dirt or grass; the ground was all cement. I heard somebody talking in a shed in the backyard, so I went in to see who it was. I saw a large green parrot sitting on a perch. He looked at me, fanned his head and tail feathers—he only had about six—and started squawking. I had never seen such a bird, especially a talking one. I stood there for a few minutes with mouth wide open listening to him. I walked over to him and tried to pet him but, he bit me hard. A few minutes later, my aunt came out and said, "Don't touch him, Johnny. He bites." She told me all about him and said he was about seventy-five years old.

My aunt asked me to sit. I sat on the floor; she sat on an old chair and started talking. She told me how wonderful it was to finally meet me. She said she had asked my father many times to bring me to New Orleans. She told me how she and my father had grown up in Louisville, a town next to Mayville. She asked me if I had met any other members of our family. I told her I had met Aunt Josie and Uncle Buck. I said that I had met uncles and cousins in Mayville. I asked, "Can you tell me anything about them?" She paused. "I think your father should tell you about them. What about anybody else? Have they said anything about anybody else?"

I said no and asked her what she was talking about. Her lips were moving, but it was as if her brain would not let her speak. I saw fear in her eyes. I begged her to tell me more, but she refused. She made me promise not to say a word about what we had talked about to my father. I promised her. I begged for more information, but she would not give me any. Shortly after that, she got up saying, "Now you promise, right?" I again told her, "I promise."

After she left, I sat on the floor for a while going over and over things. I had flashes of long-forgotten memories and tried to revive them. A few came back to me, and I knew why I had tried to forget them. My biggest question remained—*What have I done to deserve this treatment from my father?*

At dinnertime, my father returned saying nothing about where he had been. My aunt cooked a big turkey dinner. I had never seen so much food in my life. I ate so much that I thought I would explode. After dinner, my mother and father went upstairs to bed. My aunt, uncle, sister, and I sat in the second living room and talked for a while. In about an hour, they went upstairs to bed. My sister and I slept on the couches in the living rooms.

The next morning, I was up early. I went out to the shed. I made sure my aunt and uncle were not up, and I lit up a Lucky Strike, which I always kept hidden. I talked to the parrot. He just squawked for the most part as I talked. I asked him many questions. Of course, when he did talk, it was nothing about what I had asked him. After a while, I smelled bacon cooking, so I headed back to the kitchen.

After breakfast, my father announced that we were going to visit Aunt Leslie. As we were leaving, my aunt hugged me hard and whispered, "Remember, you promised!" I hugged her and whispered, "I promise."

About an hour later, we arrived. My father told us to stay in the car. He went in. He came out in about fifteen minutes and told us to go in. He drove away.

I met Uncle Jay and Aunt Leslie, another of my father's sisters. I immediately took a dislike to her. I was also introduced to their son, Randy Jr., a pale and fragile-looking kid who talked and acted a little weird. Their apartment was set up just like Aunt Mattie's except there was no parrot in the shed. We sat in the living room and talked. After about an hour of small talk, Aunt Leslie, Uncle Jay, and Mama went into the dining room to have coffee. Randy asked my sister and me if we would like to look at family pictures. Not caring one way or another, I said, "I guess so." He went to a cabinet for some picture albums. We sat on the couch, and he handed me an album and said, "We can start with the real old ones."

I opened the first page, and he started explaining each picture. He started turning the pages with one hand and massaging my thigh with his other hand. He moved his hand up and down stopping just short of my genitals. He was talking faster, and his hand was moving closer. I stood, and he tried to hang onto my thigh. I sat on another couch; he was smiling at me. I saw my sister looking at him with an expression I had never seen on her before.

He walked over, sat beside me, and said, "I have some news to tell you." I said, "Yeah, I already know." He furrowed his brow. "You know that I'm your brother?" I almost fell off the couch. I shook my head and made some unintelligent sounds but finally got out, "No! You're not my brother!" He said, "Your father is my father also, and I'm named after him. We have the same mother, but I don't remember her, do you?"

I did not know what to say. I walked out into the backyard. As I passed my aunt, she asked, "Did you and Randy talk, Johnny?" I did not answer.

In the backyard, I sat on the steps. My world had been turned upside down. My brain was screaming. I felt as if I were drowning in my own spit. I tried to talk, but nothing would come out. I could only cry.

In a while, my sister came out and sat beside me. She said, "After you left, I asked him if he was really our brother, and he said yes. He said that Mama was my mother but not yours. He said you two have a different mother ."

My mind was racing, and my tears were flowing. I asked her, "Did you know?" She never answered me; she just talked about how she and I were half-siblings. I had the feeling that she knew and was happy about that. After we talked for a while, I said, "Randy is queer." She asked, "Do you think he is?" I replied, "Yes." She said, "I'm going to ask him."

After a while, we went inside. Randy was telling my aunt, uncle, and Mama about the French Quarter and Bourbon Street. I sat, and he asked me, "Do you want to meet Uncle Ben?" Still in a daze, I replied, "I guess so." He told my sister and me to follow him upstairs.

Upstairs were two bedrooms. Randy pointed out one and said, "That's my room." He led us down the hall and introduced us to an elderly man with only one leg. I sat on the edge of his bed, and I took an immediate liking to him. I learned he was my Uncle Jay's father. Soon, my sister and Randy left. I stayed and talked with him until I was called for supper. He took his meals in his room. I wanted to ask if I could eat with him, but by then, my father had returned. I sat at the dining room table with everyone else. My father never said a word to me and hardly spoke to anyone else. The conversation during supper was not about anything.

As soon as we had eaten, my father said to my aunt and uncle, "We have to go before it gets too late." He turned to my sister and me and said, "Get in the car!" As we left, my aunt, uncle, and brother said nothing to me. My sister and I walked out and got in the car. She said, "I asked him if he was queer, and you were right, he is."

My father and Mama came out about fifteen minutes later, and we drove back to my cousin's house. Not a word was said all the way back. I sat in the rear seat. My head felt like it was going to explode.

The next morning, my father announced that we were heading back to Maple Wood, Florida.

CHAPTER 59

White Men Only

My father was stationed at a Naval Air Station. He oversaw the base hobby shop. We moved into Whiting Trailer Park, about five miles from the base.

We did not see much of my father for the first week or so. He never said anything to us when he was around. Mama, my sister, and I stayed in the trailer because we did not know anybody. I wanted to explore the woods all around us, but every time my father was leaving, he would tell me, "Stay here." He meant the trailer or the yard.

The first night he came home after those first few weeks, he walked into the trailer and said to me, "Come with me!" We walked down the dirt street and entered a cement-block building. I smelled what I thought was a cesspool. The words "White Men Only" were painted on the door. I saw a dirty, rusty sink hanging on the wall. The toilet, separated only by a narrow, wooden, unpainted wall about five feet tall, looked as if it had never been cleaned.

My father slid a deadbolt into place to lock the door. I knew what was about to happen, but I had only one thought on my mind. I blurted out, "Who's my real mother?" He backhanded me so hard that I fell across the toilet and landed on my butt on the filthy floor. My hand was in dirty, brown toilet water. He yelled, "Never ask about your mother again! You hear me, plowboy?" I got up slowly, looked down, and said in a subdued voice, "Yes sir."

"Take your clothes off and bend over the toilet!" he said.

After he was finished, I stood and started to get dressed. He gave me a backhand and said, "Remember what I said!" Head down, I replied, "Yes sir." I stood and tried to wipe the messy goo from the floor off my butt, hands, and legs, with my hands because there was no toilet paper.

CHAPTER 60

Snake!

After we moved to Maple Wood, Greg, the kid I knew from Morgan Creek, and his father and mother moved into the park. His father, also a CPO, oversaw the navy docks on White Water River in downtown Maple Wood.

Greg and I had not been close friends in Virginia, but we did not know other kids in Maple Wood, so we became close. The boat docks his father oversaw rented out wooden boats with small motors. Renters had to have military IDs to rent the boats, and they had to bring their own gas. Because of Greg's father, we were able to use a boat and motor whenever we wanted. Sometimes, renters would return boats and leave behind their gas cans. We would take any gas we could find sometimes from several cans and pour them into one, so we never had to pay for gas.

One day, we were talking about how hard it would be to get back into a moving boat. So just for fun, in front of the bridge going into downtown Maple Wood, we tied the motor in a way that the boat kept going in a circle, and then we jumped off. We tried for about a half hour but could not get back onboard the boat though it kept going in a circle. Other boats came by, and one stopped and picked us up. The people asked us what had happened. We told them that we had fallen out of the boat. They tried to get close to our boat but never could. Luckily for us, we had been fishing for hours, so there was not much gas left in the motor. We boarded it when it ran out of gas. The other boat towed us back to the dock but not before they saw how the motor had been tied. That incident got back to Greg's father, and he chewed our asses out. "If you kids ever pull a stunt like that again, you'll never use any of my boats!" Luckily for me, Greg's father did not know my father, and nothing was ever said to him.

Greg and I started doing a lot of fishing on White Water River. One day while looking for a new place to fish, we entered a small slough just off the main river near an area called The Pond. Riding slowly through, we saw a lot of ducks. Greg said, "If we had a gun, we could shoot those ducks." I said, "I have a shotgun." I said I would sneak it out when my father was not around.

A couple of weeks later, my father said he had duty and would not be back until after the weekend. Early the next morning, I slipped the gun out the back door without Mama seeing me, and I met Greg. We got a ride to the boat docks from a sailor we knew. I hid the gun in some weeds along the riverbank by the bridge. We had to wait an hour before a boat became available. Picking up the gun on the way, we headed toward the spot where we had seen the ducks.

The only shells I had were full of buckshot, but I loaded the gun. As we neared the spot, we did not see any ducks, so we kept going. Pretty soon, we came upon tree branches growing over the slough and hanging almost to the water and into the boat. I was at the bow pushing limbs out of the way when Greg screamed, "Snake!"

I quickly turned and saw a snake headed right for Greg with its mouth open. Without hesitation, I cocked the gun, aimed, and pulled the trigger. The snake disappeared right through the hole I had made in the bottom of the boat. Greg looked at me and asked, "What are you, fucking crazy?" I said, "I'm sorry! It happened so fast." Greg shut off the motor, and the boat sank.

The water was only about five feet deep, but it was muddy on the bottom. We started walking back the way we came with me holding the gun over my head. It was hard going, and it took about an hour. We eventually found our way out to The Pond and Highway 80. We walked back to the boat docks. Nobody stopped to ask two kids walking, one carrying a shotgun, what they were doing. We kept going over and over the story we would tell his father as to what had happened to the boat. We finally came up with the story that we had stopped and tied the boat up, and while we were swimming, somebody stole the boat. I didn't think he believed us, but we stuck to the story. After that, my boating days were over. Or so I thought.

CHAPTER 61

The Boat

One afternoon, my father came home and told us he was going to build a boat in the base hobby shop. He looked at me and said, "And you're going to help, plowboy."

I said, "Sir, I don't know how to build a boat."

With an unintelligible growl, he swung his dreaded left hand and caught me on the side of my face. The force knocked me across the room. As I landed against the paneling covering the front wall of the trailer, I heard a loud *crack*. The crack that was already there became much bigger. I lay on the floor. My father rushed over screaming, "Look what you've done now, plowboy!" He grabbed me by the throat, picked me up, and threw me back down forcibly. Pain racked my body as he stood over me screaming, "I said you're going to help me, plowboy! Did you hear me?" Through my tears, I said, "Yes sir." He stomped out and motioned for me to follow. As I walked out, I saw Mama and my sister sitting down to eat dinner.

I followed my father, head down and crying, as he walked toward the old bathhouse. As we approached the door, a white man was coming out. He took one look at me and asked my father, "Is everything all right?" My father said nothing; his look said it all. The man turned ashen; he turned and ran away. My father grabbed me by the back of the neck and pushed me so hard that I went flying into the room, slipped, and landed face-down on the wet floor. My nose and lips were bleeding.

That rape by my father was especially brutal as he kept hitting my head while repeating, "Don't ever talk back to me, plowboy! Do you understand?" I was trying to answer him, but between my crying and his brutality, I could not. This caused him to become more brutal. When he finished, he dressed and left me lying on the floor, naked, crying, and still asking myself, *What, did I do wrong?*

Over the next several months, I was with him at the hobby shop every night as we built a plywood boat covered in sheets of fiberglass and resin. The rapes continued, but in the men's room in the hobby shop. There were so many times he told me, "You look just like an old nigger pulling a plow," that I knew my posture had been affected. I started leaning forward more and more as I walked. Even to this day, I tend to lean forward, so I force myself to stand tall.

CHAPTER 62

Cap and Me

Many times, we played hide-and-go-seek,
From my father, near Clear Creek.
Hidden from his view, we dared to flee,
With reckless abandon ... Cap and Me.

So many nights we lay by our fire,
Eating fish, squirrel, or rabbit to my father's ire.
Moonlight and stars were our canopy,
Best friends forever ... Cap and Me.

Day and night, we conquered those woods,
Dining like kings, on Mother Nature's goods.
No need for a roof, just a need to be free,
Safe and contented ... Cap and Me.

Now decades have come, and decades have gone,
The peace he gave me, is still making me strong.
His picture is with me, and always will be,
My childhood companion ... Cap and Me.

His memory sustains me; his love warmed my soul.
The years that we shared, were worth more than gold.
But I'll find him in heaven, and once again it will be,
Peacefully and blissfully ... Cap and Me.

Our trailer park was surrounded by woods. Remembering what my father had told me about the wild animals in the area, I slowly started exploring the woods looking for them. Sometimes, Greg came with me, but most often, he didn't. He said he really didn't like going into the woods.

I ventured into the woods farther and farther. As I had done so long before, I started spending all my time there. When my father was not around—sometimes, he would be gone for three or four days—I would sneak his rifle out and spend all day and sometimes all night in the woods. As before, Mama never asked me where I had been or what I had been doing.

After walking for an hour through the woods, I found a large lake. I had brought my cane pole and fishing tackle with me from Virginia. I now brought them to the lake. Some nights, I would make a fire by the shore and would have fish, squirrel, rabbit, or whatever I could catch or kill for supper.

In midsummer 1957, a young navy couple moved into our park. Not long after they moved in, I was walking by their trailer, and the woman said hi to me. She was sitting in her yard, which was nothing but dirt like all of ours, in an old wooden chair. She was holding a baby. Lying beside her was the most beautiful German shepherd dog I had ever seen. I stopped, said hi, and walked to her. As I did, the dog rose, walked in front of her, and stopped, just looking at me. I asked, "Does he bite?" She replied, "No, but he is protective."

I slowly walked toward them. As I got closer, the dog growled and curled his lips showing strong, white teeth. She laid a hand on him, and he stopped and lay down, but he kept an eye on me. I asked, "What's his name?" She replied, "Captain of High Ridge." I laughed. "What kind of a name is that?" She laughed and said, "He's an AKC-registered dog, and that's his real name, but we call him Cap."

She told me that AKC stood for the American Kennel Club and that a dog registered there was very valuable. I told her I thought he was the most beautiful dog I had ever seen. I told her a little bit about Red. She said, "You must love dogs." I told her, "Yes ma'am, I do, and one day, I want to get another dog." She said that Cap was professionally trained and was not very friendly around strangers. She said that they had bought him as a puppy.

Over the next two weeks, I started spending as much time as I could with the couple hoping to make friends with Cap. It took the full two weeks before he finally would come over to me and let me pet him. He would sit on command at my feet.

One day, I asked them if I could take Cap with me into the woods for a walk. They were not sure, but after talking it over for a few minutes, they said I could. It took a couple of days and a lot of coaxing, but I was finally able to get him to follow me into the woods. At first, he would stop every few feet, look back at their trailer, and whine. I would walk to him and hug and pet him and say, "It's okay, Cap," and we would continue into the woods. The first time, we spent about two hours in the woods, and Cap stayed right next to me. I smiled as I realized this was all new to him.

Cap and I started spending every day together mostly in the woods. Every afternoon when I brought him home, I would hug and kiss him goodbye. Soon, every time I started toward their trailer, I would see Cap sitting in the front yard looking in my direction. Sometimes, I would walk to Mary's gas station and store combination and take him with me. The owner and his father grew to like Cap almost as much as I did. Whenever I brought him with me, they gave him some tidbits to eat. The first time he met my father, Cap growled and curled his lips. I had told him all about Cap and how he was AKC registered. My father never said a word; he just stared at him. Later, I hugged him and said, "Good boy. I don't like him either."

After a while, whenever I went outside, I would find Cap sitting by our door waiting for me. He would jump up, lick my face, and whine. One day, Cap's owners asked me if I wanted to keep Cap. I was almost speechless. For a couple of minutes, all I could do was kneel and hug him. I was finally able to say, "Yes!" They said that because of their new baby and an upcoming transfer, they did not have the time to spend with Cap that he needed. I said, "I have plenty of time!" They laughed. "We know that. We see how much you care for him, and we know he really likes you. Whenever he hears your voice or sees you in the distance, he starts whining. We tell him to go to you, and he does."

That night, I asked my father, and he agreed I could keep Cap. That was the happiest day of my life. The next day, Cap moved in with us. Every night, Cap slept on the floor below my bunk. Anytime my father would come close to him, Cap would give a little growl and curl his lips. My father never attempted to make any contact with him.

The couple left a few weeks later. The wife cried when she hugged Cap and said goodbye. He licked them all including the baby. It was as if he knew they were leaving and he was saying goodbye to them as well. I never saw or heard from them again.

For the rest of the summer, Cap and I were inseparable. We spent day and night in the woods. As in the past, when my father was gone, I would take his rifle out and we would cook and eat what we killed.

One time, Cap jumped a rabbit in some high weeds about five feet in front of us. He started chasing it, and from experience, I knew a rabbit would run and circle back to where it came from. When the rabbit started circling back, Cap was right on its tail. It was too close for me to shoot, so I used the stock of the rifle. The rabbit neared me and went right between my legs. I swung as hard as I could. Instead of hitting the rabbit, I hit Cap on his head. He went down hard and lay there looking up at me, his eyes asking, *What the hell are you doing? That's our supper!* I felt so bad; I hugged him for a long time. He finally got up, and off he went trying to scare up another rabbit. Occasionally, I saw him watching me out of the corner of his eye. I smiled and thought, *He must think I'm crazy.*

One evening just before dark, I built a fire and whistled for Cap. He had been missing for about an hour, and I was getting worried. I had shot two squirrels that I had skinned and cleaned. I put a stick through them and started cooking them. My thoughts turned to my father and how whenever he was around, he kept telling me, "Stay around the house and rake the yard." Cap and I would stay in the yard, and I would rake. Just like in Morgan Creek, it was mostly dirt, but at least I had Cap. He would just lie and watch me. Neither of us cared what I was doing if we were together.

A noise brought me back from my thoughts. Looking through the fire, I saw large, yellow eyes staring at me. It was Cap. Without any fanfare, he had found me and lay down by the fire. I was amazed at how much he looked like a wolf. *I wondered if hundreds of years ago, people sat around fires just like this with real wolves.*

After eating and putting a few more limbs on the fire, Cap and I settled in for the night. Those days, I never took any kind of blanket or anything else to lie on. I would gather pine needles, leaves, and grass to make a bed. As I lay there, my head resting on Cap, I started thinking how my life had changed since meeting him. The rapes continued—Cap would scratch and whine at the bathhouse door—but the beatings grew further apart. Every time my father came near me, Cap stood between us, growled, and curled his lips. I always rested my hand on Cap's head and watched my father hoping he would try to touch me.

There were still bad times like the one when he was leaving on a Friday morning. He announced that he had duty and would not be back until Monday afternoon. He told me, "Get that hand sickle, cut the grass, and then rake. Don't leave this yard for the whole weekend!"

After he left, I went outside and sat under a pine tree chewing on a weed with Cap lying beside me. I wondered why my father had so much duty and why he was gone so much, but I was happy he wasn't around.

Cap and I sat there for about an hour. I got up and walked into the trailer, took his rifle, walked out the back door, and headed into the woods. Cap was right beside me pressed against my leg. That day, we just wandered. At one point, Cap jumped a rabbit. The rabbit ran a short distance and dove into a hole at the base of a small scrub oak. I reached into the hole, but the rabbit was too far up for me to grab its legs. I lit a dead branch with pine needles with my Zippo and shoved it into the hole. It took only a few minutes for the smoke to get that rabbit to come out. I grabbed it, wrung its neck, skinned it, made a fire right there, and cooked that rabbit for Cap and me.

Later that afternoon, I returned home, and to my amazement, my father's car was parked in front of the trailer. I hid the gun under the trailer. I knew it would be bad. I went in to face him. I opened the door and let Cap in first. Mama was making dinner, and she told me to be quiet because my father was lying down. Right after dinner, my father went out the front door. I was sitting on the couch with Cap lying at my feet. In a couple of minutes, my father called me from his bedroom area. Walking into the bedroom, Cap right at my leg, I saw my father standing outside the rear door. He said, "Come here!" very sternly. As I got close, he reached in, grabbed me by the throat, and yanked me through the door, Cap growled loudly, and as the door closed, I heard him scratching and barking.

My father carried me into the woods behind the trailer. I was crying and telling him that I was sorry for having left the yard and that I wouldn't do it again. He said nothing as he carried me into the woods. He stopped where an old pine tree had fallen. Still holding me by the throat, he started beating me and saying, "When I tell you to stay in the goddamn yard, plowboy, you better well do it!"

I still can't explain it, but a calmness came over me. I stopped crying. I told him, "I wish I were dead. Kill me." He said, "That's what you deserve, and don't think I won't, plowboy, because you're never going to amount to anything anyway!" He told me to take my clothes off.

When he finished, he pulled his pants up and walked back to the trailer leaving me bent over that pine tree. It took two days for me to get the sap from that pine tree off my belly and ball sack.

As I was getting dressed, I heard the worst noise I had ever heard. My father was screaming and yelling in the trailer, and my heart sank. I started running, and my fears were realized. As I neared the trailer, I heard the blows hitting Cap and him howling in pain. I started crying hysterically. I opened the front door and saw my father kneeling with one hand around Cap's throat and beating him with the other. I screamed at my father to stop, and for just a moment, he did. He looked at me. I will never forget the look in his eyes. I still wake up from a sound sleep after seeing my father's face and those eyes that were pure evil.

That was all it took. Cap bit his arm and drew blood. As my father let go of his throat, Cap got to his feet and fled out the door with me right behind him. We ran as fast as we could deep into the woods until we reached the lake. We heard my father yelling for us to come back; he was firing his shotgun.

That night, we stayed in the woods. Lying with my head on Cap, I cried myself to sleep not because of what he had done to me—the rapes and beatings were pushed so far down that by then I hardly ever thought of them—but because of what he had done to Cap. Lying there, Cap just whined and licked me repeatedly as if to say, *I'm sorry I didn't protect you*. I hugged and hugged him saying the same thing over and over.

At midmorning the next day, Cap and I went home. My father's car was gone. I retrieved the rifle from under the trailer and went in. Mama cooked Cap and me some grits and eggs. "Your father is angry with both of you because you left the yard," she said. "That's why he had to whip you both." Other than that, she said nothing.

That evening, my father came home after I had gone to bed. I was not asleep; fear gripped me as I heard Cap growl when he walked by my bunk.

I stayed awake until just before daybreak. Slipping quietly out of my bunk, I picked up my shotgun, cocked it, and quietly walked toward my father in his bed. Cap was walking beside me pressed against my leg and growling. Walking right up to the bed, I pointed the shotgun at my father's head. He opened his eyes and smiled. All I saw were those eyes. I pulled the trigger. The hammer fell with a loud click, but nothing happened. My father grabbed the barrel and slammed it against my face. "You have to load the goddamn gun first, plowboy!" With Cap growling loudly, we walked back to my bunk. Once again, I had been shown that I would never amount to anything. Nothing was ever said about the incident.

CHAPTER 63

Grant

In the fall that year, I started seventh grade, my first year at Maple Wood Junior High School. I rode a navy bus, which picked us up in front of the trailer park. We lived about six miles from downtown Maple Wood.

Every morning when I walked to the bus stop, Cap walked with me. Every afternoon when I got off the bus, he was sitting in front of our trailer looking for me. When I whistled, he would come running. When he got to me, you would think he had not seen me in a year. Standing on his hind legs, he put his front paws on my shoulders and licked my face.

I met a kid named Grant on my first day at school. We sat in the back of the room across from each other. The first time we met, I thought he talked more and faster than any person I had ever met. I was very quiet and reserved, but Grant was having none of that. He talked so much. Even though I thought he was a little goofy, I found myself liking him. The biggest similarity we had was that neither of us had any interest in school. We became fast friends and stayed friends for many years, until his death in 1981. That first year, we spent as much time together as possible at school and at his house.

One day in the late fall, Cap and I were wandering in the woods when we heard a loud humming or buzzing. Getting closer and peering through the thick brush, I saw an old tree with what look like hundreds of bees coming and going into a hole about halfway up the trunk. I got closer for a better look. Cap was pressed hard against my leg, and he started growling deep in his chest; I recognized that growl as danger. Creeping a little closer all the while keeping a sharp eye on the bees, I saw claw marks on the bark all around the hole. Some of them looked fresh. Thinking a bear had made the marks and having no rifle with me, we left the area quickly. Cap and I returned to the tree on occasion but only if I had the rifle with me.

Sometime during that first year, in the winter or spring of 1958, my father bought four lots of land about a mile away near a place called Roundup Valley. The lots were at the intersection of three streets. My father took me to the lots and pointed to an area. He said, "Dig a hole here so I can build a fallout shelter. We'll use it when the goddamn Russians bomb us!"

The soil was all sand, and it took me about a week after school to dig the hole. It rained a couple of times, and some sand washed back in. My father had a company dig a well in the same area, about fifty feet away. As I was digging the hole for the fallout shelter, I heard them tell my father that they had drilled down eighty feet and had hit good, running water. After I finished digging the hole, my father had a company put a cement cesspool with no bottom but with a lid in the hole. The lie he told never bothered me because it just went down deep with everything else he said and did.

My father towed our trailer to the lot with the cesspool. Without the park bathroom available, my father reverted to raping me in the shower or in his bedroom while Mama and my sister were in the living room. For unknown reasons, he was staying away for longer times, sometimes for several days, so the rapes were not as often at that point.

I had a longer walk to the bus stop, which was still in front of the trailer park, but Cap walked it every day with me. Every morning before I got on the bus, I would hug him goodbye. In the afternoon, the bus would let me off at the end of our street. I saw Cap waiting in our front yard. I would whistle, and he would come running.

During that year, if I was not in school, I was in the woods with Cap as much as possible or at Grant's house—anything to stay away from my father. I knew from his actions that Cap still hated my father as much as I did. On some occasions when my father would try to beat me, Cap would stand between him and me. Every time Cap growled and bared his teeth at him, my father would not say anything and would walk away. It did not happen on every occasion, but I was grateful to Cap for the times it did.

One day that spring, my father came home with a young female German shepherd he named Judy. He said she was also AKC registered. As time passed, it became obvious that Judy was going to have many more privileges than Cap and I were getting. I asked Mama, "Why did Daddy name her Judy?" Shaking her head, she replied, "One of Daddy's goddamn whores."

CHAPTER 64

A New Home

Sometime early that summer, my father had a wood-frame house built. It had three bedrooms, a small bathroom, kitchen, living room, a carport with a dirt floor, and a utility room. The house was on the same lot the well was on but next to the lot with the cesspool. He had a company install a large propane gas tank in the backyard, and they installed a gas heater in the living room. They also installed a heater in the wall of the bathroom and another in a back bedroom, which my father said would be my sister's.

While we waited for the furniture to be delivered, we lived in the trailer. Water, and the cesspool, were both hooked up by some rubber hosing.

One day after school, I came home and found nobody in the trailer, but I did see my father's car parked in the driveway. Walking over with Cap right beside me, I went in and heard my mother and father arguing in the bedroom that I had been told was mine.

I walked to the door and saw my father lying on his back on a bed. He had a sheet pulled up to his groin area, and he was naked from there up. Lying on the other side of him was my sister. She was lying on her right side, and he was holding her tightly against him with his arm around her shoulders. My sister's left hand was under the sheet, and her arm was resting on his belly. The sheet was also covering her up to her waist, and she too appeared naked from the waist up.

As I walked through the door with Cap pressed against my leg and growling, Mama turned and looking startled. She said to my father, "I don't want Johnny to see this." Just as I started to speak, Mama yelled, "Johnny! Get out of here now. I don't want you to see this!"

I saw a pleading look in my sister's eyes. I hated my father more than ever, but I knew I was no match for him. I started crying and ran from the house. I went into the utility room, sat on the floor, and continued to cry. Cap was licking my face.

About ten minutes later, my sister came out of the house, entered the utility room, and sat beside me. For the first time in our lives, we forgot about all our silly sibling rivalries; we just hugged each other tightly and cried. No words were spoken, nor did they need to be. It was our silent understanding that we were just trying to survive. Cap was now licking both of our faces.

Not long after that, a big truck came and towed our trailer away. We moved into the house. On the first day we were there, my father told me to follow him. We went outside, and he made me hammer a large nail into a pine tree outside my sister's bedroom window. He told me to hang the garden hose that was still hooked to the well and had been hooked to the trailer over the nail. He handed me a bar of Ivory soap that had some string tied around it. He told me to tie the other end to the pine tree. He said, "The bathtub in the house will be used only by your sister and mother, you understand?" I nodded. He gave me a little tap on my head and asked, "Do you understand, plowboy?" I said, "Yes sir." He said I would take showers outside using the hose. To make sure I understood, he gave me another tap on my head. I am not sure if I slipped or if he knocked me down, but he left me lying on the ground. That night, I took my first of many cold showers outside.

Later that first night, he called me to follow him outside. We walked to the pine tree. After I turned the water on at the well, he told me to get undressed, and he also got undressed. As we stood naked, I saw by the moonlight that he had a full erection. He said, "Bend over and grab your ankles!" I knew what was coming. I said, "We're outside, and our neighbors can see us." He smacked me and knocked me to the ground. Dazed, I lay on the ground with the cold water hitting my hurting head. I realized that my life would never change. I looked at him and asked, "Do you hate me because of my real mother?"

Even in the moonlight, I saw the change in his eyes. He started screaming, "I told you never bring up your goddamn mother!" He stomped me with his bare feet. I curled myself into a ball and waited until he got tired and stopped. He walked into the house naked. I got up. I was bruised and bleeding. I soaped my body and rinsed myself off in the cold, refreshing water smiling the whole time. I realized I now had a hook into his anger that I could use to my advantage.

When I finished showering, I spotted my sister standing in her window watching me. I wondered if she had seen the entire incident.

CHAPTER 65

Teach This Dog

One day, my father told me to make Cap lie on a spot near the couch and against the wall. He told my sister and me, "Sit on the couch and watch while I teach this dog how to protect us!"

I sat and frowned. I was about to ask him what he meant when he walked over to Cap and started kicking him hard, hollering, "Nigger, nigger, nigger!" He started stomping on him and repeating those awful words I had come to hate.

Cap was howling in pain, baring his teeth, and growling. I ran over and threw myself on Cap covering his body with mine. "Daddy! Stop!" my sister and I were both yelling. He continued kicking and stomping me as he repeated those terrible words.

For the first time ever, Mama came out of the kitchen with a big knife. Standing in front of him, she pointed it at my father and said, "If you touch Johnny or that dog again, I'll cut your goddamn throat!" Startled, he stomped out the front door. Mama and my sister were crying and yelling, "Johnny, pack your clothes and leave before he kills you."

I walked into my bedroom with Cap beside me and started putting some of my clothes in a paper bag. Mama came in crying. Cap was sitting beside me and growling at her. I sat on my bed and put my hand on his head. He quieted down, but still had a low growl and bared teeth. She asked, "What are you doing?" I too was crying. I said, "I'm packing my clothes and leaving with Cap. We're going to live with my cousin in Louisiana." Mama begged me not to leave. My sister came into the room crying and begging me not to leave. Cap was pressing hard against my leg. We all hugged and cried. Cap licked all our tears away.

After moving into the house, my father made me keep my loaded shotgun beside the head of my bed with the full box of shells on the headboard. My father kept his shotgun, his .22 caliber rifle, and his carbine all loaded beside his bed. He kept his pistol under his pillow.

In a few minutes, Mama and my sister walked out of my bedroom. After they left, I put my clothes back into my drawers, picked up my shotgun, and walked out into the living room cocking it as I went, after checking to make sure it was loaded. Mama and my sister were standing in the living room and saw the look on my face and the shotgun in my hands. They screamed. My sister yelled, "Please don't, Johnny! They'll take you away!" Mama screamed, "He's gone." I looked out and saw that my father and his car were gone.

He did not return for many days. As time passed, it became evident to me that nobody missed him. One day about a month later, I asked Mama where he was. She shook her head and repeated, "Daddy's damned whores." I never knew what she meant, but I was glad he was gone. When he did return, nothing was said about the incident.

It was only as I was writing this book that I learned my father had returned to Mayville, Louisiana, where he worked on a dredging boat. Looking back on that incident today, I realize why Mama did not want me to leave for my cousin's house. Over the years, I learned she had kept all my father's abuse from relatives in Louisiana. She had bragged about my sister and me and how good our life was. I have learned there were many secrets kept by adults about "Daddy and his whores" as Mama put it. I believe she also meant my birth mother.

After he returned, he went to work for a chemical plant. At times, my father would walk to Cap sometimes when he was eating and without any warning kick him and say, "Nigger, nigger, nigger!" On other occasions, he would tell me to put Cap in his car and for me to get in too. He would drive to Pens, Florida and drive around until he found a corner where a few black kids were hanging out. Stopping next to them, he would reach over the seat and start beating Cap all the while yelling, "Nigger, nigger, nigger!" and holding his pistol. Of course, Cap was growling and barking loudly looking at the blacks. I would tell him to stop, but he would start hitting me saying that he was training Cap to protect us. When he drove away from these incidents, he was always smiling.

One night, my father came in the house from work holding his shoulder and cursing loudly. When Mama asked what had happened, he said, "As I got out of the car, that goddamn dog of his came out from under the house and attacked me. I believe he was going for my throat, but at the last second, I threw my arm up, and he took my whole shoulder in his goddamn mouth." He took his shirt off, and I saw bite marks and blood on his shoulder. He was talking to Mama but was staring at me with a crazy look in his eyes that made me shiver. I walked outside and called Cap. We walked a short distance into the woods, and I knelt beside him and gave him the biggest hug I could. He licked my face and looking into his eyes. I knew that he too was just trying to survive.

Cap always slept beside my bed at night. Judy always slept beside my father's bed in his room. One night before going to bed, I wanted to test Cap to see just how well he listened to me. I went into the kitchen and got two pieces of ground beef. Mama always bought two packages, one for making meat loaf and the other for my father, who ate ground beef raw.

I made sure I took both pieces from my father's package because I knew it would have his scent on it. I went into my bedroom and fed a piece to Cap. The other piece I made into a ball. I put it between his paws as he lay beside my bed. He looked at me and started to eat the meat. I said, "No, Cap," in a normal tone. He stopped, looked at me, and laid his head down without touching the meat.

My father was still in the habit of waking me up at five or five thirty every morning by throwing a glass of water in my face and yelling, "Get up, plowboy. Goddamn it, get up!"

Every morning, Judy would run in and greet Cap at the same time. On that morning, Cap woke me up growling very loudly just before my father entered the room. I rolled over to see why he was growling. Judy was eating that piece of meat, and every hair on Cap's body was standing up. His lips were curled showing every tooth. He was pissed, and Judy started backing out very fast. For the first time, I realized how smart and loyal Cap was. I walked into the kitchen and got a big piece of meat to feed him after my father had left of course.

That summer, Cap and I would hit the woods for several days at a time. On occasion, we took Judy with us. One day, I was setting snares. I had just baited one and was going to set another when I heard a yelp. I saw Judy hanging in the snare from the tree. The line had gone around her chest and on the outside of her shoulder but not around her neck. Bringing her back down and getting her out of the snare, I chastised her. She just sat looking at me then reached over and ate my rabbit bait. I laughed, looked at Cap, and said, "She's a girl. What can I do?" I patted her head. She was all doggie smiles. Cap walked over, smelled her butt, and came over to lick my face as I reset the snare. On one of those trips, a ground rattler bit her on the lip. Her lip and the side of her head were swollen so badly that she couldn't see out of one eye for almost a week. My father gave me a terrible beating saying it was my fault even though she had been off in some tall grass when it happened. I had heard her yelp, and when I went over to see what was wrong, Cap was killing the snake. I told my father exactly how it happened, but it didn't matter to him. After that, he would not let Judy go with Cap and me. I was glad because I always found her to be a pain in our asses.

Most of the time, I would sneak lettuce out of the house, but one time, I brought a carrot, for catching rabbits. That night, we ate fish. We lived off whatever we could shoot or catch—mostly snakes, fish, squirrels, and rabbits. Snakes by themselves were not much of a meal. Mostly, I would skin them, hang the meat over the fire, and add them to a fish stew with fern roots I had dug up. I usually kept a pot or two, some fish tackle, and a cane pole along with a hatchet and some small line hidden in the woods near the lake. Snake meat was usually tough, rubbery, and without much taste. On occasion when Grant came with us and we would spend a weekend in the woods, he would make a face and never eat the snake meat. I always laughed and told him how good it was. For emphasis, I would throw a piece to Cap. He always gobbled it down, and I would ask Grant, "Sure you don't want some?" as I jiggled a piece of snake meat his way. I'd laugh some more when he would say, "Fuck no!" Grant was my best friend, but he was not much for being in the woods.

One summer day, Cap and I were wandering in the woods when we found ourselves near the tree with the bees. Cap alerted me first by growling and running over to me; he pressed himself against my leg. Whenever Cap pressed himself against my leg like that, he always stayed there. But that time, I wanted to make sure he stayed, so I rested my hand on his head as we crept closer. I asked, "What is it, boy?" I heard loud growling, and it was not coming from Cap. We walked slowly through the dense brush until we saw the tree about a hundred feet away. I knelt beside Cap, who was growling constantly and loudly. I told him, "Sit, Cap," and he sat quickly. "Quiet, boy!" He stopped growling. At least very loudly. He was growling under his breath so to speak.

We saw a large black bear sitting on a limb beside the hole dipping his paw into the hole again and again and licking honey off it. The bees were swarming as I had never seen before. They must have been stinging his face because every couple of minutes, he would swipe a big paw at his nose and eyes. That whole incident lasted about ten minutes. Cap and I just watched. The bear finally shimmied down the tree backward and started running with hundreds of bees in hot pursuit. Luckily for us, the bear ran in the other direction. All I wanted was to see the bear, not shoot it. He was the most amazing animal except for gators I had ever seen in the wild. After that, Cap and I never returned to that tree.

CHAPTER 66

Tippy

By the fall of 1958, Grant and I were spending lots of time at each other's house. I never brought Cap with me to Grant's because he had a large dog. Most of the time during the school year, I would stay after school, walk to Grant's, and spend the night. His mother was one of the nicest and warmest people I had ever met. She never asked us any questions of why we spent so much time together.

On other occasions, Grant would ride my bus home with me and spend the weekend. Sometimes, Mama would ask me how long he was staying, but my father never said a word. I never made any friends at school except for Grant. I was quiet and kept to myself. I did not trust anybody, but I was starting to trust Grant, and I felt he was starting to trust me too.

I still had dreams about making money and running away. Once, I told Grant about my idea, and he said he would go with me. At first, I wanted to return to be with my friends in Morgan Creek. Sometimes, I told him that I thought Cap, he, and I could just live off the land, but he did not think that was a good idea, especially if it meant eating only what we could catch. I would just laugh and tease him about that.

Mostly I still wanted to go back to Louisiana and live with my cousin. I knew he would let me keep Cap, and I knew he was more like a real father to me. I told Grant about that plan, and he was agreeable because I thought he would let Grant stay also.

One of my new money ventures was catching flying squirrels. Cap and I would find old dead trees, that had some type of holes in them. Through trial and error, we discovered if Cap pounded on the tree hard, with his front paws, and barked loudly, one or two squirrels would come out. Again, through trial and error, I learned in which direction the squirrel would probably fly, when leaving the nest. I would then hide behind a tree in that direction and step out just in time to catch one, by hand, before it landed on that tree. I had so many bite mark you couldn't count them. Cap and I was having so much fun, I didn't care. We became so proficient at catching them that I built a cage in the backyard to hold as many as I could, though I had not sold any or had any orders. I would estimate that at one point I had twenty to thirty squirrels in that cage.

When I caught young ones, I would tie string around their necks, tie the other end to my button-down shirt, and make a small nest for them in my shirt pocket. I took them to school to show other kids and try to sell them. I was asking only 50¢, but I never sold one because even the young squirrels would bite.

In the spring of 1959, Cap, Grant, and I were hunting for flying squirrels one day when I found a newborn in a nest. His eyes were not open yet, but I took him home intending on raising him. Grant said he thought he would die soon, but I was determined. I fed him milk mixed with water through an eyedropper. I kept him in a shoebox filled with cotton on the counter in the kitchen.

One morning, Mama woke me up. "Johnny, your damn rat is dead!" I got up and looked in the box. He did look dead, but I poked him a little and thought I saw some movement. It was cold in the main part of our house, probably about forty degrees including in my room. My father liked to keep the heater in the living room off during the night, and my sister's room was the only other room that was heated, but she kept her bedroom door closed at night, with the heater on. Mama said, "The damn thing must have frozen to death."

I carried the box to the stove, picked him up by the tail, turned the gas stove on, and held him over it. Within a couple of moments or so, he started kicking and squirming. I said, "Look, Mama. He's not dead. He's just cold."

By then, I had concluded that nobody was interested in buying flying squirrels, so I let all the squirrels I had in the cage go. My closet did not have a door, but it did have a sheet for a curtain that went about three-quarters the way up and was nailed on either side of the doorway. The top was open. I now kept the flying squirrel, in the shoe box, one my head board. It grew fast and eventually made a nest on my closet shelf, from odds and ends he found around my room. One day, I was sitting in the backyard holding and talking to him. Cap was sitting right beside me, just watching. Suddenly Cap snapped at him and bit off half his tail. I had seen plenty of them with only half a tail, but I had never seen one grow back completely. Within a short time, his tail grew back pure white, so I named him Tippy. I took him to school with me as I had others in my shirt pocket. He never bit anybody. I had a few offers to buy him, but I turned them down.

About a year later, Mama said he was gnawing holes in her boxed food and eating it and pooping all over. She told me I had to get rid of him. Sadly, I took him out in the backyard. After spending some last moments with him, I put him in a tree. An hour or so later, I went to check on him. He was gone.

About a month or so later, Cap and I were again hunting flying squirrels, now, just for the fun of catching and releasing them. I went up to one old dead tree and saw a hole in the top. I banged on the trunk, and a head popped out. It was a flying squirrel. He ran down the tree, jumped on my shoulder, and started chattering at me. I couldn't believe it, but it was Tippy. I petted and kissed him and talked to him.

We both heard a sound coming from the hole at the same time. Looking up, I saw another head pop out, and out came another flying squirrel. I looked at Tippy. "So, you have a girlfriend, huh?" He jumped off my shoulder and climbed back up. They both went into the hole. I left the tree without bothering them.

About a week later, Cap and I returned to that tree. I banged and banged, but no Tippy. Even though Cap and I continued to hunt in those woods, turning all the squirrels loose after catching them, I never saw Tippy again.

Today, every time I think about Tippy, I am filled with the love and joy that he gave me for having him in my life, even if it was for such a short time. I will never forget him.

CHAPTER 67

Bandit

In the early spring of 1959, my father bought a new Chevy Impala. Grant was staying with me at the time, and my father asked us if we would like to go coon hunting. I did not answer at first; bad memories flooded my mind of being in the woods with my father. In the past when we went rabbit or squirrel hunting, I had heard my father speak of blacks as coons, so I wasn't sure what his meaning was. I looked at Grant and shook my head, but he replied, "Sure." I had no choice. I wasn't going to let my best friend go alone with my father anywhere. With great sadness, I agreed.

My father told me to get his rifle and a bucksaw. He put them in the trunk. He told me to get Cap and Judy in the car. I did, and Grant and I got into the back seat with Cap. Judy had already jumped into the front seat, so we just let her stay there. I tried to explain my fears to Grant, but then my father came out, and after he petted and kissed Judy, he drove off.

As we drove north on Highway 81, my father told Grant about how when he was growing up in Louisiana, he and his best friend, Jo Jo, used to trap and shoot muskrats, gators, and coons using a pirogue. He said they would skin them, sell the meat, dry the hides, and sell them also. As he was telling his story to Grant about all the fun he and his friend had had, I was remembering the day so long ago that he had taken me in that same pirogue out on the same waters he was talking about. I heard him but was not listening to his words. I stared out the window and asked myself, *Why, is he talking to Grant about those times?*

In about an hour, my father parked next to a bridge. I asked, "How did you know about this place?" He gave me a strange look. "Don't ask stupid questions, plowboy! I've been here before!" He drew his arm back, and I got ready to duck that terrible left fist. But then, Grant walked around the car and asked, "Where are we?" My father said, "On Cold Water Creek." I saw no houses, only woods. He made sure his rifle was loaded, and we started walking along the bank of the creek.

Cap and Judy were running ahead of us, and occasionally, we heard them barking. Getting closer, we saw that they had a big rattlesnake cornered. Judy, having been bitten once, was staying away from it but still barking. Cap, showing no fear, was close. Every time the snake would strike, Cap would jump back. My father was just about to shoot the snake when I, fearing he would shoot Cap accidently or on purpose, jumped in front of him saying, "Let me get the snake." He and Grant watched as I took out a handkerchief. Getting close to the snake, I kept flipping the handkerchief at his head, and it struck it each time. It did not take long before the snake tired, and I grabbed it by the head. Instead of killing it as my father told me to, I walked a short distance to a wet, thick, and swampy area. I threw the snake in as far as I could. I walked back and said, "The snake's gone, so you don't have to shoot it."

My father backhanded me full in the face and knocked me to the ground. Blood started flowing from my nose. As I was getting up and wiping my face with the handkerchief, my father said, "When I tell you to kill a goddamn rattlesnake, you better damned well kill it, plowboy!" I never said a word. Grant looked frightened and puzzled. I wanted to say, "Now you know the things I've been telling you are true," but I did not have to. The look on his face said it all. We continued our coon hunt with Grant staying away from my father and to our rear.

A short time later, we heard the dogs barking. I said, "Cap has something treed." My father looked at me. "How do you know what your goddamn dog is doing?" I ran toward the barking. Within a short time, we saw that the dogs had treed a coon up a sapling about thirty feet high. The coon was at the top among some leaves trying to hide. My father brought his gun up to shoot. I shouted, "It's a little one! I'd like to catch it." My father asked, "How the hell are you going to do that?" I replied, "One of us can cut the tree down, and another one can catch the coon as it falls." My father thought for a couple of minutes and said, "Run back to the car and get the bucksaw." I had always wanted a baby coon as a pet. I had heard they made great ones.

When I returned with the saw, my father said, "You cut the tree down, and I'll catch the goddamned coon." I started cutting, and my father gauged the distance. The trunk was only about four inches in diameter, so it did not take long. The tree started falling, and my father was ready with arms outstretched, but he had miscalculated. The trunk hit him in the head and knocked him out cold. Grant yelled something unintelligible and sank to the ground with the most confused look on his face I had ever seen on anybody.

The coon hit the ground running and headed toward the river with both dogs in hot pursuit. I looked at my father lying out cold, but I figured he would be okay. *If not, so what?* I was worried about my dog. I yelled to Grant, "I'm going after Cap." Grant just looked at me with his mouth open and lips moving but saying nothing. I heard Cap barking and knew I had to get to him quickly or that coon would kill him. I had heard stories about dogs being drowned it water by coons.

I got to the creek, and my worst fears were realized. Judy was standing on the edge just barking. The coon had jumped into the water, and Cap had followed. Just as I arrived, the coon climbed onto Cap's back. I knew if I didn't do something, the coon would climb onto Cap's head and he would drown. I jumped into the cold water and waded to Cap taking off my shirt as I went. I grabbed the coon and wrapped him in my shirt. He was fighting and biting mad, but I hung onto him.

I returned to my father. The coon was still wrapped in my shirt, and the dogs were jumping up trying to bite him. My father was sitting up but groggy. Grant was sitting in the same spot I had left him with that same silly look on his face. I started laughing as I sat beside him showing him the coon. He asked, "Did that really happen?" I said, "Yep. Want to go coon hunting next week?" With a queer look, he replied, "Fuck no!"

By that time, my father was up, walking around, and asking, "Did you catch the goddamn coon?" I held my shirt out. The coon, now quiet, had his head sticking out of my shirt sleeve looking around as if everything was all good.

We returned to the car. I brought the coon home, and at first, I had to tie him to some cinder blocks in the backyard. Cap and Judy would pester him, but I knew they couldn't get to him because he would go inside the blocks when they were around. I started hand feeding him and slowly introduced him to Cap. It wasn't long before he and Cap became friends. In no time, I could walk around with him on a small rope around his neck. Soon after, I could take him off the rope and he would stay right with me. Sometimes, I would carry him, and other times, he would sit on my shoulders. At times, he would walk and run around me, and Cap was playing with him as well. I let him make a bed on my closet shelf. Every time he climbed up the curtain to go into the closet shelf, it reminded me of how Tippy used to do the same thing only faster.

The biggest problem I had with him was that he liked to stay up all night playing and getting into stuff and then sleeping all day. I started taking him with me during the day to wear him out, so he would sleep at night. That did not work. It wasn't too long before Mama started complaining about the mess he was making. I tried to stop him, but I couldn't. Finally, one day, I took him to the lake in the woods behind the house and turned him loose. As soon as he hit the ground, he ran off. I never saw him again.

I had Cap for only about three years. In late fall of 1959, my father told me he had seen Cap throwing up and he needed to see a vet. I told my father I had not seen him looking or acting sick, but he insisted we take him to a vet he had heard about in Lawton, Alabama.

We drove there the next day. My father seemed to know the way right to the vet's office. The vet stuck a tube into Cap's penis up into his bladder. Cap starting growling and curled his lips. I laid my hand on his head and said, "It's okay, Cap," and he quieted down.

The vet said that Cap had kidney stones. He said he would keep him overnight and operate on him the next day. I told my father, "I don't want to leave him here. There's a good vet in Maple Wood." My father looked at the vet. I saw them nod. My father said, "The dog's staying here. Let's go!" We got into the car and drove back home to Maple Wood. Not one word was spoken all the way home.

The next morning, I called the vet. He told me Cap had died during the night. He said that he had operated on him after we had left and had tied him to a table afterward. During the night, he had tried to get loose, tore his stitches out, and bled to death. I couldn't stop crying. Every time I looked at my father, he backhanded me and said, "Goddamn it! You blame me, don't you?" I said, "Yes, I do blame you. I didn't want to take him to Alabama in the first place." Another backhand landed on the side of my head, but I was glad I had said something.

I left the house and stayed in the woods. I built a small fire in the same area Cap and I had spent many nights together. I couldn't eat. When I finally fell asleep, my dreams were filled with my father's face. Every time I closed my eyes, his demonic face would appear. I went home two days later. Nobody said a word to me, and nothing else was ever said about Cap. Mama cooked me some grits and eggs, saying nothing.

Years later, I heard that certain vets would tell people their dogs had died but would sell the dogs. The specific report I heard was about a woman who was told by her vet that her dog had died overnight. The next morning, she went to the vet's office unannounced and demanded to see her dog. He showed her one that was similar but was not hers. There was a huge scandal all over the country.

I believe my father gave or sold Cap to that vet, who lied to me about Cap dying. I also believe that my father trained Cap, just as he said he was doing, to hate blacks and that Cap was possibly given or sold by that vet to white supremacists. On occasion he still left our house, taking his guns with him and returning many days later. On these occasions he was so angry, I tried to stay away from him. By now I never asked Mama where he was.

Above all else my father ever did to me, my hate for him has never diminished over Cap. I will carry that to my grave.

CHAPTER 68

Lost Trust

I was sixteen. The sexual abuse I suffered by my father was still ongoing. I was not allowed to use the bathroom in the house; the hose hanging from the tree was still my only option for showers. Years later when my thoughts would return to those times, I remembered that we were just outside my sister's bedroom window. On occasion, I saw her standing in the window watching us. I concluded that my father had planned that.

For quite a while after Cap died, I was a lost soul. I skipped school frequently. I spent more and more time with Grant to fill the void in me. He lived in town, about six miles away. I started to confide in Grant about some of my deeper thoughts, and he started confiding in me as well. I eventually told him everything including the sexual abuse. He told me that his stepfather, Bob, would beat him, his brothers, and his mother, but he never mentioned sexual abuse.

He and I formed a plan. We would stay together at each other's house and sleep together as much as we could. We thought we would be safe if we stayed together. Many nights, Grant and I would lie in his bed listening to Bob beating his mother and siblings. I told him how while I was living in Morgan Creek, my friends and I talked about killing my father. I told him I believed that if we had stayed in Morgan Creek, I would have killed him.

At first, I was pissed. I was telling him my darkest secrets, and he was making fun of me. But his laugh was contagious. I too started to laugh. After that, occasionally, Grant would say, "Cluck, cluck!" and we would laugh.

I told Grant how my father always kept his loaded .22 caliber rifle, 12-gauge shotgun and carbine next to his bed, with his pistol under his pillow. One day when he was at my house, Grant asked me why I kept a loaded shotgun next to my bed. I told him that when I had turned twelve, my father had bought the gun for me and told me to keep it loaded next to my bed. He asked, "Would you really shoot your mother and sister?" Shrugging I said, "Those were his orders," but in my heart, I knew I would never do that.

Many times, whenever Grant and I slept at my house in my bed, we talked about and planned ways to kill my father. Sometimes, we thought we would just take the guns, go into his room, and blast away. Other times, we thought about tying him up at gunpoint, taking him out into the woods, and hanging him. I told Grant about something I had heard. A male was taken into the woods and his dick nailed to a stump. He was given a knife, and the stump was set on fire. Grant thought that was the best idea of all. But I said, "It won't work with my father." Grant asked, "Why not?" I said, "Because he has a small dick." Grant asked, "How do you know?" I shrugged and asked, "Why do you think?" For a moment, he looked at me quizzically and then said, "Oh yeah." We both laughed.

Those were the normal killing methods we thought of. Some of the others were disgusting, such as cutting his head off with his machete while he slept. One night, Grant and I took my loaded shotgun into his room and aimed the gun at him. I did not pull the trigger. Grant, standing right behind me, was saying, "Do it! Do it!" I looked at Mama lying next to him and I couldn't. Afterward, I told Grant, "We can just run away and live in the woods," but as before, he did not like that idea. My best friend was a real city boy.

Those times were brutal, but he and I made light of them as much as we could. I thank God for meeting Grant. I believe he helped save my soul at an early age.

The one thing Mama and my father started the four of us doing, was going to church on Sundays. That year, I again became an altar boy. For whatever reason, the priest took a special interest in me. He taught me the correct Latin to say for Mass. I served every Sunday, always with another altar boy or two. After a while, he asked me if I would serve Mass on Wednesdays because he said Mass that day as well. I agreed, so every Wednesday before school, my father would drive me to church. Afterward, I would walk to school. We occasionally had one or two parishioners, but mostly, it was only the priest and me.

One day, I asked, "Father I thought for you to say Mass, you had to have at least one person to hear it." He said, "Yes, that is correct. I have you, Johnny, so you're special to me." I said, "I didn't know I counted." He put his arm around my shoulder and squeezed me. He said, "Of course you do! You count to God but mostly to me, Johnny." Nobody had ever told me I had meant anything to him or her before.

That winter, Grant and I stayed at each other's house as much as possible. We mostly stayed at Grant's because he had board games. Our favorite was a metal football game that was plugged into the wall. The top vibrated, and the players, which had magnets on their bottoms, moved. Sometimes, we played for hours. His mother was so warm hearted that one time, I told Grant, "I wish I could live with you."

One altar boys had a beautiful Vespa motor scooter. I started pestering Mama to get my father to buy me one; I said I could ride it to church so he would not have to drive me on

Wednesday. So, one spring day in 1960, my father came home with a man following him towing a trailer on which was a 1949 Cushman scooter. It was navy blue and heavy. The sides were dented and showed patches of rust. There was a square, cushioned seat and a single rear brake on the floorboard. It had a kick start and was an automatic—no shifting. It was the ugliest thing I had ever seen. My father told me that a man whom he knew from work had created the scooter out of 1948 and 1949 scooter parts He told me it was mine and to take care of it because it had cost a lot of money.

The first time I started it up, I could hardly get it to move. It had very little power; my father said it had a four-horse-power engine. I got off and twisted the throttle; it moved, and I ran alongside it until it gained enough speed for me to jump on. That first day, I rode all around our area on dirt roads getting used to it. It was ugly, slow, and very heavy, but I loved it. I finally had a way to leave the house. For the first time, I had freedom. My father usually had me raking our yard, but when he didn't, I would take off on the scooter. I did not have a driver's license, but my father never said anything about that or getting plates, so I never asked.

I started riding it to Grant's, church, and school. Sometimes, kids at school would line up just to watch me run alongside it until it gained speed. They always laughed, but I didn't care. I felt a freedom I had never known. The scooter did not have the power to carry Grant and me, so I never gave him a ride.

The sexual abuse at home was becoming more intense but less frequent. He started tying my hands to that pine tree telling me as usual that I would never amount to anything. He told me that he needed to teach me about sex and what the world was about and that I had to stop fighting him. That was a lie; I never fought him because I knew it would do no good. His strength and demeanor during those times was unimaginable. I would close my eyes, grasp my ankles or that pine tree, and picture Cap standing in front of me. Under my breath, I would tell Cap how much I missed and still loved him. Every night before going to sleep, I would look at a photo I had of Cap and have a long conversation with him that would conclude with my kissing the photo and crying. I still carry that photo to this day.

On several occasions, my father heard me talking with Cap and punched me, but I didn't care. I loved and missed Cap more than anything. Sometimes afterward, I would walk into the woods and sit with my back against a tree, knees drawn up, and cry. I would listen to the night sounds and imagine that Cap was looking at me with love and trust in his eyes. I would sit and talk to him for hours sometimes until daylight. I could almost hug him and feel him licking my tears away, and all seemed better in the world. Sometimes, I would pray to God for help as the nuns had taught me I could.

Serving Mass on Wednesdays was becoming strained. One day, the priest asked, "What's wrong, Johnny? You've been very quiet lately." Little by little, I started telling him about my home life, and he always wanted to know more.

One Sunday right after Mass, he asked me to come to his residence across the street. We sat in the living room, and he asked me about everything that had happened that week. I had not disclosed the sexual abuse to him, but I had sort of hinted at it. He persisted until he finally got me to talk about it.

Crying, I told him everything—when it had started, the places where it had happened, and most of all the violence associated with the abuse. I told him all about Cap and how much I missed him. By then, I was crying harder. He sat beside me and held me close; he said everything would be all right. He offered me some wine. "To help calm your nerves, Johnny," he said. I gulped down the first glass, and he gave me another. "Go ahead and drink it. It will help." I drank the second glass as he repeated, "Everything is going to be all right."

He poured me a third glass, as I began feeling its effects. He led me to the spare bedroom, and I lay down. He said that he had to say another Mass and that we could talk some more when he came back.

About forty-five minutes later, I felt a little better. I walked across the street, got on my scooter, and drove to Grant's house. I felt stupid about what I had done and said to the priest. I told Grant about the wine. He told me that Bob, his stepfather, made homemade blackberry wine. He said if I wanted to, we could take some from him and drink it. Grant said that he had so much that he would never miss a few bottles. I told him that would be okay, but I didn't want any right then. The rest of that day was uneventful; Grant and I played baseball with kids across the street.

The following Wednesday, I showed up for Mass as usual. The priest and I were the only ones there. Right after Mass, the priest had me sit down with him in a small office. He again questioned me about my father, but mostly, he wanted to know about the sexual abuse. When I started becoming hesitant about talking, he gave me some wine and said, "It will help you to remember." I told him, "I don't need wine to help me remember. I know every detail!"

I had been raised a strict Catholic, and priests were like God—at least that's what Mama and the nuns had taught me. Because of that, I knew to never lie to priests but to always tell them everything, but I did not feel like talking to anybody especially a priest. He nonetheless persisted and kept giving me more wine.

After my second glass, he suggested we go over to his residence, so we could talk without being interrupted. At his house, he gave me a third glass of wine and asked, "Have you ever had sex with a girl?" I said, "Mama always told me to stay away from girls because they were dirty and nasty." I lowered my head and lied. "No, I have never had sex with a girl." But he kept asking. Finally, I told him about my cousin and the girl on the beach who had ripped my suit off. I was crying, but he persisted; he wanted all the details. Afterward, he said, "Your mother is right. You should stay away from girls."

He asked direct questions about the sexual abuse by my father. "What do you feel when your father enters you? Does it arouse you? Do you ever think about it at other times? Do you ever get an erection? Do you masturbate thinking about your father?"

My brain was fuzzy from the wine; I didn't understand why he was asking these questions. I asked, "Why do you need to know?" He replied, "Johnny, if I'm going to help you rid yourself of demons, I need to know everything." I was puzzled. "I didn't know I had any demons." He said, "Oh but you do! I'll help to rid yourself of them."

Still not understanding but having complete trust in him, I asked, "What demons do I have?" He said, "Johnny, you should go lie down. I can see the wine is making your brain work funny because you're not thinking or talking straight."

He led me to the spare bedroom, and I lay on the bed. He knelt beside me, folded his hands, and started asking God to help him rid me of my demons. Slowly he undressed me and started manipulating my penis. He was praying louder and louder as my erection rose. After reaching a full erection, he placed his mouth over it and started making very loud sucking and mewing noises. When I ejaculated, he grabbed my hips as my body shook uncontrollably. Afterward, he lay beside me, wrapped his arm around me, and said, "God will save you, and I will help him."

My mind was still clouded from the wine. *What just happened? Why did I do this? Is this what I wanted?* I understood nothing. I asked him, "Why am I doing this?" He replied, "Johnny, your father is putting his demon seed in you every time he has sex with you just as a girl would do if you had sex with her. What God and I just did was release some of those demons from you. Because it has been going on since you were twelve, you have many demons in you. The demons need to be released, and this is the only way to release them."

I knew what homosexuality was, but I was not a kid of wide exposure, and as I said, I had been told to listen to priests, not question them, because you trusted them. My mind was a mess, and I felt trapped not really knowing what to do or whom to talk to. As I had done in the past many times, I asked myself, *What, have I done wrong?* I fell asleep and missed school that day.

After that, I stopped serving Mass on Wednesdays. I had lost trust in the man I trusted the most. On Sunday, I told the priest that my father would not let me serve Mass on Wednesdays anymore. I never told Mama or my father about that; I would get up and leave on Wednesday mornings just as always, but I would go to Grant's house until it was time for school. I still served on Sunday mornings, but there were always others around, and I would leave right after Mass.

One thing that happened after that incident was that Grant and I stole bottles of wine from Bob. During school days, we would put a bottle in our locker. Sometimes during class, we would ask to go to the washroom. We would sneak into the locker room and drink some wine. It became a daily routine for Grant and me, at least if the wine held out.

CHAPTER 69

An Impact

Early one morning, I got a call from a detective I routinely worked with on drug cases in his town and mine. He said he had a substantial drug case going down sometime that day and could use extra help. I said I would call him back. I called my chief for permission and called the detective back saying I would meet him at his police station.

I got to his police station and was greeted by him and several other detectives from nearby towns with whom we routinely worked. After pleasantries were exchanged, we entered his war room. A couple living near a high school were selling heroin and cocaine. The detective said the male would be flying from Boston to Cleveland to buy the drugs and come back that day. I told the detective that I had information from a reliable source that a former Sandy Town resident who was living in Cleveland was a drug dealer who worked at the airport. We agreed that at the end of this case, we would turn over all information we had to the DEA.

Because of specific laws dealing with selling drugs near schools, this case took top priority. We planned for three two-man teams to keep surveillance on the residence. When the man left, two teams would follow him while one team watched the residence.

By 8:00 a.m., all three teams were in place. A travel van arrived, and the male drove off in it. The other two teams followed the van while my partner and I continued the surveillance. Within two hours, the other teams called to say the male had been dropped off at Logan Airport. We decided that only one two-man team would continue the surveillance at the residence with shift changes periodically while the other teams would wait at the police department.

During surveillance of the residence, we saw many individuals drive up, stay a short time, and then leave—typical of drug activity. Around 10:00 p.m., my partner and I were back on surveillance. The travel van arrived. Three people got out; the male under surveillance was one. They entered the residence, and I notified the other teams. Before the other teams arrived, a male and female left the residence and drove off in the van.

The other teams arrived; the lead detective had a search warrant. Because we had not determined how many people were in the house, we decided that two detectives would enter the front door and two would enter the rear door; the remaining two detectives would guard the outside. I entered the front door with the lead detective.

Inside, we quickly determined that only the couple and their three children were there. In plain view on the kitchen table was a large amount of cocaine and paraphernalia for cutting, weighing, and packaging it for sale. We also saw two empty syringes with needles on the table.

Both subjects, who appeared to be high, was placed under arrest. After reading them their Miranda rights, the lead detective asked about more drugs, and of course, they denied having any.

While one detective watched both subjects, the rest of us searched the large house. The lead detective found some heroin hidden in the male's jacket, the same jacket we had seen him wearing earlier that day when he had left and come back. We questioned them some more, but again, they denied having any more drugs.

I walked into the master bedroom and saw that the children, approximately three years old, two years old, and six months old, were wearing only diapers and were asleep on the bed. From experience, I knew that husbands and wives who were using drugs would hide their personal stashes from each other. I also knew that sometimes, heroin was cut using a baby laxative and in fact sometimes female users kept their fixes in their babies' diapers while on the babies.

I called in the lead detective to observe as I quietly and as gently as possible searched the babies' diapers. I found several syringes without needles and packets of heroin in all three diapers. A further search of the residence did not turn up any more drugs. The lead detective called for a cruiser to transport the two suspects. He also called social services to respond to the house for the babies.

Because several of the vehicles, including the travel van, had registrations leading back to Sandy Town, I asked the lead detective if he minded if I questioned the two suspects then. He said that it was late, that everybody was tired, and that could I question them at his police station. I said, "I could, but I like to strike when the iron is hot." With a sad look, he agreed.

I questioned the male, but it became obvious that he did not want to talk. After I talked to the female for about half an hour, she started to loosen up and talk a bit. After another hour or so, she started to cry, but she was answering my questions honestly. I asked her questions about whom she and her husband sold heroin and cocaine to in Sandy Town. After another hour of questioning, I had good, solid, and current information on one apartment and one house in Sandy Town. During that time the lead detective, sitting in the other room, yelled, "Johnny, I think you could get a pile of shit to talk," all the other tired detectives laughed.

By then, it was about 5:00 a.m. After the suspects were transported to the police station, I told the detectives that I had enough information to secure two search warrants. There were a few moans and groans, but everybody perked up when I told them that one subject was known to carry a handgun.

Back at my station, I filled out an affidavit in support of a search warrant, which included a report stating why, where, a description of the property, what I was searching for, and most important, a detailed reason of probable cause—why I believed the items I suspected would be there. The information had to be current, and my information was less than a day old.

I called an ATF agent I had worked with before and told him that I was obtaining search warrants and that I had information on a possible firearm at one location. He said he would meet me at my station within an hour.

At about 8:30 a.m., I had the search warrants in hand. One was a no-knock warrant used only when weapons were believed to be in the possession of suspects. I told my chief about the night's work and the search warrants. I told him that the detectives from the other towns and the ATF agent would be assisting me. He said he was very proud of the way the other detectives and I had formed a mini task force and had worked together. He told me I had his full support; he warned me to be careful and to let him know the outcome.

About a half hour later, we hit the one-bedroom apartment. I put both occupants—a male and a female—under arrest. I read them their Miranda rights; neither wanted to talk. I saw two children asleep in the bedroom. We searched the premises and found a quantity of drugs, hidden in different places including the children's diapers. I did a field test on them, and they showed positive for heroin and cocaine. DYS was called to take the children, and I called for a cruiser to take the suspects to the station to be booked for possession of class A and B substances.

The detectives, the agent, and I drove to the second location, a small house with only one bedroom, an eat-in kitchen, a bathroom, and a living room—a typical rental in the area. Because I had information that one of the suspects, the male, was known to always carry a firearm, we hit the house fast and hard.

We entered but saw no one in the kitchen or living room. I entered the bedroom and saw the male and female suspects in bed. They appeared to be in the middle of making love. I approached the bed with my shotgun pointed at him; he was reaching under his pillow. I saw the butt of a handgun with his fingers wrapped around it as he pulled it out. I told him I was a police officer with a search warrant. He let go of the gun and lay his head down on the woman's breasts, with a big sigh

After I handcuffed the subject, I pulled the handgun from under the pillow. It was a S&W 9 mm semiautomatic, fully loaded with one round in the chamber. We searched the house and found drugs. I field tested them and got positive results for heroin and cocaine. Both subjects were read their Miranda rights; neither wanted to talk. They were taken to the station in a cruiser and booked for possession of class A & B substances. A later computer search produced information that the male had been arrested previously in another state by ATF agents on several gun charges. After I cleared it with my chief, the gun charge was turned over to the ATF agent who had accompanied me.

Late one afternoon several months later, I was in my office when the front desk called me saying there was someone in the lobby who wanted to speak with a detective. I went downstairs and saw the same subject I had previously arrested. He was with a woman but not the same one I had arrested with him. He looked at me and started for the front door saying, "Fuck! You won't help me!" I followed him out and told him, "I'll help you if you need it." It took him a couple of moments before he said, "I was kidnapped and held at gun point for several hours!"

He was shaking and looked scared. I told him that we should go upstairs where we could talk, and I would take his statement. I said that I would pat him down and have his girlfriend patted down by a female officer. Both agreed, and after the pat downs, we went to my office.

He said that he was working with the ATF on motorcycle gangs and guns and was still living in the same house I had busted him in. He said that his girlfriend had left him but that he had a new girlfriend; he pointed to the female.

He said that very early that morning, two men had kicked in his front door and at gunpoint handcuffed him and dragged him out of the house. He said that at first, he thought it had to do with motorcycle gangs. The men kept calling him by a different name, and he kept telling them that was not his name, that they had the wrong guy. He said they put him in the trunk of their car and drove off. They stopped and took him out still handcuffed. He saw that they had parked in a wooded area; he thought they would shoot him.

They started asking him personal questions. Eventually, they put him back in the trunk and drove off. They stopped at a car wash where one of them made a call on a pay phone. Taking him out of the trunk he heard the man giving his description to somebody. Coming back to the car, the man said to his partner, "I have to call back in a couple of hours." They again put him in the trunk and drove off. He said that they stopped in a few minutes and that he had heard someone say, "Welcome to Burger King."

After a few hours and a few more phone calls, they took him out of the trunk and released him. "You were right," they had said. "You're not the guy we're looking for." They explained that they were bounty hunters looking for a bail jumper wanted in Vermont who they thought was living in his house.

He told them that when he had moved into that house, a guy by that name was living there, but he had moved out the year before. They told him they could legally do what they had done, and he would be better off to just forget everything. Then with a parting warning to keep quiet, one said, "Don't forget—we know where you live!"

I took a full statement. He knew about guns and was able to tell me about the weapons they had had in the trunk including sawed-off shotguns and automatic weapons. He gave me a detailed description of the vehicle with Vermont plates but not the plate number, descriptions of the two subjects, and the first names he had heard them use when talking to each other. They had also mentioned the Vermont town where the subject they were looking for was from. He said that after they released him, he had called his girlfriend. She picked him up, and they drove straight to the police station. I told them, "I'll investigate this fully."

I drove to the car wash and spoke to several people working there. I found out that a car with Vermont plates with the same general description had been seen several times that day at the car wash; one occupant had used the pay phone. I got a general description of the occupants but no plate number.

I went to a nearby Burger King. I talked with the manager, who said he would have to get permission from his boss before I saw the tape at the drive-up window for that day. I left him my card asking him to call me as soon as he got permission. After writing a full report, I contacted the Vermont state police headquarters. They advised me that they would have the officer who patrolled that area of Vermont call me.

About two days later, I received a call from that officer. I gave him the whole story as I knew it, and he said he knew whom I was talking about; he had heard rumors about how the two operated and that his information was that they did in fact carry many weapons including sawed-off shotguns and automatic weapons. He said he had never been able to get enough information on them to arrest them. I told him that I had a signed complaint and that I would apply for arrest warrants and would mail him copies. When he found them in their car, he could arrest them. The trooper gave me the personal information on both subjects.

The next day after updating my chief, I went to the courthouse with my reports and an affidavit in support of arrest warrants for both subjects. I got them and mailed copies to the trooper. About a week later, he called and asked, "What happened? I hear they turned themselves in to your court." I said I didn't know about that but would find out. I called the courthouse and learned that indeed they had turned themselves in. I asked the clerk, "How did they know arrest warrants had been issued?" The clerk did not know. I drove to the courthouse and spoke with one of the judges and a court magistrate officer I knew through my work. I explained to them what had happened; the judge said he would find out exactly what had transpired and let me know.

The next day, the clerk magistrate said that the judge had found out that copies of the arrest warrants had been mistakenly mailed to the two suspects. I called the Vermont state trooper with the news. We were very disappointed. I drove to the complainant's house and explained to him everything I had done and what had happened. I told him that I would still go forward with the charges but that I would still need him to testify in court. Because of the way everything had gone down, he was afraid for himself and his girlfriend, who was now pregnant.

I spent the next hour talking with him. He told me stories about his upbringing and how his father, who was a very domineering person, had raised him to handle guns and hate the government from early on. He said he had never met a cop he liked. He thanked me for first believing him and then investigating his incident. His girlfriend was there while we talked, and she wanted to make sure I knew that she was pregnant and that they were afraid of retaliation. When I left, he shook my hand thanking me. His girlfriend hugged me and thanked me. I did go back to that house several times, but I never saw them again.

Back at the station, I updated my report. I leaned back, closed my eyes, and thought of the entire case. I hoped that our chance meeting on that case would change their lives forever. I reflected on my own life and how meeting one man had had an impact on me that I still feel today.

CHAPTER 70

Coach

I rode the scooter everywhere during the summer of 1960, but I had trouble with it. The engine ran fine even in the rain, but because the body was so heavy, the drive chain started breaking. I didn't tell my father because I was afraid he would take it and what freedom I had away.

Whenever it broke, I would fix it usually with wire I started carrying with me to connect the links. By the time school started in the fall, it was breaking down constantly. One day just as it was getting dark, I was on the way home from Grant's house when once again it broke. I pulled off the road, retrieved the chain from the roadway, and put the scooter on its stand.

I was lying on the grass trying to get the chain back on, but it was hard to see in the dark, and I was cursing. A car pulled up behind me; its headlights were shining right where I needed them to, so I could see what I was doing. The driver got out and slammed his door. His shadow loomed large as he approached. I was still working under the scooter trying to get the chain back on. He asked, "Having trouble?" I let out a string of curses ending with, "I wish my father had never gotten me this fuckin' scooter!"

The next thing I knew, I was being dragged out from under it still holding the chain. I saw my father's contorted face. I wanted to die—whatever it would take. He grabbed the chain from my hand and started beating me with it, screaming and yelling unintelligently. He sounded more like an animal than I had ever heard him. I was bruised, bleeding, and crying. "Get in the car, plowboy!" I watched from the back seat as he pushed the scooter farther off the road and threw the chain into the woods. He came over, got in the car, and drove home. Not a word was said all the way.

When we got home, it was full dark, and I was covered with blood, grass stains, and grease from the chain. "What happened, Johnny?" Mama asked. My father said, "He fell off the scooter." Mama said, "You need to stop riding it." My sister was pointing at me and laughing. My father said, "He won't ride it anymore." I wished I were dead. I tried to clean up in the kitchen sink, but my father grabbed me and pushed me out the back door saying, "Go take a shower, plowboy."

Out back, I took my clothes off and started my shower. The water was very cold, but I hardly noticed. Bruised and bleeding, I started crying. My father came out shortly, took his clothes off, started backhanding me, and said, "So you know about fucking, huh? I'm going to show you fucking!" The rape that night was brutal—one of the worst ever. I never saw the scooter again.

One day during physical education class, the head football coach split up the class for touch football. The coach of course played quarterback for both sides. Mostly, everybody just went downfield, and he would throw us passes. He threw several to me, which I always caught and would make a good run afterward. I did not know it then, but I later realized he was just scouting for new players for the high school football team, and it was a lucky day for me.

Soon, he started throwing more and more to me. They were getting harder to catch, but for the most part, I caught them. After a while, he called me over and asked, "Johnny, have you ever thought about going out for football?" I told him no. He said, "Why not come out to practice this afternoon?" I said I would. I told Grant what the coach had said and asked him if he would like to try out too. He said, "Sure! Why not?"

After school, Grant and I spoke with the coach, who had a team trainer set us up with practice uniforms. That first day was rough, but we got through it without losing our minds or breaking any bones. Most of the time, there was more running than I had ever done before, but Grant and I toughed it out.

One Friday after practice, the coach called Grant and me into his office. He said, "Johnny, somebody said you and Grant were smoking in downtown Maple Wood a couple of days ago. Do you smoke?" The easy lie was right on the tip of my tongue—*He'd never know, right?* Grant was waiting to see what I would say. I looked into the coach's eyes and saw something. "Yes, Coach, I've been smoking since I was nine." He asked, "Do you think you can quit?" I said, "I don't know, but I'll try." He looked at Grant. "What about you? Can you quit?" Grant looked at me and said, "I'll try too, Coach."

Grant and I practiced that next week, and the coach said nothing to us. On Friday right after practice, he called us into his office and asked, "Johnny, did you quit smoking?" I did not speak. The silence was deafening. Coach was staring at me and waiting. I stared back and thought, *What, would one more lie be? No big deal. What would be so different now?* But there was something about Coach. In only two weeks, I had found myself believing in something I was doing. I was in pain physically from all the running and exercises, but it was a good pain. Sure, there was a lot of yelling, but everybody got yelled at, not just me. For the first time ever, in my heart I knew that football was something I could do, and Coach was somebody

I could believe in. The clock on the wall was going *tick, tick, tick*. I thought, *One little word. That's all I have to say, and I could be out of here—no more practice, no more pain*. I could run and hide as I had done so often before. I took a deep breath. Grant was staring at me intently. "I tried, Coach, but I couldn't stop." He seemed a bit amused at that. I think he had thought I would say, "Yeah! I quit." With seriousness in his voice, he said, "Okay, Johnny. It will make you short winded, but keep on trying, okay?" I replied, "I will, Coach," and I meant it. He only had to look at Grant, and he quickly said, "Me neither, Coach." At the end of the next week, Grant left the team.

That first year of football was the toughest thing physically and mentally I had ever done. I did not have my scooter, so I had to walk the six miles home after practice. When I had first gone out for football, I told Mama about it, and she had simply said, "Okay."

We played on Friday nights, so usually on Fridays after school, I would walk to Grant's house with him and then head back to the school to dress for the game. Before home games, the team ate at 5:00 p.m. in the cafeteria. For away games, we met at the school and rode school buses to the game. I hardly played my first year. During practice, I felt like a tackle dummy. I knew I had a lot to learn, so I wasn't dejected. I loved every minute of it. Not only was I learning the basics of football, I was also learning teamwork, but most of all, I learned respect, trust, and gentlemanly conduct on and off the field.

I started trusting myself; though I was discovering my limitations, I always tried to overcome them. For the first time, I had trust in somebody else. I trusted my teammates that they would do their jobs and I would do mine for all of us to be winners. At the time, I wasn't aware that my self-esteem was rising even if it was ever so little.

School was still very hard for me; I had no interest in it, but my behavior changed as I learned from Coach. Sometimes after practice, I would go to Grant's house and spend the night. I think now of how many times I stayed with Grant and how many times his mother fed me. I know there must be a special place in heaven for her because she never said no to me and she always welcomed me with open arms.

My father spoke to me only once about football that first year. One night, we had had an away game. After arriving back at the school, I again walked home—six miles—and got there about 1:00 a.m. I had been up since five thirty that morning, the usual time my father woke me up. The house was dark. I headed quietly to my room. My father came out of the darkness from his bedroom, grabbed me by the neck, and dragged me to the back door not saying anything. He didn't have to. I knew what he wanted to do. Once outside, he let me go, and I walked in the dark to that pine tree and waited for his instructions. He hit me on the side of my head and knocked me into the tree. I fell to the ground, and he yelled, "You think you're a goddamn football player! You'll never ever be one, and you'll never amount to anything. You're too stupid!" He grabbed me by the throat and pulled me to my feet. He bent me over and yanked my pants off tearing them. As he raped me, he kept saying I would never be a football player. When he was finished, he hit me in the back of my head and knocked me to the ground. I just lay there dazed, my torn pants around my ankles.

After a few minutes, I got up and pulled them up. As I did, I looked up and through the dim light of the moon and stars, I saw my sister in her bedroom window. She immediately walked out of view. I did not go back into the house. I walked and wandered not really knowing or caring where I was going.

The next morning, I found myself in the wooded area behind Grant's house. I sat with my back against a tree and my knees drawn up. I fell asleep. I don't know how long I slept, but Grant woke me up by shaking my shoulder. I got up, and we talked. Nothing was asked or said about why I was there; it was understood.

We walked to a corner store, where he kept the clerk busy as I stole some junk food including canned Vienna sausages and a couple of soda pops. For the rest of the day, we hung out at his house playing his electric football game. That night, I slept at his house. We hung out the next day, and we went to school on Monday. I had on the same clothes; Grant's mother had given me some safety pins to pin up my ripped pants.

I stayed with Grant for about a week. He gave me one of his shirts. I went home the following weekend; nobody asked me anything. It was as if I had never been gone. I knew my father was in my sister's room because whenever he went in with her, he shut her bedroom door. Mama just asked me, "Are you hungry?" I said, "No ma'am." I walked into my bedroom and heard jumbled voices coming through the thin walls from my sister's room.

I was in tenth grade. For the rest of the football season, I tried hard because I wanted so much to show my father that I could indeed be a football player.

After football was over for the year, Grant and I spent as much time together as possible at each other's house. My father never said a word about Grant staying at our house or about our sleeping together.

One day after Grant had been with us for about two weeks, Mama asked, "Johnny, when's Grant going home?" I said, "I don't know. When he wants to I guess."

Nothing else was said, and the next day, Grant and I left to spend time at his house.

CHAPTER 71

Our First Time

My father was doing shift work at a chemical plant. One day, he left taking his guns with him as he had done before. After he had been gone for a week, I asked Mama where he was normally I did not ask, but this time I did. All she would say was, "He'll be back." When I persisted, she said, "I don't want to talk about it." I did not ask again.

That spring and summer were the best I had had in a long time. Grant and I started fishing, swimming, and playing baseball with kids in his neighborhood. To go swimming, we would walk for miles on the railroad tracks to the train trestle that crossed White Water River on the other side of Highway 91. We would spend the day jumping off the trestle with other kids. Sometimes, we played chicken with trains. Whoever was the first one to jump was the chicken. Grant and I were proud because we were never the chicken. Of course, we were all on the lookout for the railroad dicks, who would come around occasionally trying to nab us, which they never could.

A rope hung from a big pine tree about forty feet high on the riverbank. The rope was a good thirty feet long, and we had to climb another tree about twenty feet high to reach the rope, hold onto a knot, and swing into the river.

I had two rods and spinning reels, I had brought from Virginia. I also had a couple of long cane poles. When Grant and I were at my house, we would fish at the same lake Cap and I used to go to in the woods behind my house. Other times, Grant and I would fish at White Water River, which was not too far from his house. We dug for big earthworms pretty much everywhere. We found one spot that we had to sneak into that had the biggest ones. I told him how when I was little and lived in Louisiana, I dug some big ones in a graveyard, so we started digging in a graveyard not far from school. We caught a few fish, cleaned them and I would build a fire and we ate them.

One day, Grant said that somebody had told him about good fishing in Escambia Bay. I knew where it was but not how to get to it—it was a long way. We bought frozen shrimp at a Piggly Wiggly and hitchhiked to a fish camp in the Beach area. The same train tracks we jumped from in Maple Wood ran by the fish camp and over a Bay. Beside the railroad tracks were telephone poles and wires running across the bay. After walking almost all the way over the bay, we came to a spot where there was one telephone pole missing. We decided to stop there and fish, and it became our favorite spot. We fished from pilings below the tracks so whenever a train came by, we were never in the way. After a while, the engineers would blow their whistles and grin at us. Because we never messed with the trains, I think they liked seeing us, and we sure liked hearing those loud train whistles.

Grant and I would walk at times to the naval base about three miles away and go to the outdoor pool. One day, I was in the pool and noticed swim goggles lying on the side of the pool. For a little while, I watched to see if anybody was using them. Nobody was. I swam over, grabbed them, put them on quickly, and swam toward the deep end of the pool. I did not see anybody looking my way, so I continued diving in the deep end.

When I came to the surface on one occasion, I noticed two women who looked to be in their mid-twenties standing on the edge of the deep end. One of them started swimming across the pool toward the other side just as I dove under water. I naturally looked in her direction and saw that her bathing suit top had come completely off. I stayed underwater until she reached the other side and fixed her top. I surfaced and tried to look inconspicuous, but I stayed in the area.

She started swimming back to her friend on the other side. Of course, I dove underwater and saw the top of her bathing suit come off again. She had the biggest breasts I had ever seen, but of course, I had seen only a couple.

I swam to Grant and told him what I had seen. We swam back to the deep end and took turns using the goggles whenever she would swim to the other side. After one of her return trips, Grant and I were at the same side of the pool as she was. Shortly she called Grant and me over. We looked at each other sheepishly and went. The woman said, "You two are naughty boys watching me when I'm swimming." Grant and I denied looking. The women laughed and started talking to us; they did most of the talking, and Grant and I nervously hung on their every word as we stared at her breasts almost popping out of her bathing suit.

As it turned out, they were navy waves stationed at the base. Their names were Jenny and Joyce. Jenny, whose bathing suit had kept falling off, asked us if we wanted to go to the Maple Wood drive-in that night. Grant said, "Yeah! We'd like to!" Jenny said she would drive.

Grant and I went into the pools locker room, showered, and changed into our street clothes. I was very skittish and told Grant I did not want to go, but he was very excited about going to a movie with two older women; he talked me into it.

We went out; Jenny and Joyce were waiting for us in Jenny's car. She told me to get into the front seat with her; Grant got into the back seat with Joyce. They were still in their bathing suits. Joyce immediately pulled Grant over to her and put her arm around him. Jenny patted the seat right next to her and motioned for me to sit there. I shook my head and stayed where I was—as close to the door as I could get. She shrugged and drove off.

Jenny drove to their barracks and said they would change into their street clothes. While they were inside, Grant was talking a mile a minute, but I just kept shaking my head and saying, "I don't want to do this." But Grant was my best and only friend, so it did not take much talking for him to convince me to go.

The women came out. Joyce got into the back seat with Grant and started kissing him right away. I was still squeezing myself against the passenger door, but Jenny reached over, took me by the arm, and gently pulled me next to her. She gave me a long kiss and stuck her tongue in my mouth. I guess you could say that was my first French kiss. She smiled. We drove to downtown Maple Wood and stopped at the Park More Restaurant. They went in and came back with burgers and fries for Grant and me.

She then drove to a package store and bought two six-packs of beer. In the parking lot, they said they did not feel right about going to the drive-in. I looked at Grant and asked, "Then what are we going to do?" They laughed as we drove off. Grant and Joyce were making a lot of noise in the back seat. I looked and saw that he had his hand under her blouse as they were kissing.

Jenny drove for about forty-five minutes before pulling into the woods by Cold Water Creek. Jenny told me to bring the beer. She pulled a heavy woolen blanket out of the trunk and headed to the water. Grant and Joyce stayed in the car. She spread the blanket out near the water, sat, and said, "Come on, Johnny, sit. I won't bite." For a while, we sat and talked, with her doing most of the talking. We were drinking beer. She asked me about school and home life. I lied about everything, telling her school was great and that home life was wonderful. I even told her my father had been stationed at the base before retiring.

She lay back on the blanket, sat her beer down, and gently pulled me down onto the blanket beside her. "Johnny, have you ever made love to a girl?" I laughed nervously and said no. That was the truth. What I had experienced years ago was not making love. Jenny put my hand on her breast and said, "That's okay." I lay there as she slowly undressed me and quickly undressed herself. She started kissing me all over and eventually placed her mouth over my semi-erect penis. She started a slow, up-and-down head movement until I was fully erect, and she rolled onto her back and pulled me on top of her. She gently reached down and guided me into her. She took my face in her hands and kissed me long and hard with her tongue again going deep into my mouth.

Though I had never "made love" to a girl before, I knew just what to do; an age-old motion took over my body. It did not take long, and after ejaculating, I started to roll off her, but she said, "No, Johnny. Stay with me." We stayed entwined for a few minutes, and then I rolled off. She rolled with me and held me in her arms saying over and over, "It's okay, Johnny" though I was not responding or saying anything. I lay there thinking how I was going to go to hell and wondered if I would confess this to the priest at my next confession. I made love with Jenny two more times. I thought that if I were already going to hell for the first time, two more times would not hurt.

After a few hours, Grant and Joyce got out of the car and came over. We all talked and drank beer. Sometime after midnight, they drove us to within a mile of my house. All night, Grant wouldn't stop talking about Joyce. He asked me several times about how it had been with Jenny, but I refused to talk about it.

We went to the pool many more times that summer, but we never saw them again. The rest of the summer passed way to fast, and my father returned. I never found out where he had gone, but he seemed angrier when he returned with his guns.

Many years later, I learned that there had been unrest between blacks and whites in Bogalusa, Louisiana, and I wondered if that was where he had gone.

CHAPTER 72

Freida

In the fall of 1961, I started eleventh grade. I could not wait to play football. On the first day of practice, I promised myself to try hard to make first string, so my father would be proud of me.

I had been active over the summer though I was still smoking; I felt I was in good shape.

Practice started, and boy was I wrong; the first week, I was so sore that I felt I wouldn't make it. It was hard, especially when we would do one-on-ones. That involved two dummies lying on the ground and one offensive and one defensive player and one running back with a ball were placed between them. The object was for the player with the ball to run between the dummies, the offensive player to block, and the defensive player to tackle the runner. It seemed that Coach watched me extra close that year maybe because I was a smoker. I worked hard, and by then, I was working out with the first string. I was feeling good about myself. When you played first string for Coach, you were on offense, defense, the punting team, the kickoff team, and the return team. I was playing offensive end and defensive tackle. I loved both positions, but my favorite was defensive tackle. I loved the hitting.

On the field, I learned teamwork and respect but most of all how to listen when Coach spoke. I always did what I was told and sometimes more. Off the field, my only real friend was Grant. We were pretty much inseparable and had a lot in common. Both of us were terrible in school, and we never did homework. One day, an assistant football coach put me in the drivers' education program, which I enjoyed; I ended up with a Florida driver's license.

That fall, a chief petty officer at Whiting Naval Base rented a trailer in our neighborhood. He brought with him the most beautiful silver German shepherd I had ever seen. His name was Chief. He was kept day and night chained to a pine tree in their yard. With memories of Cap guiding me, I soon made friends with Chief. I would see chief petty officer come out of his trailer and Chief start barking and jumping on him trying to lick his face. He would yell at him, hit him on his head, and knock him to the ground. The poor dog never understood and would get back up and again try to approach him, but it was always with the same result. He always smelled of liquor; I don't ever remember seeing him when he was not drunk. Several times, I asked him if I could take Chief for walks, but he always refused me.

He was married to a Philippine woman named Freida, who did not speak a word of English. She only smiled and nodded at me, and I would smile and nod back. One day, he asked me, "Johnny, do you fish?" I replied, "Yes I do." He said, "My wife has been bugging me to take her fishing. I don't fish. Will you take her?" Thinking it might help me get to take Chief for walks, I replied, "Sure I will, anytime." He asked, "How about tomorrow?" I said, "Okay."

Early the next morning, she knocked on our door. She was under five feet tall and was wearing sandals, a baggy dress that hung to the floor, and a huge, brightly colored sun hat that looked like it was made of bamboo. She smiled and showed some missing teeth. With a couple of gestures, she indicated she was ready to go fishing. I retrieved my two cane poles, dug some worms in my backyard, and headed toward the lake through the woods. She had very short legs, and she dragged her feet, but she was always smiling. It took us an hour to reach the lake.

Somebody had left an old, leaky, wooden boat about ten feet long at the lake. It had three seats, and everyone who came to the lake used it. It had an old oil can for bailing water and a couple of old boards for paddles. I did not like the paddles, so I had a long sapling I had cut and had hidden in the brush near the boat that I used to pole the boat with. The area had no fast-moving water, so an anchor was not needed. I poled to a good spot, and we started fishing. We were catching what I called and still do, shit eaters. I threw mine back in, but she wanted to keep hers.

There was always an inch or two of water in the bottom of the boat, so she just threw them in there. It was funny to see them flopping around and her sitting there with a big, toothless grin. She looked happy, and we smiled a lot at each other. After a while, I heard a loud crunching noise. I turned and saw her biting the head off a small fish. Blood and guts were running down her chin as she ate that entire fish. I just smiled and turned back to fishing.

Occasionally, I would hear another crunch and would figure she was eating her fish. I laughed and remembered catching crawfish and eating them raw—shells and all—but not the heads. When we left, Freida did not have any fish to take home, so I figured she must have eaten all she had caught.

A couple of days later, I saw the chief petty officer. He said his wife told him she had had a great time fishing with me and asked, "Will you take her again?" I said, "Sure! Oh, by the way, can I take Chief for a walk?" He said no, but I did take Freida fishing again. I never could talk to her, but I laughed a lot, she smiled a lot, and we enjoyed our time together as she ate raw fish. They lived near us for only a few months. They left while I was at school one day, and I never saw them again.

I told Grant about the fishing trips and how Freida had eaten the fish raw. He said, "You're lying," but I convinced him it was the truth. I even invited him to come with us one time, but he said, "What are you, fucking crazy? I'm not going to watch some woman eat raw fish. Fuck no!" "Fuck no" was Grant's favorite phrase for everything, and it always made me laugh.

CHAPTER 73

Navy Reserve

One day, Grant told me that a marine recruiter had been at school talking to kids about joining after graduation. I asked some other students about what had been said, and after hearing about the training the recruits went through, I decided it was something I would love to do.

That night, I told my father that I was going to join the Marines after I graduated; he did not say a word. A few days later, he woke me at five thirty saying, "Get in the car!" I got dressed and went out to his car. In a couple of minutes, he came out, and we drove off through the woods on dirt roads without saying a word. I knew better than to ask where we were going; I quietly stared out the window.

We arrived at a house. A man dressed in a navy CPO uniform opened the door and ushered us into a room set up like an office. He and my father started talking, and it didn't take long for me to realize that this CPO was a recruiter for the navy reserve. He had a stack of papers in front of him that were all filled out; he pushed one to me saying, "Johnny, sign here and you're in the navy reserve." I looked at my father and then at the recruiter and said, "But I want to join the Marines when I graduate."

Because I was looking at the CPO, I did not see my father's hand. He backhanded me in the mouth and knocked me out of my chair. My father and the CPO were staring daggers at me. My father said, "So help me God, you'll never become a goddamn marine." The CPO said, "Johnny, you don't want to become a marine. It's a dirty job, and nobody likes them. Besides, right after basic training, they'll send you to Vietnam, you'll get killed, and then what will your mother do?"

My father yelled, "Sign the goddamn papers, plowboy!"

I signed the papers, and we left. My father said, "I don't ever want to hear you talk about joining the goddamn Marines!" I said, "Yes sir." He went into the house and I walked into the woods. I stayed there until it was time for me to catch the bus for school.

At school that day, I told Grant what had happened. Grant, my best and only friend, also joined the navy reserve. We went on duty the third weekend of every month at the Naval Air Base in Pensacola, Florida. My father drove us for those weekends.

For the first few months, we went only to classrooms. During Christmas break, the navy sent about twenty reservists, including Grant and me, to boot camp for two weeks. When we left Florida, it was about seventy degrees. When we got off the plane at O'Hare Airport, it was just ten degrees. We took a bus to a train station, where we were met by kids from other states. We took a train to the base. It was cold and snowing, and we were in our summer whites—no coats—and were freezing. Some kids were crying. They made us run carrying our sea bags all the way to an empty warehouse. We stood outside for almost an hour at attention. Finally, a CPO arrived. He told us that he was sorry for having made us wait but that he had to finish watching a wrestling match. I looked at Grant and shrugged. I remembered my first winter in Morgan Creek and how cold I had been. My brain turned the cold off. It was one more experience I shoved deep down inside.

About a half hour later, we were taken into the warehouse, which was unheated. We stood at attention as one by one we were called up to a desk. We answered questions and signed papers. That took about four hours. Around two o'clock that morning, we were taken to a barracks, the first heated place we had been in for hours. We put our gear away and got into our racks—bunk beds—around three AM.

At five sharp, which became normal for us, all lights were turned on and the CPO and other instructors came in yelling and banging on metal trash cans. I thought, *At least they're not throwing cold water in our faces.*

I did not find boot camp hard except for the classroom work, which totally bored me. We had to stand watches at night, two of which were outside—the outside clothesline watch and the dumpster watch. It snowed and was bitterly cold every night. During those watches, we could wear pea coats and gloves. We washed our clothes in the latrine and hung them on the clothesline outside. Every night, we stood watch over the drying clothes that froze solid.

One night at the end of one shift, a sailor on the dumpster watch could not be found. They woke us up, and we scoured the area. It took about two hours before we found him. He had crawled inside the dumpster, covered himself with trash to keep warm, and had fallen asleep.

For the rest of the night, all of us had an outside watch at different locations including a latrine even though it was not used in the winter. The sailor who had fallen asleep was going through boot camp just as we were, and he was our captain. Of course, he did not stand another outside watch that night. He made up a story about how the next sailor was sick and he had volunteered to take his place. Because he had been on two watches back to back and the sailor relieving him was late, he had crawled inside the dumpster to get warm. Not wanting to abandon his post, he accidently fell asleep. I didn't think the CPO believed or cared about his story. I thought he just wanted to show us that when one failed, we all failed. I just smiled and did my job knowing that was the same principle Coach had taught us.

That sleeping sailor had been appointed our captain. Time after time, he lied to the CPO and other instructors about us all. On one night while some sailors were on outside watch, the rest of us were up all night, cleaning the inside latrine with our toothbrushes. One sailor dumped too much soap on the floor, and we wound up with suds about two feet high. It took half the night and all morning—no time for breakfast—to get it all out. That was the last straw. He had to go.

The next night about three in the morning, eight sailors covered him in a blanket head to toe in his rack as he slept. They held the blanket with one hand and beat him with a bar of soap inside a sock with the other. He made so much noise that he woke up the CPO, who was asleep in an adjoining room. By the time the CPO came in, all of us were back in our racks and he was crying and saying how we had beaten him. There were no marks to prove anything, but he continued to blame us. A few days later, the CPO removed him, and we never saw him again. We got to choose our own captain, and that was me. I maintained that position for the rest of boot camp.

Other than the soapsuds incident, which we all laughed about many times, an incident stands out in my memory. One sailor, the biggest of all of us, stood about six five and weighed 220. He was always talking about his girlfriend—how pretty she was, how sexy she was, and how they would get married and have twelve kids. No matter what the conversation was, he started talking about his girlfriend. All the sailors sleeping around his rack knew what he was doing. I happened to sleep in the rack next to his; both of us slept on a top rack. I had a straight line of sight of him every night. About three o'clock one night, the CPO walked into our compartment and yelled at the sailor. The CPO pushed over his rack. He fell out, and his falling rack hit mine and knocked it over.

The CPO yelled, "If you're going to masturbate, then you'll masturbate in front of the entire company." Everyone was awake. All the lights were turned on, and the CPO had us carry a large table to the center of the room. We put a chair and two buckets of warm water on the table. The sailor had to climb on the table, sit in the chair, put his feet in the buckets of warm water, and masturbate. The CPO made us sit in a ring around the sailor and watch until reveille.

I smiled and laughed. I knew what Coach had taught us; he had shown me a path in life I could follow. Grant asked, "Why do you always smile during these things?" I told him what Coach had made me realize—when one fails, we all fail. He didn't get it. Grant said, "Bullshit. He's just a masturbating fool, and this has nothing to do with us." I was saddened for my best friend, but I didn't force the issue.

CHAPTER 74

Home Sweet Home

I came home from boot camp thinking my father would be proud of me. I walked in wearing my uniform and carrying my sea bag. I looked at my family, who were eating. The three looked up, but only my sister said, "Hi, Johnny."

I went into my room, unpacked, stored my sea bag, and changed out of my uniform. Not wanting to sit and talk to my father, I walked past the table toward the back door. My father yelled, "Hey, plowboy, I want you to clean up the goddamn carport. It's full of cat shit!" Our carport had a dirt floor that the cats used as a litter box. Originally, we had had two cats, but at that point, we had about eight. They stayed outside, and some were afraid of people. Sometimes, kittens just disappeared.

One day when a cat was having kittens, Mama yelled and screamed for me to come help her. She was beating the cat with her broom and yelling, "She's eating her babies!" I grabbed the broom, laughed, and said, "Mama, that's how she cleans them after they're born. The cat licks them clean and eats the afterbirth." Mama made a face. "Disgusting damn animals."

I shoveled the cat shit into a bucket and dumped the mess in the woods. I reflected on my past two weeks. It did not bother me going to boot camp over Christmas vacation; my family did nothing for Christmas anyway. Only twice in my past did I get anything for Christmas. The first time, my sister and I received a package from my cousin Drew. He had sent me a pocketknife, which I loved. The second time, about two weeks before Christmas, my father said, "Come out to the car. I want to show you something." He opened the trunk and showed me several boxes. I saw from the pictures on the boxes that they contained a toy kitchen set. He said, "First, I want to tell you that there's no Santa Claus." He pointed to the kitchen set. "This is your sister's present from Santa."

He opened a box and showed me a pair of moccasins that had to be laced with rawhide. One moccasin was already put together, and the other was about halfway put together. He told me sternly, "This is your present, and on Christmas morning, you'll act surprised in front of your sister. You better not say anything to her about there being no Santa!" Just to make sure I understood, he backhanded me and knocked me to the ground. Twice, he made me say, "I will not tell my sister there is no Santa Claus." He left me there, wiping blood off my face. I was nine then.

I never said anything to my sister, but I told Lance, the boy living behind us. With no thought for his feelings, I said, "Lance, there is no Santa Claus. Your parents have your Christmas presents hidden in the trunk of their car." He did not believe me; he got the keys for the car, and we found all his presents in the trunk. He went crying to his mother and father.

That night, my father gave me one of the worst beatings ever. In the process, my pocketknife fell out of my pocket. He picked it up, opened the blade, and said, "You don't need no goddamn pocketknife either!" I never saw that knife again. I was heartbroken for a long time. I always hoped my cousin would send another present, but he never did.

That Christmas morning, my sister and I saw the boxes with the metal kitchen set stacked up on the living room floor all wrapped up. My sister opened them and was thrilled. I did not see the moccasins. My sister woke our father with hugs and kisses. He came out and helped her put the set together. I was trying to sneak outside, but he made me sit on the floor and watch them.

I thought that I did not deserve the moccasins that Christmas. But what I could not understand was what occurred about a month later. One evening, I walked into the trailer and saw Mama sitting alone in the living room and smiling. Beside her was the box with the moccasins I had seen that night in the trunk. They were in the same condition I had seen them in. Smiling, she said, "Johnny, this is your Christmas present. Your father spent a lot of money for them, but he doesn't have time to put both together, so you finish them, okay?"

Without answering her, I took the box, grabbed a knife from the kitchen, and walked out into the woods. I cut both moccasins up. I gathered some wood, sat the box on top, and set them on fire with my Zippo. I sat smiling as they burned. Nobody ever asked me anything about them. I started crying. I looked toward my house, where my family was eating dinner. I hated and blamed myself. All I wanted was to die.

For the rest of that winter, I took showers under that hose hanging from the pine tree. The weather was cold, but it did not seem to bother my father, and I had no choice. We showered only about two or three times a week. During that winter, he raped me only occasionally.

I now realize he was preparing me for what was coming.

CHAPTER 75

The Bug

One Saturday morning in the spring of 1962, Hal, a young sailor stationed at the navy base, who had worked for my father there, and his wife, Laura, visited us. They were from Yonkers, New York. Hal was a very funny man, and I enjoyed his company. His wife was very quiet but nice also. Hal had a car I had fallen in love with—a black and yellow '56 Chevy convertible. When he came to visit, I would beg him to let me take it for a drive. By then, I had a driver's license. He always let me, but he would go along.

One time as I was driving along Highway 81 toward Maple Wood, Hal asked me if I would like to buy his car. I immediately said yes and asked him how much he wanted. He said, "Johnny, I know how much you love this car, and knowing you're in high school, you'd look awesome driving it. I'll sell it to you for six hundred." I was totally amazed at the cost. At the time, I was working part time at a gas station and planned to work there, full time during the summer. During the day, Ray, the owner, usually worked with his father, and after school, I would work with his father and Ray would go home. He lived right behind the gas station, so if we got into a pickle, he could come right over.

I was making about $10 per week pumping gas, patching and changing tires, and whatever else needed to be done. I told Hal I could pay him $5 or $6 a week; I needed some money for gas. He said, "I'm sorry, Johnny, but I need cash to pay off a debt. I've been playing poker with some people off the base, and I owe them six hundred. If I don't get them the money in a couple of weeks, I don't want to think about what they'll do to Laura."

Letting out a big sigh, I said, "You know how much I want to buy your car, but the money will have to come from my father." Hal said, "I know, but there's nothing I can do about it. I really need the cash." I said, "Okay. I'll talk with Mama and see what happens."

We drove to a Dairy Queen for a shake. I had always enjoyed doing that, but that time, I was depressed. I knew there was no way my father would ever buy that beautiful car for me. I remembered the old Cushman scooter that looked as if it had gone through World War II.

I drove home slowly; I thought it would be the last time I would get to drive the car, and I wanted it to last if possible.

We got home. My father was gone. When Hal left, I asked Mama about the car. She reminded me that my father had spent good money on the scooter and that I had never appreciated it or thanked him for it and had just left it on the side of the road for somebody to take. I said, "Ma'am, that's not what happened!" She said, "I don't want to discuss it. You treated your father terribly, and you deserved to have that wreck when you fell off it." But I begged her to speak to my father about buying it, and she finally agreed to do that.

I worked that afternoon and told Jay, Ray's father, about my morning with Hal and how he wanted to sell me his car. He was curious about the convertible and asked me all kinds of questions about it though he had seen it many times as he or I gassed it up for Hal. After talking about the car for some time, he pointed at his car, a beautiful, black-and-white '56 Mercury two door. "Johnny, I'll sell you my car for six hundred."

I had admired his car but had never driven it. He said, "I don't need it anymore, and I hardly ever drive it." I was floored. In one day, I had gotten chances to buy two beautiful cars I had always admired. I reminded him that once summer started, I would start working full time. I asked him if I could make payments every week. He said, "I'm sorry, Johnny, but I prefer cash." I told him that the money would have to come from my father. He said, "Okay, no rush."

I spoke with Mama about this different car. Again, she was not enthused about the idea, but she said she would speak to my father about both cars.

Days passed, weeks passed, but I heard nothing from Mama or my father, and my hopes vanished. I worked every afternoon with Jay, but he asked me only once if I was going to buy his car. I told him that my father had not given me an answer yet. I never heard from Hal, and I never saw him at the gas station either. In my heart, I knew he was gone.

Early one morning about two months later after school had let out for the summer, my father woke me at five thirty. I did not get right up, so I got the usual glass of cold water in my face. He said, "I don't want you leaving this house today, do you understand me?" I was half asleep. I said, "I'm supposed to start working full time at Ray's gas station today. I have to be there at seven." He backhanded me and knocked me back onto my bed. "You heard what I said, plowboy. Don't talk back. Do you understand?" Lying on the bed, I said, "Yes sir." He walked out of the house. I heard him start his car and drive away.

I got dressed, made my bed, and walking to the kitchen. Mama asked me if I wanted some breakfast. I told her, "No thanks, ma'am." I walked out the back door. For the rest of the day, I just hung around the house not doing anything but trying to understand what I had done wrong that time. Because of the way the morning had started, I did not think of calling Ray to tell him I couldn't come into work that day.

About four that afternoon, I was sitting on my bed looking at a *Playboy* magazine Grant had given me that I kept hidden under my dresser. I heard a strange car pull into our driveway. I went into the living room; Mama was standing in the front door. She said, "Your father's home." I looked out as my father was getting out of a light-blue VW Beetle. With a frown on my face, I backed up as my father came stomping through the door. He told me, "I paid nine hundred for this goddamn car for you." He handed me a set of keys and said, "Let's take it for a ride. You drive!"

I got into the driver's seat, and my father got into the passenger's seat. The car had a manual shift; I had driven only automatics, but from conversations with other kids, I knew a standard shift car had a clutch pedal as well as gas and brake pedals. I started it, put it in first, and let the clutch out. The car lurched forward. I pressed on the clutch just as my father yelled at me, "Put it in reverse, goddamn it!" I put the car in reverse, and the car started going backward bucking as it moved slowly. I backed onto the dirt road and put the car into a different gear. It started forward bucking and lurching. After I drove for a distance, the engine was racing. My father yelled, "Shift it, goddamn it!"

I was shaking uncontrollably. After shifting into another gear—I was only guessing where the gears were or how many there were—I continued to drive as the car bucked and jumped. "Goddamn it! Shift again! Do I have to tell you everything, plowboy?"

I shifted gears, and the car lurched and bucked again. Fearing the worst, I pulled away as far as I could from my father leaning against my door. Nothing happened. Stepping on the gas pedal, I continued driving to the end of the road, where I stopped.

Looking both ways, I put the car in gear and started to pull out onto Highway 81. The car bucked hard and then stalled. I turned to my father, and in a small and shaking voice, I said, "Sor—." That's as far as I got. He punched me full in the mouth, drawing blood. "Goddamn it! Can't you ever do anything right, plowboy?" The back of my head hit the doorjamb, and I became fuzzy headed.

Looking down through the blood and tears, I tried to start the car, but it was in gear, and I had not depressed the clutch. My father backhanded me. I heard a loud ringing in my ear. He said, "Goddamn it! You'll never amount to anything!"

I pulled the keys out of the ignition and threw them at him. For the first time in my life, in a broken and defeated voice, I screamed, "Keep the fucking car! I didn't want the goddamn thing anyway!" I got out and started stumbling toward my house.

I got home and sat on the couch. My head was hurting, the ringing in my ear was loud, and my lips were bleeding. Mama got a dish towel, put some ice cubes in it, and handed it to me. "What happened? Did you have an accident? Where's your father?" I told her I had given the keys back to him and told him I did not want the car. She said, "Your father spent a lot of money on that car for you. He traded his car in for two of those VWs. He bought one for himself and the other for you. Don't you dare talk back to him, do you hear me?"

Before I could answer, my father stomped in the house. He threw the keys onto the table and said, "There are the keys. The goddamn car is yours whenever you decide you want to drive it! The gas tank is full, but you'll get a job and put your own gas in it!" I got up and walked out of the back door as he screamed, "You'll never amount to anything, plowboy!"

The next day, somebody came to pick my father up, and they left. A couple of hours later, my father came back driving a black VW Beetle. The blue VW was still in the driveway. I walked to Ray's gas station and gave him a story about how I had fallen and hurt myself, and that was why I had not come into work the day before. My face was black and blue, and my lips were swollen and cut. My ear was still ringing. I knew he knew the truth because he knew my father. With sorrow in his voice, he said, "I'm sorry, Johnny, but I have to let you go. My father is old and not well. If I can't depend on you, I'll have to find someone else." I pleaded with him. "My father has bought me a car, and you can depend on me. Please, I really need this job." He said, "I'm sorry, Johnny, but I have to find somebody else."

I walked home and told Mama that Ray had fired me. She said, "Well, you better find a job quick before your father finds out."

That afternoon, I walked to Grant's house. He looked at my bruised face and shook his head. Nothing needed to be said, but I did tell him about the car. He asked me why I had not driven it to his house. I told him I really did not want it. He asked, "Are you fucking crazy?"

We talked and laughed about what we could do with a car. When I told him, I had gotten fired at Ray's and I did not know where I could get a job, he said, "Somebody told me that farmers in Allentown were hiring workers to pick and load watermelons." I said, "We don't know anything about picking and loading watermelons, but how hard could it be?" I slept at his house for a couple of days. When I got home, the VW was still in the driveway.

For the next week, I just hung around the house looking at that car. Grant's words were ringing in my ears. Every time my father saw me, he would look at me with a scowl; I saw hate in his eyes. I avoided him as much as possible.

One morning after he had awakened me with that hated glass of water, he left for work. After hanging around the house for a couple of hours, I drove the Beetle to Grant's house. I had a couple of shifting mishaps, but nothing serious.

Grant came out all excited. He got in, and off we went. We drove all over town not going anywhere in particular. We had a full tank of gas. My father had said that the car would get about thirty-five miles per gallon. He also said that if I ran out of gas, I could pull a lever and would have another gallon of reserve gas.

I didn't have any money, but Grant said he had a couple of dollars. He also said that he had just heard that the Piggly Wiggly store needed people to pass out flyers. I drove to the store, and we spoke to the manager. He said he would pay each of us $10 per week for passing out flyers every day. We took the job knowing we would not get paid until the end of the week.

I drove, and Grant stuck flyers in mailboxes and doors in just about every house in downtown Maple Wood. We still had a huge stack of flyers left, so we drove to the outskirts of town and distributed the flyers. We handed them to passers-by as well. We were putting two or three in each bundle we handed out because we had so many. By the end of the week, we hated our job. We received our $10 and quit.

A couple of days later, we met up with two friends from school, Sandy and Ryan. All four of us were interested in getting jobs. Remembering what Grant had heard about farmers hiring people to work in their fields, I drove the four of us to Allentown. We stopped at a neighborhood store and asked about jobs in the area. The owner said he knew a farmer who was looking for workers to pick and load watermelons. He made a phone call, and then he told us to be at the store by five the next morning and the farmer would meet us there.

I stayed at Grant's house that night. We got up at four, picked up Sandy and Ryan, and got to the store at four forty-five. At five, a farmer drove up in an old truck. We got into the back of his truck, and he drove us to a field near Cold Water Creek.

That day, we loaded his old truck several times with watermelons and ended up sore. But as the days went by, the soreness left us, and we started enjoying the hard, hot work. We were working Monday through Friday sunup to sundown and making $4 a day, which was top pay then. The work was hard, but we were young and enjoyed it. I don't know how many melons we loaded and unloaded from that old truck into tractor-trailers, but I do know that by the time watermelon season was over, I swore that I never wanted to see, much less eat, another watermelon ever.

Soon, we gained a reputation, as hard workers in the area. Every morning, we showed up at the store early, and several farmers would show up wanting us to work for them. We did not want to split up, so we worked only for the farmers who would hire all four of us. The first day after melon season ended, we showed up as usual, but no farmers did. By five thirty that morning, we figured we would have to find jobs elsewhere. We were just about ready to leave when a new pickup truck driven by a well-dressed man arrived. His truck bore the name of a farm we recognized; it was owned by the owner of a bank in Maple Wood. The driver introduced himself as the foreman and said he wanted to hire all four of us for top pay five days a week, sunup to sundown, for the rest of the summer. We all accepted, and I started driving us right to the farm.

The work again was hard, and the weather was hot. Sometimes, we helped clear land. Other times, we picked corn, peanuts, and cotton. When hay was cut, we would load the bales, which weighed between 80 and 110 pounds, onto a trailer and then into the loft of a barn. On some days when we had to work late, sometimes until two or three in the morning, we were paid an extra dollar for that day.

In the fields, we worked next to black men who were earning $4 per day just as we were. Sometimes, their wives and kids worked in the fields, but they were usually paid only $1 per day. After learning that and without telling anybody except Grant, I told the foreman to add my and Grant's extra dollars—Grant had agreed to this—to one black family's wages. The man, his wife, and his four kids ages six, seven, eight, and nine worked in the fields right beside us. The foreman agreed, and nothing else was ever said by the foreman or Grant and me.

As the summer got hotter and hotter, the foreman would give us an hour off for lunch. Every day, the four of us drove over to Cold Water Creek and played football in the water. It was only about two feet deep in the deepest section we played in, but it was refreshing.

In August, football practice started. I went in that season tanned and feeling in the best shape I had ever been in. One day as the players were going to the locker room after practice, Coach said, "Johnny, you're doing very well. Do you feel in shape for the season?" I replied, "Yes, Coach, I feel great." He said, "Good. I think it's going to be a great year. Maybe we'll win them all."

That year, the Maple Wood High Panthers went undefeated. We averaged over forty points per game. Our closest game was 28–21. That Monday's practice was so hard that I believe you can find people in Maple Wood who still talk about it today.

Other than football, school still held no interest for me. I believe if I had not been playing football, I probably would have dropped out. My grades were terrible, but I just made it through thanks to football. I learned more from Coach than I ever learned at home, or elsewhere. During one game, our running back was being tackled at the line of scrimmage every time he ran in my direction. Coach pulled me aside at halftime and asked, "Johnny what's your blocking assignment on thirty-three trap?" I said, "Inside gap next to widest man." He asked, "So who have you been blocking?" I said, "There's no man in the inside gap, so I've been blocking the man head-on our tackle." Coach said, "Johnny, the middle linebacker is the next-to-widest man. You've been blocking the wrong man, and that's why we can't run anything your way." I said, "Okay, Coach, I'll block the right man from now on." The Coach said something that I have kept with me and used my entire life. He said, "Johnny,

I don't ever want you to block the wrong man again, but if you do, I want to see you put that man all the way to the ground, so he will always remember you after that block. Do you understand me?" I replied, "Yes, Coach."

His words became an inspiration for my life. I started entering situations with the intent of seeing them through, not stopping, and doing everything to the best of my ability. I have gratefully passed on that attitude over the years to kids I coached, in baseball and football. Kids I also met as a juvenile officer.

During the football season that year, I met Gina, a cheerleader for the junior football team. We started hanging out together a lot. The local radio station would broadcast our Friday-night games. Every Saturday morning, I would drive to her house, and Gina, her mother, and I would listen to a repeat broadcast of the game while they cleaned up and bandaged all my bumps, bruises, scratches, and cuts. I loved every minute of their doting on me.

But they did not realize that only a few of my bruises and scrapes were due to football; the rest were from my father. One time, he hit me so hard that my bottom teeth cut right through my lip. I showed Gina and her mother that I could stick my tongue through the gash. I told them it had happened the night before during the game. Other than Grant and until the writing of this story, I have never told anybody the truth about how that had occurred.

After the football season was over, Gina's father, who was in the navy, was transferred to Tennessee.

During the fall of 1962, I always took showers after football practice or a game. I was also coming in later at night trying to avoid my father's sexual abuse. For the most part, it worked. The rapes were occurring only about every two weeks but at no set time. Sometimes, he would wake me up in the middle of the night and say, "Let's go take a shower." After so many years of physical and sexual abuse, I had accepted that as part of life. I never discussed it with anybody except Grant, but by then, there was not much more to say about it.

In late 1962, after football was over and through the winter of 1963, Grant worked pumping gas at a station across the street from Sky Line Heights, a subdivision on Highway 81 outside Maple Wood. Grant called me the day he got the job. He told me he would split his weekly pay, $25, if I would help him during his shift. I agreed even though the shift was from 6:00 p.m. to 6:00 a.m. He said we could take turns sleeping, but as it turned out, neither of us could sleep very much. Much of the time, we used his cash bank and played poker.

My most memorable moment that winter was one cold, windy night. It was raining real hard. We were playing poker when a car pulled up to the pumps and the driver started blowing his horn. Grant and I kept signaling to the driver that we did not want to go out in the pouring rain, but he continued blowing his horn. Finally, Grant and I played rock, scissors, and paper, and I lost. I ran out to the car, and the young man rolled his window down and said, "I'm sorry, but this is all I have." He handed me 17¢. Gas was 25¢ a gallon. I took his money and gave him a full gallon. He again said, "I'm sorry, but that was all I had." I said, "That's okay." He drove off. He never knew I had given him an extra 8¢ of gas. I went in and told Grant, and we had a good laugh. I said, "That's something we'll remember for the rest of our lives, huh?" He laughed and said, "Fuck yeah." True to our laugh, I included this story here.

I had told Mama about Grant getting the job and me helping him out. When I told her the hours, she asked, "What about school?" I told her we were taking turns sleeping at the station. Nobody at home questioned me that winter.

In January 1963, the sexual abuse abruptly stopped. I thought maybe he was proud of me because I had a job. Grant had weekends off, so we spent the time together.

The last day of school, a group of us decided to wear only T-shirts. We were sent to Mr. Casey, the assistant principal, and he said, "Go home and put on regular shirts. Don't come back until you do." I had driven Grant to school that day, and he and I had shirts in my Bug, but we left school for a couple of hours just to get away for a while and drink some of his stepfather's wine. We put our regular shirts on and went back to finish the school day.

The day of graduation was just like another day for me. Nobody from my family attended. The talk that day was about a party at the home of our biggest football player. That night right after dark, Grant and I drove to the party. Just as we got out of the car, I heard somebody I recognized yell out that he had a girl's bra and was wondering where she was. Somebody yelled that she had just taken off to the beach with the host. Grant and I walked around for a while. Though we knew all the kids there, we felt out of place among them. We stayed only for a short time. I knew where we could buy beer and wine, no questions asked. We bought a six-pack of Blue Ribbon and a bottle of cheap wine, and we drove out to Cold Water Creek. Grant and I built a fire, talked, and drank. School was over. We had no idea what we wanted to do.

CHAPTER 76

Graceland

Grant and I were still going to the navy reserve meetings once a month. One time, we went aboard a DE—a destroyer escort. Sometimes, the ship went to sea just for the weekend.

One day, a farmer called me and said he had heard about me and my work ethic from other farmers. He asked me if I would be willing to work for him full time Monday through Friday for $5 a day with an extra dollar when we worked into the night. The hours were the standard sunup to sundown and included supper.

I found the farmer to be honest and hard working. Every evening at five, we ate supper fixed by his wife. Every meal included some type of corn. My favorite was her creamed corn.

As it had been the previous summer, the work was hard, it was hot, and the hours were long. The farmer owned cattle, so most of his crops were corn, peanuts, and cotton. He had a corn-picking machine, but it wasted about four rows of corn. To offset that, I would drive his pickup over two rows and pick the corn on either side. I put the corn in sacks that I emptied into the bed of the truck. When the truck was full, I would drive to the barnyard and unload the corn into a bin that was hoisted and dumped into the top of a silo. The farmer had many acres of corn, so it took a few weeks to complete this task.

Later, after he had driven the corn picker through the entire field, I drove the pickup back over the downed stalks and repicked the area. The farmer was very appreciative saying, "I lose about a ton of corn a year due to the picker."

Several times that summer when things were slow for one reason or another, he would give me his old, bolt-action, single-shot .22 caliber rifle and told me to go in the fields and woods and shoot as many crows and squirrels as I could. He said that he lost another ton of corn a year to such varmints. Because I had done a lot of squirrel hunting, that was an easy job, and I loved it. Whenever I came upon a squirrel eating corn, it would climb a tree and sit still—an easy target. To make it a little more fun, I would throw a stick to make it run, and then I would shoot it. I skinned and cleaned the squirrels and gave them to his wife, who cooked them for dinner the following night usually in a stew.

I had never hunted crows. I knew that when some were on the ground, others were perched in high places watching for danger. What I did not know was that some of these watchers were noisy, but that was a distraction because I found out they also had some that were very quiet. If you did not know where the quiet ones were, you never saw them until they sounded the alarm. There was only one occasion when I was able to shoot a crow. One early fall day, the sun was hidden by clouds and the wind was blowing. It took me about an hour before I finally was able to spot the silent crow. I snuck up close enough to shoot a crow that was feeding on corn. When I shot it, it started cawing very loudly. All the other crows flew to the downed crow, even the crows that were on watch, as if to help. They saw me and did something I had never seen or heard about—they attacked the silent crow that had been on watch; they pecked him relentlessly, they flew away. He was just lying on the ground bloodied and unable to fly. I walked over and saw that his injuries were massive. I shot him. After that, I was never able to sneak up close enough to shoot one of those crows.

That fall after work at the farm was finished, I had saved some money and decided to drive to Tennessee to see Gina and her family. I happened to mention it to my friend Ryan. A couple of days later, his mother called me. She said that she was originally from Tennessee and asked if I would take her and her daughter with me and Ryan. She said she would pay for the entire trip.

The day I was leaving, I told Mama, but she asked only, "When will you come back, Johnny?" I told her in a couple of weeks. Giving her Gina's phone number in case she needed to get in touch with me, I left. Having not seen my father in more than a week, I never mentioned him to Mama.

It took the four of us two days to drive to Tennessee in my Bug. I dropped Ryan, his mother, and his sister off at his aunt's house in Memphis. I then drove to Gina's house. Her family was happy to see me, and I was thrilled to see them, but I could tell the feelings between Ray and me were not the same. We went out two nights in a row, but both times, she brought her girlfriend along. They sat in the back seat and spent the entire evening talking giggling with each other, ignoring me. I felt hurt and left out. I liked her a lot, but between my father's abuse and Mama's always telling me to stay away from girls, I couldn't bring myself to say, it.

After spending two nights of feeling rebuffed by Gina, I did not want to put her through a painful reunion, so I left on the third morning. I drove to Memphis and stayed with Ryan and his family, who gave me a warm welcome.

That night as I was falling asleep, my thoughts returned to Gina. I realized our relationship in Maple Wood had been based on football. I had graduated, and her family had moved; I realized that she had moved on, but I was stuck in the past. With a smile, I thought, *Good for you, Gina. I wish only the best for you, and I love you.*

Wanda, one of Ryan's aunts, was full of life, and she laughed a lot. She was fun to be with. She told us about a blind date she had had in high school. At the last minute, she had canceled the date. She found out much later that her date had been with Elvis. For the rest of her life, she kicked herself for not going on the date.

Several times, she drove Ryan, his sister, and me past Graceland. One time as we were driving past, I asked her, "Do you think we could go inside and see it?" She said, "I don't know." There was a side gate with a guard where she pulled up and parked. All four of us got out and approached him. He was an elderly man probably in his sixties. Wanda asked if we could go inside, and he said, "No, I'm sorry, but you can't." She asked if Elvis was there, and he said, "No, he's in Hollywood making a movie."

While they were talking, I saw that he had a spinning rod and reel and was trying to untangle the line. I asked him about it, and he said, "Elvis gave it to me the last time he was here, but I'm having a terrible time with it. It keeps on getting tangled up every time I use it." I said, "I have one myself that I've used many times. I could get it straightened out for you and show you how to use it." With gratefulness in his voice he said, "Thank you." He handed the rod and reel to me.

While I worked diligently on the tangled mess, Wanda asked the guard many questions about Elvis. It took me a little while, but I got the line untangled. I showed him the proper way to cast a spinning reel. I even showed him how to do it if he was casting under a tree. He was so thankful that he let us go inside the gate. We did not go up to or inside the house, but we did get a closer look at the pink Caddy under a carport. Wanda was beside herself. She must have thanked me a hundred times for getting us inside.

Late one afternoon, Ryan's mother asked me if I would drive Ryan and his sister to the store to pick up some items for supper. Before I had a chance to answer, a cousin of Ryan's who lived next door said, "I'll drive them." The three of us got into her car, and she drove to a store. Ryan, his sister, and I went in to buy what his mother had requested, and she drove us home. As I was about to get out of the car, I said, "Damn. I forgot to buy some Lucky Strikes." I asked Ryan and his sister, "Would you guys like to ride back to the store with me?" Before they could answer, Ryan's cousin said, "I'll drive you, Johnny. Ryan, why don't you take the items in to your mother." Thinking nothing of her offer, Ryan said, "Okay. See you later, Johnny."

By then, it was after dark. She drove me back to the same store, where I bought a couple of decks of Lucky Strikes. We drove off, but she was not heading back in the same direction we had come in. When I asked her about it, she said, "I want to show you a very beautiful spot before we go back." After driving for about half hour, she stopped on a hill overlooking the Mississippi River with the bridge going to Tupelo, Mississippi, in the background. I marveled at the view and told her so. Looking straight ahead, she said, "This is a beautiful spot, and it's very special to me. Johnny, do you find me attractive?" Taken aback, I said, "Yeah, I guess so." I lit a Lucky with a shaking hand. She moved over next to me, took the Lucky out of my mouth, threw it out of the window, and kissed me passionately, pushing her tongue deep into my mouth. Pulling back, she started unbuttoning my shirt, and by then, I was caught up in the moment as well.

We made love twice for what seemed hours; I smoked two Lucky Strikes in between. Finally, she said, "I better get you back." She drove me back. As we sat in the driveway, I kissed her and asked, "Can I see you again?" She didn't answer, so I got out of the car. She smiled and said, "Goodbye, Johnny," and drove off.

When I got inside, Ryan's mother asked me if I was hungry. I said, "No ma'am," and went into the living room to watch TV with Ryan and his sister. Nobody asked me why I had been gone so long.

I never saw Ryan's cousin again. I learned later from Ryan that she had gotten married right after our visit.

CHAPTER 77

Viva Mexico

A couple of days later, Mama called. She was upset. "Johnny, I've been trying to locate you for several days. I called Gina's family, but they said you'd left three days ago and didn't know where you had gone. I remembered Ryan's last name and talked to his father. He gave me this number." I asked, "Okay, ma'am, why are you calling?" She said, "The navy called. You're supposed to go on a two-week cruise next week. You need to come home now!" I told Ryan and his mother, and we left for home the next morning.

I got home, and my father and sister were not there. Mama said, "Daddy took Dora to Sears in Pensacola for school clothes." She never asked anything about my trip, so as I had always done, I didn't give her any information. I walked into my bedroom, sat on the bed, and took my clothes out of the paper bags they were in. I took my clothes to the utility room next to the washing machine. I walked to the backyard and sat under that pine tree. I looked at the hose and reflected on the past year. I felt crushed that my father had never taken me shopping for new clothes. I felt I must have been a very bad kid. I knew if I wanted to impress him, I would have to try even harder. I drew my legs up and cried.

Later that evening, my father and sister returned. She was very happy and wanted to show me her new clothes. I ignored her and walked to my room. My father said, "I want to see you outside." He walked out the back door. I followed thinking we were headed for our nightly shower. He was waiting for me in the carport. His eyes were shining brightly in the dim light coming through the door from the kitchen area.

I stopped and heaved a big sigh and looked down. He said, "Goddamn it, when I get your sister in a happy mood, don't spoil it for her. Do you understand, plowboy?" I said, "Yes sir, I do, but—" That was as far as I got. He punched me in the head and knocked me down. My head hit hard, and for a few moments, I lay there dazed. I started to get up. He grabbed me by the throat, pulled me to my feet, and slung me toward the middle of the carport. As I fell into the sand face-first in cat shit, he screamed, "Clean up all this goddamn cat shit, plowboy!"

He went inside, and I tried to wipe the cat shit off my face. I had to use my shirt to get the shit out of my nose and eyes and off my lips. I shoveled the cat shit into a bucket and pitched it into the woods. I washed the cat shit off with Ivory soap under the hose.

I walked inside. Mama was cooking supper. My father and sister were nowhere in sight. I walked toward my bedroom and saw that her door was shut. I heard giggling. My father was talking, but his words were muffled. I went in my room for a clean shirt and left. Mama never said a word to me though she had seen me entering and leaving.

I drove to Grant's house, and we went to a diner for burgers and fries. We talked about our upcoming cruise. I never mentioned the run-in with my father. Grant saw the redness on the right side of my face but said nothing. No words were needed.

I spent several days and nights at Grant's. As we had before, we heard his stepfather beating his mother and brothers. Even today, I can hear their cries of despair. During those days, Grant and I helped ourselves to his stepfather's homemade wine.

The day before we were to report for duty, I went home but made sure it was when my father was at work. I packed my sea bag with my uniforms and personal items—a toothbrush and a partially used bar of Ivory soap that I wrapped in a pair of underwear. I left the house without either my sister or Mama saying a word to me. I was feeling good because I knew I would be away from my father for two weeks.

That night, I slept in my VW after buying a bottle of wine from a place where no IDs were asked for, a store owned and operated by a black man. He also sold moonshine, and he was always trying to get me to buy some. Grant and I did by a Mason jar of it from him once, but it was too strong for us; beer or wine was our fix.

The next day, I drove with Grant to the naval base in Pensacola, and we boarded the USS *Bird,* a navy reserve ship. We left port and docked in Key West, Florida, a few days later. That was a fun time for Grant and me. For the first time, I felt like a grownup in my uniform. Shipmates and people, I met treated me as an equal, not as a kid. Grant and I drank in many bars; draft beer was cheap, and we were never asked for IDs.

On our third night on liberty, Grant and I along with several shipmates were in a bar, The Tomato Patch. We had just started drinking when I suddenly thought of home. I guess you could say I got homesick or something worse; I am still not sure. I started drinking faster. I drank so much and got so drunk that I didn't remember what happened after that. Grant and my other shipmates told me about it later.

Grant and another shipmate half-carried me back to the base. After going through the front gate, I broke away from them and walked to a submarine used as an advertisement for the navy. I started beating on it and yelling, "Why? Why are you doing this to me?" Days later, Grant told me he knew why I was yelling, but everybody else had just laughed.

Grant and another shipmate half-carried me to the ship. At the pier, I again broke away from them and jumped into the murky water ten or fifteen feet below. Earlier that day, a barge had been tied up there. Grant told me, "If that barge had still been there, you'd probably have died from the fall."

I asked Grant for more information. At first, he didn't want to tell me. I said, "Grant, you know what I've been living through at home. I need to know what I did and why!"

He said, "Okay. Just as you jumped, you yelled, 'Fuck it! I don't care!'"

I asked him if I said anything else; he said no. I have always thought there was something else I said, but my friend never told me. I had never told him I wanted to commit suicide, but I had said, "I wish I were dead" and "I wish I had never been born, many times." Looking back, I believe that was my first attempt of suicide, even though I was in a drunken stupor.

He said he and another shipmate had climbed down a ladder and pulled me out. He said it had taken some talking to get me to climb up the ladder. In the water, I had lost one shoe, my hat, and my kerchief. Upon reaching the top of the pier, I had collapsed, and Grant and another shipmate carried me aboard to the mess deck and tried to get me to drink black coffee. Unsuccessful they carried me to our berthing compartment, undressed me, and put me in my rack.

My first memory after being in the bar was waking up in my rack. Finding myself very thirsty, I walked over to a scuttlebutt—a drinking fountain on a ship. I could tell the ship was underway. I got a drink, went back to my rack, and fell asleep.

My next memory was me sitting on a deck in the engine room, where my duty station was. I had a shit can—a metal bucket used for just about everything—between my legs, and I was throwing up into it. I looked up asked a third-class shipmate if I could go back to the berthing compartment. He was disgusted with me. "Get the fuck out of here!" he said. I was only a reservist, and he was regular navy, so I now understand his uncompassionate statement.

The next day, I was back to work in the engine room. The first assignment I was given was to go to the boiler room with a shit can and bring back a bucket of steam. Arriving, first-class boilerman sent me to another location, the people there sent me to another, and the people there sent to yet another. In all, I was sent to about six locations for a bucket of steam. Eventually, a chief set me straight and sent me back to the engine room. All my shipmates had a good laugh, and I laughed with them. It felt good that they would include me in a joke.

That night, I was in my rack asleep when my first class from the engine room woke me at midnight saying, "It's your watch to go up on the bow and watch for the mail buoy." I had to get in uniform and carry a flashlight to notify the bridge when I saw the buoy. Standing on the bow in the rain, I could hardly see anything, but I kept at my post for hours. Just after daylight, it was still raining. I wondered why I had not been relieved after four hours. An officer approached me. I came to attention. He asked, "Sailor, what in the hell are you doing out here?" In what I hoped was a professional voice, I replied, "Watching for the mail buoy, sir." Covering is mouth he chuckled. "Son, there is no mail buoy." He ordered me to report to my work station. As I was walking away, he laughed and said, "Mail buoy. That's a good one." My shipmates in the engine room had another good laugh. Thinking of the lessons coach had taught me about team work, I again laughed with them.

Later that day, I saw Grant, and he too laughed saying, "The whole ship knows." For the next several days, I was in a deep depression. The night before we were scheduled to dock, I found myself on the fantail—the rear end of the ship. I investigated the dark water and thought about my life. I felt I did not mean anything to anybody. I thought about jumping overboard and ending it all. But a voice in my head said, *don't do it. You can and will prove to your father that you can amount to something.* Out loud, I asked, "When? How?" The voice said, *You will.* With confusion and a big sigh, I returned to my berthing compartment. That night, my dreams were filled with happy times I had had with Cap.

The next day, the ship docked in Veracruz, Mexico. Following all the old sea dogs, Grant and I went to all the bars they did. After our first liberty in Key West, Grant and I had only $10 between us. We exchanged that for 150 pesos and thought we were rich.

On our second night on liberty, I met Juanita. I had fifty pesos left, and Grant had sixty. Beer was very cheap. She wanted to take me across the street for ten pesos. Her girlfriend wanted to take Grant for the same amount. We offered to pay only five pesos. We haggled with them, but our lust won over, and we agreed on ten pesos each.

We walked across the street with the laughing girls who were speaking in Spanish. I told Grant, "I should have paid more attention in Spanish class." Grant asked, "You took a year. What did you learn?" Looking at him with a stern gaze, I said, "Si," and we broke out laughing.

The girls took us to adjoining rooms. The floor was dirt. A bed sat in a corner. A hose hanging from the ceiling completed the room's furnishings. There was a continuous drip from the hose that ran onto a piece of wood in the dirt. The puddle of water ran under the wall and out of sight. The room had no roof.

Juanita undressed, lay down on the wooden bed, and with open arms motioned for me to join her. Instead, I sat at the foot of the bed still in my uniform. I couldn't take my eyes off that damned hanging hose. With shaking hands, I pulled a rubber from my pocket keeping my back to her. I had never used a rubber before. I took it out of its wrapper slowly. The ship's doctor had stood on the gangway as we were leaving to go on liberty and passed out rubbers to all of us. I unwrapped it and saw it was rolled up. I blew into it as if it were a balloon to check for leaks, as the Doctor had told us to do.

Juanita was now sitting behind me speaking in Spanish with her legs on either side of me. I felt her large breasts pushing into my back, and she was laughing. Grant's girl in the next room yelled something in Spanish, Juanita yelled something back, and they laughed. I was blowing hard, but the damn thing would not blow up. I kept at it until finally it started to balloon out. Juanita hit me on the back saying, "Let's fuck." At least that is what it sounded like. When she hit me, the rubber, which was ballooned out, slipped from my hand and zoomed away. I was horrified as I saw it land in the dirt. I picked it up and tried to brush the dirt off it. Juanita was laughing hysterically. She knocked the rubber out of my hand and started undoing my belt saying over and over, "Let's fuck." I was not sure, but I thought that was the only English she knew. I stood there in a fog as she undressed me. Standing in the dirt naked and barefooted, she pulled me on top of her as she lay back on the bed.

I think the act took about a minute. She pushed me off and walked to the hose. As she started talking to me in Spanish, her face turned into my father's. I heard him yelling and screaming at me. I saw he had a full erection. As tears filled my eyes, I jumped off the bed and started for the door naked. Juanita grabbed my arm and pulled me toward the hose. Instead of fighting her, I became docile, ready for my punishment. Juanita did not know the demons I was fighting, but she did know something was wrong. With concern on her face, she hugged me hard, her engorged nipples pressing into my chest. Within a couple of minutes, my mind returned to the present. She wiped the tears from my cheeks and kissed me passionately. She put water in a rubber bag with a long tube that was hanging on the wall. She motioned for me to hold the bag. She inserted the tube into her vagina and motioned for me to squeeze the pouch to push water into her.

We got dressed and walked back to the bar, where she immediately went over to another sailor. Grant walked in a few minutes later, and as in the past, he wanted to talk all about our experiences. I let him do the talking.

That night as Grant and I boarded the ship, we turned to the town and hollered, "Viva Mexico!" I don't know why we did that, but we did. Within a few days, we were in our home port in Florida.

CHAPTER 78

Home

I went home and walked in in full uniform and was all smiles when I said hi to my family. I hoped my father would be proud of me. He was on the couch with my sister trying to teach her to play an accordion. I heard Mama in the kitchen. He said with a snarl, "Shut your goddamn mouth, plowboy." Standing he hit me in the mouth and said, "Can't you see I'm trying to teach your sister how to play this goddamn accordion? Go clean the cat shit up. It hasn't been picked up since you've been off playing sailor!"

My sister was pushing the accordion keys; it sounded like a dying dog. I thought, *if that's her best, she'll never learn.* I sighed, went to my room, and sat on the bed for a couple of minutes trying to clear my head. My sister and father walked by heading to her room. My father glanced in and said, "Goddamn it! When I tell you to do something, you do it now!" "Go clean up that goddamn cat shit like I told you!" I said, "Yes sir."

I wiped blood off my face with a shirt from my closet. Still in uniform, I walked past Mama in the kitchen and went outside. She did not say anything to me, and I did not say anything to her. I shoveled up the cat shit and threw it into the woods. As I had so many times in the past, I sat with my back against a pine tree. I relived the past two weeks; I thought of the fun Grant and I had had—the beers and the things we had seen for the first time. My thoughts turned to Juanita. I smiled thinking she must have thought I was a complete nut trying to blow up that damn rubber. Laughing, I said out loud, "Thanks, Juanita. I'm with you."

My thoughts were interrupted when my father asked, "What the hell are you doing out here, and who are you talking to? Go inside and unpack your goddamn sea bag so your mother doesn't have to do it!" I got up and headed to the house. As I walked past him, he kicked me so hard that he lifted me about a foot off the ground. I fell to the ground crying in pain and thinking he had broken my ass. He kicked me in the stomach. "Get up plowboy! It doesn't hurt that bad!"

It took about fifteen minutes for the pain to subside enough so that I could go in and unpack my sea bag. I went to bed but couldn't sleep. I wondered where life would take me. Grant and I had talked about what we were going to do next. I said, "I have the car, and I've saved a little money. I want to go back to Louisiana, and I'd like you to come with me." He said, "I don't want to go to Louisiana. I want to stay here and get a job." I said, "What about California? We could find a whole new life out there." But he said, "No, I just want to stay here." He had not mentioned anybody, but I thought a girl was keeping my best friend in Maple Wood.

As I lay in bed, I looked at my shotgun several times. Each time, that little voice kept telling me, *No, don't do it. You can and will prove to him you can become something*. About 5:30am, I heard him getting up. I got up, got dressed, and went out before he could throw that glass of cold water in my face. I walked across the street and into the woods, where I waited for him to leave. I knew he was not going to work, but I had no idea where he was going. Every morning working or not, he left and did not come home until late afternoon to take a nap. "Home sweet home. *Why even come back*?" I thought.

CHAPTER 79

Tarpaper Shack

I spoke with Ray about working for him again. That time, he was more receptive. His father was not feeling well, and Ray really needed somebody to help him. The hours were from noon to eight six days a week—Sundays off. He still paid me $10 per week. It took less than $5 to fill my Bug up once a week. I had about $100 stashed under my mattress. I wasn't seeing Grant a lot those days; he always seemed to be busy when I called or stopped by his house. I told him that after I saved up a couple of hundred dollars, I planned to go back to Louisiana. I kept asking him to accompany me, but he kept turning me down. However, he did say he was involved with a girl. I smiled. I knew I couldn't compete with that.

I started spending all my time working or just hanging around by myself again, sometimes at the lake in the woods. A few nights, I built a fire and reminisced. I felt so alone and didn't know what to do. One day, I drove to Bagdad, a town next to Maple Wood, and fished in a creek I had fished before just to pass the time. I spent much of my fishing days with two black families who fished there. Maybelle, an older black woman, had two teenagers who fished with her. Mee Maw and her son were there as well.

The first day I fished there, I laughed when one of them cast a line and the cane pole made a loud whap when it hit the water. Mee Maw gave me a long stare. I told her how when I was little, I used to fish with a cane pole and it used to make the same loud whap. Just for fun, I did the same thing with my cane pole, and everyone laughed at that. It had been a long time since I had been able to relax, enjoy myself, and not worry about my father showing up.

I started fishing every day before work. We talked about family and told funny stories. I told them about living in Louisiana when I was younger. I skipped all the bad stories, but Mee Maw always gave me a look that told me she knew there was more than I was telling. I liked her. She had been born and raised in Bagdad. She had never gone to school, but I listened to her intently whenever she spoke. After about a week, she said, "Johnny, just call me Mee Maw. That's what everybody calls me," yes ma'am I replied.

For bait, they always used worms they had dug up. An old black man sold red wigglers not far from the creek; they were like those I had used so many lifetimes ago in Louisiana. He had a large worm bed in his backyard filled with sawdust and dirt. The sawdust kept everything loose. For a couple of dollars, I could buy a hundred, many more than I needed, but when I left, I gave the remaining worms to the black families because I knew they could not afford to buy their own. I didn't keep any of the fish I caught either; I just enjoyed fishing. I gave what I caught to them.

One morning, Mee Maw invited me to supper that night. I told her I had to work until eight, but I could come on Sunday, my day of. She asked me to come the next Sunday at five. I said, "I'd love to. Thank you, ma'am." She laughed. "Don't call me ma'am. That makes me feel old." Sorrow Mee Maw, I forgot. She had told me a lot about her husband, and I was anxious to meet him. She didn't live far from the creek; she told me how to get to her house.

On the following Sunday, my father drove all of us to Mass as usual. Back home, I changed clothes, took some money out from under my mattress, and started out the back door. My sister's door was closed. I thought my father was in her room, so I was surprised to find him standing outside staring into space. As the screen door slammed shut behind me, he said in his usual demonic voice, "Don't let the goddamn door slam, plowboy. What's wrong with you?" I said, "Yes sir, I won't do it again." I started walking to the Bug, but he put my shoulder in a vice grip and spun me around. "Where the hell do you think you're going?" I said, "To meet Grant. We're going fishing." "No, you aren't, plowboy. You're going to clean up the goddamn cat shit. Let me know when you're finished!" I said, "Yes sir," and picked up the bucket and shovel. He went in letting the screen door slam loudly.

I cleaned up the shit in about ten minutes. I dumped the mess in the woods across the street. I walked into the house but could not find my father. My sister's door was still closed, and Mama was in the kitchen making a Sunday dinner of black-eyed peas, rice, collard greens, sweet potatoes, and her great homemade biscuits.

I sat on the couch and waited for about fifteen minutes. My father never appeared, so I got up and said, "Goodbye, ma'am," and walked out. I drove to Grant's, but he was not home. I drove to Bagdad and saw that everybody except Mee Maw was fishing, so I bought some red wigglers and fished with them. I laughed with them at some stupid story being told.

We fished all day, and I gave them my fish. I was thoroughly enjoying their company; they were all very family oriented. I never heard a cuss word, or anyone take the Lord's name in vain. When Mee Maw spoke, everybody listened to her; she was very well spoken. It wasn't so much the words she used but the way she said them. I listened to all of them laugh and talk and could not understand how my father could talk so badly about blacks. They were nothing like he had said they were.

We fished all afternoon and took a lot of fish to Mee Maw's house. I left the Bug by the creek. Her house was what my father called a tarpaper shack. Her husband was in a rocker on the front porch smoking a pipe. Everybody else went inside, but I sat on another rocker and spoke with him. I lit up a Lucky Strike and offered him one, but he refused and pointed to his pipe. He was quiet and soft spoken. I was interested in his stories about World War II, but he spoke sparingly about that.

That day, I came away with a new meaning for the word *nigger*— "perseverance." My father had tried to beat into me his thinking about blacks; I realized my father's hate was more intense than I had ever imagined. Leo's stories about the treatment of blacks during the war were sobering. I asked, "Leo, you were fighting for this country, right?" He looked at me with the saddest eyes I had ever seen. "Yes, I was." With sadness overflowing my heart, I said, "I'm sorry, Leo." He simply said, "Thank you, Johnny." Leo was the most remarkable black man I had ever met.

Mee Maw called us in for supper. I followed Leo into the small house. There was an eat-in kitchen with a table and six chairs all homemade. There were two bedrooms; one had only blankets on the floor; it was apparent where their four kids slept. In the kitchen was a hand pump that emptied into a well-worn, porcelain basin. She said, "The outhouse is out back if you need it, Johnny."

She was frying fish on an old, cast iron stove. I walked out back and saw that the outhouse was just like the one I had used in Louisiana. I smiled as I saw it was also a two-seater. Inside was what I thought was a thick Sears catalog, which were always plentiful.

Afterwards, I returned to the kitchen; her four kids were at the table. As her husband and I approached, she made the youngest get up and let me use his chair. He sat on the floor. After putting the fried fish, hushpuppies, and collard greens on the table, Mee Maw sat. I started to say a silent grace but stopped when I saw her take a son's hand, and he in turn took his sister's hand, and it continued around the table; I took her husband's and a daughter's hands. We bowed our heads as Leo said grace.

During supper, talk was light, but never a foul word was spoken. After dinner, everybody went out to the front porch; Leo and I sat in the rockers. I lit up a Lucky Strike and offered him one. That time he accepted. In a few minutes, Mee Maw came out. With a smile on my lips and respect in my heart, I gave her my rocker and sat on the floor with her kids. There was not much talking; I realized it was their quiet time. Everybody was saying goodbye to another day and lost in their thoughts, including me.

Because they had no electricity, I figured they probably went to bed right after dark. As soon as darkness settled in, I left with a newfound respect for black people. I wasn't naïve enough to think all blacks were like this family, but I sure knew that all blacks were not as my father purported them to be. I had found Mee Maw and her family to be religious, well-mannered, polite, and humble. They may have been living in a tarpaper shack, but the house was clean through and through.

She had invited me into their home with no intention other than to share a simple meal with them. I came away with tears running down my face, a curse on my lips, and a renewed hatred for my father. I had no hatred or fear of these simple folks. I had left all the money I had—about $22—and my deck of Lucky Strikes in the outhouse. I never returned to that fishing creek, and I never saw Mee Maw or her family again. My shame over what my father had taught me over the years kept me away, but I have never forgotten the day I had dinner in a Tarpaper Shack and the lesson it had taught me.

CHAPTER 80

Alone

One day about a week later in 1963, I walked through the woods to the lake where Cap and I had spent so many nights together. That night, instead of catching a squirrel, a rabbit, or a fish, I caught a big water snake. I skinned it, and as I was roasting it on a stick, my thoughts turned to Cap. I laughed when I remembered the first time I offered him some snake meat at this same spot. He looked at the snake, looked at me, and then looked back at the snake as if asking, *Are you for real?* I laughed and hugged him, and he licked my face. I ate a piece, which was tough and rubbery, not to mention it didn't have much flavor. I again offered him a piece, but he backed away growling. Amused and laughing, I said, "What's the matter, Cap? Are you afraid?" I kept poking the piece of snake at him, and he kept growling.

I called him to me and put a piece of snake in my mouth. Rubbing my tongue around on it, I pulled it out, and taking Cap's head in my hands, I looked into his eyes and said, "It's okay, Cap. You can eat it." I held the piece of snake right in front of him. He looked at me, sniffed the snake, and ate it. He immediately looked for more, and he never refused snake again.

Remembering those times, I fell into a troubled sleep beside the lake. My dreams were filled with the times Cap and I spent days in those woods. I don't know if it's possible to cry in your sleep, but I think I did.

The next morning, the birds woke me just before dawn. I sat up and called out, "Cap? Where are you?" Then reality set in. My thoughts returned to the present. I made sure the fire was out and slowly walked home. As I reached the house, my father was just leaving. I stood still not speaking to him; he said, "Don't leave this yard today, plowboy!" I said, "I have to go to work at Ray's today." He started toward me with that crazy look on his face and said, "Goddamn it! You do what I say, plowboy!" Before he could reach me, I said, "Yes sir," and walked into the house.

I spent the day cleaning my room and hanging out in the yard. My thoughts were on my father and wondering what was coming next. I couldn't think of anything I had done wrong. I tried not to think about him, but I couldn't stop. I asked Mama, "Ma'am, do you know why I have to stay here today?" She said, "Johnny, don't ask questions, and do what your father said." My sister stayed in her room all day with the door closed, so I didn't see her.

Around three that afternoon, I was sitting under the same tree in the backyard I had turned Tippy loose in so long ago. Staring at the hose hanging in the pine tree I hated so much, I heard my father drive up. In a few moments, I heard him talking to Mama in the kitchen in a loud voice. I heard my sister's door slam shut. I got to my feet with a huge sigh and my head hanging low. I walked into the house through the back door. I did not see Mama, but I saw my sister's bedroom door shut, and I heard my father talking loudly and my sister crying in there.

I walked into my bedroom and sat on my bed. A few minutes later, my father came out of her bedroom and told me, "Plowboy, get into the goddamn car!" I walked out; Mama was in the front seat of his VW. I got in the back seat and asked, "Ma'am, where are we going?" She said nothing; she just stared straight ahead.

My father came out, got into the car, and without saying a word starting driving. As we passed Ray's station, I said, "I'm going to lose my job again." Nobody said a word as my father drove to downtown Maple Wood and headed west on Highway 91, still saying nothing. He drove for about an hour west toward Alabama. He exited Highway 91 onto another paved road and kept driving, making several turns. He drove onto dirt roads and continued for another half hour, again making many turns. He stopped in the middle of nowhere, turned the car around, and looked at me. "Get out, plowboy!" in the worst and cruelest voice I had ever heard him use.

After I got out, he called me to his window and asked, "Do you have any money?" I was puzzled; I stammered, "No sir." He handed me a dollar, and before I had a chance to say anything, he drove off. I stared as he disappeared into a cloud of dust. I felt the most alone I had ever felt. I wanted to cry, but I wouldn't let myself.

I yelled, "What the fuck did I do now?" My first thought was he had found out about Mee Maw, and that was his way of teaching me just as he had taught Cap. I yelled, "Her family is more of a family than ours will ever be, and you're a fucking liar," knowing he couldn't hear me.

My mind was racing going back over the past few days. I could think of nothing I had done to deserve this. I thought I must have done something bad when I was young, but I could never remember what it was. Looking in his direction, I said in a subdued voice, "I'm sorry, Daddy. I'll try harder."

It started to rain hard. Thunder boomed, and lightning filled the sky. Soaking wet, I walked to the side of the road, sat, and pondered my situation. I could not understand why he had done this. *Is he checking my survival skills? He must know by now I can survive in the woods.* I couldn't think of any reason other than Mee Maw why he would do this. *Surely, he'll come back for me at some point.*

As dark inched forward, the storm intensified. I saw an old, dead tree about a hundred feet from the road. It looked as if it had been struck by lightning many times. I had always heard lightning wouldn't strike the same place twice. I went to it and sat huddled in the dark, legs drawn up tight, my chin on my knees.

After a couple of hours, the rain became a drizzle and the thunder and lightning stopped. I found an old tree with lots of low-hanging branches, found some branches on the ground, and lit a fire with my Zippo. I had a full pack of Lucky Strikes, most of which were dry. Sitting with my back against the tree, I stared into the fire. I lay down after a few hours still hoping he would come back. I fell into an uneasy sleep, but I woke occasionally to keep the fire going.

CHAPTER 81

Decisions

The next morning, I put the fire out and started walking in the direction my father had taken the previous day. I hoped I could remember the turns as I came to them, so I could make my way back to Highway 91 and hitchhike home. I walked for what seemed hours but saw only one car. I tried to hitch a ride, but he would not pick me up.

I came to a bridge over a creek. I was wearing shoes with no socks, underwear, jeans, and a white T-shirt. I was thirsty and had not eaten since breakfast the day before; Mama had made me bacon, grits, and eggs when I had gotten home. I saw some minnows in the water but had nothing to cook them in. I thought about eating them raw. Then I saw some frogs, and I managed to catch a few. I built a fire, but having no knife, I had to tear their legs off. I cooked them over the fire. They tasted like a million bucks. I sat with my feet in the cold water and contemplated the day. Within a short time, I decided to head to the one place I missed the most in my life—Louisiana. I spent the night under that bridge sleeping soundly with my plan made.

The next morning, I was up early as usual and again started walking in the same direction. A few cars passed me, but I didn't bother with hitchhiking. I walked for what I thought was hours. I came to a store with a gas pump in front. Going inside, I saw an older woman behind the counter. She kept a sharp eye on me as I walked around. Someone drove up to the pump and started blowing his horn. The woman asked, "May I help you, son?" I asked, "May I use your bathroom, ma'am?" "The outhouse is out back," she replied as she started for the front door.

After she went outside, I stole some junk food, some mystery meat, and a few cans of Vienna sausages. I wanted to keep the only dollar I had for as long as I could. I went out the back door as if I were going to the outhouse. I stayed at the side of the building until she finished pumping gas and went back into the store. I continued walking.

By then, I was walking on paved roads, but I was not sure it was the same road my father had taken. I had not paid attention to where he was taking me; my thoughts were on what I had done wrong. I walked for a short time before going into the woods. I ate the junk food but saved the canned meats. I kept walking, and eventually, as dusk was approaching, I saw another bridge. I didn't remember crossing a bridge with my father and mother. It was bigger than the one the day before.

I went under the bridge and saw an elderly man sitting next to a small fire. He was a big man with long, matted, and dirty hair that hung to his shoulders. His beard was long and matted as well. His hands were big but clean. His clothes were old, dirty, and torn in places they shouldn't have been. His face was wrinkled and tanned from years being in the hot sun. He squinted as he stared at me. I started to turn and walk away, but instead, I walked over and asked his permission to sit by his fire. At first, he did not answer, so I just stood quietly for a few minutes. When he still had not answered, I started to walk away. He said, "Sit down, young fella." I did and said, "Thank you, sir."

We stared into the fire deep in our own thoughts. After about a half hour of silence, he got up, threw some more wood on the fire, sat down, and asked, "How come you so polite?" Smiling, I said, "My folks taught me to be polite to my elders." He laughed. "They taught you well, son."

After that, talking came easy. He said, "My name is Joe, but people call me Red," pointing to his thick beard and long hair, all bright red. I laughed and said, "That's a good name. I once had a dog named Red. He was a good dog." He laughed and said, "Well, if that don't beat all! I was named after a dog." I asked him what he was cooking in his old pot hanging on a stick over the fire. He replied, "Lima beans." I said, "I have a couple of cans of mystery meat." He smiled. "Well hell, son, let's open them up." After we ate, we washed it down with a half pint of blackberry brandy he had.

We talked late into the night. I told him a little bit about how I had come to be there. I mentioned how my father had forced me to join the navy reserve. He told me that he had been in the army in World War II and that his luck had lately seemed to have run out on him. He had lost his job, his family, and everything he owned. He gave me lots of advice about life, so I wouldn't make the same mistakes he had made.

"You should go over to your naval base and tell them you want to go on active duty," he said. I told him my plan was to hitchhike to Louisiana and live with one of my cousins or maybe go to California and start a new life. For the next hour or so, we discussed my life's path and what it might hold for me. I said goodnight and fell into a deep sleep dreaming of white, sandy beaches and surfer girls.

The next morning, I said goodbye to Joe, and that was hard. He had touched me in an understanding way I had not been used to. I gave him my remaining canned meats and left feeling good. I walked and hitchhiked back to Highway 91. I knew I did not want to go home; it was either west to Louisiana or east to the naval base in Pensacola. I chose east. The first car to pick me up was a sailor going there.

We arrived at the gate. I had no ID. My wallet with my driver's license and navy ID were at home along with my money under my mattress. It took a lot of talking to the guards. They finally called somebody, and a shore patrol wagon soon showed up. The shore patrol put me inside and took me to a lockup. In a rambling kind of way, I explained to them who I was and why I was there. I figured because of my appearance and my dirty, stinking, and messy clothes, I must have looked like a hobo. I had been wearing the same clothes for days. They did not believe me.

I lay on a metal bed with no mattress and closed my eyes. My thoughts wandered back over the past few years and continued right up to the present. I remembered what Coach had said: "Johnny, even if you're going to block the wrong man, I want to see you block him all the way to the ground." I realized what I had to do. I called out to one of the shore patrol repeatedly, but he kept saying, "Shut up!" He finally came over to my cell, and I asked him if he would call CPO Charles Gates, who, I said, could vouch for me. He said he would. In about a half hour, CPO Gates was standing in front of me. I was let out of the lockup. As he was driving me to headquarters, I closed my eyes and wondered where my screwy path of life was taking me.

CHAPTER 82

A New Beginning

One bright, sunny day in July 1985, I was sitting at my desk in the detective division going over reports of the day when the front desk called saying that there were two federal agent's downstairs wanting to speak with a detective. I asked the officer to send them upstairs.

In a few minutes, two well-dressed men knocked on my door. They introduced themselves as being from the ATF Boston office and were following up on a report that had been filed by the Sandy Town Police Department and forwarded to their office about a certain Ronnie Barthwell. I had not filed that report, but I knew all the information. I said Ron was involved with three other men. They owned and ran a takeout restaurant called Brothers in Sandy Town's Brant City section. The information we had was that all four were previous motorcycle gang members. We also suspected they were involved in drugs but had not had enough information to obtain search warrants.

The information about Ron was that he sold Valium from his house for $10 a pill. The information stated that when you walked into his house, there was a loaded .50 caliber machine gun on a tripod pointed at the front door. I had heard about another former biker who was a machinist that he had worked on the gun to make it operational. I had my doubts about the information, but I passed it on to the two agents. They asked me if I could show them Ron's house. I told them I could, but it was a very close-knit neighborhood. I told them that he lived on a short, dirt, dead-end road and that watching the house would be almost impossible. I said Ron liked to hang out on a seawall by the beach in Brant City.

We left the police station, and I showed them the area and the rented house where Ron lived. I also showed them the seawall and the takeout restaurant. I gave them a copy of an old arrest photo of Ron and a full description of him, including the clothes and headbands he liked to wear. They said they would start surveillance the next day. I submitted a report to the captain, so the department would know that federal agents would be working in Sandy Town.

For the next two weeks, I did not hear anything from the agents. Then one evening while I was in the field, I got a radio call from the station saying that a federal agent was at the station wanting to speak with me. I advised them I couldn't come for about an hour. I was told the agent would wait.

When I got back to the station, one of the same ATF agents I had met told me they had found the suspect where I had told them he would be and had followed him around every day but had never seen any suspicious activity. They said that when he would leave the beach, he would drive to a different house other than the one I had shown them. Laughing I told him Ron didn't have a car. I told him that I would meet them in the area the next day and try to figure out what was going wrong.

The next afternoon, I met the two agents near Brant City. We walked to the area where they had been watching the suspect. They pointed him out. I said, "You've been watching the wrong suspect."

Once that was straightened out, the agents began intense surveillance on the right subject. They checked back with me and said they were getting nowhere. Eventually, the suspect was brought into the station and questioned by the agents. He denied everything concerning the machine gun and selling pills. He allowed a cursory search of the house he shared with a female; nothing illegal was found.

During and after the investigation, Ron and I formed an unlikely relationship. One night while I was on duty, a cruiser responded to a disturbance call. I heard on the radio that the officers were bringing Ron in under arrest for disorderly conduct. After he was booked and placed in a cell, I spoke with him through the bars. Even though he had been drinking, he told me, "I didn't get arrested for being drunk but because I was mad and having an argument with somebody. Johnny, I could give you some good information if you'll help me." I took him out of the cell in cuffs to the conference room to talk in private.

I read him his rights and had him sign a Miranda rights card as a precaution. He told me about a house he had been in in the past two days. He said the owner was a guy named Chad Breen. He said he had bought a small amount of weed from Chad for his personal use. Ron said he had been shown some guns including rifles, shotguns, and handguns that Chad said had been stolen. Chad wanted to sell them.

We talked for about an hour, and he told me about several houses that were selling drugs and were in possession of various firearms. I asked him about the machine gun and its whereabouts. He laughed and said he had disposed of it. I told him that I was worried that somebody might do unimaginable things with it including hurting innocent people. Ron was quiet for a while before he said, "Johnny, I won't tell you the location of it, but I will tell you that nobody will ever use it. I cut it up into pieces and threw it in a waterway." I don't know if I believed him, but that machine gun was never found.

I asked him about selling Valium. He said, "That wasn't me. It was my roommate." I later learned that in fact his roommate was the one selling the Valium and was getting them from a doctor I knew. I told the doctor face to face that based on the information I was receiving, he was probably the biggest supplier of prescription drugs in the area. He asked, "Do you really think so, Johnny?" I gave him a resounding yes. I warned him that if he continued in this manner, only danger and incarceration would result. I knew the doctor was a speed freak. He had told me he was taking a lot of his own medications by way of pharmaceutical samples.

One morning not long after that, he called me and asked me to come to his office right away for a talk. I told him I had to go on duty at 4:00 p.m. and would come over after that. When I got to his office, he was upset, scared, and paranoid. He was talking so fast that I could hardly understand him. After calming him down, I learned what was bothering him. "Druggies are banging on my rear office door. Some are trying to kick it in. Others are coming in through the front office, walking past my receptionists, and entering my private office. They're threatening me. They want more prescription drugs. My real fear is that they'll find out where I live. As you know, Johnny, I have a wife and a child we just adopted." I asked, "So what are you doing about it?" He said, "I'm scared, Johnny, so I write the prescriptions. Johnny, if you'll be my private bodyguard, I'll pay you a lot of money. I need you to protect me and my family."

I could tell he saw the amazement on my face, when I said no, because he couldn't sit still. He walked around, sat, jumped up, and yelled, "Why won't you do it? Do you want them to kill me?"

"Doc, sit down and be quiet." He sat and became quiet, but he was squirming. I put two hands on his desk, leaned forward, and said, "I warned you to stop. Now you want me to work for you?" That means I would become a part of the drug trade I hate so much. I've known you for years, but you disgust me to no end. I'm going to turn the information over to the state police." I leaned in closer and said, "Fuck you, you are an asshole. You deserve what you get." I walked out of his office and heard yelling, screaming, slamming walls, overturning his desk, and talking unintelligibly. I never spoke to him again.

Later, I did report him to the state police. Within a year or so, he lost his license to practice medicine. Ironically, that was not due to any drug-related activity but of sexually nature; I believe his own drug addiction had caused that. I considered him just one more drug dealer who was put out of business.

Ron again asked me if I could help him get out of jail that night. I said, "I'll see what I can do." I returned him to his cell and called the bail clerk. He said that because the charge was only disorderly conduct, he could get out for $25. In about an hour, the bailsman came in, and I paid the $25. I drove Ron to a coffee shop. We sat in the parking lot while he drank coffee and we talked more. I drove him around town, and he pointed out several houses including the house where Chad lived. I drove him to Brant City and dropped him off. He said his female roommate had kicked him out after the feds had come snooping around.

He said, "Johnny, I swear to you it was not me selling the Valium, it was my roommate, but I've become addicted to the Valium." I asked him if I could take him to a clinic for some help with his addiction. He declined. "Johnny, I've gone that route before. It didn't work." He shook my hand and said, "I've never met a cop I liked until I met you. Thanks for doing what you say you'll do." I said, "Ron, you can trust me." He said, "I know I can." An unusual relationship was born.

Back at the police station, I pulled out a file. I had made numerous notes on a Chad Breen. I added information on the firearms Ron had spoken about. In about a month, I had received enough information from other informants; with that and with what Ron had given me, I obtained a search warrant. I arrested Chad and seized drugs, drug paraphernalia, and guns.

Over the months, Ron and I talked several times. On some occasions, he would give me some drug and gun information. I always followed up on his information along with other informants' information and received and executed several search warrants. Once, we seized a sawed-off, double-barreled shotgun.

Ron's mind was burned out on drugs and alcohol; most people in the area hated or feared him. He looked like a real badass. At times, I would buy him coffee. He would ask me for some change, and I would always give him $10 of my own money. I told him to buy food and other necessities, and he said he would, but I knew he'd buy alcohol. Since having been kicked out of his house, he was not using prescription drugs anymore according to him; he was living on the street.

One cold, rainy night as I was driving past a Liquor Store, I saw him outside. I stopped and watched him asking patrons on their way in something. I walked over to him. He was a mess. He still wore the same clothes I had seen him in over a week before. He stank terribly, and he had defecated in his pants, but worst of all, he was shaking so badly he could hardly stand or talk straight. I saw that he was in the throes of alcohol withdrawal. I begged him to let me call somebody to have him admitted to a detox center, but he refused. After much deliberation, I bought him a pint of Southern Comfort. I told him to get in the car. I gave him the bottle, and he started chugging it down. I said I would drive him to wherever he was staying. I wanted to get him away from the store and trouble. He gave me directions to where he was staying. I dropped him off knowing he would be safe and would not be seeing anybody else that night.

About a month later another cold, snowy day, one of the same federal agents from before was waiting for me at the station when I went on duty at 4:00 p.m. He said that he had been looking for Ron and had heard that I might know where he was staying. Before I gave him up, I wanted to know that Ron would be treated right. The agent convinced me that he wanted only to talk to him and get some information on a Boston motorcycle gang. I agreed to take him to see Ron. I have always regretted that decision.

We drove for about three-quarters of an hour; I took the slow way with many turns. Ron's place was off a dirt road in the woods. About two years previously, a house had burned down killing a young man who had been staying in the people's basement. On the dirt road in front of the house was an old car that had been sitting there for years. It too had been burned. Ron had covered the car with an old, large canvas and was living inside.

I yelled, "Ron, its Johnny. Don't come out with a gun or anything. I have a federal agent with me. He wants to talk to you." Ron said, "Okay, Johnny, I'll be right out." He came out and spoke with the agent at length as I stayed in my car. Afterward, the agent got in the car and said, "Okay, I'm all set." I never asked what they had talked about.

I did not see Ron for a few months even after checking his home in the woods. One day, my wife and I were out shopping when she exclaimed, "Oh my God! That guy is heading toward us!" It was Ron walking away from a medical center with bloody bandages on his head and arm. His thick, black beard and long, stringy, black hair were matted with dried blood. He was dragging one leg as he approached my car. I smiled and chuckled at my wife, who was looking like she was trying to crawl under the seat. I said, "It's okay, honey. I know him."

Ron reached us, and I rolled down my window. "Hey, Ron. You okay?" He replied, "No, Johnny. I need to talk to you, and I could sure use some money." I gave him a twenty and said, "I'm going to drop my wife off at home. I'll meet you at the Dunkin' Donuts down the street." He said, "Okay, I'll see you in a little while."

About an hour later after dropping my wife off at home, I returned to the Dunkin' Donuts, though my wife had begged me not to go. I bought coffee for Ron and me, and we sat and talked in my car. He asked, "Will you drive me back to the woods? I have some information I want to give you." I knew he meant the old car. I said, "Sure, Ron." We stopped at a liquor store, and I bought him a pint of Southern Comfort.

Arriving at his home, he said he had something to give me. He went into his old car and came back with a double-barreled, .38 caliber derringer. "Johnny, I've been helping the feds with information on a motorcycle gang in Boston. I was given this gun by one of them and told to dispose of it. The biker said that a woman was murdered for a hundred bucks because another woman was having an affair with her husband and the murdered woman was in the way. All I know was that the woman was found in a stairwell in Dorchester." I asked him repeatedly for any other information, but he said that was all he knew. I took the gun with my handkerchief not putting my prints on it.

Ron and I sat in my car and talked as he drank his liquor. Finally, the conversation turned to him. He told me a little about his previous life and how when he was young, he had been sexually abused by his mother, father, and others. He said that his stepfather, who had also abused him, had thrown him out of the house when he turned thirteen. He said he had been on his own ever since and had hooked up with a lot of bad people. He said now all he wanted was to live quietly and die in peace. I asked him about the feds, and he said, "I still have some more work to do for them, but I'm afraid because I'm not the same person I was years ago." I told him he should tell them he was finished. He said, "I wish I could." To me, that meant they had something on him and were working him to gain information they needed.

The temperature was dropping fast, and snow was falling heavily. I asked him if he would be okay, and he said, "Oh yeah, I have plenty of blankets in there to stay warm." As Ron got out of my car, we shook hands. I looked at him with a heavy heart and said, "Stay safe, my friend."

I spoke with my captain about what Ron had said concerning the murder without giving him Ron's name. He said, "You do know that in a murder investigation, you can be made to make your informant known." I said, "Yes, I know." He advised me to follow it up with the Boston police. I called and spoke with a detective in the Dorchester Division. He said that without more-specific information, it would be hard to find the exact case. I told him I would give him the gun; maybe that would help them. Later, I met with the detective and gave him the gun; I told him everything Ron had told me. I never heard from him again.

One night while I was going over some reports, I received a phone call from an informant. He asked, "Did you hear about Ron?" He said Ron had been beaten very badly by some motorcycle guys, gone into an abandoned building in Boston, and died.

I reflected on how Ron's and my lives had been similar, up to a point. His life had led him down a path of crime, drugs, and booze, and he had ended up burned out and beaten to death. I realized that my life could very easily have gone the same direction. My thoughts returned to that day at the naval base when my life restarted; it was a new beginning simply because I had followed through with what Coach had taught me.

That day in December 1963, I signed papers and became a sailor on active duty for two years. I was given a Greyhound bus ticket and traveling orders; I was told to report to duty in, South Carolina. I hitchhiked to the bus station and I rode a bus for three days with just the $1 my father had given me. When the bus made stops, I would steal a few junk food items to eat, mostly candy. By the time we reached South Carolina, I had 13¢. I had taken a shower at the base, but I was still wearing the same clothes I had been wearing when I had left home. Nobody wanted to sit next to me.

I got off the bus in downtown. I asked an older sailor in uniform where the base was and how far away it was. He said, "It's about ten miles. You can take a taxi or a city bus." I told him that I did not have the money for either and that I would walk or hitchhike. He put his hand on my shoulder and said, "It's okay, son, I'm taking a taxi there. You can ride with me." I thanked him, and we got into a taxi.

The ride to the base took about half an hour. Nobody talked. The sailor and the driver kept their windows rolled down, even though it was cold, because of my odor. I stared out the window and contemplated what life meant to me. I could not think of any reason to keep on living. I felt defeated, abandoned, useless. I did not feel I belonged anywhere much less in the navy. I blamed myself for being where I was, but I still could not figure out what I had done wrong.

We arrived at the base, and I thanked the sailor. Marines on the gate directed me to the on-duty officer, a CPO. I gave him my papers. He looked at me and asked, "Son, when was the last time you ate?" I told him it had been more than three days. He took me to a mess hall and got a cook to feed me. I don't remember what it was, but I ate until I thought I would burst.

The CPO showed me to a barracks where I would stay until assigned to a duty station. The first thing I did was take a long, hot shower. The CPO had scrounged up some clean boxers and a T-shirt. That night as I was falling asleep, I was under clean sheets and a wool blanket. My thoughts returned to home. Tears welled up in my eyes as I thought of Mama and my sister. Sure, I missed them because I never even had a chance to say goodbye to either but mostly because I was frightened for them—I had no idea what my father had planned for them.

The next morning, I received a chit—a purchasing order—for new clothes. I was directed to the base clothing store, where I bought new uniforms, work clothes, and a sea bag. I returned to the barracks and took another long, hot shower. I balled my old clothes and shoes and took them outside to a dumpster. I held them to my heart for a few minutes; saying goodbye to them was an emotional moment. I don't think I cried. I believe it was the cold air that was making my eyes water.

Within a couple of days, I was assigned to a destroyer. I told them that my prior duty station as a reservist had been in the engine room. I was informed that since I was nonrated, I would be placed where I was needed. I was assigned to the forward fire room and became a boiler man, also known as a snipe.

My first few days in the fire room were a real test. I was caught between my new life and not wanting to be there. On my second day, I caught the eye of Player, a second class who also worked in the fire room. He called me over and asked, "Johnny, what the hell is wrong with you?" I stood quietly with my head down. "Johnny? Do you hear me? What the hell is wrong with you?" Tears started running down my cheeks. I raised my head and said in a choking voice, "I don't know" while shaking my head. He grabbed my shoulders and shook me. "Oh my God! Are you fucking crying?" He let go of my shoulders, heaved a big sigh, and yelled, "Johnny!" I looked at him. He said, "Son, do you know what I do when I feel like you do?" I could only shake my head. He sighed again and said, "I get fucking drunk!"

In a breaking voice, I whispered, "I'm not twenty-one. And besides, I don't have any money." He said, "Don't worry about either one. You're coming on liberty with me tonight." With those few words spoken between us, a genuine friendship ensued. Somehow, Player had our liberty days and duty days matched up.

That night while on liberty in uniform, he brought me to one of many bars not far from the base that were so much more than the bars Grant and I had gone to in Key West. Loud music was blaring from a jukebox, and the cigarette smoke that filled the room stung my eyes right as we entered. Mostly sailors and a few marines filled the place. Women were everywhere. A bare-breasted woman was sitting on the bar talking to two sailors seated on stools in front of her. Player and I walked up to the bar and sat on the only two empty seats in the place. A tired and harried-looking female bartender came over and said, "Hi, Player. What will you have? The usual?" He nodded and said, "Johnny, meet Rose. Rose, meet Johnny, a new shipmate of mine." Rose nodded and asked, "Hey, Johnny, what'll you have?" Player said, "The same as me, and put them on my tab." Rose said, "Okay" and left. She returned shortly with two warm draft beers in dirty glasses she had filled from a pitcher at the other end of the bar. Picking up his glass, Player turned to me and made a toast. "Here's to you and to many more beers, and may you forget." We clinked glasses. As I tasted that nasty beer, I thought, *Here's to you, Dad. Thanks for helping me become a man.* How naïve I was at that time of my life.

Payday was every two weeks, so Player took me to that bar every night we had liberty for two weeks. The ship went to sea for a short time, and Player even bought me cigarettes. I was still smoking Lucky Strikes, and I could by a carton for $1 from the ship's store once we were more than three miles out. The draft beers were only 25¢. Some nights, I watched Rose wring out her bar rag into those pitchers of beer on the bar. I was usually in a drunken stupor, and I would just laugh.

On payday, I received $22. I repaid Player $1 for the Lucky Strikes and bought the beer all night. I believe I spent a total of $6 that night. The bar closed at 2:00 a.m., and as everybody was leaving, Rose asked, "Johnny, can you hang around for a little while?" Player looked at me, winked, and said, "Oh boy. Have fun, Johnny." After locking the doors, Rose and the others cleaned the place for about an hour. I sat at the bar, and Rose kept refilling my glass for free.

About 3:00 a.m., everybody was leaving. Rose took my arm and led me outback. I could tell she also had been drinking as the two of us headed toward a car parked behind the bar. She opened the door, pulled the seat forward, and got into the back seat. She motioned for me to join her. I got in the back seat, and we started kissing and continued with some light petting.

After a few minutes, she pulled out what I thought was a cigarette. Lighting it with my ever-ready Zippo, I realized it was no regular cigarette. After taking a couple of hits, she offered it to me. I declined. "I've not tried it often, so I'm not sure what it will do to me." She laughed and again offered it to me. "Don't worry, Johnny. It won't hurt you. It'll make you happy and a little horny. I promise you the sex will be great."

After taking a few hits with her egging me on, I found it wasn't too bad. I am sure that the beer and the marijuana did help me forget, and the sex was just as she had promised. We made it last a long time—twice, or was it three times? I don't remember. She gave me exactly what I was looking for—closeness to another person who made me feel wanted.

I walked back to the ship around six that morning hungover, legless, and very sore. I realized why Player had laughed said, "Oh boy." That morning after muster, Player looked at me and said, "Oh oh, looks like you had a good night." I smiled and said, "Oh yeah."

That night, we had duty. He told me, "I want to give you some pointers about woman." He taught me to always have something to drink handy. He kept blackberry brandy on the ship, and that night, we shared some. He talked, and I listened. I came away with three critical points. The first, which I carried with me for a long time, was, "Johnny, fuck them, leave them, but never get serious with a woman." The second was, "Johnny, when you're fucking, never let a woman wrap her legs around you because she's trying to trap you by getting pregnant." The third was, "This one is easy—keep drinking and you'll forget whatever it is you're running from." I thought Player was the wisest man I knew.

After that night, I started branching out alone to other bars. As time passed and drinking became a way of life, my thoughts of home faded, and I found myself forgetting. By then, I was having sex every night with different girls. Some nights if one would ask, "When can I see you again?" I would laugh, make a disparaging remark, and leave.

In a while, I had saved some money and bought two pair of cheap civilian clothes. For $3 a month, I rented a locker in a back room of the bar where Rose worked. After that first night, she always treated me well, sometimes not charging me to drink. Occasionally, we would wind up in her car but only when it was her idea, not mine. I eventually bought a cheap iron and a can of starch. The locker room had showers, so I would sometimes shower and wash my clothes at the same time and hang them in my locker to dry. The next time, I would iron them before going on liberty.

One night while in a bar on the strip, I was sitting at a table with two women when I heard a familiar voice. I saw a group of sailors entering the place and spotted my best friend, Grant. I jumped up, ran over to him, and shouted, "Hey man! Good to see you!" From his reaction, I could tell he wasn't as glad to see me. He asked, "Hey, how are you?" But then, he wandered off with his shipmates. I stood there, grief stricken as everything I had been trying to forget came rushing back to me.

I returned to the table, but the two women had left. I had other things on my mind, so that didn't bother me. I drank and watched Grant and his shipmates laughing, drinking, and having a good time. Old memories of Grant and me and the secrets we had shared flooded my brain. The longer I sat there, the madder I got that Grant was ignoring me. After about an hour and a few more beers, I walked up to him and grabbed his arm. "Grant, I need to talk to you!" I pulled him to my table and said, "Grant, you're my best friend. Why are you ignoring me?" He said, "You left and never said goodbye or anything. I didn't know where you were, so I called your house. Your mother said you had run away. She didn't know where you were. I figured you went back to Louisiana as you had said you wanted to do." I said, "Grant, you should have known I would never have left like that without talking to you first." He said, "Well, I didn't know, and I was pissed at you."

I gave him a quick rundown of what had transpired and how my father had left me in the woods. He said, "I'm sorry for being mad at you. I didn't know. We should have killed him that night." I said, "I know." After talking for a few minutes, I joined him and his friends at the bar for the rest of the night. He introduced me to them as a friend from back home.

Grant was stationed on a different ship, so after that night, I saw him a few times over the next few months. We drank, laughed, and had a good time, but I could tell our friendship was not the same as it had been; it was strained. But my old life was slowly slipping away. Alcohol and at times marijuana were doing their jobs and becoming a major part of my life.

The last night I saw Grant, I told him my ship was leaving and was being transferred to Boston to go through fram. He asked me what that was, and I said, a rebuilding of the ship. I wanted to hug him and tell him that I loved him and would miss him. But the best I could say was, "Well, I'll see you." He said, "Fuck yeah."

CHAPTER 83

Lost Soul

Early in 1964, we unloaded most supplies from our ship, all our munitions, and most sailors before sailing to Boston; only a skeleton crew remained onboard for the trip. A few days later, the ship arrived in Boston. A northeaster snowstorm had delayed our arrival by two days. During that storm, I realized why the destroyer had the nickname Tin Can.

After the storm, the ship docked in Charlestown. The first night, I had liberty and I went ashore to check out this new and exciting place with Player. We passed several bars that were playing loud music. We found a small bar on a side street that had no live music but a jukebox playing old, soft music. There were no men in uniform, and half or more of the patrons were older women. The bar was a perfect place for some serious drinking by two guys looking to forget.

We sat at the bar and ordered beer. Maybe because we were in uniform, no IDs were asked for. After about an hour, two women came over and started a conversation with us. Eventually, all four of us moved to a table and talked and drank for the rest of the night; the women were at that point paying for our beers.

At closing time, 2:00 a.m., one of the women asked if we wanted to go to her house for a drink. She lived a short distance away, so we walked. We sat at her table and drank beer. One pulled me to my feet and led me to her bedroom. I guessed she was in her forties. I thought, *Yep, this will help me forget.*

It was pure sex—no foreplay, no talking, just sex. Afterward, she thanked me, and I walked out into the living room, where Player was waiting for me. As we were leaving, one of them said, "Hey, the next time your ship is in port, come over and see us." We looked at each other and laughed. I said, "No fucking way, whore." She threw a beer bottle at me that smashed against the door. She yelled, "Fuck you, asshole!" Player and I laughed all the way back to the ship. Player said, "Johnny, you're learning. Keep it up!"

Within a few days, the ship entered a dry dock, and we moved into barracks. At that time, we could go on liberty in civilian clothes. I had just turned twenty-one and I eventually wanted to hang out with a younger crowd, so I started drinking heavily in a bar called The Blue Mirror just outside the main gate. I started drinking Cutty-Sark, and beer. If I was lucky, women would buy me drinks. I moved from woman to woman, never staying with one very long, and most times, it would be only one-night stands. Eventually I tired of younger girls, mostly because they wanted to know more about me—where I was from, how my home life was, etc.—always with the questions. I started hanging out with older women because they wanted only one thing from me, no questions asked, and besides, they would supply me with all the whiskey and beer I could drink, not to mention the sex.

For that year while we were living in the barracks, I lost weight because I was drinking so much but not eating. I had feelings that I did not understand; I felt like a lost soul. Every time a feeling from back home came up, I would drink more until I reburied it. I was always looking but did not know what I was looking for. I spent a lot of my time with Player again, because he never asked questions or wanted anything from me. He had taught me to drink and forget.

I started out being a quiet and shy kid, and with all the drinking, I was sinking further into that black hole of despair. Eventually, I felt I had nothing to live for. Every morning, I woke, and looking through glazed eyes and a foggy brain, I wondered, *Is today the day it'll all end?*

On Christmas Eve in 1964, I had been away from home for more than a year with no contact with my family. After drinking all day, I went to the YMCA in Charlestown, and they let me call home. Mama answered, "Hello? Who is it?" I said nothing. She hung up.

A few minutes later, I called again, and she asked, "Hello? Who is this? Johnny, is it you?" I heaved a big sigh and said, "Hi, Mama." She asked, "Johnny, when are you coming home?" I said, "Mama, I'm never coming home." She started crying. I said, "Now Mama, stop crying. I just can't come home." She said, "I know," and she hung up.

That night, I went to The Novelty, a bar in downtown Boston's combat zone; a high crime area and met two women; they bought me drinks as fast as I could down them. At midnight, they said they were going to midnight Mass. I told them I was Catholic and would like to go with them. They laughed and tried to shoo me away. "You're not Catholic. You're just a drunk." I said, "I was drunk—I mean I am drunk—no, I mean I'm really drunk, but I'm also a Catholic." They did not believe me and left.

I stumbled down the street following them. They walked into a church as Mass was starting. I went in, spotted them, walked over, and stood next to them. That was a mistake. After a while, I started talking in a drunken stupor quite loudly, as I sort of remember, to God. I asked him why he had not helped me when I had asked for help. I had a lot of other questions, but I don't remember them. At one point, two priests—at least I think they were priests—asked me to leave. By then, everybody including the two women had moved away from me.

The next morning, I woke up lying in the bushes next to the church bruised, beaten, bloodied, and hungover. My wallet was empty of cash. It was a long walk back to the ship.

In the early part of 1965, coming out of dry dock, the fram completed, the ship sailed to Guantanamo Bay, Cuba, for a shakedown cruise. Player was transferred back to South Carolina, and I never saw him again. He had always been there for me when I needed him, and I missed him.

While on liberty in Gitmo—Guantanamo Bay—there was not much to do except drink at the only place we could go, the EMC, the enlisted men's club. There were absolutely no women, only sailors. At 1:00 a.m., the club closed, and as all of us came out in uniform, shore patrol was waiting outside, and they would separate us according to our ships. They loaded us on what were called cattle cars, old hay trailers transformed into transports. A truck would pull several at a time with all us sailors in them. The doorway had no doors, but there was a vertical bar in the middle with two shore patrol hanging onto them as the trucks headed to the different ships to drop us off. Of course, at 1:00 a.m., drunken-sailor fights broke out. The first thing that happened was the two-shore patrol were kicked off, and then everybody started fighting. Beating people felt good. It was a nightly routine I enjoyed.

One morning, I woke up with a very bad hangover on the ship, and I had a big bruise on my jaw. It had been a particularly bad fight the night before. My whole jaw was hurting, and I couldn't open my mouth. As I was heading out of our berthing compartment to go see the doctor, the first class I worked for was standing next to his locker cleaning it out. He handed me a knife with about a three-inch blade and asked, "Hey Johnny, do you want this?" I said, "Sure," and I stuck it in my back pocket.

I spoke with the ship's doctor, who said he was sending me over to the tender, a hospital ship tied to the dock, to see a dentist. I was still fuzzy brained and hungover; I just said, "Okay."

At the tender, I saw the dentist, a lieutenant junior grade. He was very angry and told me I was drunk, and he would send a report to my ship's doctor about that. I sat in a chair, and the knife in my back pocket stuck me in the butt. I reached behind me and pulled the knife out. I held it resting on my leg, the blade shining brightly. The dentist, who was standing beside me, gave out a shrill yell, as if I had grabbed his testicles hard. He jumped back. I saw him nod, and two sailors grabbed me from behind. Not knowing what was going on—I knew the alcohol was clouding my brain a little—I struggled with them. Within a minute or so, the three of us were rolling around on the deck with them trying to subdue me. I was still clutching the knife, and I was trying to stab them. "Remember the Alamo!" I yelled for some reason. Through all the hullabaloo, I heard the dentist yelling in his high, shrill voice, "Hold him down! Grab him here! Grab him there!" Another sailor joined the first two, and between the three of them, they were able to hold me down on the deck, the third one sitting on my chest.

Through it all, I had said nothing other than the Alamo thing. I growled a few times because my jaw was still hurting. I couldn't open my mouth, and my hangover had my brain in turmoil. The dentist knelt, grabbed my upper and lower jaws, and ripped them wide open. I gave out a loud scream of pain. The stench was so bad that the dentist gagged and almost vomited on me. The sailor sitting on my chest had to cover his mouth; he rolled off me. The other two sailors, who were holding my arms, let go and scooted away gagging.

I rolled on my side and vomited all over the deck. I was then strapped in a chair, and my wisdom teeth were pulled. I don't believe they needed or used any Novocain. Afterward, the dentist said that when I had been hit in the jaw, my wisdom teeth, which were probably already impacted, had spread an infection overnight because of the alcohol. He was very angry with me and said he had called my ship's doctor. I nodded and went to sleep.

Within a couple of hours, my doctor came over and got me. On the way back to our ship, I told him what had happened. He laughed and said, "Don't worry about it."

We operated out of Cuba for about six weeks. During that time, we pulled liberty in different ports in the Caribbean, including San Juan and Jamaica. In one bar, I had my first taste of rum; a rum and Coke cost 45¢. That made me a big fan of rum.

Arriving back in the United States, the ship was stationed in Newport, Rhode Island. As I had done in South Carolina, I rented a locker downtown for my civilian clothes. I developed a good relationship with the night clerk, so some nights after I had drunk heavily, I could sleep on the pool table in the locker room, if I hadn't hooked up with someone.

My past abuse had been bad, but alcohol was helping me forget it. Without realizing it, however, I was becoming something else that could kill me just as easily—a drunk. I know now that the difference between what I was becoming, and an alcoholic was that I didn't have to attend those damn meetings. Besides, I had girls helping me forget.

While I was sober, I put all my effort into working and learning the boiler room. It helped with the pain I was trying to forget. Sometimes, it worked, but other times, it didn't. I started having problems with my stomach. At times, I would pass blood from the top and bottom of my body. I went to see the doc, and he gave me a bottle of Maalox. He said to take every four hours and stop drinking for a little while to give the medicine a chance to work. I took the bottle and said, "Okay."

While the ship was docked, during the day, some of us would sneak out the back gate and drink our lunch at a bar. One day, I was sitting at the bar enjoying a rum and Coke when the doc walked in. He saw me and yelled, "Johnny, I told you to take the Maalox and stop drinking for a while!" I picked up the bottle, showed it to him, and said, "I have it with me. I take a slug after every drink." The doc shook his head and said, "All right, but keep drinking the Maalox." He sat at the bar and ordered his drink.

CHAPTER 84

Cherrie

In November 1965, knowing I was due to get discharged in December, I was torn between going home or re-upping. During that time, we were told our ship was going to Vietnam right after the first of the year. We were told about a ship like ours the Viet Cong had tried to board and take over. We were warned not to tell anybody that we were going, including our family, because of spies in the United States. My decision was made. Wanting to do my part in the conflict, I went to the engineering officer and volunteered to go. That got me a discharge extension.

Those days, Vietnam was a hot item that was in the news every day. There were many protests nationwide; those in the military who were returning from Vietnam were called baby killers. One night in a bar, I heard a drunk say some awful things about returning men. He was a sailor wearing a peace pin. I walked over and tapped him on the shoulder. He turned, and I hit him square in the mouth as hard as I could. Of course, a huge fight broke out. So many chairs, tables and other items were broken that the bar had to close for two days.

When the news came down that we were going, most sailors on the ship tried to get a leave before departing; some did, but others did not. I was lucky; all my hard work had paid off, and I was granted a ten-day leave. I borrowed some money from one of my shipmates running a slush fund (for every $5, you paid back $7). It was illegal but a needed service since I was making only $22 every two weeks. I borrowed $100.

I started my leave a few days before Christmas. On the day of my leave, I rode a bus to my locker room for my civilian clothes. In full uniform, I hitchhiked to Logan Airport in Boston for a plane to Florida. Because I was in uniform, I was able to buy a standby ticket; not a full priced ticket, but no guaranteed seat. I had to wait until the plane was near ready for takeoff; if a seat was available, I would be allowed to board.

I had called Mama about my going home on leave; she seemed happy but reserved about that. I told her I would call when I arrived in Pensacola. She told me that my father had taken a job on a dairy farm, about twenty miles north of Maple Wood. She said she and he were living in a small house on the farm though they still owned the house in Maple Wood. She said she would try to find somebody to pick me up.

I arrived in Pensacola the next day about 11:00 a.m. I did not see anybody I knew, so I called home. Mama said that Earl, the farmer she worked for, would pick me up. An hour and a half later, I saw a man in coveralls and a straw hat walk in. I asked him if he was Earl; he said he was. We got into his late-'50s Ford truck and drove to the dairy farm. There, I got out, thanked him, and walked into the old, run-down house. Mama and my sister, who was home from college, came out to greet me. My father was nowhere in sight.

That evening, Mama made a big pot of black-eyed peas, rice, and cornbread. She gave me a gallon jar, and my sister showed me where to fill it from a large vat of fresh milk. Onboard, we had homogenized milk, and it did not taste as good as this milk. It was kept at a temperature just above freezing. It had been a long time since I had tasted fresh milk. It reminded me of trying to get milk from Aunt Josie's old cow, and I smiled. I felt good to be with family once again after two years.

After supper, Mama, my sister, and I sat in the living room talking. I told them my ship was going to Vietnam—that was why I was home on leave. Mama started crying, or maybe I should say wailing. My sister hugged me as she cried. Just then, my father walked in, saw Mama and my sister crying, and grabbed an axe handle next to the door. He said, "God damn you, plowboy! Come here and make your mother and sister cry? I told you you'd never amount to anything. I'll kill you!"

He started toward me axe handle raised high, but Mama stood and said, "Daddy, Johnny told us he's going to Vietnam! That's why we're crying." He had that wild look in his eyes. The axe handle was still raised over his head. "I don't care! Get out of my goddamn house!" Sadly, I left.

I walked down the dirt road and sat at the edge of the woods. It was very dark, and I heard only the usual night noises of insects and small animals. A kind of calm and peace fell over me. I felt at home. All the old feelings I had tried so hard to forget came rushing back. I said out loud, "I'll never be free. My life is useless. I haven't become anything, just like he told me."

About fifteen minutes later, I heard my sister calling me. I answered, and she walked over and sat beside me. She said, "Mama is talking to him to see if he'll let you back in the house." She wanted to walk back and sit on the front porch, which had a light on; she did not like sitting in the dark. As we walked back, I put my arm around her and said, "Sorry I came home, sis, and started all this trouble over again." She leaned her head against me and said, "I'm glad you came home, Johnny."

She and I sat on the front porch talking for a couple of hours. Eventually, Mama came out and said I could come in. My father had gone to bed because he usually got up at 4:00 a.m.

to milk the cows. The house was small and had only two bedrooms. I slept very lightly on a sofa in the front room. It was so small that half my legs hung off its end.

I heard my father get up, get dressed, and walk out into the front room where I was. I did not open my eyes, but I could sense him standing over me and staring. He said, "God damn you!" and walked out. I fell into a fretful sleep which tormented by dreams.

Later that morning, Mama fixed grits, eggs, and homemade biscuits. After that, my sister and I walked down to see the dairy farm's owner, to whom she introduced me. They seemed to be real nice country folks. Mama, my sister, and I spent the day sitting and talking. At one point, my sister said she was going to meet some friends at a juke joint that night and asked if I wanted to go. She said they had a real nice country and western band there. I told her I didn't know any of her friends and would feel out of place. She said, "You know Cherrie, Grant's aunt." I said, "Oh yeah, I know her. Is Grant home yet?" She replied, "No, not yet."

About 7:00 p.m., my sister and I left the house; she was driving my old VW Beetle. As soon as we got down the road about a mile, she told me I could drive. She said she didn't want to start any trouble while at the house.

A short time later, we arrived at the juke joint. The band was playing a slow country song; the words and music gave me a comforting feeling I had not felt in a long time. Out on the floor, eyes closed, couples were hanging onto each other as they slowly danced, their bodies pressed hard against each other. As I watched, my eyes filled up as a longing flooded my heart and soul. Suddenly, I said, "Is she out there? I know she is!" At that moment, a young girl in a short skirt and cowboy boots walked by, smiled, and said, "Keep looking, cowboy."

I smiled and wiped away my tears. I shoved my feelings deep down with all the others, where nobody would ever see them. My sister and I sat at a table with five of her friends. Somebody pulled chairs over for us. I sat next to Cherrie, and we exchanged greetings. My sister introduced me to her friends. We all ordered drinks, and everybody started talking. I spoke mainly with Cherrie.

When the band started playing a fast number that I liked, I asked her if she would like to dance, but she declined. She and I talked while the others did a lot of dancing. After about an hour, the band played a real slow number. Cherrie asked, "Well, Johnny, are you going to ask me to dance or what?" I am sure I had a stupid look on my face. I said, "I thought you didn't want to dance." Giving me that "silly boy" look, she said, "I didn't want to dance to that jitterbug song, but I like to slow dance." Very pleased with myself, I asked, "Cherrie, would you like to dance?" Laughing, she said, "Of course I would."

After that, we danced every slow dance holding onto each other like two lost lovers reunited. We moved our chairs closer together, and I sat with my arm around her. We smiled a lot at each other without saying anything. Occasionally, I would look at my sister, who was watching us with a huge smile on her face, pleased I was sure.

At the end of the night, I asked Cherrie if I could drive her home, and she accepted my offer. She rode up front with me while my sister rode in the back. Cherrie was living in an apartment behind the courthouse in Maple Wood. She and my sister kept up a stream of conversation all the way there. I walked her to her door. I looked at her in the moonlight and asked, "Do you want to go out tomorrow night?" She said, "Boy, Johnny, you don't waste any time, do you? Yes, I would." I said, "I'll pick you up about six." I could tell that she was waiting for a goodnight kiss, but something held me back. I finally said, "Goodnight. I'll see you tomorrow." With a deep sigh, she said, "Okay" and walked inside.

On the way home, my sister asked, "Are you going to see her again?" I replied, "Yes, tomorrow night." She asked, "Why didn't you kiss her?" I shrugged. "I don't know." The truth was that I had been afraid to. I had known Cherrie only as Grant's aunt, and I had not wanted to make unwelcomed advances. Cherrie was different from the typical bar girls I was used to.

The next evening as usual, my father was not around. I took the Beetle and picked Cherrie up. We went to a restaurant on Highway 91, and we talked for hours. She wanted to know what I had been doing in the navy and where I had been, but she spoke sparingly about herself. The more we talked, the more I realized she was nothing like the women I had met in the past two years. I now believe that I started to back away for that reason; because I had known her for years, I felt I did not deserve her.

She had to be at work early in the morning, so I took her home at eleven. We walked to her door; it was obvious that I was not leaving without giving her a kiss. She stepped close to me, and as I kissed her, she closed her eyes. Her body pressed into mine as our lips met. I recognized a desire in her. I had the same desire, but it scared me. She asked if we were going out the next night. I told her, "Yes. I'll pick you up at the same time."

I got home about midnight. My father met me at the door. With an angry shove, he opened the screen door so hard that it almost came off its hinges. It knocked me off the porch. Standing in the door and holding that axe handle high, he said, "I'm saving that goddamn VW for your sister. You're not to use it again. You hear me, plowboy?" I said, "Yeah, I hear you." He took a menacing step toward me, swinging the axe handle, still raised, and screamed, "What did you say?" I said, "Yes sir, I hear you." I had jumped back so he didn't hit me.

He was mumbling under his breath as he walked into the house and to his bedroom. I sat on the front steps and smoked. I wondered if I should just head back to Boston. At least there, I knew women I could stay with to finish my leave. Then I thought of Cherrie. I thought it wouldn't be fair to just leave her like that.

About four hours later, I was still on the porch when I heard my father getting up to milk the cows. I walked into the woods behind the house until I saw him leave. I went inside and lay on the couch. I closed my eyes. My thoughts returned to my memories, and I wondered as I had so many times in the past, *what have I done wrong to have him still treat me this way. Hadn't I become a sailor like he wanted me to?*

Later that day, I called Cherrie and told her my father would not let me use the Bug anymore. She said, "That's okay, Johnny. I'll pick you up. I want to say hi to your mom." I gave her directions to the farm.

She arrived about 6:00 p.m. in her '58 Chevy. She hugged Mama and my sister and talked with them for a few minutes. My father came home. Cherrie was standing next to me, and as my father entered, she moved even closer to me. My father walked up to us, leaned in, brazenly stared at her breasts, and asked, "Cherrie, you want to go see the cows?" Of course, Cherrie said, "No thank you." My father said, "I can take you down back on the tractor" as he reached for her. I stepped into his path, and Cherrie stepped behind me. As his hand hit me in the chest, I said, "She said she doesn't want to go with you!" He angrily said, "God damn you!" He grabbed the axe handle. I knew what he wanted to do. I stood and waited, fists clenched, wanting to finally get this over with.

As he raised that handle above his head, I turned to made sure Cherrie was out of the way. She was already headed for the door. My father had a crazed look in his eyes. "Get out of my goddamn house and take that bitch with you!" He brought the axe handle forward but missed my head. Bringing it back quickly, he raised it and got poised for another swing. Before he could swing, I walked out. Cherrie had already reached her car, and I joined her. After opening her door, I went to the driver's side and got in. She was crying. She said, "Oh my God! I've never been so scared in my life!" With tears in my eyes and disgust in my heart, I said, "Cherrie, I'm so sorry you had to see that. I promise you I'll never bring you here again." She said, "Thank you." As we drove off, we saw my father standing on the porch with axe handle raised.

That night, Cherrie and I parked down by the White-Water River. She was still shaken up, so I put my arm around her, and we talked for hours. Late that night, we drove back to Jay. I got out of the car about a mile from the farm. While she waited, I walked to the house. It was before milking time, so I knew everybody would be asleep. I slipped into the front room, retrieved my bag with my uniform and other items, and left as quietly as I had come in. I stopped on the porch, and in the darkness with tears running down my cheeks, I said, "Goodbye."

After walking back to Cherrie, I had her drop me off at the house in Maple Wood. Cherrie said she would pick me up the next day. The doors were locked, but in my youth, I had never latched my bedroom window, and it was still unlatched. Inside, everything was as I had last seen it. My father's guns were beside his bed, and my shotgun was beside my bed. I checked if it was loaded. It was. I put the barrel under my chin and my finger on the trigger. I was so angry that I wanted to die, but then I saw Mama's face all screwed up and screaming, "You'll go to hell, Johnny!" Relaxing my grip on the gun, I said out loud, "But aren't I already in hell?"

I drifted off into a light sleep, the gun still resting on top of me. My dreams were once again filled with Cap and me roaming the woods. I wondered if he was dreaming of me. I knew he would be because our feelings and love for each other ran deep.

Lying there, suddenly, I saw my father's face twisted up in a ghoulish way, axe handle raised and ready to strike. I yelled, "No!" Opening my eyes, I realized it was only a dream. Sunlight was pouring through the bedroom window. I put the shotgun back in its resting place. I made sure there was no evidence of my having been there, and I climbed out the window. The hose was still hanging in that pine tree, so I undressed and showered. Having money in my pocket, I walked to Ray's gas station to grab something to eat, mostly junk food. I sat our front with Ray's father and sometimes helped him pump gas. We talked for the better part of the day. In the late afternoon, I called Cherrie to tell her where I was.

Early that evening, she picked me up, and we drove to Pensacola Beach stopping along the way to grab a bite to eat. I had not had a drink since the night I had arrived, and I didn't feel the need for one. We spent that night parked by the beach and talking. I had my arm around her. She was soft spoken and gentle. In the wee hours of the morning, I had her drop me off down the street from our house in Maple Wood. I kept a sharp eye out to make sure my father was not around. I was going to go inside the same way as before, but something stopped me. Instead, I walked through the woods until I reached the lake. I built a fire and made a bed out of leaves and brush. I used my sea-bag as a pillow. I fell into a troubled sleep.

That afternoon, I headed back to the house. My heart sank when I saw my father's Bug in the driveway. Wanting to avoid a showdown, I cut through the woods and walked back to Ray's station. I called Cherrie to let her know where I was.

I spent Christmas Eve in my old bed alone but with the shotgun handy in case my father came in. Now, I believe I would have used the gun. Luckily, he never came.

Cherrie spent Christmas Day with her family. She invited me to go with her, but I thought I would feel out of place, so I declined. For the rest of my leave, Cherrie and I spent the evenings together, and I came to realize she was a very special hometown girl with great values. I knew she had feelings for me, but I just wasn't feeling the same about her; I never made any sexual advances toward her.

She drove me to the airport and asked me when I would be coming back. I told her I didn't know. I said something totally out of character for me. "Cherrie, I'm not the guy for you. I drink too much, and I have so much anger in me and so many unresolved issues that I would only hurt you. I don't even know where my life is taking me." With tears in her eyes, she said, "I know, Johnny." I held her hand, kissed her tenderly, and said, "Goodbye, Cherrie." I knew it was for the best for both of us.

CHAPTER 85

Old Habits Return

The flight to Boston was long. Most passengers slept, but I stared out the window pondered my life such as it was. On the plane, I had a little more than my share of drinks. Being in uniform, I don't believe they would have cut me off unless I passed out.

I took a train from Logan Airport to downtown Boston. I walked to the Hill Billy Ranch in Park Square, where a band was playing good bluegrass music. The crowd was loud, and the clinking of glasses and ice was a recognized and welcome sound. In full navy blues, I attracted a lot of attention.

I walked by a table, and a girl sitting with a couple grabbed my hand and pulled me into an empty chair beside her. She said her name was Sally; she introduced the couple as her sister, Janet, and her sister's boyfriend, Rod. I said I was Johnny. The boyfriend asked me what I would like to drink, and I said, "Rum and Coke with lime." He ordered drinks for everyone and paid for them giving me a big smile. I smiled and thanked him, but I wondered what he was up to.

He bought round after round. After my third rum and Coke, I started relaxing. By midnight, I had consumed six or eight rum and Cokes. Sally said, "I'm hungry. Can we get some Chinese food?" The others agreed. Sally asked, "Can I bring the sailor with me?" The boyfriend said, "Sure, bring him along." She grabbed my hand. "Let's go, sailor."

I had only $5, enough for a bus ticket back to Newport while in uniform. My brain was feeling that familiar fuzziness from alcohol, and it felt good to be back in that space. Having heard stories of sailors being rolled for their money, I excused myself saying I had to visit the head. There, I put my $5 bill in my sock.

When I got back, I saw that the couple had left but the girl was waiting for me. Excitedly, she said, "Let's go!" I followed her outside and across the street to the boyfriend's car. We got in the back seat, and she was all over me. The couple laughed and said, "Hold on, kids! We're going to eat first."

The boyfriend drove us to Chinatown in the combat zone, which wasn't far. We entered a restaurant named China Wok and ordered food. Again, the boyfriend paid. Afterward, we returned to the car, which was parked in a dark alley. I again got in the back seat with the girl. She lit up, and I smelled that familiar scent of marijuana. We passed the joint around.

I heard zippers being unzipped, clothes being taken off, and heavy breathing coming from the front seat. I heard the car squeaking and felt it moving as the couple engaged in the age-old act of love. By then, the girl had my uniform off and was sitting on me trying to insert me inside her; she was cursing because I wasn't cooperating. With a big sigh, I rolled her off and climbed on top of her to fulfill her wish. As I finished in a shuddering gush, I rose and screamed, "You got what you wanted! Can I do anything else for you, ma'am?"

She started crying, and the couple in the front seat sat up and asked, "What's going on? What's wrong?" I said, "Everything's wrong with you people. I shouldn't be here." I got dressed, and as I got out of the car, the girl screamed, "Johnny! Come back! I love you!"

I wandered the area for an hour and ended up in Boston Commons, a park known to be unsafe at night. I was cold, tired, and sleepy. I sat on a bench as it started to snow.

I opened my eyes, and all I saw was white. I thought, *Well, you finally did it. You're dead. But why the clouds? I thought for sure I'd see fire and the devil.* For a few minutes, I just enjoyed the freedom of the moment—no pain, no feelings, no memories, just floating through the air not feeling anything. *Wait a minute. My hands are numb, and I can't feel my feet either.* With a big yell, I sat up throwing snow everywhere and scaring a woman walking by so badly that she screamed and ran off looking as if she were pissing in her pants. I realized that it was daylight and that I had fallen asleep on the bench. Falling snow had covered me.

I got up and walked away. People watched me closely as if they thought I would attack them. I walked to the Greyhound bus station and bought a ticket to Newport; I had enough for coffee. I sat next to a window and settled in for the ride. An older gentleman sat next to me and tried to get me into a conversation, but I was not interested, so he soon gave up trying.

I looked out the window as the bus slowly made its way out of Boston. My thoughts turned to Cherrie. I liked her, but I thought she was too close to me and my family, and I knew in my heart she was not prepared to deal with me and my troubles.

CHAPTER 86

Around the World

Our ship left for an around-the-world cruise. We went through the Panama Canal, and our first liberty was in Panama City. As I walked out the gate the first time, a young boy ran up to me and shoved a newspaper in my face and babbled in Spanish. He ran off after a couple of minutes taking my wallet and ID with him. My money was safe because I had put half in one shoe and the other half in an inside pocket of my blouse. The next day, my ID was returned to the ship.

As had become my custom, I drank heavily every day while on liberty as Player had taught me. I thought I was erasing my pain, but looking back on those troubled times, I know all I was doing then was masking it.

Five of us young sailors went on liberty together. Just outside the base on the first day, we hired a Panamanian named Pedro, who drove an old, black '57 Caddy. He was quite a character. He was about five feet tall and weighed about 200 pounds. He wore very bright and multicolored shirt and pants, and he wore a ridiculous-looking straw hat and sandals. He spoke so fast that we had to keep telling him, "Slow down, Pedro! We can't understand you."

The city was very congested; he drove like a maniac all the while talking to us and not paying much attention to his driving. He kept saying "Bar, beer, girls, I know them all, and I take you." He was so funny that he kept us laughing.

That night, he drove us to about six bars. He would wait outside in his Caddy while we were inside drinking and carousing with the girls. I have never contracted any venereal disease. Most of the bars had small bedrooms off the back that the girls rented by each use. It should have been by the quarter hour. A couple of the bars turned out to be off limits for some reason. The shore patrol would show up and take any sailors into custody. While we were inside one, Pedro came running in telling us, "Shore patrol! They arrest you! Let's go." He got us out just as the shore patrol arrived.

At another bar, he came in again yelling, "Shore patrol coming!" All the bar girls herded all the patrons into a room behind the bar. The walls were just boards nailed up; we saw them, and they saw us, but the shore patrol was not allowed to go behind the bar, so no one was taken into custody.

The city was the dirtiest place we had ever been, but Pedro kept us out of trouble and took good care of us. We tipped him very well in American money when he dropped us off at the front gate that night.

Our next stop was Los Pueblos, which turned out to be for only eight hours to refuel before we left for Hawaii. Most of the sailors were on the pier calling home for the last time in the United States. I thought about calling Cherrie, but after some real soul searching, I decided not to. I knew it would only upset her, and that was not what I wanted to do. I knew I could not drag it out. *Haven't I already ended it?*

Our ship was only a few hundred miles from Hawaii when a distress call came in about a small plane reroute to Hawaii that was running out of fuel and was about to ditch in our vicinity. Our sister ship, the *Fish* and ours, the *USS Bonita*, both destroyer, were dispatched. Our captain was very good when it came to inform us about such situations; we heard everything over the speakers. When the information was relayed that the plane was coming in for a landing between the two ships, I went topside to watch. I saw a twin-engine, plane coming in and hitting the water. The nose went down, and the plane flipped over on its top; the wheels were sticking straight up. The two inside, were able to climb out just after the plane flipped and before it sank in about ninety seconds.

The pilot and passenger were bobbing in the heavy seas in life jackets. The plane landed close to our ship, so one of our lifeboats with three sailors was launched. The pilot and passenger were rescued and brought aboard. As they were being brought onboard, only about ten feet from me, I saw that the pilot had a hole about the size of a pencil right in the middle of his forehead that was bleeding. They were ushered straight to the sickbay to see the doc. I knew they would be in good hands.

I walked to the fantail, the rear of the ship, and my friend Fred, not the Jim from back home, came up out of the aft boiler room. As we walked and talked, I saw a wallet floating by the ship and pointed it out. We saw lots of bills stuffed into the wallet with some hanging out. Those we saw were all hundreds. The ship was rocking back and forth. Thinking we would receive a nice reward, I lay on the deck underneath the safety lines, and as the ship rocked toward the wallet, I reached far out, but just the tips of my fingers touched it. I told Jim, "Hold my feet! I'll reach farther out on the next roll." I squirmed way out with Jim gripping my feet; the ship rolled back, and I grabbed that wallet.

Just at that moment, an old CPO who had just come up out of the aft fire room, yelled at the top of his voice, "Fred! Let go of Johnny! Johnny! Get up!" Fred, being the good sailor, he was, obeyed the command—he let my feet go. My head went into the wave that was hitting the ship. Seawater washed all over me, and my legs bent up catching the life lines and stopping me from being washed into the sea. The CPO chewed our asses out well. We told him we were trying to retrieve the wallet for the pilot, but he didn't care.

Oh, the wallet you ask. I dropped it when my head went under and seawater filled my mouth. Right after that, another sailor who had also seen the wallet floating by got a long-handled net, but by then, the wallet had drifted away. Later, the rumor going around the ship was that the pilot had lost his wallet with over $10,000 in it. Fred and I were sad because we figured we could have used a good reward.

Right after the rescue, the ship left at full speed for Hawaii. Originally, we were scheduled to stay in Hawaii for four days, but troubles that had plagued the *USS Bonita*'s number-one evaporator, a machine that turned salt water into fresh water, acted up again, so we stayed an extra day. I rented a VW Bug and toured the island for four days even driving over Diamond Head and completely around the island. four of my shipmates and I visited all the monuments. My thoughts about all the lives lost during the attack in 1941 were sobering, and we hadn't even started drinking yet.

During our four days there, we engaged in several fights over some ladies of the night, as they liked to be called. On our last day of liberty, the five of us started drinking early that day. As on previous nights, we spent most of that night on what was called Hotel Street because of the bars and girls. Once again, I was hoping the pain would dissipate, but in fact, though I did not know it then, it was eating me up inside. I continued to have stomach pains, and sometimes, I would pass some blood when throwing up or defecating. That night, all of us got so drunk that we started a fight over something I still can't remember. Leaving the bar, I drove the Bug on top of a stop sign. We could not get it off, so we just left it there, walked to the base, and went aboard drunk, battered, and bruised.

Our next port of call was Midway, where we stayed only overnight for refueling. Jim and I went on liberty. I bought two six-packs of beer at the PX, the basic store on naval bases, and sat in a park watching Gooney birds, the funniest things we had ever seen. They built two-foot-high nests on the ground made of mud. The baby—we saw only one in each nest—was almost hairless and had a small head but a large bottom. They looked like one of those old inflatables that when punched bounced away but bounced right back up again. The adults were very funny to watch. To take off, they ran almost in slow motion but went faster and faster. As they picked up speed, their feet sounded like horses' hooves, and they would eventually rise into the air. Once airborne, they soared gracefully. To land, they came in fast, hit the ground, and rolled over several times before righting themselves and walking like ducks to the nest to feed the young. It was so funny that Jim and I spent our whole liberty drinking beer, watching the birds, laughing, and having a good time, but most of all forgetting for a few hours.

Our next port was Guam, again for refueling. There was absolutely nothing to do, so Jim and I bought a couple of six-packs, found a quiet spot, and drank to pass the time. I talked about some of my old life but not in detail—just some of the highlights. Fred talked about his home life, and in general, he had a good family. The worst part he hated was that his mother and father had moved from South Carolina to Maryland.

We then steamed to Subic Bay in the Philippines. We had only two days of liberty, and we were told not to go off the main road. Four shipmates and I walked off base and found bars two stories high lining both sides of the dirt street. Brightly lit and multicolored jeeps took us wherever we wanted to go. The drivers were like those in Panama; they knew what we were looking for.

The best part of liberty in Subic Bay was that we got everything we wanted for $10. Marijuana was a big part of life in Subic Bay. For a few pesos, we could by a small bag of the drug or a rolled joint from any of the drivers. I did smoke, inhaling often, but my real drug of choice was beer and hard liquor. I was still doing anything I could to erase my memories. My friends and I were involved in several fights that night; I was now getting into fights very quickly and often.

After liberty and on the way back to the base, we found a vendor on the bridge before entering the base who sold actual monkey meat on a stick that he cooked to order over a grill–25¢ a stick. While we ate, we would throw quarters into the murky water below. Kids would dive to retrieve the quarters and would come up with them in their teeth.

On the second night after drinking heavily and smoking, we were drinking in one of the bars we had never been in before. The band was just starting to play after a break. I asked the lead singer if one of my friends who liked to play drums could play for a little while with them. He said, "Fuck no! Sailor no play." One of my friends heard what he had said, and he came up to the stage. By then, my anger was erupting. I looked at the singer and saw my father's face all screwed up and yelling at me. I hit my father's face as hard as I could, knocking him down and into the rest of his band. A big fight broke out. They should have let my friend play because afterward, most of their instruments were ruined. After tearing up the bar, the five of us left through the back door just ahead of the shore patrol. We went to another bar trying to find a nice, quiet place to drink. We never found a quiet place, but we sure found lots of drinks and women.

In one of the other bars later that night, all five of us found ourselves with women on the third floor. It was lined with bedrooms that were simple but contained what was needed—a small bed with only a dirty mattress and a bedside table with an old, worn bowl containing dirty water and a rag hanging on the side. I sat on the bed, looked around, and in a drunken stupor thought, *this is where I belong. I'll never go any further in life.*

The girl and I got undressed and finished smoking. We were just getting right when I heard one of my friends yelling, "Johnny! Help!" I put on my boxers, grabbed the rest of my clothes and my shoes, and ran to his room. As I entered, my other friends were right behind me. The shipmate who had yelled for me was lying naked on the bed, and his girl, also naked, was standing next to the bed holding his wallet. I asked, "What's going on?" He said, "She's stealing my money!" The girl started screaming, and three short, sumo-wrestler types came through the door carrying long, curved swords. We were all yelling. They apparently spoke no English, but they made it clear with throat-cutting motions that they were going to cut our heads off.

My friend on the bed got up; with his business hanging down for all to see, he was standing beside us yelling just as loud. He grabbed his wallet, and the five of us went out the back window onto a roof and jumped in the street out back. It was too late; we hadn't remembered our one order— "Never go off the main road."

We found ourselves in the worst place we had been in, and we were in varying stages of dress. We were walking in mud a good foot deep. Back on the main street, we found a water faucet on the side of a bar and cleaned ourselves up the best we could. We were done drinking for that night, so we headed back but stopped long enough for some monkey meat.

CHAPTER 87

A Fight For Freedom

The next story is a shortened version of a ship and her sailors I was proud to serve on; she made a great contribution to the defense of the United States and the rest of the free world. It is the story of about three hundred men who sailed halfway around the world to meet and engage the enemy in direct combat operations with very few hours of relaxation. The *USS Bonita* fired her guns numerous times, *in anger for the first time*.

I dedicate this story to the fight for freedom and to the brave men who have fought and died in faraway lands. I hope the telling of our story will underscore the struggle this country faces every day in the fight for world peace.

Vietnam was only the beginning of a long and hard battle against oppression. I have empathy for those around the world who have neither the power nor the knowledge to fight it alone. It would be such a shame if help for the greatest nation in the world did not come to their aid. I am not saying that the world should become Americanized, but I believe all people should be free to decide under what conditions they live.

In 1974, when South Vietnam fell to the North, I was in my easy chair at home, the same as millions of other Americans watching it on TV. It did not affect me directly, but I wept for those poor souls it did.

I fly the American and the POW flag in my yard every day, in honor of those brave and proud men who fought and died abroad.

CHAPTER 88

Vietnam

The following story, in part, is taken from my around the world cruise book I received, while serving in Viet Nam in 1966.

Leaving Subic Bay, we steamed toward Vietnam. We went on plane guard duty in the Tonkin Gulf for the USS *Ticonderoga*, a large attack aircraft carrier, whose planes conducted operations in South Vietnam.

Ships on plane guard duty were a very important part of the war effort. For two weeks, we followed the carrier prepared to pick up survivors if a plane didn't make it to the deck and had to ditch. In the fire room, we had both boilers online always because there were times when we would be doing ten knots and a minute later would have to do twenty knots. Our watch was eight hours on and eight hours off. The worst part of that duty was that the temperature in the boiler room was about 135 degrees all the time and it was very noisy. Most of the time, I slept on the deck, too tired to go back to our berthing compartment.

Next, we were sent on an antiaircraft picket station to watch a Chinese Communist–held island. After that stint, we were sent to observe and follow a Russian intelligence-gathering trawler. We then went on gunfire-support exercises. After forty-two days at sea, we went into the port of Kaohsiung, Taiwan, for some well-deserved R&R. We had no pier to tie up to, so our ship anchored in the harbor.

Kaohsiung was like Subic Bay on steroids. There were so many bars and girls that everybody fell in love immediately. In fact, the scuttlebutt was that two sailors on our ship went AWOL and married local girls. I never did find out what happened to them. We had two days of what was called port and starboard liberty—half the crew went on liberty the first day and night, and the other half went on liberty the second day and night. As everyone else, I drank myself into a stupor when on liberty.

I remember seeing a small boat with two Taiwanese in it come alongside our ship and all our garbage being dumped in it. They pawed through the mess and ate whatever they could as fast as they could. It was so sad to see; my heart went out to them. A woman named Soo Lin owned a business that took out our garbage and cleaned the outside of our ship. She would also take our uniforms to be cleaned, pressed, and returned the next day. All hands thought she was awesome.

Leaving Kaohsiung, we steamed to Hong Kong for a five-day liberty. I wasn't expecting Hong Kong to be so modern. There were lots of bars and girls, however, and many high-rises, parks, and monuments as well as the usual stores. I bought a watch with a rocket as the second hand. I was so proud of myself because the owner started off wanting a hundred dollars, Hong Kong dollars, that was. If I remember correctly, ten of their dollars were worth one American dollar. That night, I showed my shipmates my new pride and joy. Another sailor laughed and showed me his watch, the exact same one, saying he had bought it on the pier for twenty Hong Kong dollars. I had the last laugh when I told him I had paid only five. Sadly, it lasted only about a month before it quit.

The last night on liberty, Jim and I had been drinking since early morning, and sometime around ten that night, we realized we had not eaten all day. I asked the bar girl for something to eat; she said all they had was chicken soup. She brought us large bowls of it and chopsticks, which I still have to this day. I told her I needed a spoon, and she went to get one. She was gone so long that by the time she came back with a large cooking spoon, I had learned to use those chopsticks and had eaten the soup. I do not think the meat was chicken, because it was very dark and tough. Could it have been cat? I don't know, but maybe.

We sailed back to the Tonkin Gulf for another month and half of duty that included ASW—antisubmarine warfare—operations and gunfire bombardment for support of marines in the Da Nang area, who were taking heavy gunfire from the Viet Cong. After that, we again pulled plane guard duty and then served as a gunship for the USS *Bainbridge*, a nuclear-powered missile ship. After that, we were sent on a mission that is still classified. The scuttlebutt was that it was not a normal operation for an ordinary destroyer, but I never found out what we did.

We then steamed back to Kaohsiung, Taiwan, for much-needed R&R. During that liberty, I could stay overnight one time. But afterward, the engineering officer told me, "I'm sorry, but you weren't supposed to stay overnight," so I wasn't allowed to stay overnight again. During that time, both boilers needed some complicated repairs, and only the chief, other rated sailors, sailors with and little more training and of course made more money and I, who was nonrated, were kept onboard for two days around the clock to handle the work. All other nonrated sailors from the boiler room went on liberty for five days.

After that, my engineering officer told me, "When we return home, put in for early liberty for two weeks. I'll approve it." I was beside myself thanking him. Of course, nobody in the boiler room knew that during those two days, I had done most of the work while the chief and the first class drank coffee. I liked thinking that somebody knew I was worth something after all the hard work I had put in onboard.

We left Kaohsiung and headed back to the war zone. We spent ten days of around-the-clock bombardment while at general quarters, or battle stations, the entire time. We fired more than two thousand five-inch shells into the Mekong Delta. We were in the Saigon River's shallow waters, our ship had a shallow enough draft to operate in the river but on one occasion, our ship was stuck on a sandbar. I went up and looked past the fantail; our ship's propellers were throwing sand up maybe fifty feet in the air as the ship tried to get off that bar.

As before, the captain had the entire assignment piped through the ship's speaker system. Every time something would come over the speakers about our having hit our target, we heard cheering from all over the ship. Reports later said we had hit more than a hundred Viet Cong sites.

We were summoned from our upriver position several times to help in emergency gunfire support for the South Vietnamese army. Our guns pounded structures and earthen emplacements twenty miles up the coast as they were attacking a Viet Cong camp. The scuttlebutt over the loudspeakers was that we had silenced the ground fire aimed at our spotters and had demolished the VC structures and emplacements leaving an unknown amount of VC dead. The *USS Bonita* received reports of excellent effect and outstanding coverage about its gunfire support, and our captain congratulated the entire ship for our hard-earned success.

A few days later, the captain ordered a cookout on the fantail with swimming in the world's biggest pool, the South China Sea. Sailors with machine guns mounted on an upper deck and other sailors with automatic weapons in two lifeboats circling us as we swam. It was a well-deserved break in the action after being at sea for most of the deployment. Oh yeah—no sharks even though it was rumored that neither the North nor South Vietnamese would ever dare swim in those waters.

The *USS Bonita* earned the nickname The Steaming demon because of the great percentage of time we had spent underway—more than any other ship in our squadron. But problems with our number-one evaporator persisted throughout our deployment. Because freshwater was first and foremost needed for the boilers to make steam to propel the engines, our captain came up with a grand scheme to help all us smelly sailors. Every time rain was near, he steered the ship back and forth through the storm so all us hands had a chance to shower outside. What a sight—dozens of naked sailors soaping up on the fantail.

After completing gunfire support, the *USS Bonita* joined the rest of our squadron in Subic Bay for a couple of days of R&R. We steamed home via the Indian Ocean, the Suez Canal, and the Mediterranean.

CHAPTER 89

The Return

When we arrived back in Newport, Rhode Island, I was lucky enough to go topside to see the eight ships in our squadron met by a small fleet of navy fireboats, water hoses spewing high into the air imitating those rounds fired, a coast guard cutter, and many pleasure boats. As we entered the harbor, a historic Newport artillery company fired its old cannon, which was something to see. I was impressed by seeing what I thought were thousands of people, I learned later it was more than ten thousand, waiting for loved ones or just to greet us. It was good to be home and to step onto solid ground in the United States of America, where we were all free.

I went on early liberty, meaning liberty right after muster in the morning, for the first two weeks; the engineering officer had kept his word. After that, I took a thirty-day leave. As I was trying to leave my ship, I saw a girl, Helga, I had known briefly the year before. She was standing on the deck next to the gangway. I did not want anything to do with her because without my permission or knowledge, she had contacted Mama. I had received only two letters while in Vietnam, both from my sister, and she had told me about Helga first writing and then calling Mama telling her how much she loved me and how she wanted us to spend the rest of our lives together. I was worried I could not leave the ship without her seeing me, so I asked Fred to distract her, so I could slip by.

As he was talking with her, I put my sea bag on my shoulder and hid my face; I slipped past her and moved quickly toward the pier. I had just reached the gangway when suddenly Helga jumped on my back, wrapped her arms around my neck, and started kissing me and screaming how much she missed me, how much she loved me, and very loudly—how much she wanted me. People around us were looking and laughing. One young woman looking sorrowfully at me and shaking her head, said, "You can do better than that, sailor." I smiled and shook my head. I walked off the ship with her hanging onto my arm and talking a mile a minute. I walked up the hill toward the buses.

She said, "I have my car. I can drive you to your locker club." I agreed but told her I was mad at her. As we drove, I told her why. She cried and told me how much she loved me. I told her very angrily that I had no feelings for her. She didn't believe me; she said, "You love me, but you just won't admit it!" Her crying brought up memories of me crying, and I hated her more and more. My anger got the best of me, and I started yelling and calling her a "fucking slut." Of course, that made her cry harder.

By the time we arrived at my locker club, I had a pounding headache and needed a drink badly. Getting out with her still crying, I retrieved my sea bag from her back seat. As I was walking into the club, I saw her driving away. In the club, I met the same night time clerk from the year before. I had told him that my ship had been deployed for about a year. He welcomed me back, and because he had saved my locker, which was next to the shower and toilets, I gave him several oriental paintings that were on black velvet and lit up under black lights, which he had previously told me he liked. They had cost me only a few dollars, but it was worth it to see the smile on his face and to have him save my locker.

After stowing my uniforms and liquor and changing into civilian clothes, I walked to the nearest bar and was welcomed back by the barkeep and a couple of the bar girls I knew as well as a couple of new ones. I downed some shots of Cutty-Sark and sipped my Blue Ribbon. I was just starting to feel good about being back when one of the bar girls, Lauran, strolled past and whispered in my ear, "Trouble coming, honey."

I turned and saw Helga walking toward me with a huge smile. She sat on the bar stool next to me and said, "Aren't you going to buy a girl a drink?" Looking at her with disgust, I felt my anger rising. I was on the verge of yelling at her when Gena, standing behind her, caught my eye. She had a scared look on her face, so I said nothing and bought Helga a Tom Collins. She started a conversation with the barkeep acting as if nothing had happened.

We sat and drank until the band started playing around eight. She tried to get me to dance, but I refused. She tried to get me into conversation, but I refused. As we continued sitting and drinking, I got madder and madder. By 2:00 a.m., I had drunk about half a dozen shots of Cutty-Sark and a six-pack of Blue Ribbon. She was still talking, but by then, all I heard was *blah, blah, blah.* It was closing time, and she was looking pretty good, at least from where I was sitting.

I took her arm and said, "Let's go." She hopped off the stool, and we headed out. As I passed Lauran, she looked at me shaking her head. Helga had parked in the alley behind another bar; she said she had surfed the strip looking for me. I drove us out to a spot overlooking Narragansett Bay called *Make Out Point*. She climbed into the back seat and beckoned me to follow. For a moment, I looked at her and thought of how much I hated her for what she had done. Then the alcohol and lust took over, and I came back to reality. It was past 2:00 a.m., and I had no other place to go. I said, "What the hell. One more for the road won't hurt."

I climbed into the back seat and saw that she was lying down, undressed, arms outstretched, and legs splayed; her womanhood beckoned me. I saw that she had a couple of six-packs of Blue Ribbon on the floor. I opened one and took a long swallow as I undressed. I saw her long hair cascading across the seat and shimmering in the full moon. Her breasts, with extended nipples, proudly pointed up, and she was smiling. I gasped at how beautiful she was. I said out loud, "Too bad you're such a slut," but she just smiled at that. She grasped my shoulders and pulled me on top of her with a big sigh. With a deep sigh of resignation, I let lust take over. As I entered her, I started crying; I hated myself for what I was doing and thinking.

After my explosion, I lay on top of her as my body was racked with sobs. She held me close and wrapped her legs around my waist. She tried to wipe my tears away and said, "See? I told you that you loved me." Even in my drunken stupor, I hated myself more than I hated her, but not saying anything made me hate myself only more.

We sat up and drank several Blue Ribbons. We made love two more times before falling asleep, still entwined with my manhood nesting firmly inside her. A loud banging woke me up. At first, I thought I was still in Vietnam and we were pounding the shore with those big guns. I remember yelling, *"Kill the bastards!"* Opening my eyes, I saw bright sunshine was pouring through the car windows. I closed them, hoping the noise would stop, but it didn't.

I opened my eyes again. This time shielding them with my hand. I saw the cause of that awful noise that was making my head hurt—my father. My mind and body froze. I closed my eyes and opened them. I was waiting for that cold glass of water in my face. When it didn't come, I realized where I was. A cop was banging on the window and yelling, "Hey! You guys okay in there?" I couldn't get words out, so I gave him a thumbs-up. The cop wasn't buying the thumbs-up; he was demanding we get out of the car.

Our clothes were in a heap on the floor. Helga, still lying under me, woke and asked, "What's going on?" I said, "My father wants us to get out of the car." She sat up. "What? Your father?" I shook my head to clear my brain. "I mean a cop." She opened the door, clambered out, and started talking to the cop. She was naked. I screamed, "Leave her alone!" but he ignored me. I climbed out too. The cop looked at me standing there in all my nakedness, looked Helga up and down several times, and said, "You damned sailors get them all. Get dressed and get the fuck out of here!" I picked that moment to puke my guts out. Before we got back in the car, I washed the puke off myself with some beer, gulping down the last half.

I was standing with my back against her car trying to hold it up, I think; Helga reached in and brought our clothes out. I popped open a fresh Blue Ribbon just to take the edge off while getting dressed. As I drove us back to Newport, she started talking again. She figured that after the previous night, everything was forgiven, and I would be going home with her to Fore River, Massachusetts, for the weekend. I didn't say anything about being on a thirty-day leave.

Arriving at my locker club, I stopped the car on a side street right in the middle. I got out and said, "Goodbye," leaving the door open and the car running. As I walked away, she was screaming and crying. She chased after me and put her arms around my neck interlocking her fingers. She went totally limp, and I dragged her down the street hoping she would let go and return to her car. I heard angry drivers stopped behind her blowing their horns because her car was blocking the street just as I had planned. She paid no attention and clung to my neck, crying and screaming how much she loved me and saying, "Please don't leave me!"

I approached my locker club and saw a brunette leaning against the building waiting for a bus. She smiled and asked, "Having a rough day, sailor?" I smiled and said, "Oh yeah."

I entered the club with Helga hanging on my neck and screaming; Steve, the manager, said, "Lady, this is a men's locker room—no women allowed." She didn't respond; she grasped me even tighter. I had a *What can I do?* look on my face and said, "I can't get her off me."

Another club member came over, and between the two of them, they got her hands unclasped from around my neck. I bolted for the club area downstairs. She tried to follow, but the manager and the other club member held her back. I looked back in time to see her kick the manager in the balls. As he was falling to the floor, she punched the other club member in the mouth and ran out.

I went to my locker, undressed, and took a long, hot shower. A short time later while I was dressing, the manager approached. I saw a large lump in the front of his pants and figured he had an ice pack covering his gonads. He leaned against the pool table and in a strained voice, he asked, "Johnny, is that your girlfriend?" With a sorrowful, bad-puppy look, I replied, "Steve, I'm so sorry. I never thought she would act that way, and no, she's not my girlfriend, just a girl I picked up in a bar last year." I promised him I would never let her get that close to the club again.

I lay down on the pool table for some shut-eye. I remembered that cop banging on the car and wondered why I had seen my father's face in him. I concluded that he was right, that I would never become anything in this world. Finally, with a pounding head, I fell into a restless sleep filled with visions of my father telling me how bad I was.

I left the club a couple of hours later. I walked down the street stopping to have a few Blue Ribbons and shots of Cutty-Sark on the strip while I kept a sharp eye out for my possessive lover. No way in hell would I allow her to follow me to my next destination.

It was 12:15 p.m. Looking around the room for one more quick check, I walked past the bar area and nodded to Alice, the barkeep. She smiled and gave me a knowing look. That was not the first time I had used the back door to slip away. As I made my way through the stacked cases of beer in back, I placed my empty in one and grabbed a full one. I walked out the back door, jumped off the landing, and walked swiftly to the ferry. I crossed the gangway and paid the fare–10¢ for sailors. I breathed a big sigh of relief as it pulled away from the pier.

Back at the bar, I had called Gina and her family; her father was then stationed in Quonset Point, and because it was a Saturday morning, I knew they would be home. I crossed the bay and was met by her father. He welcomed me back, and as we headed to his home, I filled him in on my trip to the Far East of course leaving out all about the drinking and the girls.

His family happily greeted me. I had brought gifts for the family, and I had a special one for Gina I had bought in Hong Kong—a beautiful, hand-crafted, musical jewelry box decorated with the image of a rickshaw. It played beautiful oriental music, and the rickshaw's wheels turned slowly in time to the music. I had fallen in love with this piece when I had first seen it, and I was very proud of myself for giving her this beautiful piece of art. Her family loved it.

Gina's mother made us a late lunch, and her father gave me his credit card saying, "If you want to go out tonight, you need to gas the car up first." I thanked him but declined the credit card saying I would put gas in it. I drove his car to the nearest gas station, gassed up—at that time, you could gas up before you paid—and reached for my wallet as I walked to the station. To my surprise—no wallet. I quickly checked inside the car, but still no wallet. With great embarrassment, I went inside; the attendant let me call Gina.

Within a short time, Gina's father showed up; a friend had driven him there. He paid for the gas. On the way back, I told him I wasn't sure where I had lost my wallet. I said I had a couple of hundred in cash and a large check in it. We got to his house; the family had already looked around but had not found it. With a sinking heart, once again, I knew I was doomed.

I called Helga from their house. Helga simply asked, "So, are you coming back?" With defeat in my voice, I said yes. She said, "Don't worry. All your money is safe." I said, "I know. It's not my money you're after, it's my soul. She laughed as I asked, "Are your mother and stepdad home?" She said, "No, they went away for the weekend. Why?" I said, "No reason, just wondering." But I was hoping her mother would not be there.

The previous year when I spent a weekend with Helga, she was called in to work on a Saturday morning. Her stepdad was working as usual. Since we had been out late the night before partying, and Helga was at work, I figured I could get a little extra shut-eye. I did not know how much time passed, but suddenly, I felt Helga slide into bed behind me. Her naked body pressed hard against my back. We had made love before she had left for work, but my body was responding to this new intimacy as she reached over me and massaged my manhood to full erection. I rolled over, and to my surprise saw that it was Helga's mother.

This thirty-something-year-old woman had emigrated from Germany when she was pregnant with Helga and had her when she was only a teenager. I realized where Helga had gotten her beautiful body. Her lovemaking was much different from Helga's—it was hard, fast, and loud. I was worried that neighbors in the next apartment would hear her.

After that, occasionally when I called the house looking for Helga, her mother would answer. Several times, she convinced me—though it did not take much—to meet her. She would drive to Newport to pick me up. We never went to a bar; instead, we bought alcohol, drove out to Make Out Point, and spent several hours making love. She would then drive me back to the strip in Newport. I would usually get drunk with that big question buzzing in my head, *What the hell are you doing?* By the time we left for Vietnam, I was glad to go.

I told Helga to pick me up at the ferry on the Newport side in about two hours. She said, "The ferry! I never saw you get onto it, but okay, I'll see you there." I now knew that yes, she had been following me but that my old trick had worked. Gina's father dropped me off, and I caught the 4:00 p.m. ferry back to Newport, where she was waiting for me.

She put her arms around me, gave me a huge hug, and then kissed me hard pressing her soft body into mine. She reached into her car for my wallet and handed it to me. With a sigh of relief, I put it in my back pocket. I never checked for the money, as I drove us to her home in Fall River.

Late that afternoon to my dismay, her mother and stepdad returned. Helga and her mother wanted the three of us to go out that night for a drink. I declined saying I didn't feel like drinking. I suggested Helga and I go to a drive-in.

As we were leaving the house, her mother came out of her bedroom carrying a blanket. Handing it to me with a lopsided grin, she said, "Just in case you two get cold in the back seat." Helga giggled as we headed out the door.

On the way, I stopped for two pints of blackberry brandy. Helga said, "I thought you didn't feel like drinking tonight." I lied. "I wanted to spend time with you." She snuggled in close and kissed me hard. At the movie, I had both pints to myself because she didn't like blackberry brandy. After the movie, we did use that damn blanket in the back seat right in her driveway. I saw her mother standing in the living room window watching us. My brain saw my sister standing there watching. I had a feeling if I didn't get away from those people, bad times would result.

The next day, Sunday morning, I lied about having to get back to my ship by Monday morning. We hung around the house for the rest of the day. In the early afternoon, her mother and stepfather went out; her mother told us with a big smile, "You kids have fun."

Of course, after she left Helga pulled me into her bedroom. As we were lying there afterward, I lit up a Lucky, and she asked me if I would come back next weekend. Lying, I told her sure if I didn't have duty. She said, "Okay. Call me and let me know."

As we lay there, I heard the front door open. I said, "Get dressed! Your mother's back!" I slipped my pants on just as her mother walked past the open bedroom door. Helga had not moved; she was still lying spread eagle on the bed. I looked at her and then at her mother, who was standing in the doorway. Motioning with her hands so Helga could not see her, she pointed to me and then herself and nodded *Yes?* I looked down, and she continued to her bedroom. The stepdad was nowhere in sight.

That afternoon, Helga drove me back to Newport. She wanted to drop me off at the base, but I told her I needed to go to my locker club, take a shower, and change into my whites before going back to the ship. She wanted to wait, but I talked her into going home with the promise that I would see her the next weekend.

After she left, I took a shower but changed into civilian clothes. I used the back door and made my way down to the waterfront, a dangerous place for any sailor to go—at least that was the word around town. On some occasions, my shipmates and I had gone down there usually late at night if we hadn't scored women on the regular strip. That night, I met a bar girl who was a full-blooded Apache named Chrystal, or as she was affectionately called *she who sleeps around* by her friends mainly because she was seven-and-a-half-months pregnant but didn't know who the father was. She took a quick liking to me as I was drinking Blue Ribbon and playing pool for a dollar a game. She warned me that these guys were good. I walked away with an extra fifty bucks that night and did not have to buy my beers either; she bought all night long for the promise that I would come back and see her another night.

That night, I got so drunk that she called me a cab because she was afraid some of the locals would "do you harm," as she stated. The cabbie took me to my locker club. I barely remember arriving and going downstairs with the help of the night clerk to fall asleep on the pool table.

I was awakened by violent shaking. It was the night clerk, and he was more pissed than I had ever seen him. I saw that I had puked all over the pool table and myself. While he continued screaming, I stripped down and practically crawled into the shower. When I got out, he was still mad as he was trying to clean the puke off the table. I put my boxers on, sat on the bench by the shower, and went back to sleep.

The next thing I knew, someone was shaking me and saying, "Johnny, wake up. It's time to go." It was the first class I worked for in the fire room. After a few minutes, he was able to get me up. He reminded me that we had made plans on Friday before I had left the ship to meet up. I was still drunk, so I wasn't remembering much, but he was excited. "I'm taking you to buy that GTO you've talked about!"

I got dressed, and we loaded my civilian clothes and the five gallons of liquor I had into his car. I crawled into the back seat and promptly went back to sleep.

CHAPTER 90

Dodge Charger

He drove straight through to Reading, Pennsylvania, where there were many car dealerships. He pulled into one and woke me. We walked inside, and I headed straight to the men's room, where I puked up everything else that was in my stomach. I had a huge headache, I was sick to my stomach, and I was hungover and maybe still a little drunk.

I went back to the showroom and told a salesman that I wanted a '67 GTO. He said smiling "I don't have any GTOs." I told Steve, "Let's go," and turned to walk away. The salesman said, "I don't have what you want, but I do have a car that will eat that GTO up." I asked, "What is it?" With a big smile, he said, "A Dodge Charger." Steve said, "At least look at it." I did not feel like arguing. The salesman took us out back and showed us a '66 navy-blue Dodge Charger. It had a style I had never seen before. The inside was also navy blue with four bucket seats and a four-speed. I immediately fell in love with it, mostly I think because of the navy-blue color.

It was parked next to a dirt track behind the main building. The salesman asked, "Do you want to take it for a test ride?" I said, "Sure, let's go." He got in the driver's seat and motioned for me to get into the passenger seat. He drove around the track two or three times doing about thirty miles per hour. He smiled and asked, "What do you think?" I looked at him; he seemed to have two heads and four eyes. I said, "I need to drive it now." I believe the blood left his face. He asked, "Are you sure you're sober enough to drive?" I said, "If you want to sell the car, I need to drive it first." He sat there saying nothing; he looked worried. I got out and walked around to the driver's door. "Of course, I'm sober enough." He got out, I got in, and he got in the passenger seat.

After I drove around the course twice, he was screaming, "Let me out now." I didn't get it. I had been keeping it under a hundred. After two more laps with him making shrill noises like a girl, I pulled the car up behind the building and said, "I'll take it." He raced out of the car and into the building. Steve said, "You scared him pretty bad, and me too." I shrugged. "He shouldn't have let me drive then."

We went inside. The salesman was nowhere in sight. Another salesman said, "I'm going to help you because the other salesman is feeling ill." I looked at him and thought, *How funny. This guy has two heads too.* I told him I wanted to buy the Dodge Charger out back. He looked me up and down and asked, "You're in the navy, right?" I said, "Yes." He asked with a smirk, "Do you have any credit or collateral?" I thought about how stupid he was. He was going to make this sale but had done nothing; the car itself had closed the deal. Laughing slightly, I said, "No." After a few more moments, I said, "But I have a check." His demeanor immediately changed. "Yes sir, come right this way."

My friend and I followed him into an office, and I gave him a government check. I signed the back, and he prepared the paperwork. It took only about an hour to get everything changed over to me. I received the change from my check as they put on a Pennsylvania temporary paper plate, serviced the car, and filled the tank. I said goodbye to my friend and headed out with a new car, cash in my pocket, and five gallons of my favorite beverages. Life was good, but I should have remembered that some changes happen, but some others don't.

I drove for two days stopping only for gas and bathroom breaks, not always in a bathroom. When I stopped, I would grab something to take with me to eat, and I had all that booze, so I was sipping it all along the way.

I arrived back home in Florida; I made sure I timed it, so my father would be out milking the cows. I went in and surprised Mama, who was already up as usual. I gave her a big hug, and she started to cry just a little, saying, "You should have told me you were coming home." I lied. "I know, Mama, but I wanted to surprise you." I was half drunk and on thirty days' leave. When I started driving, I had no idea where I was going; I just got in and took off. On the way to nowhere I decided to go home. While Mama was cooking breakfast, I woke my sister up. She gave me a big hug and came in the kitchen and joined us for breakfast. She was now out of college.

After eating, I drank coffee, smoked, and told them about our around-the-world cruise. I was surprised to see that my sister had started smoking. While we were talking, I brought up the subject of Helga with Mama. She was happy and smiling as she talked about her. She said that one day out of the blue, she had gotten a letter including a picture from a girl named Helga. She wrote that she knew and loved you very much. She also said that you told her you loved her also and wanted to spend the rest of your life with her," She said, "She had given Helga her phone number and they had spoken several times." Mama said, "She's a very nice girl and very pretty too."

I felt tingling in my hands moving up my arms as I gripped the coffee cup almost to the breaking point. My shoulders were twitching. My neck started to heat up, and I felt the hairs on it rise. My pulse was racing, and the blood rushing into my ears was causing ringing loud enough that I was sure Mama and my sister heard it. My eyes burned; I literally saw red as the blood continued its path into my brain and past. I ran my fingers through my hair expecting to feel blood shooting out of the pores of my scalp. Smiling, I calmly said, "Mama, you don't really know her. She's not a nice girl, and I'm never going to see her again." With a frown, she said, "Johnny, you always were too choosy with girls." With sadness in my voice, I said, "Well, Mama, you're the one who always told me stay away from girls because they were dirty and nasty, remember?" Mama turned and walked away.

My sister said, "I'm meeting some friends tonight at the same bar as last year, and Tammy, my old high school girlfriend, will be there. You're welcome to join us." I thanked her and said I would.

Being very tired and still in a fog from all the alcohol I had been drinking, I lay on the old couch. I don't know how long I had been sleeping before I was awakened by a violent punch that knocked me off the couch. My head hit the floor hard, and I was dazed. Not knowing where I was, I yelled, "Let's get the fuck out of here, boys!"

I was jerked to my feet and shoved so hard that I crashed through the screen door, onto the front porch, and down into the dirt in the front yard. Shaking my head to clear the cobwebs out, I stood and realized it had been my father who had attacked me. Standing there dazed, I saw Mama behind him and my sister beside her crying. I don't know why, but I took a step toward the porch with fists clenched when I saw he was holding that axe handle high. His look told me he would kill me. Even though my brain was fuzzy, I looked him in the eye and asked, "Why? Why are you doing this? What have I ever done to deserve that? Does it have something to do with my birth mother?"

He started screaming and swung the axe handle down. It caught the roof of the porch. He lowered it and with a menacing jab toward me with the axe handle said, "Get the hell off my goddamn property!" I knew it really wasn't his property, but I figured things would get only worse if I stayed. I walked to my car and said, "Bye, Mama. Bye, sis." I drove off throwing dirt and gravel and left in a cloud of dust. In the rearview mirror, I saw him standing alone on that old porch with axe handle raised.

Luckily for me, I had not taken any clothes or liquor into the house. I headed toward Grant's house in Maple Wood. It was good to see him again. We had not spoken since my ship had left. When I had been home the year before and was dating his aunt Cherrie, Grant was still on active duty. He was home again, off active duty and working as a male nurse in the Maple Wood hospital. Of course, he wanted to see my new car, so I took him for a ride, and we stopped, parked, and talked for a while at the park on White Water River not far from his house. I still had some of the five gallons of whiskey, so we didn't have to buy any. As we drank, I told him about my visit home and my father's reaction. "As far as I'm concerned, I never want to see him again." I asked him how Cherrie was doing; he said she was fine. He asked, "Are you going to see her again?" I told him no and explained why. "Grant, she's a nice girl, but I just don't feel a connection with her." He agreed, but with a laugh, he called me a shithead. I laughed and said, "Yeah, you're right, but I just need to find the right girl, or I'll never settle down." I told him that my sister was meeting friends including a close high school friend, Tammy, that night. I asked him if he wanted to come along. He said, "Yeah, but I heard Tammy's married." I replied, "I didn't know that, but we'll find out tonight."

We went back to his house, and his mother greeted me with warm hugs. I enjoyed being around her because she always treated me as if I were one of the family. She still had a huge, warm, and giving heart. I showered and changed clothes. We talked for a while and then played a game of football on Grant's old electric football game. Later, we went to the Park More, a restaurant, for a bite to eat.

CHAPTER 91

The Race

In the early evening, Grant and I headed to the bar to meet up with my sister and her friends. Walking inside, I heard the band playing country music, which I loved. My sister and her friends were there. She introduced Grant and me to all of them except Tammy, whom we already knew. I bought a round for the table; everyone asked me about Vietnam. With the music blaring in our ears, it didn't take long before my trip became history and everybody, but Tammy got up to dance. I moved next to her, and we started talking. I asked her if she was married, and she said, "Yes, but my husband and I are separated. I moved back home. I'm living with my parents in Maple Wood."

We talked throughout the night. I asked her to dance, but she said, "I'm not much of a dancer." So, we drank and listened to the music while watching everyone else dance. By the end of the night, I had consumed my usual amount of Blue Ribbon and Cutty-Sark and was feeling no pain. Even though Tammy had come with a couple at the table, I asked her if I could drive her home to her parents' house. She said, "Yes. I was hoping you'd ask."

She and I drove Grant home; she and I spoke just a bit on the way because we were constantly staring at each other. I woke Grant up at his house. As he got out, I said, "I'll see you tomorrow." Laughing, he replied, "Yeah, sure you will."

After he got out, I asked Tammy, "Do you want to go home?" She replied, "No." I said, "Okay." I drove to the park Grant and I had been to earlier that day. It did not take long before we were in the back seat. We made love for several hours, taking breaks in between to smoke and sip my whiskey. We fell asleep entwined.

We awoke with the sun beating down on us through the window. Tired and hungover, I was thirsty. All I had was the alcohol. She refused, but I took a few long pulls from a bottle. It was the one thing in my life that I always trusted, knowing it would never let me down. Meeting Tammy again brought up old feelings, but in a strange way I could not explain, the feelings felt comfortable.

We got dressed, and I drove her home. I went in to see her parents, whom I had not seen since my high school years. Walking inside, I was greeted first by her mother, who after giving me a hug, looked at Tammy and stated very sternly, "See? I begged you to wait!" Not knowing what she meant, I looked at Tammy, but she only looked down and shook her head.

In a couple of minutes, her father came into the living room and happily greeted me with a hearty handshake and an invitation to dinner. "I'm making my fried mullet you used to like." I told him, "I remember yours was the only mullet I ever liked, so thank you, I'll be back."

I headed back to Grant's, but he was not home, so I headed to our old house, and I found my window still unlatched. I climbed in and took a bath. I left after making sure nothing was left to show that I had been there.

I climbed out the window and was about to get into my car when someone said in a hard, gravelly tone, "Stop right there or I'll shoot!" I turned and stared into the twin barrels of a shotgun pointed right at my head. I saw the grizzled, old, bearded face and long, white hair of our neighbor Mr. Winters. When I was fifteen, his wife had run off, and he told everybody, "She's run off with Johnny" even though I was still there.

Eventually, he had gone to Chicago, where she was from, and convinced her to return. She had stayed only a few months before leaving again. That time, he did not go after her, but he told everybody she had left because "She's in love with Johnny." Of course, everybody knew he was just a crazy old coot, but with him standing in front of me with a gun locked and loaded, I did not know if he meant to kill me.

Slowly, I said, "Mr. Winters, it's me, Johnny." Squinting his eyes, he asked, "Who is it?" I replied louder, "It's me, Mr. Winters, Johnny." Dropping the barrel of the shotgun slightly, he said, "Well, boy, what are you doing back here? I almost shot you." I replied, "I'm home on leave from the navy." He said, "Your folks don't stay here. They're living on that old cow farm." I replied, "I know. I just came by to see the old house." He said, "Well, you better git, or somebody might shoot you."

I got in my car and drove away. He stood there watching, shotgun still cocked, just to make sure I left I guessed. *Man, he's still the same old coot.* I reflected on how many times I had seen him shoot that gun. Once late at night, we heard a shot and ran to his place. He had shot his dog, Bear, through the screen door with both barrels. He said, "Bear's got that hippophobe, and she's gone mad." We couldn't tell much because her head was blown off. It was winter, and we figured the poor dog just wanted to get in out of the cold.

The next day, he asked me to help him bury her. He told me to pull the heavy metal cover off the cesspool, and he just threw her body in. With great sadness, I put the cover back. I had sat and petted her many times in the past and found her to be a very gentle animal.

One time, she had pups from mating with my Cap. Mr. Winter had taken the pups and tried to sell them as Florida field shepherds with papers he forged as AKC registered. He sold one pup for $750. Within a month, the couple brought it back because it had distemper. Afterward, he threw that pup and all the others into his cesspool.

I drove to a bar a couple of miles away near Sky Line Heights, where Gina once lived. I saw couple of guys I knew. Everybody wanted to see my Charger. Showing them, I was all smiles. They made me feel important, as if I had status.

We talked about our high school days and played pool for beers. I won a few, and by the time supper came around, I had had my usual amount of Blue Ribbon. That time, knowing I was headed to Tammy's parents' house, I didn't have any Cutty-Sark. I told the guys I would probably be back later with my friend Grant and a girl. The liquor was flowing freely, and everybody said they couldn't wait.

At Tammy's house, I was again greeted with friendliness and warmth. After a great meal of fried mullet, hushpuppies, and a couple of beers, I called Grant. He was home and eager to go out. Tammy and I left her house to pick up Grant. Of course, we had to make a quick stop in a secluded area I knew about, so Grant was a little worried when we showed up thinking that we had forgotten about him. Grant hopped into the back seat and looked at the two of us. He laughed and said, "Oh sure, I have to wait for hours while you two were making out." Tammy and I looked at each other, and we all laughed. After taking a long pull on a bottle, I handed it to Grant, and we headed to the bar.

We were met with loud whoops and wolf whistles. Laughing, Grant said, "Oh guys, you shouldn't have," and the stage was set for a night of drinking, fun, pool, and a good mix of country and rock blaring from the jukebox. We had enjoyed ourselves for about two hours when the front door flew open and two burly fellows came in asking, "Who owns that damn Dodge Charger out there?" Everybody pointed at me just as I was about to take my last shot on the eight ball for another Blue Ribbon. I glanced at the intruder but went back to my game. He grabbed the eight ball and said in a loud and menacing voice, "I asked, who owns that damn Dodge Charger?"

A quiet fell over the crowd. Several males and females moved in to surround the two. Straightening up with stick in hand, I quietly asked, "I do. Why?" In a more somber voice, he asked, "I own that Chevy SS out there. You want to race?" Before I could answer, Grant yelled, "You bet your ass we do, and we'll fucking beat you too!" I saw that the crowd was anxiously waiting for my answer. Looking back at this pompous ass, I said, "Sure, why not? Three out of five for a hundred bucks." He replied, "Okay, let's go out on the old Munson Highway." A great cheer rose from the crowd as Grant and I left the bar with Tammy following.

Having owned only the VW Bug, I had never drag-raced before, but I had been a fan of that great movie featuring James Dean, *Rebel without a Cause*, so I knew what I had to do. I figured if we raced five times, I would have a decent chance of winning. As we drove off, Grant said, "Wow! Look who's following us." Looking back, I saw a dozen cars filled with patrons.

We got to a remote part of the highway in twenty minutes. The other cars lined the side of the road, their lights on. The crowd was standing beside them whooping and hollering as the driver of the Super Sport and I revved our engines. Two of the cars had moved down the highway about a quarter mile away to mark the end of the race. Both of us had given one of the patrons a hundred dollars to hold for the winner.

Tammy gave me a disgusted look and asked, "Are you sure you want to do this?" I didn't answer her but showed her my best alcohol-induced, knowing smile. Grant, standing about ten feet in front and between us, a white scarf he had borrowed from one of the females in his raised hand, jumped up and came down dropping his hand. With engines screaming, tires smoking, and the smell of burning rubber, we started down the road with a tremendous roar. I saw the onlookers raising beers and yelling. Silly boy. I beat him by a good car length. Returning to the starting point, Tammy said, "I don't want to ride with you again."

I asked her if she would be our starter and use her panties as a flag. As you could imagine, alcohol was doing its job. Reluctantly, she agreed. She climbed into the back seat, took her pants off, and pulled off her panties. She threw them at me. Laughing, I said, "I want to keep them afterward." Grant excitedly rode shotgun. As we sat and waited for Tammy to drop the starting flag—her panties held high—and with the crowd going wild, Grant asked, "What the fucks with her?" Taking a long pull on one of my jugs, I replied, "She was scared, that's all." She was pissed at me.

On our second race, I again beat him, but on our next one, I missed third gear, and he beat me handily. Lining up for our fourth race, the other driver yelled over, "How about we make it two hundred?" Looking at Grant, I laughed, and he yelled, "You're fucking on."

With a tremendous burst of speed in first gear, I pulled a car length ahead. Grant was yelling, screaming, and jumping up and down in the shotgun seat, banging his head against the roof. After hitting second gear, the Super Sport pulled beside me as we roared down the road. That time, I made sure I did not miss third gear. I pulled completely away from him and won by two car lengths. Arriving back at the starting point the other driver came over to congratulate me and pay up. Shaking my hand, he said, "I've heard how fast Chargers were, but I never believed it. I sure do now, though. That is one fast fucking car."

Leaving the race area, I asked people if they wanted to go to Cold Water Creek and party. Most agreed, and off we went, arriving around midnight. We built a huge bonfire and spent the night sitting around it, reliving the race repeatedly. By dawn, only Grant and I were awake. Tammy was sleeping beside me. We were pretty much played out.

I fell into a restless sleep, and I dreamed about Grant and me traveling the country and drag racing. In late morning, I was awakened by somebody shaking my shoulder. It was Tammy saying she needed to go home. I got up. My head felt like an overinflated balloon, my mouth tasted like a buffalo had shit in it, and my entire body was hurting. I woke Grant up and told him we had to go. Grudgingly, he got up, crawled into the back seat, and went to sleep.

After dropping Tammy off at her house with the promise that I would pick her up that evening, I drove to Grant's. There, we took showers and lay down. That afternoon, we drove to the Park More restaurant for a bite. Afterward, I dropped Grant off at home telling him I was going to pick Tammy up and spend the night with her somewhere.

CHAPTER 92

Love or Lust

I picked Tammy up, and we headed for the beach area, looking for a new watering hole. We found a bar that was quiet. We had a few drinks and headed to the beach. We took a blanket that she had brought from her house and walked to the beach. We took one of the three bottles of alcohol I had left.

We spent the night drinking, skinny dipping in the warm gulf waters, and making love. The next morning, we found a small diner and had a bite to eat. We spent the day driving around the area and talking. That night, we headed back to Maple Wood and spent the night at the beach area on Cold Water Creek. We finished that bottle of alcohol, and I bought a six-pack of Blue Ribbon. We finished that also.

The next morning, she said she would like to go home. After dropping her off, I headed to our old house. I was very tired and hungover, so instead of climbing through the window to bathe and change clothes, I crawled into the back seat and fell into a troubled and restless sleep.

I don't know how long I had been sleeping when I was awakened by a loud thump. I thought, *Wow. This dream is so realistic I can feel the car moving.* I opened my eyes, and my dream turned into a nightmare—I saw my father's contorted face outside the window. I rose on one elbow. He motioned for me to come outside. I got out and stood in front of him wondering, *what in the hell does he want now?*

He was holding his shotgun with that ominous barrel pointed at my chest. Before I could speak, he screamed, "Are you shacking up with that goddamn bitch? She's married, and all the neighbors have called the sheriff's office on you. I'm going to call them myself!"

My alcohol-induced reply was, "It's none of your goddamn business what I'm doing with her!" With an unintelligent growl, he swung the stock of the shotgun at my head. I was still fuzzy headed, but I was ready for him. I stepped out of the way, and the stock hit my car with a thump, the same noise that had awakened me.

I heard a tremendously loud bang as he pulled the trigger. The recoil from the shot caused the gun's barrel to hit me in the head. I had not been prepared for that. I dropped to my knees and screamed, "What are you, fucking crazy?"

"Get off my property and don't come back or I'll shoot you!"

I jumped to my feet and saw old man Summers, our neighbor, coming out of his door and running toward us, his shotgun held in a menacing way. Believing he would fulfill his promise, I got into the car and drove to Grant's house thankful I had not gone inside and fallen asleep.

Grant had just gotten home from work. We sat in my car; I gulped down as much liquor as I could. I told him what had happened. Grant got real serious for a moment and said, "Johnny, we should have killed the bastard when we had the chance and we still can." With a big sigh, I said, "Well, maybe we should."

That night, Grant and I picked up Tammy, and we headed to the bar. I wasn't in good spirits and didn't feel like playing pool, but I bankrolled Grant for his lost games. By the end of the night, I was in a real fog. I was drunk, but I was still asking what I had done so wrong to be treated that way.

After dropping Grant off at his house, I drove to our usual place on Cold Water Creek. I told Tammy what had happened that afternoon with my father. I asked her if he had ever tried anything with her. At first, she shook her head, but I could tell there was more to the story. I persisted, and she eventually told me that one day when she had been at our house visiting my sister, my father had tried to separate her from my sister, and when that didn't happen, he tried to grab her and throw her onto my sister's bed. Getting away from him, she left the house and never allowed herself to be put in that circumstance again. She was crying as she relived the incident. I put my arms around her. "He'll never hurt you. Grant and I are going to kill him."

I spent the rest of my leave with Tammy and Grant. The three of us talked many times about killing my father, but of course we didn't. The last night, Tammy and I spent some time with her parents before heading to Cold Water Creek. She said, "I'd like to come to Newport and live with you. We could get an apartment." I never did answer her.

The next morning, I dropped her off at home. As we were sitting in the car, she started crying and said, "Please let me come with you." With a heavy heart, I looked at her and thought, *Is this love or just lust?* In my alcohol-clouded brain, I didn't know. I kissed her and said, "I really have to go, but I promise I'll keep in touch." I could tell she wanted much more from me than I had to offer her.

CHAPTER 93

The Flat

After saying goodbye to Tammy, I headed to Grant's. We spent a couple hours talking. He asked me if I was serious about Tammy; I said, "I don't know. The sex is great, but I don't feel that real connection with her, you know?"

Saying goodbye to Grant and his mom was hard, but I had to head north. I didn't have any alcohol left. After leaving Santa Rosa County, which was dry, I bought a few bottles of blackberry brandy. I put that Charger through its paces, sometimes reaching speeds of 150 mph. I had a flat tire along the way—thankfully not at high speed.

I reached Quonset Point, Rhode Island, in under twenty-four hours. The brandy was gone, and I hadn't eaten since leaving Maple Wood. I pulled into Gina's house, and her family came out to see my new car. Taking one look at me, her mother fixed me something to eat and made me go to bed right afterward. I still had two days left on my leave, so I spent them with her family trying to sober up before heading back to the ship.

I left her house the next day and headed to Newport and my locker club. There, I showered, sent my civilian clothes out to be cleaned, changed into my uniform, and drove to the base. My shipmates wanted to know all about my leave. Had I met any girls? They especially wanted to know about my new car. I told them about the drag racing and how I had won $200. I told them I had dated a girl I knew from high school, but I didn't give them any details even though they begged for more. I never mentioned Mama, my sister, or my father. I did tell them about Grant, though. A couple of them thought it was cool that he had become a male nurse, but a couple others thought it was gay. Personally, he was my best friend and I didn't care what he did.

That first weekend back, my friend Fred and I headed to Boston and the Hill Billy Ranch in Park Square for some fun on Friday night. By now I was rolling in money. My pay was about eighty-two dollars month. I don't know why, but I wasn't interested in meeting any girls that night. I think my mind was still in a fog, so we just got drunk.

After closing time, we walked across the street to the parking lot. I saw that my right front tire was flat. Fred asked, "Do you have a spare?" I laughed and said, "Sure do, but it's flat too." We sat on the pavement, leaned against the car, and laughed. I finally got up and said we needed to find a good tire.

We walked around the combat zone looking for a tire at 2:00 a.m. After walking for about an hour, we came across an older pickup. Still a little bit drunk, I thought the tire size was the same as my car's. The doors were unlocked, and we found a jack and a lug wrench behind the seat. We jacked the truck up and took a tire off. We heard yelling, and we saw two big and fat men coming toward us. They were so fat that they couldn't run. I picked up the tire, rim and all, and Fred and I took off running laughing foolishly all the way.

We didn't go straight to the car; we thought they might have had friends in the area who would follow us, so we ran a silly zigzag path. Finally, totally out of breath and still laughing our asses off, we made it safely back to my car. I got my jack out; we jacked the car up and took the flat off. When we tried to make the stolen tire fit, we had no luck. All the holes were missing, or the lugs were in the wrong place. In our drunken stupor, we couldn't figure out which it was. Eventually, we did find out that my car's tire was fifteen inches and the tire we had stolen was sixteen inches. We sat and laughed. As I fired up a Lucky Strike, it started to rain, so we laughed harder and drank some of the whiskey and blackberry brandy I always kept for emergency use in the trunk.

It was only a passing shower, so we sat there soaking wet for a few hours. After daylight we saw a taxi coming down the street. Fred ran out to the curb to flag it down. I brought the tire over and explained our problem to the driver. He laughed but said he knew an all-night gas station and would take us there. I asked him where it was, and when he told me the area, I knew how to get there. He said he would take us for a flat fee of $20—no meter. An argument ensued over the amount, and we ended with him taking us for $10.

He dropped us off at the station, and the attendant agreed to fix the tire but wanted $25. Another argument ensued, but he refused to lower the price, so we paid him but only after he fixed the tire by putting a plug in it. It took him two hours to fix the flat, and afterward, I called a taxi. It was not the same one who had brought us to the garage, and it cost only $3.25 for the return trip.

After putting the fixed tire back on the car, Fred and I crawled into the back seat and fell asleep. The parking lot attendant came on duty at 8:00 a.m. and woke us up saying he needed to collect more money if we were going to keep the car parked there. It was only $5 for the day and night, so I paid him, and we went back to sleep after asking him to wake us up at noon, when the Hill Billy Ranch opened.

Good to his word, the attendant woke us up, and we walked across the street to get our first beer of the day. The restrooms were downstairs, and they could be locked from the inside, so Fred and I took turns cleaning up. On the wall of the men's room was a machine that dispensed everything from condoms and aspirin to Aqua Velva towelettes for 25¢ each. We spent the day talking to the barkeep, an older woman who liked to tell jokes. I think it was just her way of keeping us talking and of course buying beer and Cutty-Sark.

CHAPTER 94

The Girls

We left the Hill Billy Ranch just before closing time and walked next door to the Trailways bus station. I was drunk, and Fred had to help me get there. I can't imagine what we must have looked like—two drunks helping each other down the street.

We walked into the restaurant that was part of the bus station. Sitting at one of the tables were Sparkle, a young black girl, and Ginger, an older white girl. They were working girls we knew. When they were hanging out at the bus station and not working, we had a lot of laughs with them. They could tell some funny and sometimes not so funny stories.

One of their more memorable ones, as they told it, was about a cold winter night when they were standing on a corner in the combat zone at about 1:00 a.m. They had just discussed leaving because the few people who were out were not interested in sex. Suddenly, a dark panel van pulled up; the driver asked them if they wanted to go to an after-hours party. As cold as it was and with nothing else happening, the girls said yes. A price was agreed on, and the driver took them to a house in Dorchester, a suburb of Boston. A large male was at the door collecting money and patted down all males who entered. They were not allowed to bring any weapons into the party. Of course, none of the girls was ever patted down, so all the males would give their weapons to the women to bring inside.

They found a party in full swing with a three-piece band, a room filled with males and females, a mix of black and white. All kinds of drugs were right out in the open. For three hours, the girls worked the party and made lots of money. The girls laughed when telling how the basement was just one big room and any sex acts had to be done against an outside wall but in full view of everyone. There were no chairs, beds, or any other furniture, so the floor had to suffice. Most of the sex acts were just blow jobs—quick and easy and on to the next one.

Around 5:00 a.m., the girls were tired. They had made a good amount of money in a short time and were standing in a corner drinking beer. A young white boy approached them. He looked about eighteen, but after talking with them, he admitted he was only sixteen. He said he had never been with a girl before and wanted to pay both for sex. Ginger said they laughed and told the kid, "Go home to Mommy, kid," but the kid persisted. Sparkle gave the kid an outrageous price just to get him to leave. The kid agreed and pulled a large wad of money out of his pocket. Seeing the money, the girls said, "That's for each one of us." The boy agreed and gave them the money. He said he had a car parked outside where they could go for the sex.

By then, the girls were ready to leave the party anyway, so they agreed to go with the kid. He led them to an older Ford station wagon around the corner. The girls found another young boy inside. Of course, they were upset and questioned the first one about this boy. He told them that he was his friend and he had never been with a girl either; that's why he had agreed and had paid for both.

Looking at each other, the girls decided to follow through with the deal. It was very windy, and they were glad to get into the car and out of the blustery cold. One girl got in the front seat while the other got into the rear seat with the other boy. Things progressed fast after that, and after all four had gotten undressed and were just about to fulfill the young boys' dreams, gunshots rang out from the direction of the party. All four sat up in the seats as more gunshots were heard. Suddenly, blue lights and cops filled the night all around them. As cops were banging on the windows, the girls, still naked, climbed into the way back and covered up with some items there.

The two boys, also naked, were trying to get dressed when doors on both sides of the car were yanked open. Cops reached in and pulled both boys out. The girls heard them yelling as the cops dragged them away. The girls said they lay naked in that car for three hours until the cops finally left.

They got dressed and started walking away through the then-quiet neighborhood when an old man standing in an old bathrobe on a porch asked them, "Hey, how would you young ladies like to make twenty bucks?" Laughing, they kept walking. They took a taxi home. I usually did not ask the girls how much money they made in a night, but after that story, I did. They said they had made over $2,000, each.

I smiled and lay down on the bench as they laughed at me and at how drunk I was. I am not sure how long I slept, but when I woke up, only Jim was at the table. He also was lying on a bench next to me sound asleep. I could only rest my arms on the table, put my face in my hands, and groan a little. Simon, a young gay boy who worked at the restaurant said, "You look terrible, honey. Would you like something to drink?" All I could do was nod. In a couple of minutes, he returned with a glass of a cold liquid that I thought was some type of apple juice. In the past, Jim and I would sit in the restaurant and drink keeping the bottles hidden from view from other patrons but known by Simon. I gulped down about half the glass; the supposed juice hit my belly like a rock and came up like a rocket, hitting the table and spewing out onto the floor. Of course, it was a whisky. The look on poor Simon's face was priceless—pure astonishment. I wiped my mouth and said, "Sorry." I headed for the restrooms still puking along the way with a hand clamped over my mouth. Simon was standing in the vomit gagging and lurching. After cleaning up, I woke Jim up. We were leaving as Simon was cleaning up the mess, gagging and throwing up himself.

CHAPTER 95

Lies, Sex, and Alcohol

It was Sunday morning; Fred and I returned to my car and talked about what we wanted to do next. Fred said he would like to return to Newport and maybe go back to the ship to get some rest for Monday morning. I told him I didn't feel like driving, so we climbed into the back seat and slept for most of the day.

In the late afternoon, we went back to the bus station to get a bite to eat after first cleaning up in the restroom. The restroom had the same problems as others in the area had with homosexuals. I went up first while Jim sat at our usual table against the wall. Standing on either side of the stairway, two homosexuals were waiting for young men to use the restroom. As I started up the stairs, one went in front of me and the other followed me. I had seen that many times in the past and knew exactly what I was going to do that time.

In the men's room, the first one walked up to one of the three urinals. As I entered the room, the one behind me brushed past me and walked up to a second urinal leaving the only open one right in the middle of the two being used. I walked up, unzipped, and started urinating. Because no walls separated the urinals, the two men were standing next to me and almost touching my shoulders. The man to my left had a huge smile as he started to masturbate. The one to my right was doing the same. He looked at me, smiled, and said, "Relax and enjoy yourself." Because I had drunk so much the night before and had not peed all day, my stream was like a fire hose; it was so strong that I thought I could have put out a fire.

I stepped back and peed to my right and then to my left. I started peeing back and forth as the two men, who were dressed in suit pants, hopped around like little kids. I kept peeing on them until they finally ran downstairs and out of sight cursing about "All you damned sailors." With a big smile, I continued peeing. The dispensing machine was like the one in the Hill Billy Ranch, so I was able to clean up. I went downstairs; Fred was laughing. He asked me what I had done to them. Telling him made him laugh even harder.

After eating, we decided to go to The Novelty Bar. Fred had changed his mind about going back to Newport. We returned to my car, and I drove there. I parked on a side street next to a group of motorcycles. Inside, we saw a long, horseshoe-shaped bar that was crowded. Just inside the door was a group of motorcyclists. Walking past them, we found only two seats available. Sitting next to us were two girls who were by themselves. I started talking to the pretty blonde next to me; she told me her name was Lola. We changed seats, so Jim could sit next to Beth, the other girl. For the rest of the night, we mostly sat and drank because the girls were not much on dancing. I was able to convince Lola to dance to a couple of slow numbers because I just wanted to cop a feel or two.

By closing time, 2:00 a.m., we were all feeling pretty good. I didn't have to ask to drive them home because Beth asked, "You're driving us home, right?" Before Fred or I could answer, Lola said, "Of course they are, if they want to get laid" while looking at me. I had a big smile on my face and said, "Of course. And I want to get laid too."

We went to their place, an apartment in Dorchester above a liquor store. For the rest of the night, we partied, drank, and smoked a little weed. We found out that both girls were part-time bartenders at The Novelty Bar. At 6:00 a.m., we said goodbye to the girls; we left them naked and tired and headed for Newport. We had only an hour and a half to get onboard for muster, which we made with fifteen minutes to spare. That was because I had not obeyed the speed limit; I had again put that Charger through its paces.

Fred wasn't interested in a relationship with Beth, but I wanted to see Lola again, so I went back the next time I had liberty. Walking into the bar, I found her bartending. Sitting at the bar, I put a $10 bill down and ordered my usual—a Blue Ribbon and a shot of Cutty-Sark. She had to work only until 8:00 p.m.; she was relieved then by Beth. Lola and I had a few drinks; then, she grabbed my hand and said, "Let's go home." I was a little taken aback by her remark, but who was I to turn down free alcohol and whatever went with it? As we were leaving, I saw that my $10 bill was still lying on the bar, so I left it for Beth.

That night was a weeknight, so I set an alarm clock on her headboard for 5:00 a.m. Of course, I slept through it; by the time I woke up, it was 6:00 a.m. I took off for Newport doing a hundred. I reached the ship; the ship we were tied to was running drills, so I couldn't go onboard right away. As soon as I could, I boarded, changed, and went to the boiler room.

Not long after that, I was called up to speak with the chief. I knew what he wanted. I lied and said that I had been on the pier buying stuff from the gedunk truck—the same as a roach coach—and couldn't get back onboard because the ship next to us was running drills. That worked for the time being.

That night, I went back to Boston and started all over again. That time, I put her alarm clock in a metal pot, but that still did not wake me. I was late again. I had to give the chief another lame excuse. He warned me that if happened again, I would be restricted to the ship. As I was leaving, he asked, "By the way, Johnny, how is that new girl? Is she nice?" I smiled. "Chief, she'd break your old dick." The chief had been in my shoes at one time; he knew the score. Laughing, he said, "Lucky swab." After that, I saw Lola only on the weekends and would leave early Sunday night from her house of course. I was never late again.

After a few months, Lola was becoming very possessive. If I did not show up right on time after getting off on Friday afternoon, she would get very mad. She was irritated constantly because I wouldn't come see her every night even though she knew about my being late two mornings in a row. She started accusing me of having an affair with Beth, her roommate.

On one occasion, Lola had left for work at noon and I was still asleep. Beth walked into my room wearing a flimsy robe that was wide open and woke me up. She did not have to say anything; her being there said it all. Afterward, we agreed that once was enough; we had just wanted to know what it was like. I told Lola, "No, Beth and I are not having an affair." I knew it was all about the lies, sex, and alcohol, but it had been only once, that wouldn't hurt, right?

My ship was due to get underway for maneuvers. When I told Lola, we were going to sea for three weeks, she got mad and said I was lying, but then, she gave me a huge hug with lots of crying. When I left that last morning, I gave a big sigh of relief and left Dorchester behind me with smoking tires.

After only two weeks, the ship returned to Newport on a Friday. Normally during the week when we pulled liberty, we would stay in Newport and frequent the bars on the downtown strip because we had to be back onboard the next day. Having weekend liberty, I asked Jim and two other shipmates if they wanted to go to the Hill Billy Ranch in Boston. All three said yes, so we went to downtown Newport first to change into civilian clothes and headed to Boston.

One of our other shipmates had just returned from two weeks' liberty after going home. His father had bought him a new Ford with a 390-cubic-inch engine, and he kept telling everybody how fast it was and how he could beat my Charger. Before leaving the ship, I had made plans to meet him outside Newport; I wanted to see if his Ford could run. My friends were excited when they learned of it.

Arriving at the designated spot, I found the Ford already there. We lined up, engines revving. A shipmate stood between and in front of us with one of my old white hats raised above his head at the ready. At the drop of the hat, we roared off down the road with tires squealing and rubber burning. It wasn't even close—I left that Ford in the smoke; he saw nothing but my taillights. The kid was mad but tried to pay me the hundred bucks we had bet. I just laughed and said, "That's okay. Go get drunk on me." With downcast eyes, he said, "Thanks, I will."

CHAPTER 96

Tickets

It was now late fall of 1966. Leaving Newport, we drove to Route 24, a four-lane divided highway, went through Fort River, Massachusetts, and headed to Greentree, Massachusetts. Just after passing a rest stop with a Howard Johnson restaurant, I was still feeling great about the race and wasn't watching my speed. I heard a siren and saw blue lights behind me. I pulled over. A Massachusetts state trooper approached my car on foot. He was polite as he asked me for my license and registration. At the time, both were from Florida. I gave them to him along with my navy ID card. He asked me to sit in the car for a minute. I saw him in my rearview mirror talking on his radio. My friends were laughing and joking about me getting stopped by the police.

In a few minutes, the trooper returned and asked me to step out. I did, and he asked, "So you're in the navy?" I replied, "Yes sir." I said that my friends and I had just returned from Vietnam and that I had just bought the car and we were on our way to Boston for some fun. I apologized for my speed saying I just wasn't paying attention to how fast I had been going.

We talked for a couple more minutes; he told me that he was a former marine and had served in Vietnam also. He said, "Sorry, son, but I have to arrest you for speeding." He asked if any of my friends had a driver's license so one of them could drive my car and he would not have to have it towed. I told him, "Yes, my friend Fred does."

After checking his license, he told me to get into the back seat of his cruiser. He did not handcuff me. His cruiser had bucket seats in the front with a shift on the floor. As he started driving, I leaned forward, and we started talking. I told the friendly trooper, "I think I could beat you in a race." He laughed and said, "You think so, huh?" I laughed and said, "Yes, I think I could. How fast did you clock me on your radar?" He chuckled and said, "A hundred and forty-nine." I laughed and said, "Guess I'll have to get my speedometer fixed." He asked, "Don't you think you were going that fast?" I said, "No, faster. My speedometer was registering a hundred and fifty." He laughed and said, "You're going to have to learn to slow down, son." I said, "I didn't see you. Where were you hiding?" He said, "In the Howard Johnson's parking lot."

As he drove to downtown Greentree, we talked pleasantly. The trooper told me that because I had an out-of-state license coupled with speeding, he was allowed by law to arrest me. He also warned me to be very polite at the Greentree police station. "Last year, a driver came through town and hit a child. After he was arrested, he had shown a navy ID, so he was released on bail. Later, the child died, and when they went looking for this sailor, they found out it was a bogus ID card. He was never found. Now, the Greentree police have a real hard-on for sailors."

I said, "Thanks for the information. I'll be a perfect gentleman," which I was. The trooper wrote me a speeding ticket for 75 mph; I paid a $25 fine to the clerk, who bailed me out.

After that, my friends and I headed into Boston for some fun and excitement, which we found in the Hill Billy Ranch. I stayed away from The Novelty Bar and the combat zone. That night, all four of us hooked with different girls and went in different directions. Our SOP—standing operating procedure—was always after splitting up to meet the following night at the Hill Billy Ranch, as we did on that occasion.

On Saturday night, none of us had any luck scoring girls, so we headed back to Newport and got to the locker club about 3:00 a.m. Two of my friends slept in my car, which I had parked on a side street, while Fred and I slept in my locker club. I slept in my usual place—the pool table—while Fred slept on a bench.

On Sunday morning, my two friends in the car wanted to go back to the ship, so I drove them there. Fred and I went back to the strip and started drinking as soon as the bars opened. That night, I hooked up with Chrystal— "She who sleeps around"—and Fred slept at my locker club. I did not spend the night with Chrystal, so I picked Jim up at 5:00 a.m., and we returned to the ship in time for reveille at 6:00 a.m.

One week later, Friday afternoon and at the same spot on Route 24 in Greentree, I was again stopped, that time by a different Massachusetts state trooper for speeding. I was again arrested but taken to Bridge street, Massachusetts. I asked the trooper, "What speed did you clock me on your radar?" He said, "A hundred and fifty. Why? Do you think you weren't going that fast?" I replied, "No, my speedometer was registering a hundred and fifty." Again, the fine was $25. After those two tickets, I learned my lesson, and I have never gotten another speeding ticket.

That Friday night, my friends and I stayed in Boston drinking at the Hill Billy Ranch, but on Saturday afternoon, we headed to Newport and the bars we knew so well on the strip.

CHAPTER 97

Fate

One warm summer night in July 1979, my partner, and I had just gone on duty at midnight. Requesting permission as policy dictated, we had gone to a donut shop for coffee. On the way back to our assigned area, we received a radio call; the dispatcher directed us to a house off Surf Avenue for a simple lockout. Knowing the area, I asked if the fire department had been called. The dispatcher replied, "No, she asked that we not call the fire department."

We arrived in a few minutes. As I pulled the cruiser up to the house, I said, "To my partner, why don't you have your coffee. I'll handle this. I'll probably call the fire department anyway." He smiled, opened his coffee, and started looking for his favorite, a French cruller, as I got out.

At the front door was a woman who looked to be in her thirties wearing a nurse's uniform. She had long, red hair tied in a bun. She was about five feet six inches tall but with a muscular build. I thought, *Boy, I bet she can handle some of the drunks who go to the ER*. She said, "Officer, I'm so glad you're here." I checked the door just to make sure it was indeed locked. I said, "We usually call the fire department; they have a door spreader and can usually get the door open in a couple of minutes." With a girlish giggle, she said, "Please don't bother the firemen. They'll come with their lights flashing and carrying those big hoses." I told her I didn't know what else I could do, except to call a locksmith. "Oh no, I can't afford a locksmith!" She said, "I keep all my windows locked and drapes closed so nobody can peek at me, but I do keep my bathroom window unlocked. If you could give me a boost, I could get in."

She led me around to the side of the house. Because there was a bright moon and a nearby streetlight, I saw the window clearly. It was about eight feet off the ground. I asked, "Are you sure you can get through that window?" She said, "OH 'yes." She told me that another time when she had locked herself out, a neighbor had come over with a ladder and she had climbed up and through the window with no trouble.

With a little skepticism, I locked my fingers for the old ten-finger lift. She stepped into my hands, and I started to lift. Her weight was bearing down on my hands, and she started to wobble. I started losing my footing in the sand. She started to wobble more and more with me trying to get underneath her. Somehow, I got completely turned around. She put her knee on my shoulder. Her dress went over my head, and she said, "Now officer, don't you look up my dress" with that same girlish giggle. She put her other knee on my shoulder. Still holding onto her ankles, I thought, *Shit why not*. She stood up on my shoulders, legs spread, and I looked up. She was wearing pink bikini panties. I gave a gasp when I saw the hairiest pair of balls I had ever seen with the old, one-eyed monster between them staring back at me. She gave a little jump and got halfway through the window.

At that moment, my partner came around the corner of the house, looked up, and said, "What the hell—" stopping in midsentence as his flashlight shined up and he saw what I had seen as she slipped out of sight through the window. Without saying a word, we walked to the cruiser. As we walked past the front door, I heard her say, "Thank you, officer" again with that girlish giggle.

I said, "Boy, I need a drink!" My partner said, "Let's go to my house." It was only a couple of blocks away, and we drove there in silence. He went in with our coffees and came out quickly. I was not sure what he had put in the coffee—gin maybe—but we gulped it down. I said, "Thanks. I needed that." He said, "Me too."

A short time later, we answered another call. After we cleared, I drove to the beach section of Sandy Town and parked. We still had not spoken about the incident. After a few minutes, he asked, "Were those real?" I replied, "They looked real to me." He laughed and said, "Oh yeah! You saw them up close." I lit up a Lucky and thought about those days so long ago when drinking was my daily routine and things like that didn't bother me. Alcohol always helped, but when I thought real hard, I knew that it only covered up my problems and that sometimes, fate could change your life also.

For the rest of the weekend, we stayed in Newport, and if I did not hook up with anybody by 10:00 p.m., I would go to the bar where Chrystal worked. At the end of the week, she complained that I came to see her only for sex. Laughing, I said, "No, I also come for the free beer and Cutty-Sark." She hit me with an empty beer bottle.

That following Friday while still aboard ship, I decided to stay in Newport for the weekend. I suggested to my friends that we go to The Binnacle, a bar only a block away and behind my locker club. That bar was different from the bars on the strip, and the girls who frequented it were not run-of-the-mill bar girls. They were younger and nicely dressed; some were not long out of high school. For the most part, we avoided going to that bar for those reasons. We were not looking for long-term relationships; we wanted a little fast love and a good time. So, our plans were made. Leaving the ship and arriving at my locker club, I found that my civilian clothes I had sent out to be cleaned had arrived pressed, starched, and ready to wear.

We started off drinking on the strip; later, we decided it was time to head over to The Binnacle. We paid the cover charge of $2 and went in. A band was playing a slow number as couples on the dance floor held on tight to each other. The rest of the bar was one big room filled with tables and chairs. About fifty people, mostly sailors, were there. We sat and ordered drinks. Two of my friends went over to ask a couple of young girls to dance. I saw two young girls I recognized from other nights at The Binnacle, so I walked over and asked one to dance.

As we danced, she moved in close and held me tight. I was not moved. These young girls just did not do anything for me. I liked older, more-experienced women, not young girls although I had to admit the sex with them was terrific. I tried to convince my two friends to go back to the strip, but by then, they were dancing and sitting with some young girls at another table. Fred was still sitting at our table. I tried to convince him to leave, but he just wanted to drink. I decided to do the same.

More people arrived. Among them was a pretty, short-haired blonde who looked to be in her late twenties. She looked out of place with this crowd of younger girls. She was nicely dressed in a short skirt and a tight-fitting blouse that covered her ample breasts. She sat behind Fred and me at a table by herself. She ordered a drink and looked around as she sipped it. She looked my way, and our eyes locked. I smiled at her. She smiled, but her gaze quickly moved on. I thought she must have been waiting for somebody.

But a half hour passed, and nobody showed up. The band started to play a popular slow song. I was about to walk over and ask her to dance when one of two sailors sitting next to her asked her. As they danced the sailor, who was talking fast, was making his move. Watching her closely, I could tell she was ignoring him and kept looking around. I watched as they returned to her table after the dance. She sat, and the sailor stood beside her still talking, but she continued looking around. He must have asked her if he could sit down because suddenly, she looked at him and shrugged, and he sat.

After that, they talked, and he bought her a drink and then another, but they did not dance. Another hour passed, and I was still very curious about her, so when the band started playing another slow song, I walked over and asked her, "Would you like to dance, ma'am?"

The sailor sitting with her said, "She's with me, sailor!" The girl looked at him, stood, took my hand, and led me onto the dance floor. She smiled at me, and as I smiled back as we started to dance. I said, "I wanted to ask you to dance earlier." She asked, "Why didn't you?" I said, "I thought you were waiting for somebody. I didn't want to bother you." She looked at me and said, "That's a cute line." I smiled and said, "Yeah, but it's true."

She did not reply. We danced in silence with me holding her close. When the dance ended, I held her hand and asked, "Will you meet me here tomorrow night at seven? If you're willing, we could go to Boston for the night." She paused before saying, "Yes, if I can." I smiled and walked her to her table then returned to mine. I continued to watch her for the rest of the evening. Occasionally, our eyes would lock; I would smile, and she would smile back.

Just before the last song of the night, she left alone. The sailor who had been sitting with her returned to the table with his friend. He was mad; he slammed his fist on the table and knocked over their full beer bottles. He said, "That fucking bitch!"

After last call, Fred and I looked around for our two friends, but they had left, evidently with the two girls they had been sitting with. Leaving the Binnacle, Fred and I walked to my locker club, and he fell asleep on a bench. As I lay down on the pool table I thought, *has fate intervened in my life*.

CHAPTER 98

Puppy Love

The next day, Jim and I met up with our two friends over lunch. The other two gave us the details of their night with the two girls. Nobody but I had anything planned for that Saturday night. I told them about the blonde and how she had said she would meet me at The Binnacle that night if she could. We were up for another night there.

That afternoon, we started off slow and went to a bar on the strip that we called The Peanut Bar. They had barrels of peanuts around the bar that were free for the taking. Of course, the more peanuts we ate, the more beer we drank. We loved throwing the hulls on the floor. Usually by the end of the night, patrons were walking on peanut hulls rather than the floor.

We drank and played pool until about 7:00 p.m., when we headed to The Binnacle. We paid the cover charge and entered the bar. The band was setting up. I saw about twenty to thirty patrons, most of whom were sailors as usual, and only about six girls. I did not see the blonde. I walked over, with my friends, to the same table we had sat at the previous night.

Betty, a waitress we knew, took our orders. I said, "Betty, I'm supposed to meet an older blonde ..." I meant a girl older than the usual girls coming to the bar. "...and I want to know if you saw her before I came in. She's about five feet, eight inches tall, a little meat on her bones, and she has nice boobs." I illustrated how big with my hands. "She'd be alone." Laughing Betty said, "Johnny, if a girl like that came in here alone, these sailors would be all over her like crabs on a dead fish."

It was 7:30 p.m. I was feeling a little blue, or maybe I was a little drunk. But I did not stop drinking or hoping. The band started playing, and at eight, more girls and sailors started coming in. I kept a sharp eye on the door. By eight thirty, my two friends were off dancing as Fred and I sat at the table talking. He told me about how his mother and father had moved from South Carolina to Maryland and his father had gotten a job at a Pontiac dealership as a mechanic. As he was talking, I saw four girls walking past the stage. I grabbed Jim's arm and said, "Look." I pointed at them. He said, "The one in the back is mine." I said, "The girl with her hand over her heart is beautiful." He said, "Oh no, not this time. That one's all mine."

I couldn't keep my eyes off her as she walked with her girlfriends straight toward us. The closer she got, the more boyish I felt. The girls sat at the table next to us; she had her back to us. My hand holding my beer was trembling. I felt like a young kid with a huge crush on his teacher except that she was not old enough to be a teacher. I took a long drink of beer, looked at Fred and said, "Wow." He asked, "What?" I said, "I've never seen a more beautiful but innocent-looking girl in this place after all the years we've been coming here. Did you see the way she had her hand over her heart and the innocent look on her face? Fred, all of that was for real." He smiled and said, "We'll see."

With those words, the race was on. My two friends returned to the table from dancing and started asking about the four girls sitting at the table next to us. I ignored their questions and listened to her as she ordered a Coke. Her voice was soft, sweet, and innocent. Even with all the cigarette smoke, I smelled her enticing perfume. *This girl is something very special, and I need to treat her that way.* It was puppy love at first sight.

I watched and listened as her girlfriends talked; I could tell they were regulars at the bar, but she did not take part in the discussions; I could tell, she was taking it all in for the first time. Normally, I would not have thought twice about a girl like her, but there was something I couldn't explain.

The band started playing "Mustang Sally," a fast-dancing song. I stood and started toward her, to ask her to dance, but Fred did the same. I gave an empty chair, sitting between us, a hard shove. He tripped over it and landed on the floor with a loud thump. She turned to her left and looked at him on the floor; At the same time, I tapped her right shoulder and asked, "Would ya'll like to dance, ma'am?" With an innocent and surprised look, she looked at me and then at her giggling girlfriends and asked, "Well, would all of you like to dance?" She was smiling as I took her hand and gently escorted her onto the dance floor. "Mustang Sally" was mesmerizing because her body seemed to glide through space. As we danced, my thoughts turned to mush. Try as I might, I could not stop myself from grinning at her and feeling like an idiot.

When that song ended, the band went immediately into a slow number. I took her hand and without asking, put my arm around her and started to dance, still grinning. She smiled at me but said nothing. I didn't know if she was feeling it or not, but somehow and for some reason I couldn't explain, I knew my life was going to change forever. As we danced, I held her close and felt her body shudder ever so slightly; I now knew she too was feeling it. Across the dance floor, our bodies moved as one; all the other dancers disappeared. For the first time ever, I closed my eyes, and it felt as if our hearts were beating as one. I could not explain it, then nor can I explain it today, but I knew from the bottom of my feet to the top of my head that I had found my soul mate. Folks, that's how love happens.

As the dance ended, I gave her a little twirl and completely out of character for me while still holding her hand, I introduced myself, and she introduced herself as Samantha. Our fingers interlocked as if we never wanted to let go. I walked her to her table. Pulling her chair out and pushing it in after she sat, I asked, "May I sit with you?" She smiled and said, "Yes, please." I pulled over the chair I had tripped up Jim with.

Her girlfriends were giggling and talking among themselves, but they focused their attention on me, and she introduced me. I still have no idea what she said about them or me. My eyes and thoughts were only on her. Samantha asked me all about the navy and where I was from. I had been in the New England area for almost four years at that point, but I still had trouble understanding some girls when they talked, they talked so fast. When Samantha talked, however, she was very clear, and I understood her every word. Maybe it was because I was listening intently to everything she had to say; I wanted to know more about this amazing young woman.

I bought a round of drinks for the table, and Samantha and I danced a few more times. I excused myself to go to the men's room. Upon my return, she said, "Some guy just came over and gave me something. I don't know what to do with it." I asked, "What is it?" She reached into her purse and came up with a full pint of Southern Comfort. I said, "You're not allowed to have that in here." I looked around to make sure no bouncer or waitresses had seen it. I pushed the bottle down the front of my pants and said, "I'll take it out to my car." I stood and saw that my pants were so tight the pint made it look as if I had an enormous erection. One of her friends audibly gasped and asked Samantha, "What in the hell is that?" Samantha replied, "Oh, that's just a little Southern Comfort." Her girlfriends laughed, and I had a big smile on my face, as I walked away.

As the night progressed, Samantha and I sat, talked, held hands, and danced. Her girlfriends danced with other sailors, some of whom I knew. At closing time, a sailor I knew named Marty was sitting with one of her girlfriends, Kate, at our table. The four of us left the bar and went to an all-night restaurant. The place was full of late-night partygoers, but we were able to get the last table. We ordered breakfast and watched the antics of a drunk at the counter; he was trying so hard to stay awake and eat his spaghetti and meatballs, but he missed his mouth every time. Sometimes, he would put it in his nose; sometimes, he would put it in his hair; and other times, the forkful would fall on his shirt or pants. One time, we saw a meatball fall off his fork and roll across the counter next to another customer's plate. The poor drunk tried to stand to retrieve it, but when he couldn't, he just reached over with his fork and kept stabbing at the poor meatball. He never did retrieve it; a waitress picked it up and put it back on his plate. Nobody else seemed to be watching him, but the four of us had a great time.

Just as we were paying our bill, the drunk lost it and went face-down into his plate of spaghetti. A short time later we left. As we walked by him; I lifted his head and said, "Hey mister, you're sleeping in your spaghetti." He threw up in the spaghetti and again went face-down in it. I told the waitress, "You might want to get his face out, so he doesn't drown in his own puke." With a tired look, she said, "Yeah, okay, thanks."

It was a little past 3:30 a.m. I drove us to the mom-and-pop motel Samantha, Karen, and the other two girls were staying in, which was near the base. I parked, and the four of us talked for a few minutes. Then we all started making out until well after daylight. Kate went in the motel, and the sailor left. Samantha and I were alone for the first time. We were just talking. It was obvious that neither one of us wanted to leave, but she was tired and wanted to sleep. I kissed her goodbye, as she went into her room. I promised I would come back later to drive her home.

She had told me she worked for the Prudential Insurance Company in Boston and was living with her grandmother in Arbury. I drove to my locker club and found Fred sleeping on the bench, so I went to sleep on the pool table. Later, Fred woke me up, and I showered and changed clothes. It was Sunday afternoon. I told him I was going back to pick Samantha up, so he decided he would go back to the ship. I told him I would drive him.

CHAPTER 99

Lola

In front of my locker club was a city bus stop. As Fred and I were leaving the locker club, I saw the pretty blonde, the same one I was supposed to meet the night before, at the Binnacle. It was obvious she was waiting for a bus. I walked past and smiled at her. She smiled back. I drove Fred to the base. As he was getting out of the car he looked at me and said, "You are a lucky dog." We both laughed. After I dropped him off at the base I headed over to the motel to pick up Samantha.

She had her suitcase packed and was ready to go. I drove slowly; I wanted to spend as much time as I could with her. When we got to her place in Arbury, she introduced me to her grandmother and grandfather, who were very nice and warm hearted. I took an instant liking to them, and it seemed they liked me also. I spent the afternoon and evening with them thoroughly enjoying myself. Around 10:00 p.m., Samantha said she had to work the next morning and she needed to sleep. I said my goodbyes to her and her grandparents.

Leaving Arbury, I thought about how I had lied to Lola about going to sea for three weeks. Still thinking about her, I decided to go by her apartment and say goodbye. She was home alone. I told her the ship had just come in that day. She wanted me to spend the night, but I told her I couldn't. I said a long-distance relationship between us wouldn't work out. I told her the driving back and forth was tiring and costing me a lot. She said she would give me money to help pay for gas, but when I told her I would never take her money, she surprised me by saying she was willing to relocate to Newport and get a bartender job there. That really set me back a moment; I did not know what to say.

Finally, I said, "Look, I'm sorry, Lola, but it's just not going to work. My ship goes to sea a lot, and a long-term relationship won't work." We talked for a while as we drank a few beers. I was getting ready to leave around 1:00 a.m. She started crying again. She grabbed my hand and pulled me toward her bedroom, which I let her do.

Later, as I stood beside the bed looking down at her nakedness lying there sleeping, I said in a quiet voice, "I'm sorry, Lola, but I've found the one I want to be with forever." I left about 3:00 a.m. and have never seen or thought of her again until this writing.

CHAPTER 100

Honey

I don't know—I may have been drunk or I may just have been blue,
The night was filled with music and sailors whom I knew.

It was four girls from Boston all looking for love,
But the night was young, and all it took was a shove.

Girls everywhere but not another one did I see,
From the moment we met, I knew it would only be you and me.

After our first dance to "Mustang Sally," I bought you a drink,
And for the rest of that night I knew my ship would never sink.

After fifty years, we have never parted—this marriage of two,
With all our highs and lows, I can still say, "Honey, I love you."

I started driving back and forth to Arbury as much as I could to see Samantha. She wanted me to meet her parents, who lived in Sandy Town, about thirty-five miles south of Boston. She told me they were a strict Irish Catholic family. I told her that I also was Catholic, but I had reservations, as did she, about my meeting them. First, according to her mother as told to Samantha and me by her grandmother, I was a twenty-three-year-old sailor with more up my sleeve than just my arm. Second, I was like a rebel without a cause, and her father did not trust rebels. It took three months and a lot of persuading by her grandmother before we all agreed to meet.

I went to their house on a Friday; I did not get there until 10:30 p.m. They had given me the town's name as Sandy Town, but I went to another closely named town. It took me a while to straighten that out and get to their place. I was there for only half an hour before her father said I should leave. I was mad, as was Samantha, but there was nothing we could do about it. I told her I would stay in my car overnight and would return the next day.

I found a wooded area and slept in my car. The next morning, I waited and nervously returned around eleven. After we talked through my mishap of arriving so late the night before, her mother and father were friendlier and offered me breakfast. Samantha had three younger sisters and one younger brother. All of them were extremely happy to be around me, and they treated me as an older brother.

After breakfast, Samantha and I went to meet some of her high school friends. As I was opening the car door for her, Lilly—one of her sisters—stuck her head out a window and shouted, "Samantha, keep him! Look at that car!" Samantha was smiling as she got in. I laughed and waved at her sister.

I started driving to Sandy Town every weekend, and eventually, her father let me stay overnight with a little push from Samantha I was sure. I slept in Samantha's bedroom downstairs right next to her mother and father's bedroom, and she slept upstairs with her sisters. Her whole family had a good laugh when they saw how my legs hung off the end of her bed by about two feet.

Sometimes, I would drive to Sandy Town during the week just for the night and get up at five to return to Newport. Though I was seeing a wonderful girl, my drinking continued, and I asked myself, *what am I doing?* I had never planned to settle down, and I was having doubts about myself. I certainly did not want to bring any hardship to this wonderful young girl. Of course, by then I had learned she was only seventeen.

Even with all the turmoil in my mind and life, it took only about two months, right after her eighteenth birthday, before I knew I wanted to spend the rest of my life with this beautiful young woman. With no hesitation one night as we were sitting in her driveway, I asked, "Honey, will you marry me?" With a sob, she said yes, and we kissed passionately. She said I would have to ask her father for his permission and blessing. I looked at her with pure fear. She laughed and said, "Oh honey, don't worry about it." With a relieved sigh, I smiled and said, "I love you so much, and I always have," meaning that even before we had met, I knew in my heart she was out there, just waiting for me, as I was for her.

CHAPTER 101

A Band of Gold

Days passed, and Samantha kept asking me when I would speak with her father. I kept putting it off until one night when we were standing in her kitchen, she asked me again. Her mother, sisters, and brother, who were also in the room, waited to hear what my answer was. With a big sigh, I said, "Okay, I'll ask him."

I walked into the living room, where he was watching TV. I stood in front of him and in a choked-up voice said, "Sir, I would like to ask you something." Samantha and her siblings were crowded near the doorway, and her mother was sitting on the couch beside him. As I spoke, she leaned forward as if she knew what was coming and waited. Her father turned the TV off and waited for me to continue. Without hesitation but still in a choked voice, I said, "Sir, I would like to have your permission to marry your daughter." He said nothing. I glanced at Samantha and her siblings with the fear of rejection written all over my face.

In a loud voice, he asked, "Which one?" I panicked. I said in a small, squeaky voice, "Samantha." With a big smile, he stood and said, "Of course you have my permission, son. I know you're the one." With a big sigh, I said, "Thank you, sir" as he gave me a big hug. Her mother gave me a big hug also as did her sisters and brother.

I took a box containing a band of gold out of my pocket. I knelt in front of Samantha and asked, "Honey, will you marry me?" Crying, she said, "Yes." I slipped the ring on her finger as everyone including her father and I started crying.

CHAPTER 102

Confusion

In early 1967, I was transferred to Pennsylvania, to attend a naval school. I continued to drive to Sandy Town every weekend. She and her family planned a June wedding, but the more time we spent together, the sooner we wanted to get married. We approached her parents asking for their permission to marry quickly, but they refused. Samantha continued to ask on her own when I was not there, and they eventually conceded; the wedding was moved up to April.

Samantha's father and I had several conversations about my mother and father attending the wedding. At first, I told him that they had said they could not come to the wedding because of his work. I had not told them about the marriage. Each time he and I spoke, he put more pressure on me to ask them to attend. Finally, one day, I called home. Mama answered, and I told her about the wedding. There was no crying, no tears—just dead silence. "Mama, did you hear me?" In a raised voice, Mama asked, "Johnny, why are you marrying a damned Yankee?" I said, "Because I love her, Mama." Mama said something I had never heard her say: "You know your father hates Yankee nigger lovers!" My blood was boiling. I hung up. I couldn't understand Mama's reaction.

The next time I spoke with Samantha's father, I said, "I've spoken with them again, and they still say they cannot come." I could tell by the set of his jaw and the look in his eyes that he was mad, but I was happy. I did not want either one, but my father mostly, to come to the wedding. My sister never entered my mind.

Samantha made all the wedding plans. On occasion, I would return to my ship in Newport to visit with my shipmates and tell them about my wedding. I asked my friend Fred to be my best man numerous times, but he declined each time saying, "I don't want you to get married. Besides, you stole her from me." Laughing, I replied, "Yes I did, and now she's all mine."

As the wedding date got closer and closer, my thoughts were more and more confused; I still wondered if I was making the right decision. Each time, I told myself yes, but in the back of my mind, I still had doubts. My mixed-up feelings had nothing to do with sweet and innocent Samantha; they were all about me. I felt as my father had told me many times, I was nothing who would never amount to anything. I had no self-confidence and no plans beyond the navy. Sometimes, I would cry when thinking that I was taking her and her family down the long, miserable broken road I was on, but I did not know what to do. Each time I was with her, I saw how happy and excited she was about our wedding. I knew I had to put aside my feelings and the self-pity I was wallowing in. With great resolve, I put her ahead of and above me. I told myself, *for the first time in your miserable life, Johnny, do the right thing.* While stationed in Pennsylvania, my drinking got even worse.

One of my shipmates at the school was a sailor I had known previous and meeting him again only furthered my drinking and gambling. One day while in the barracks, about twelve of my shipmates and I were shooting dice and drinking. We were in the back of the barracks next to a door that opened into an empty room. The door opened, and an officer was standing there. He confiscated all the money and liquor and made us stand at attention while he called for the head of our school. He wanted to send us all to the brig.

It took about a month before everything was smoothed over. After that, we still drank and gambled, but we were more careful about it. At one point, I was drinking so much and not eating that I started passing blood again. Eventually, I went to the base dispensary, and they in turn sent me to the navy hospital, where I stayed for about two weeks.

While I was there, one doctor asked me about my drinking. For some unknown reason, I started talking about my home life, before the navy; I wasn't ready to talk about all of it, but I did talk. I also talked about my upcoming wedding and my confusion if I should or not. In the end, he just laughed everything off saying, "I think you have pre-wedding jitters as a lot of young men getting married do." He talked about his own wedding and how he had handled it. To my relief, my past life and drinking were ignored. The only person I ever had any trust in was my best friend, Grant. Looking back, I do not blame that doctor, but I believe that if we had talked more in depth, everything would have come out sooner.

I got out of the hospital and returned to the school, but I was put in a different class. I met another young sailor also going through the school, and he and I became fast friends; we were drinking every night during the week. Every Friday, I would drive to Sandy Town, about six hours away, and drink blackberry brandy on the way. During the week, we went to a local bar, not far from the base, and another bar over the river in New Jersey, which I called The Pool Bar because it was a small, quiet bar with about six pool tables. The two of us could hold our own and managed to win many beers, leaving me some money for shots of Cutty-Sark.

During that time, drinking was so natural to me that I didn't give it a second thought. I now know that the massive amounts of alcohol I consumed did not erase my memories or worst fears, but only enhanced them.

I want to give all my readers a lesson I learned. Find someone and sit down with that person. Talking and writing helps. Opening your heart and soul is the way back. I can't describe to you how much writing this book has brought me back from hell. I drank trying to shove all my feelings down deep, hoping to erase them. I now know that drinking made my life much more miserable and could have had dangerous consequences beyond my control.

CHAPTER 103

Evil and Hate

One Friday afternoon, the weekend of the wedding, I received permission to leave school early. I had gotten written permission, from the navy, to marry Samantha. I arrived at Samantha's house at four that afternoon. On the way, as was usual for me, I had drunk a pint of blackberry brandy. As I was getting out of my car, I was taken aback when Samantha and my sister ran toward me. Samantha was all smiles as she hugged and kissed me. My sister, bubbling with excitement, gave me a big hug and asked, "Johnny, why didn't you tell me you were getting married?"

I did not have time to answer because she kept talking about everything. With dread in my voice, I said hi to Samantha. Taking my hand in hers, Samantha asked, "What's wrong, honey?" sensing my tension. With a weak smile, I shook my head, meaning nothing was wrong.

As I went in, my worst fears were realized. I felt the blood drain from my face. Sitting on the couch were Mama and my father; Samantha's father was doing all the talking. Samantha's father smiled and said, "Hey Johnny, look who made it after all!" I walked to the couch and said, "Hi, Mama." She looked at me saying nothing. Looking at my father, I recognized the look on his twisted-up face—pure evil and hate.

My father got up and walked out the door. I followed him outside and confronted him on the walkway. He turned and pulled a large kitchen knife out of his pants and started tapping his leg with it. "Mama and I both brought knives to protect ourselves from these goddamn Yankee nigger lovers." That frightened me to my core. I was visibly shaking with the brandy affecting me only slightly.

I thought of all the years I had borne the brunt of this man's words. His actions filled my head with the speed of a locomotive. With words spewing out of me, as if I were vomiting, I ignored the knife and stepped closer. "They are not goddamn Yankee nigger lovers. They're nice Catholic people, and I'm marrying this girl because I love her. They're nothing like you."

I saw hate in his eyes as he said, "Well, you won't do anything I say because you never have, and I see why you're marrying her, and it isn't because of love, as he stuck his tongue out, licking the dribble from his chin." I knew what he meant. I had seen the way he had stared at Cherrie's breasts while asking her to go see the cows. He was still holding that knife, now inching it closer to my stomach. I didn't know what he was planning, but I knew that whatever it was, he would have to kill me first.

My sister came out and ran to us. Looking at the knife in my father's hand, she said, "Daddy, put that away. You don't need it." He put the knife back in his pants and put his arm around my sister. As they walked into the house, he gave me a look of pure evil that sent a chill straight through me.

CHAPTER 104

The Wedding

Because Fred had refused to be my best man, I asked Josh, another shipmate, to fill that role. I asked two other shipmates, Al and Little Rick, to be ushers. Shortly after my arrival at Samantha's house, they arrived from Newport. It was great to see them. Meeting them outside in the driveway, I was able to shove my tensions down deep.

Samantha had been firm about her wanting me to wear my navy uniform for the ceremony. I had brought mine and wanted to make sure they had brought theirs. They said they had. The night was young, and everything was going as planned, right?

That night, my friends were staying at a motel. Later that evening after drinking several beers and a bottle of wine, the four of us went to the Beacon, a local bar, for a few drinks for my bachelor party. Little Rick was driving us in his car. As I got into the car, I saw that my friends had come to the wedding ready to party. The back seat was filled with beer, whiskey, blackberry brandy, and bottles of Tango, a mix of vodka and an orange drink.

A band was playing rock 'n' roll music, and my friends started whooping it up. We were able to find a table in the back. I ordered drinks, and my friends went looking for girls to dance with. As the night progressed, my two ushers seemed to be hitting it off with two girls. By the end of the night, they had been sitting with the girls for a couple of hours. The lights went on and off several times, to indicate it was time to leave. Al came over to talk with Josh and me. Al and Little Rick wanted to take the girls back to the motel and wanted us to find something to do "Just for a couple of hours," he said. We laughed and said in unison, "Okay."

They left with the two girls apparently in their car leaving us Little Rick's car, which I drove. We went to the Brant City section of Sandy Town and parked by the waterfront. For a while, we looked at the ocean without speaking. Josh broke the silence by asking, "Are you really going to do this?" With just a slight hesitation, I said, "Yes, I have to or I'm going to die."

We drank and talked for several hours. I felt close to Josh, and I trusted him enough to talk about some personal things but not in detail. At some point, I told him that so many times in the past, I had wanted to just die. He did not laugh, point fingers, or try to give me advice. Looking at me with a long stare, he said, "Well, maybe this marriage is what you need." He was a good friend.

We saw a police cruiser pull up behind us, shine a spotlight into the car for a moment, and then drive on. Around 6:00 a.m. and fully drunk, I drove back to the motel and found our two shipmates passed out and still with the two girls, who were naked. We went back to the car and fell asleep in the front seat.

A few hours later, I was awakened by Little Rick banging on the window. I saw the two girls getting into their car. I woke Josh and the four of us went to a diner for breakfast. We were hungover if not still drunk. We went back to the motel, got dressed, and headed to the church for the wedding. I asked my friends for a favor. "Anything you need, Johnny, just ask. It's your day," they said. I said, "Will you guys keep a sharp eye on my father? If he starts anything, well ... kill him." They all looked at me. I said, "Yeah, kill him." They said, "Okay." We entered the church.

We were married in Saint Ann the Catholic church Samantha had attended since she was young. Dressed in our navy blues, my best man and I were standing in front of the altar with the priest as Samantha's father walked her down the aisle. During the entire walk, which seemed to take hours, Josh kept saying, "Johnny, don't do this. The car's parked out back, the engine's running, and the doors are open. We could leave fast. Nobody would catch us. Let's go get drunk at The Hill Billy Ranch. You don't need this. You don't want this." But his words fell on deaf ears. I heard him, but I was thinking, *My God, she's the most beautiful woman I've ever seen.*

Samantha's father kissed her goodbye and put her hand in mine. I turned to Josh and for the first time, I realized that over the past few years, my shipmates had become my support system by always being there for me. I had also been their support system with my leadership abilities. Looking at him for a long moment with sadness on my face but love in my heart, I smiled and said, "I'm sorry, but she's the love of my life, and I'm going to spend the rest of my time on this earth with her." With tears in his eyes, he said simply, "We all know, Johnny. You look great together. I love and respect you, man." I knew that what he had been saying was only to make sure I really wanted to marry Samantha. Turning to Samantha, I took her hand and gave out the biggest sigh of my life. I smiled at her, and we turned to the priest.

When the vows were read, and it was my turn to say I do, I had trouble getting the words out. It took three tries, with Samantha looking at me in horror. As I squeaked out "I do" in a shaky and barely audible voice, I heard some subdued laughter behind me from a few of the wedding guests. I felt a sharp pain on my arm as Josh hit me with his elbow while saying, "Johnny, it's okay. You can do this." Embarrassed, I said, "I do" again, only that time, it was so loud that the entire church laughed, and I think a few others across the street in their houses also laughed and giggled. I took a deep breath, held it for a moment, looked into Samantha's eyes, and said softly and in a normal tone, "I do." The priest said, "I pronounce you man and wife. You may now kiss the bride," I lifted her veil and took her face gently in my hands and said, "I love you, ma'am" as I kissed her softly. I took her hand, and we turned and walked down the aisle.

I saw true happiness on the faces of my wife's family and friends. On some of her male friends' faces, I thought I saw a little envy, and I gave them the biggest *Too bad! So sorry!* smile I could muster. I looked on the other side of the church and my smile turned into a frown. My sister was smiling, but Mama was staring straight ahead with a blank look. My father was nowhere to be seen.

We approached the door, Al and Little Rick, looking tired but for good reason, opened the doors for us. I saw my father standing over to the side on the steps. Unbelievably, he was dressed in a suit and tie, but he had a disgusted look on his face as he stood there staring at Samantha's breasts, saying nothing. For the first time ever, instead of hating him, I saw him in a new light. He looked so small and pathetic. I felt only pity for him. We walked down the steps and went next door to the community center.

CHAPTER 105

The Reception

I went through the reception as if I were dreaming. Samantha and I could not take our eyes off each other. People entered the hall and put wedding gifts on two long tables. I was amazed at the number of gifts. I had never attended a wedding before, and I had no idea how many people were there. It was like being in a crowded bar.

The priest had made it clear to Samantha during the planning of the wedding that no alcohol other than a champagne toast would be allowed. On one table was a large punch bowl. I told my friends about the no-alcohol ruling, but of course they were not going to let a lonely priest stop their fun. I saw the priest take a sip of punch. His eyes almost bugged out of their sockets. He looked around and gulped down the entire plastic glass and got a refill. I smiled. I knew that my friends had fulfilled their promise: "Johnny, no fucking priest is going to ruin your wedding!"

Samantha's father and I seemed to be in a race to see who would get drunk first. I am not sure who won, but I do know we got drunk. As the reception progressed, I watched the three members of my family. Seeing my sister dancing, drinking, and having a great time with my three shipmates filled my heart with an emotion I had never experienced before—happiness. During one trip to the restroom, one of my shipmates followed me and asked, "Johnny? I—" I stopped him before he could finish. I said, "Go ahead, my brother, but just remember, she's my sister, so treat her with the same respect you treat me with." With a big smile and a huge sigh of relief, he grabbed my hand and said, "Thank you for your blessing, Johnny." Mama and my father sat by themselves, not drinking, eating or socializing with anybody. Eventually, Samantha changed into a beautiful blue traveling suit as we prepared to leave.

I was talking with Samantha's mother when suddenly looking beyond me, she saw something that drained the blood from her face. She turned and walked away hurriedly. Wondering what she had seen, I turned and saw my father standing behind me. He asked, "Do you want me to help you load all this goddamn Yankee plunder into your car?" With a big sigh, I said, "No thanks" and walked away.

Taking Samantha's hand, I led her to my Charger and left. Samantha and I had only that Saturday night as a honeymoon. To this date, we have never taken another. We drove one town over and stayed in the Cape-way, a rundown motel in a nearby town and had dinner at the Hearthside restaurant. For many years afterwards, whenever possible, we ate there on our anniversary.

CHAPTER 106

Taking Samantha Away

The next day, we drove to Samantha's parents' house in time to go to church at Saint Ann's with her mother. Her father did not go. I smiled and thought, *At least I got up and am going even with this hangover.*

We learned that after the reception, my three friends had been in a crash and had totaled Little Rick's car; the other driver was the only one arrested. I was hoping to see them, but they were not around having headed back to Newport earlier that morning by bus. We also learned after the reception, my parents had caused some trouble at Samantha's parents' house. As little as she was, Mama had grabbed one of Samantha's uncles and physically threw him out the front door with my father's help. We never found out the full story; nobody wanted to talk about it. Mama, my sister, and my father had already left for Florida, by bus.

Later that afternoon, Samantha and I headed to Pennsylvania. That leaving was the most wonderful and emotional separation I had ever seen. She and her family cried so hard and long that I thought we would never leave. I shed tears but for a different reason. The memory of my father driving off and leaving me on that dirt road all alone was flooding my thoughts. I knew that Samantha's family were feeling a loss but with a good feeling. When her father hugged and gave me a wet kiss, he sobbed and said, "Johnny, please take care of my little girl." Hugging him back, I said, "You know I will, Pop."

Arriving that evening, we stayed at a motel for a few days until we found an apartment not far from the base. We lived there for several months until I finished school.

CHAPTER 107

Our New Life

We drove to back to Sandy Town to say goodbye to Samantha's family and friends the day I finished school. I was transferred to California and I had been given a fourteen-day leave to get there. We stayed for two days in Sandy Town, and our parting was only slightly less emotional than the first.

We packed everything in the Charger and headed to Florida for our new life. I was anxious for Samantha to meet my friends and family in Florida and Louisiana. On the way, the first night out, I had been driving for hours; Samantha asked if she could drive a while to let me rest. I told her to just keep driving on Interstate 81. I got in the passenger's seat and dozed for I don't know how long. She woke me saying, "Johnny, I ran off the road."

I woke up fast and looked around, but I couldn't see anything because it was dark. I asked, "Where are we?" She said, "I don't know." I tried opening my door, but it wouldn't open all the way because it was hitting against the ground. Confused and mad, I yelled, "What happened?" She was crying. "A car's headlights were in my eyes, and I couldn't see." Still mad, I said, "Well, at least you woke me up before you killed me."

She was sobbing uncontrollably; I felt like a real jerk for what I had said. I put my arm around her. "I'm sorry, honey." She had told me that she had poor night vision and avoided driving at night unless it was necessary. I realized it was my fault and I should not have let her drive, especially at interstate speeds. I again apologized taking full responsibility for my actions.

She could not get out of the driver's door because the car was almost on its right side. Eventually I had to climb out my window, walk around to her side, open the door and help her out. It was hard, but because of the big engine, I was able to get the car back onto the blacktop. It was the first of many fights. It was my fault, and I blamed myself, but I couldn't understand why I had gotten so mad.

Late the next morning, we were in Tennessee when I saw a tractor-trailer entering the highway in front of us tip over on its side. I stopped as did other drivers and ran over to see if the driver was okay. I reached the cab first and saw diesel fuel pouring out of his tank onto the ground. I climbed up and looking through the open window saw the operator with blood covering his face. I asked, "Can you get out?" He replied, "No! My legs are jammed under the dash." They looked bent and crooked. I said, "There's diesel fuel all over the ground out here, but I'll get somebody to help me get you out." Several other drivers arrived. I said, "His legs are trapped under the dash, and he can't get out." Myself and two drivers climbed up on the cab, opened the door and reached in, trying to pull the operator out.

I saw another driver standing on the ground who was smoking. I yelled, "Get rid of that cigarette!" and pointed to the diesel fuel he was standing in. He looked down and then back at me and continued smoking. I again yelled for him to get rid of the cigarette, but again, he ignored me. With disgust, I yelled at the two men trying to get the operator out, "Watch out! This guy's smoking down here, and he won't put the cigarette out." I ran back to my car. Samantha asked, "What's that smell?" I said, "Diesel fuel. Some stupid guy is standing in it smoking and won't put his cigarette out." She said, "Please don't go back." I said, "I'm not. Some other guys are trying to get the operator out because his legs are stuck under the dash." I drove off thinking how stupid some people were.

We continued driving. I was thinking about home. I thought, *at last I was married, had served in the navy, as my father had wanted me to and had become a man. Surely, he'll be proud of me now.*

CHAPTER 108

I Knew

Early one afternoon in 1986, I was changing the oil in my car when my daughter, Bella, came home with her new boyfriend. He was driving. I saw the happy smile on her face, and I smiled at her. Her boyfriend got out of the car, and she walked over to him, grabbed his hand, and led him to me. She was filled with joy and happiness; she gave me a big hug and said, "Daddy, I'd like you to meet David, my boyfriend." He stuck his hand out quickly, and I shook it saying, "Glad to finally meet you, David." Seeing a quizzical look on his face, I said, "I've heard about you." He laughed and said, "All good I hope." I just smiled. They walked into the house to see my wife, Bella's mother.

About a month later, my daughter said, "Daddy, I have an important question to ask you." I replied, "Ask anything, honey." She said, "Some kids I know are saying that David is cheating on me with a black girl in town." With sadness in my heart, I asked, "What do you think?" She said, "I don't know, but the kids keep telling me he is. I asked him, and he laughed and denied it." I saw the hurt in her eyes. I badly wanted to tell her that I knew the truth, but I didn't want to break her heart. I said, "Give it some time. I'm sure it'll all work out for the best, honey." I watched as my lovely daughter walked away and knew what I had to do.

A couple of nights later, I was just getting out of my car, in my driveway just after dark, when my daughter and David arrived. My daughter got out of the car happy and smiling as usual. She said, "Hi, Daddy," and walked toward the house. As David walked past saying, "Hi, Detective." I said, "David, I'd like to speak with you, if you don't mind." He replied, "Sure."

I took him around to the other side of his car. About six inches separated us. I said, "David, my daughter thinks you're cheating on her with a black girl." He said, "I told her I—" I stopped him in mid-sentence saying, "David, I know who you are, and I know you work for Harold, selling his cocaine and weed. I also know you're dating his sister, Mary. Since they are black, the rumors are true. Besides, I've seen you with her. I also know that Harold's supplier is a cocaine dealer named Big James. I believe they asked you to start dating my daughter, so you could get close to me and learn whatever you're able to." He tried to step back, but he was up against the car. I placed my arms on the car on both sides of him to trap him there. "David, if you do anything to hurt my daughter or if you let somebody else hurt her, I want you to know that because I'm a detective in this town, I know where all the bodies are buried."

Even in the dim light of the moon, I saw his face pale and his lips quiver as he tried to wet them with his tongue. He said in a shaking voice, "I would never hurt your daughter, and I would never let anyone else hurt her, I promise you, Detective." His eyes darted left and right; he was looking for a way out, but he had nowhere to go. I got right in his face, with only a couple of inches now separating us. Looking deep into his eyes I said, "Remember what I said." I stepped back. He said, "Yes sir Detective I will," and ran toward the door of the house looking back nervously over his shoulder at me.

About a week later, my daughter came in the house crying. I asked, "What's wrong, honey?" She stated, "David broke up with me." As any dad would, I hugged her hard and said, "It's okay. He didn't deserve you anyway." Still crying, she said what a daughter would say—"Thanks, Daddy."

About two years later, my wife and I were having a buffalo steak dinner in a restaurant in a nearby town. I always carried a piece when off duty. In my peripheral vision, I caught two people approaching me quickly. Because of the work I was doing in those days, my peripheral vision was so good, I think I could have seen my ears. I reached in my dinner jacket and rested my hand on the butt of the gun I carried in a shoulder holster. I saw David followed by a young woman who was carrying a baby.

Head down, looking scared, and in a shaking voice, David said, "Detective, I would like you to meet my wife, Jane. This is our baby, and she's pregnant with our second child." I smiled, stood, and shook hands with them. "Congratulations to you both."

With his head still down, David said, "I want to thank you. The talk you gave me that night scared me and changed my life. I now have a good job, a family, and I've been drug free for two years." His wife said, "Detective, I know about what David had been doing. He told me about the talk you gave him, and I know how much it changed his life for the better. Thank you."

I saw fear but hope in their eyes. "Son, hold your head up high. I'm very proud of you. I know it must have taken a lot of courage on your part to do what needed to be done, and I can't tell you how much I commend you for doing the right thing. That night, looking into your eyes, I knew there was goodness behind them. I knew that if I helped you with a little push in the right direction, you could change your life."

He replied, "I'm so glad you said what you did. It made me see what I was becoming, and I didn't like it. Your talk changed my life forever. We both thank you." They left.

Sitting down I saw my wife was crying. "Honey, did they scare you?" She replied with a smile, "No. That was just the nicest thing I've ever seen you do." I said, "It was all him. I just coaxed him in the right direction."

I never saw David or his wife again, but I believed them and hoped they continued their path to recovery. One day years later, I told my daughter some but not all of what had transpired between David and me. If she reads this book, she'll know the whole truth. I hope she can look back on the experience and forgive David as I have.

That night, I lay under the cool sheets and reflected on the unexpected and joyful meeting of David and his wife. I remembered the first time my father met Samantha as my wife. It was nothing like when I had met David's wife earlier that night.

CHAPTER 109

She Knew

It took us three days with just short rests to reach Florida. I timed it just right; we got to the house around 6:00 a.m., when I knew my father would be milking the cows.

Mama greeted us and fixed us something to eat. I told her we had been driving for days and needed to rest. My sister had gone back to college, so Samantha and I used her room. By the time we got up late in the afternoon, Mama was making dinner. My father was nowhere in sight. Samantha and I showered and changed clothes. After dinner, we headed to Maple Wood, so I could introduce her to Grant and his family.

At Grant's, she met him, his brothers, mother, and stepfather. Afterward, we took Grant out for a few beers. Samantha, being only eighteen, drank Coke as Grant and I played pool at the same bar we had been in before.

Later, we dropped Grant off, drove back to mama's and found the house in the darkness. We still had not seen my father. We quietly slipped into our bedroom and shut the door. I woke the next morning and got dressed. I noticed the bedroom door was open. I found Mama fixing breakfast. I asked, "Mama, did you come into our room and wake us up for breakfast?" She had a strange look on her face. She said, "No, but I was just about to." I had a feeling there was more to her answer. When Samantha joined us a little later, I didn't say anything to her about what I suspected—that my father had been in our bedroom poking around and staring while we were sleeping. I had not told her much of anything about my life growing up, but I think that in the short time she had seen my father before the wedding, she had made up her mind about him.

Samantha and I spent the morning talking with Mama. Even though nothing important was said, I knew theirs would be a strained relationship. Around midmorning, my father came in from milking the cows. He didn't say anything to us; he talked briefly with Mama in the kitchen while Samantha and I were in the living room. He went to lie down. Samantha and I continued to hang out with Mama just talking.

Later that afternoon, my father woke up and walked into the kitchen while Mama, Samantha, and I were still in the living room talking. The kitchen and the living room were one big room with no separation, so we saw him banging pots and pans. Samantha got up saying she was going to see if she could help him. She approached him and asked, "What are you cooking?" He said, "A big pot of crabs. Do you want to have some with me?" Samantha laughed and said, "I know I'm from New England, but I've never liked shellfish. I promise you I've tried it all, and I'm still a big disappointment to my mom and dad for not liking it." His expression changed quickly, and she took a step back. He growled, "Who the hell do you think you are, you Yankee bitch, turning your nose up at my good food? We had to eat every bit of the shit your family served at your home and your wedding! We couldn't even say we didn't like any of it!"

I quickly got to the kitchen. With fists clenched, I stepped in front of Samantha and yelled, "This is my wife! Don't you ever talk to her like that, not now and not ever!" He hadn't lost any of his speed; with one swift move, he reached behind the table and pulled out his axe handle. He raised it, his eyes glazed over, and he started to swing it at me. In a split second, Samantha, a gentle and soft-spoken girl, was in front of me. She had picked up a butcher knife from the counter, and she leveled it as his belly. She said, "Go ahead, hit him just one more time." His face registered confusion. He stopped in mid-swing. Samantha said, "As long as I live, you'll never hit him again. You touch him, and I'll gut you like the filthy pig you are!" My father stopped, the axe handle still raised. Looking into his crazed eyes, I stood there with fists clenched waiting for that first swing and hoping he would because I was ready to end this now. Samantha, still holding the knife pointed at his gut, said, "I meant every word I said."

He looked at me and Samantha. He lowered the axe handle and screamed, "Get out of my goddamn house and take this nigger loving bitch with you!" Samantha and I walked into the bedroom, gathered our clothes, and headed to the car. I looked back just as my father walked out on the porch. I backed away from the house yelling out loud, "You'll never be around my wife or any children we have for as long as I live."

That day changed my life. I finally felt that I had found my true following, my path in life, and it was with Samantha. That was the last time I ever saw my father alive. He was standing on the porch, with axe handle raised, yelling, his eyes spewing hate and anger.

We drove to Maple Wood to say goodbye to Grant and his family. After that, we found a motel for the night and had dinner at the Parkmore. That night as we lay in bed, sleep would not come to us. For the first two hours, we lay back to back trying to find sleep, but it just would not find us.

I turned and put my arms around her. I pulled her in close. I whispered, "Honey, I'm so sorry you had to see that. I love you. I hoped with you being my wife, he would approve and life between us would change. It seems as if nothing has changed. I promise you that I'll make sure he will never be around you or any of our children."

I felt Samantha shudder as she rolled over to face me. Placing her hands on my face, she said, "Thank you, and I meant every word I said. I would have killed him if he had touched you. You don't have to apologize because from the moment I first met that man, I knew what he was like mostly because he kept staring at my breasts and moving his tongue as if he were licking my nipples like a pervert. You're right. We'll never allow him to be around any children we have."

We fell asleep in each other's arms. My dreams that night was interrupted by the image of my father standing on his porch with axe handle raised and screaming obscenities at us.

CHAPTER 110

First Trip

The next morning after breakfast, we headed to Mayville, Louisiana. I was anxious for Samantha to meet my relatives. It took us only six hours driving the old US 91. We stopped in the beach area in Mississippi, for gas and lunch. Samantha fell in love with the area because it reminded her so much of her hometown by the water. That was Samantha's first trip ever, and I wanted her to enjoy it.

We stopped in Mayville and stayed with my cousin Drew. I took Samantha to New Orleans to meet aunts, uncles, and cousins. I especially wanted her to meet my aunt Gray and her husband, who was originally from Chicago. He absolutely loved Samantha; he said, "I'm so delighted to have another Yankee in the family." My aunt laughed and asked, "What happened, Johnny? Did you have four flat tires? Is that how she caught you?" Smiling, I put my arm around Samantha and said, "I love her." She smiled and said, "She's a sweet girl, Johnny, and I can see that you both love each other very much."

We went back to Mayville before leaving for the West Cost. A cousin, who I had not seen in a long time, told us that her dog, Maggie, had recently had six puppies, and she thought a puppy would be a great wedding gift. He weighed about five pounds and was black and tan with a black ring around one eye. His tongue was almost completely black, and when he licked our cheeks, we smelled that puppy smell. His fur was as soft as goose down. We fell in love with him immediately, named him Blacky, and thanked her repeatedly. After visiting for another day, we headed to California.

CHAPTER 111

Blacky

My car did not have air conditioning; Texas was very hot. We set up a small bed for Smokey on the console. We also kept a plastic bottle of water and a dish for him within arm's reach. We traveled on Interstate 10. Signs in Texas read, "Drive Safely"; there seemed to be no speed limit, but I kept my speed at sixty-five during the entire trip. I was in love and did not have one drink.

Without alcohol to help me forget, my thoughts returned to my father and my past life. Though I had apologized to Samantha and truly meant it, I was doubting myself and still wondering why I had married this young, innocent girl and brought her into my messed-up life and family. I realized I had lived my life in a depression; I was afraid I was going even deeper and was dragging Samantha with me. What I didn't know at that time was that I wasn't dragging her along—she was coming of her on accord and knew some of what my life was about.

In these volatile times with the horrors of Vietnam being broadcast almost every day, I found myself looking at Samantha as my hero. As with any hero, I wanted to treat her with respect, but looking back as years passed and some of my buried demons surfaced, I feel I let her down.

One morning, we stopped at a truck stop in western Texas for breakfast. We had not been eating very much mostly because of the high heat. When we walked into that restaurant, country music was playing loudly from a jukebox that looked a hundred years old. The smells of ham, bacon, eggs, and coffee made our mouths water. A waitress asked us in a real southern drawl, "May I help y'all?" I smiled and nodded. "Yes ma'am. We would appreciate some hot coffee."

We looked over the menu. I had never seen so many breakfast choices that included so much food. When the waitress returned, Samantha ordered the smallest item on the menu, but the smells had taken over my senses, and I ordering two of the "Trucker's Special." The place was crowded, but within ten minutes, our waitress came with a platter containing three large eggs over homemade hash, a half-pound of bacon, a slab of ham that was so large it was hanging off the platter, two large homemade sausages, and a heaping amount of home fries. That is not to mention two biscuits and of course a big bowl of grits. Samantha looked at the platter and laughed. "I know you can really eat, Johnny, but I don't think you'll be able to finish that." I said, "We'll see."

The waitress laughed and looked at Samantha. "Honey, this isn't his. This is your breakfast." I laughed as Samantha was speechless for the first time since I had met her, her mouth was wide open, but nothing was coming out. Within a couple of minutes, the waitress brought my order, and another waitress brought my other order. The waitress looked at me and said, "Enjoy it, honey."

We ate as much as we could and started wrapping some of the meats in clean napkins. The waitress saw us and asked, "Would you like me to put your food in to-go boxes?" I said, "No thanks. We have a puppy with us, and we wanted to take some of the meat for him." Smiling, she said, "Oh honey, don't take that food. I'll get you some good food for that puppy."

She came back shortly with a to-go box containing several uncooked, quarter-pound, all-beef burgers. When I paid the bill, I saw that she had not charged for the burgers, so I gave her an extra tip. The whole bill was only a little over $5. In the car, we fed Smokey a patty, which he loved because it looked and felt like a pound of meat.

We stopped frequently, so it took us what seemed days to cross Texas. Arizona and New Mexico were even hotter, but it was so dry that we didn't sweat at all. One day, we stopped at a rest area behind which was a large lake that appeared to be man-made. Very high mounds of sand beside the lake contained tracks from big machines like bulldozers. About ten feet of grass and a chain-link fence separated the lake and the rest area. We were stretching our legs and letting Smokey run around and do his business in the grass when suddenly, he darted under the fence and headed for the lake. At the edge was an embankment of pure sand that dropped about twenty feet to the lake. I called and whistled for him, but he continued his romp. At the edge of the embankment, he didn't stop in time and tumbled over and down.

By then, I had vaulted over the fence, which was only about four feet high. I ran to the edge of the embankment just in time to see him hit the water. He went under and out of sight. But in a few seconds, he surfaced and started doggie paddling.

I was screaming his name, whistling, and saying, "Come here, boy!" He started swimming to the other side of the lake about a quarter of a mile away. I took off my shoes, shirt, and pants and slid down the embankment. When I reached the lake, Smokey was about twenty-five yards out and still headed toward the other side. In warm water up to my knees, I yelled,

"Blacky! Come here, boy!" By some miracle, he started swimming back to me. I snatched him up as he tiredly flopped into my arms. I hugged him.

The loose sand made climbing with one hand and holding Smokey with the other hard to reach the top of that embankment. But making it I walked to the fence and handed him to Samantha, who had tears in her eyes. Several other motorists who had also stopped to walk around and walk their dogs had watched the incident and were taking pictures. They clapped and said, "Good job!" I realized I was standing there in just my boxer shorts. Embarrassed, I hurried back to put on my pants and shirt among all the laughter from the onlookers. After that, we always tied a cord around his neck every time we walked him. Looking back on that incident, I am glad the internet hadn't been invented yet.

On our second day, we were in some mountains doing sixty-five with our windows down and enjoying the day. In my rearview mirror, I saw a tractor-trailer coming up behind us. Not seeing anything out of the ordinary, I dismissed it. At the time, I was driving down a steep incline and the road was winding back and forth. Within a couple of minutes, a very loud air horn sounded right on my bumper. I looked in the mirror and saw that the tractor-trailer was very close to us. I picked up speed, but the truck stayed right on our bumper. After we reached speeds of over a hundred, Samantha was screaming while holding Smokey, "What does he want?" I put my hand out of the window and waved the driver to pass us, but he kept right on our bumper. I increased my speed as did the truck. I finally yelled to Samantha, "He must have lost his brakes. He can't pass because of the winding road."

At the bottom of the hill, the empty road was now visible, and the truck passed us with a tremendous amount of relief, I slowed down and pulled over. In a few minutes, Samantha and I were back to normal, and we continued our way. Within about a mile or so, we came upon the truck. The driver was sitting on the ground in front of it with his head down. I stopped and asked out the passenger's window, "Are you okay?" He nodded. "I lost my brakes coming down the mountain. Thank goodness you folks are okay." I asked, "You need help?" He shook his head. "No, I'll be okay."

We finally entered the mountains of southern California; a refreshing coolness was in the air. We drove up to a checkpoint a few miles from the border. There were about a dozen cars in line ahead of us. As we got closer to the checkpoint, we saw a sign that read, "No Plants. No Vegetables. All Animals Will Be Quarantined for 10 Days." We were devastated thinking they would take Blacky away. When it was our turn, I pulled up to the guard with my window down. He looked at Blacky in his bed on the console and asked, "Do you have any plants or vegetables?" I said, "No, officer, we don't." Still looking at him he said, "Okay, go ahead." As we drove off, Samantha and I looked at each other with wonder and amazement. Samantha gave Blacky a hug and said, "I love you." He licked her face.

CHAPTER 112

Los Pueblos

We reached Los Pueblos that evening and contacted some friends I had known in Maple Wood. I had a couple of days left on my leave, so we stayed with them while we searched for an apartment.

A very nice, matronly, elderly woman was the manager of our first apartment that was one of a dozen apartments set up like small cabins. There were six on each side facing each other. Our cabin was small but clean; it had a living room with a couch, one chair, and an end table with a lamp. There was no TV, but one of Samantha's grandmothers had given us a twelve-inch, black-and-white TV as a wedding present. There was no outside antenna, so we used the rabbit ears that came with it. Reception was lousy, and we could get only a couple very fuzzy channels.

The bedroom had a twin-sized bed with headboard, a table with a lamp, and a very small closet. The kitchen was tiny, but it had some pots, pans, and utensils. The bathroom was clean, but it was so small that when I sat on the toilet, my knees were up around my chin. There was a very small tub with a printed shower curtain and an old-style sink that hung on the wall with an old metal toothbrush holder screwed to the wall. One light was over the mirror above the sink.

The rent was $50 a month, and we did not have to sign a lease. The utilities were included, but of course there was no air conditioning. She told us that normally, she did not allow animals, but because we had just come to town, she allowed us to keep him if we picked up his poop and nobody complained especially about barking. Outside in the yard was one main walkway down the middle with well-kept grass on either side; walkways led from it to each cabin. At the street entrance was a three-foot, white picket fence. Samantha loved it, and I saw why—though the complex was old, it had been kept up beautifully.

A few days later, I checked into the base. The drive there from our apartment was too long. We stayed at that apartment for only a month; we found an apartment complex in Chula

Mist, a lot closer to my base. That apartment was much bigger but still very simple. It had carpet throughout. A large couch, a coffee table, two chairs, and an end table with a lamp were in the living room. The kitchen was spacious; it had a table with four chairs and a good amount of pots, pans, and dishes.

The bedroom had a queen-sized bed with two nightstands with lamps, a dresser, and a full-sized closet. The bathroom had a full-sized tub with sliding doors, a regular-sized toilet, a sink in a vanity, and a linen closet. The rent was $85 a month including utilities. Samantha's military dependent's check was just enough to pay the rent. I was now bringing home $145 a month. That complex had what they called cable TV, something we had never heard of before. We still had only that twelve-inch TV, but the picture was crystal clear.

Life aboard ship was demanding on both of us. Every week, the ship went to sea and returned on the weekends. All crew members had port and starboard liberty. Every weekend when I got home, Samantha would open the door, look at me, run to the bathroom, and throw up. It did not take long to find out that she was pregnant. That was a first for us, and it did not go well. Arguing and fighting became normal for us. I began to hate that tour of duty; my drinking continued and became even a little worse. My suppressed feelings started to rise to the surface as our arguing continued; I was now blaming Samantha for everything. Our marriage was in trouble right from the start.

One Sunday while on duty on the ship, I was repacking a valve to keep it from leaking. Having done that many times in the past, I thought it would be easy. I had removed all but the last of three or four pieces; no matter what tool I used, I couldn't remove that last piece. Frustrated and angry, I used a rattail file on it. I broke the tip off but continued using the broken end to get the last piece of packing out. I pried real hard, and the file broke again; a sharp piece flew into my eye. I tried to wash it out. When that didn't work, I tried pulling it out, but I couldn't. I went to sickbay, and I was sent to the base infirmary with instructions to get back quickly because the ship was getting underway the next morning.

At the infirmary, I was told that a large piece of metal was in my eyeball; they could not remove it there, so I was sent to the naval hospital. At the hospital, they said they had nobody available for surgery to remove it. I was kept overnight; they said they would contact the ship.

The next morning, with better equipment and a special doctor, I underwent minor surgery to remove the metal and was kept overnight again for observation. A bandage with numbing medication and a black patch was placed over my eye.

I left the hospital the second day. My ship was underway. For the next week, I was assigned to a barracks where I worked every day until liberty call, when I went home for the evening.

During that week, the patch stayed on my eye; I had to go to the infirmary every day to have the dressing changed and more of the numbing medicine applied.

The following Saturday, a doctor removed the patch. I had vision, but it was cloudy and only lasted temporarily. Regardless, they let me return to my ship. Of course, I was given duty for the entire weekend. Many sailors told me that they thought I had faked the injury. I looked at them with disgust and said, "Yeah, sure. I jabbed myself in the eye with a file just to get out of going to sea for a week."

After that, I totally withdrew from shipmates and kept to myself when onboard. I hated my life, the navy, and my ship.

Life at home continued to be strained, and my depression deepened as I continued to drink. My anger was surfacing more and more. Eventually I returned to Massachusetts, leaving Smokey with friends, where I was hospitalized and given an honorable discharge.

CHAPTER 113

The Job

We stayed with Samantha's family in Sandy Town for a short period. Her father was disabled, and still having three sisters and a brother at home, money was a problem for them. I started looking for a job and found one the first week with a construction company making $1.25 per hour as a laborer. I worked from 7:00 a.m. to 4:00 p.m., but I was paid for only eight hours. After taxes, I was bringing home just over $30 a week. Most of that went to Samantha's mother for room and board. I kept $10 for gas and what not.

Working in freezing temperatures was new for me, and I did not like it. My drinking and anger were coming out sideways. I could put blame on the job with some of it going to Samantha's mother for taking most of our money. Arguments and disagreements became a daily routine between Samantha, her mother, and me. Her father never said anything.

I was drinking blackberry brandy at work and coming home in a bad mood. Drinking covered my thoughts but did not erase them; it made matters only worse. In late February, we moved out of their house and into a room in a florist's shop next door to the police station. The room, which was just eight by twelve, was used as the office for the florist shop, but a small bed, an old-fashioned, plug-in icebox that had only one shelf and kept a few items cool but not cold, and a small electric heater were brought in for us.

During the day, the entire building was heated, but at night, the heat was turned off even in the bathroom that was used by those in the florist's shop and was down a hallway. Utilities were included in the rent. We bought an electric hot plate for cooking, which was very limited. We had no phone, but we could use the florist's phone for local calls.

During the day, Samantha helped in the shop for no pay, but her work went toward the rent—$25 per week, which included Samantha's work. She was very pregnant at that point and was limited to how much she could work. Even though we had only about $30 per week for ourselves, Samantha always found a way to make things work out. When I look back on those early days, I don't know how or why she put up with my anger and drinking.

My first job was to drive an old pickup truck into the woods in north Sandy Town and pick up large boulders from very old rock walls. I would take them back to the shop, where I loaded them into the bucket of a front-end loader for loading into a dump truck. Once I filled the dump truck, Gino, an old brother of the company's owner, drove us to a house in Boston where the company had been building a stone wall. Gino would drive down the long driveway and help with the building of the wall. My job was to unload the truck by hand and cart the large rocks down to the jobsite by wheelbarrow. We worked on that job every day for a week to complete it. I liked working with Gino because he always had wine with him. I was still bringing blackberry brandy, so the cold was not as bad. Gino and I got along very well.

My next job was in a basement of a house in the hills section of Sandy Town. The company owner drove me there in the mornings. The first day, he drew a circle about three feet across with chalk on the basement floor's four-inch-thick cement. He handed me a six-foot iron bar pointed on one end and said, "I want you to dig a hole through the cement to the dirt below. The hole has to be as big as the circle I've drawn."

As soon as he left, I unpacked my lunch box, which contained just two pints of blackberry brandy. I sat and took a few long pulls from the bottle. My anger was consuming me. Trying hard until my head hurt, I couldn't figure out why I still felt so much anger. I knew only that it was eating me up and I couldn't do anything about it. At one point, I yelled at the top of my voice, "I'm trying! Can't you see that?" to nobody.

To help with my thoughts, I did what I had been doing for the past five years—I drank the first bottle of brandy. I thought about just getting into my car and driving to Louisiana. I had always felt my roots had been in Louisiana, and still do today. By then, I had a loud ringing in my ears, and my head felt like it would open, and everything would come oozing out.

Looking at that bar, I thought how easy it would be to jab myself with it and end it all. I closed my eyes, and Samantha and our unborn baby popped into my mind. Something I couldn't explain overpowered me, and I started to cry uncontrollably. As my sobs racked my body, I screamed, "Why?" Afterward, with Samantha's soft face framed behind my closed eyes, a great love filled me. I knew I couldn't do that and leave her that way.

After about an hour of sitting there and feeling sorry for myself, I picked up the iron bar and started digging the hole. Chipping away at that concrete was slow going. I had no gloves, so blisters covered both hands. At the end of the day, the owner picked me up. He was very upset with the little progress I had made. He said that if I wanted to work my way up from being a laborer, I needed to work harder and faster. I asked him if he had any gloves, and he said, "No I don't. You have to supply your own." That evening, I popped the blisters and covered them with Band-Aids. I borrowed some gloves from Samantha's father though they were too small.

Every morning, my boss drove me to the job, and every afternoon, he picked me up. On the third day, he came in to see how much I had done. The hole was only about half the size he wanted. He said, "Goddamn it! You have to work faster." Of course, I was spending the first hour of every day drinking and feeling sorry for myself. Old memories flooded me as I told him, "I need some different tools, maybe a jackhammer." He said, "The neighbors don't want any noise, so all you have is the iron bar." He walked over to a wall made of six-inch-thick cement, drew a circle about the same size as he had drawn on the floor, and said, "I made a mistake. I need you to dig a hole through the wall, not the floor."

For the next three days, I chipped away at that wall. The work was even harder because it was sideways, not straight down, and that bar was heavy. I was drinking two pints of brandy those days.

CHAPTER 114

An Era Ends

On Friday evening, March 1, 1968, Samantha and I drove to her parents' house after work. Her mother came out and stood on the steps. Samantha said, "Something's wrong." As we were getting out of the car, she yelled, "Johnny, your mother called. Your father's dead. Come in and call her."

I went inside and called Mama collect. She was so upset and crying so hard that I couldn't understand anything she was saying. I asked her to put my sister on the phone. My sister was crying too, but I was able to understand her when she said, "Daddy was walking over to the barn to milk the cows and had a heart attack. He fell in cow shit. The people who owned the farm saw him drop and ran to check on him. They called for an ambulance, but it took about forty-five minutes for one to respond. They took him to a hospital, but he was already dead."

I talked with my sister for about an hour. I said I would call back the next morning to talk to Mama after she calmed down. I told Samantha's parents that I needed to go home quickly but didn't have any money. I asked them if I could borrow money from them for the flight from Boston to Pensacola and back. They said they did not have the money either but would see if they could borrow it from a friend.

That night, I told Samantha I had mixed feeling about him dying. I did not know if I was happy or sad, but she held me in her arms as I cried myself to sleep thinking only of how much Mama and my sister was crying, hurt, and alone.

The next afternoon, we returned to Samantha's parents' house. Her mother told me she had found out how much a round-trip ticket would cost and had borrowed that amount from a friend. I thanked her and called Mama. We talked for an hour or so with her mostly crying. I told her I was flying home and would let her know when to except me.

I made reservations for a flight on the following Monday. I called the owner of the construction company to let him know what had happened. He was not happy at all. He said, "If you're not back to work by next Monday, you're fired." I said, "Okay, I'll do my best."

Samantha's father drove me to Logan Airport in Boston Monday morning for my flight. Our first layover, only about an hour, was in Newark, New Jersey. I had brought four pints of blackberry brandy; those days, passengers were not searched. I was seated next to a nun, so I had to be careful about my drinking. I bought a drink of whiskey and sipped it slowly, so after drinking my brandy, nobody would question me about my slurred speech.

We stopped in Birmingham and Montgomery, Alabama. One incident during the flight got everybody, even the flight attendants, a little shook up. The plane was flying along at about 30,000 feet when suddenly it dropped for a few seconds. The captain came over the intercom telling everybody how sorry he was; the plane had flown throw an air pocket or some such thing, but everything was back to normal. With all the screaming and crying in the cabin, it was hard to hear exactly what he was saying, but I didn't think everything was back to normal. With my buzz on, my only complaint was that I had to order a new drink, which was given to me at no cost.

While sipping brandy on the sly, I thought about my father's death. What I had told Samantha was the truth. I didn't know how I felt—relieved or at a loss. It was as if my brain had two voices talking to me. One was saying, *fuck him*, and the other was saying, *he was your father, and you were brought up to respect you parents, remember?* With the alcohol's help, I eventually fell into a troubled sleep and had to be awakened by the nun when the plane landed in Pensacola. Smiling, she said, "Don't worry, son. God will forgive you." I tried to think of what she meant, but without an answer, I said, "I don't believe in God." She gasped as I walked off the plane.

My sister was waiting for me, still driving my old '61 VW. She was very happy to see me. As we sat in the car, she tearfully told me about our father's death. She said he had recently been on some crazy diet of boiled eggs and spinach and had quickly lost about a hundred pounds.

It took us about an hour to reach the farm. When we got there, Mama had a nice lunch of red beans and rice with cornbread ready. Taking a half-gallon glass jar, I walked to the main house to speak with the dairy owner and his sons. I thanked them for taking care of and helping Mama out during that time. They told me that Friday morning, they had been in their kitchen having breakfast and had seen him approach the barn. He had grabbed his chest, dropped to his knees, and fell. They had called the sheriff's office. There was no ambulance in Jay, so one had to be summoned from Maple Wood, about twenty miles away, and it took about an hour to arrive.

I again thanked them for helping Mama and my sister out and asked if I could get some milk from the vat. They told me to get as much as I wanted. I went to the vat, opened a spigot, and filled the jar with cold, raw milk.

After eating, Mama, my sister, and I sat and talked. Mama said arrangements had already been made to ship his body to Louisiana by train. She said she was waiting for me to arrive. Tickets had been bought for her, my sister, and me to take the same train. The next day, one of the dairy farmer's sons drove us to the station in Pensacola. Mama did not want to board the train until after she saw the coffin loaded. The ride to New Orleans took only a few hours with a few quick stops in Alabama and Mississippi. We were met by my cousin Drew, who took us to his house in Mayville. My cousin had arrangements with a funeral home to pick up the casket, and a wake was planned for the next evening at seven.

Mama and my sister stayed with my aunt Beth and her daughter and me. I stayed with my cousin Drew. That night, I sat with him, his wife, and a few relatives who stopped by; they could not attend the wake the next day. Everybody had already heard that my wife and I were expecting our first baby, and of course they wanted to know all the news—how I liked living in the north, would I consider moving to Louisiana, and many other questions. I still had two pints of blackberry brandy, so the evening went by slowly but comfortably for me.

Before his death, I had withdrawn into myself, but after his death, I started withdrawing even further as my confusion settled in. The questions were coming, but I wasn't answering many; I was mostly just nodding. We didn't get to bed until after midnight.

The next evening, my cousin drove me to the wake. I stayed outside telling my cousin I needed some time alone. He said, "I understand" and walked in. I was still in a confused state of mind about his death. I finished my last bottle of brandy. One of my aunts poked her head out the door and asked, "Johnny, are you coming in?" I nodded. I wiped away tears as she went back in. With a big sigh, a shudder, and a cold spot in the middle of my back, I went in and down a short hallway stopping at another closed door. I heard voices inside. I felt a resigning quietness fill my body as I opened the door and entered. I saw a coffin surrounded by flowers and with an American flag draped over it at the other end of the room. About two dozen people were talking among themselves sitting or standing in small groups. Mama, my sister, all my aunts, and my cousin Betty Ann were in a kitchen area off to my right; they were laughing and talking.

As the door closed behind me with a loud click, a deathly quiet filled the room as everybody turned to look at me. I stopped and asked myself, *What the hell did I do wrong now?* A chill ran up my back raising the hairs on the back of my neck. Even if they had continued talking, I would not have heard them due to the loud ringing in my ears. I shook my shoulders and walked slowly to the casket; everyone watched me intently. I felt as if I were in a slow-motion movie. The silence was deafening. I stared straight ahead, afraid to investigate the casket but afraid not to. I stepped closer. My heart was pounding so hard that I thought it would tear right out of my chest. My hands were squeezed so tightly that my fingernails drew blood. I looked at that evil man who had dominated me for my entire life for reasons I did not know and felt I never would.

As I leaned in and stared at him, tears rolled down my checks and fell onto his cold hard face. I kissed him full on the lips and said out loud, "I love you, Daddy." I heard gasps and crying. A voice I recognized as my father's twin said, "Oh Lord." I stood alone and fell into the most peaceful state I had ever known. My sister came up and put her arms around me. We cried together.

Eventually, my sister and I left the casket, and I never returned. That long night, I met relatives I had never seen before and some I had not seen in years including my brother, Daddy, who stayed in the background and did not mingle with everybody; he mostly talked with my aunt, his adoptive mother. At one point, I tried to engage him in conversation, but he blew me off, so I ignored him. Shortly after that, I saw him leaving with cousins from New Orleans, and I knew he was going home.

Sometime after midnight having seen around a hundred relatives coming and going, all of us close relatives left; I went back to my cousins for the night. I went out onto the front porch and finished one of two pints of brandy a cousin had bought me on the way back.

The next day, we returned to the funeral home. There were not nearly as many people for the funeral procession. We buried my father. An era ended I thought as I walked away from his grave that day.

CHAPTER 115

The Blame

Mama, my sister, and I stayed in Mayville with my cousin for a couple more days before returning to Florida. The night we returned, I sat with Mama to find out what her plans were. She was adamant that she wanted to go back to our home in Maple Wood. She asked me several times if I would move back to Florida. I told her I would have to talk with Samantha. She said something that broke my heart: "I blame Daddy's dying on Samantha." I stared at her. I asked, "Why, Mama? Why would you say that?" She said, "Because she's a nigger-loving, carpet-bagging Yankee." I yelled, "That's my wife you're talking about!" She never had any other explanation.

After arguing with her for several minutes, I realized it was useless. Even when I brought up the crazy diet he had been on, she still believed that my wife had somehow killed my father, and I realized there was no way I would change her mind.

The next day, I made a reservation for a flight back to Boston. On the flight back, I had a lot of thinking to do about moving back to Maple Wood with Samantha. I was not looking forward to those discussions, and I knew I would have to tell her what Mama had said.

Though I asked Mama many times over the following years about what she had said, she never spoke to me about it again. The only conclusion I ever came to is that my father hated Samantha for standing up to him that day with the knife or maybe simply because his thoughts of her was also as a "nigger-loving, carpet-bagging Yankee," so in Mama's eyes, the blame was on Samantha, who killed him through his own hate, I guessed.

CHAPTER 116

Bella

I got back to Sandy Town on Saturday, March 9; Samantha had stayed with her parents. At that time, I did not bring up the subject about moving to Florida. On Monday morning, I was back to work putting that hole in that basement wall.

Because Samantha was due to have the baby any day, we decided to stay with her parents for that week and sleep in her old bedroom. That night about midnight while Samantha and I were lying in bed, she went into labor. An ambulance was called, and she was taken to a hospital.

I drove to the hospital with one of her sisters. I requested permission to go through delivery with Samantha. I was asked if I had had any childbirth classes. When I told them no, they said I could not go into the emergency room to see her or go through delivery. They instructed me to sit in the waiting room; they would let me know when the baby was born.

For over thirty-two hours, we stayed in the waiting room sleeping on the most uncomfortable chairs imaginable. Hour after hour, I kept asking the front desk for updates, but the only answer I ever received was, "Not yet." Every time I asked to see her, I was told no.

On Wednesday, March 13, I was finally told I could see her, but when I asked if the baby had been born, I was told, "I don't know." I went upstairs and found Samantha; she looked exhausted, but she was able to talk for a few minutes. She told me I was the daddy of a baby girl.

After a few minutes, she went to sleep, and I walked to the newborns' area to see my daughter. I looked at her through the window and could not hold back tears. A million thoughts went through my mind. *Please God, if you're real, let me be a good father and protector, and I'll give all the love I never received to this beautiful, innocent baby.*

The first time I held her, I looked into her closed eyes. Her tiny hand held my finger tightly and with tears flowing, I said, "Bella, I promise you I will always protect, respect, and love you with my entire being until I die." I looked at Samantha lying beside us; she too was crying. I squeezed her hand and said, "Honey, I meant every word."

Samantha stayed in the hospital for three days after Bella was born. The hospital told us that because we did not have insurance, we would have to leave the baby there until the bill was paid. After that meeting, I found out why some women were known as she-devils. Of course, we took Bella home.

I missed work on Tuesday and Wednesday. The company owner was very mad at me, but he put me back to work with the stipulation that I would work on Saturday in that cold basement. Because I had missed two days and pay, I agreed. By the following Tuesday, I had a six-inch-wide hole through the wall when the owner came into the basement. He said that because I was so slow in finishing that job, he was pulling me off it and putting me on another.

He drove me to work with Angelo, one of his relatives, building cement steps at a house in Sandy Town. We spent the first two days in the woods in North Sandy Town picking up rocks from old stone walls, putting them in that old truck, and taking them to the jobsite.

On that job, I learned three things from Angelo about building steps. The first was that because the rocks were on somebody else's land, we picked them up out in the woods where nobody saw us, so there was no cost for them. (Years later, I found out that there was a rock quarry nearby that sold rocks by the pound.) The second thing was that we filled the framework for the steps with the rocks to save on concrete though the homeowner was charged for large amounts of concrete. And third, I learned to mix cement by hand rather than with a mixer; that took more time, so the job hours added up quickly.

I worked for that construction company for two more weeks. Of course, I still had my blackberry brandy. During that last week, Samantha and I discussed moving to Maple Wood. I told her how Mama blamed her for my father's death. Even with that information, she agreed to move. That Friday afternoon, I told the company owner that I was quitting and moving to Florida. He wasn't mad and said that he had been expecting me to leave. He said, "Spring's close, and laborers are cheap and easy to hire for the summer."

CHAPTER 117

The Move

I received about $31.50 after taxes every Friday, and I had to pay $25 a week for rent. By the time we were ready to move to Florida, we had no money. I called Mama and told her that we would move to Maple Wood but that I didn't have the money to make the move right then. She said she had gotten life insurance money from my father's death and would send me enough to get to Florida. The next day, she sent $200 via Western Union to a store in Sandy Town.

After getting the money, I went to a Chrysler dealer to have the oil changed in my Charger. The service manager said, "Your right rear tire looks low, and it has wear on it. I happen to have that tire in stock, and I can mount, balance, and install it for fifty bucks." I followed him out to the service area and looked at the tire. I saw some wear but not enough that I thought I needed a new tire, and it did not look low. The manager said it would go flat soon and I would never make it to Florida. I disagreed and said, "Just change the oil."

About a half hour later, he returned and said, "Your car's ready." I paid the bill, and with him following me, I walked out to the service area. That tire was completely flat. Smiling at me, he said, "I told you." I looked closely and saw a small puncture in the sidewall. I asked him about it, and he replied, "I don't know anything about that." Mad as hell but not able to prove anything, I went to the front desk and called Samantha's father. I explained the situation to him and asked him to come to the shop. When he arrived, I jacked up my car, took off the flat, and put it in his trunk. I gave him $25 to buy me a new tire.

While he was gone, I sat in my car just to make sure nothing else was done to it and to sip brandy. The manager was stomping around the area mad as hell and telling me I needed to get my car out; so, he could bring other cars in to work on. I just looked at him and smiled.

When Samantha's father returned with a new tire mounted on my rim, I put it on the car. I told the manager, "You better hope and pray nothing else happened to this car." He backed away quickly saying, "You're fucking drunk." I stepped closer saying, "So what?" He stormed away with no further outburst. The floor inside of the shop was very smooth, and I burned rubber on my way out filling it with smoke. Some of the mechanics were cheering as I left.

The next day after a lot of crying and hugs between Samantha and her family, we left for Maple Wood.

CHAPTER 118

A Special Moment

When we arrived in Maple Wood, the first thing I did was stand in front of that pine tree in the backyard. My feelings erupted; my anger boiled over. I pulled the hose down and cut it into many pieces with an axe from the utility room. I chopped the tree down and cut it into four-foot pieces. I put the pieces of hose in an old barrel we used to burn trash, splashed gas over them, and set them on fire. I put pieces of that tree in too. It took several hours for all of it to burn, but I stayed there until the last embers. I said out loud, "I just want to know why!"

I had not noticed that Samantha was standing behind me. I didn't know how long she had been there, but she hugged me from behind. You could have heard my yell all the way to Massachusetts. For a second, I thought my father had reached out for me from the grave. I turned around, and we laughed. She didn't try to get me to talk; she knew it was a special moment for me.

The boat my father and I had built at the hobby shop was in the backyard. Within a few weeks, I cut it up and disposed of it at the Maple Wood dump. I had to make several trips. As I drove away on the last trip, I again visited those memories so long ago, but that time, I smiled, knowing I would never see it again.

My sister had been going to college in Alabama since 1964 but had not received a degree. She moved back home after my father's death and took up residence in her old bedroom, so Samantha, Bella, and I took over my old bedroom.

A neighbor told us about a Dollar Store in downtown Maple Wood that was hiring. Because we needed money, Samantha got a job for $1 per hour. My sister was driving my father's '61 VW. Samantha was driving my old VW to work, and Mama gladly babysat for us.

I quickly got a job at a chemical plant for $2.05 an hour. I was working in an airconditioned lab, testing the products being produced, which was great for the summer. Those in the lab had to work one hour per shift in the production area. Working out there, I became friendly with those employees and started drinking and gambling with them after work.

Over the next year and half, I became friends with the production workers and eventually transferred to that area. I again started drinking heavily. Quite a few of the workers had cars or trucks they liked to race. Of course, I went right along with them betting on my Charger. At first, winning was easy, but after a while as I won more than my share, nobody wanted to race me.

The last race I ever ran was with a young man from a nearby plant. He came over just after midnight as we got off work that night. A good-sized crowed gathered because we had heard of the old truck with a big engine. The young man bragged how he had put a 396-cubic-inch motor in the truck and it was the fastest thing around. As we sat around in the parking lot drinking and placing bets, I said to him, "Let's race for titles." He asked, "Are you fucking crazy?" I laughed and said, "Okay. A hundred bucks then?" He agreed.

We drove onto the main road leading from the plant. Many cars and a lot of people lined the road in front of us, headlights shining brightly. We lined up. A female worker in front of us was holding a white shirt. I downed the rest of my bottle of blackberry brandy, threw the empty on the passenger's seat, and smiled at my adversary. He was staring intently straight ahead. I saw that his knuckles were white as he gripped the steering wheel. I chuckled. I looked at the girl holding the shirt. A great calmness came over me—the pint of brandy was taking effect.

I revved my engine. The tach needle rose into the red as the girl raised the shirt. My engine was so loud that it drowned out the girl's screams as she jumped up with the shirt held high. Her arm came down hard bringing the shirt with it. I let out the clutch, and my Charger came to life in my hands. Both of us roared down that road side by side. Within a short distance, I shifted into second gear and pulled ahead. I knew that third gear was not my strongest, so I kept it in second longer than usual. As I hit third, I saw the quarter-mile mark coming up fast.

I passed it and looked in my rearview mirror. I thought I saw headlights off the road, and they seemed to be rolling. I turned and went back. The truck had indeed gone off the road and rolled. It was lying on its side, and the young man was standing beside it. Everybody got there, including one of the guards on the gate. The young man was shaking up—a little bloody but okay. He handed me my winnings and said, "Damn. That Charger is fast."

A bunch of us righted his truck, which had damage to the front, the roof, and both doors. He drove off. We never saw him again. After the race, I met most of the onlookers at a bar. We drank with me buying, and we played pool for beers. I made it home about 2:00 a.m., and Samantha was so mad that she wouldn't talk to me.

The next day after Samantha went to work, I took a walk in the woods. I went to the lake where Cap and I had spent so much time. I built a small fire, sat, and thought about how simple my life had been. I thought about my current life and what I was doing with it. I didn't like what I saw. When Samantha came home that afternoon, I talked with her, apologized to her, and made promises I knew I wouldn't or couldn't keep.

CHAPTER 119

The Chair

In 1969, I sold the Charger to a neighbor for $500. Samantha, very pregnant with our second baby, had been complaining about the VW's lights, horn, and windshield wipers not working. After hearing her complaints repeatedly, I decided to fix the problem. After drinking two or three Blue Ribbon beers and sipping on my eternal pint of blackberry brandy, I collected my tools. I drilled a hole in the dash. Opening the trunk, which was in front on a Bug, I pushed wires through the hole. By trial and error, I found the solution. Twisting two wires together would start the engine. When I wanted the lights on, I twisted two other wires together. To blow the horn, I could just tap two wires together. Windshield wipers were also no problem—just twist two more wires.

One day, the state of Florida decided to put all cars through inspections. A new building was erected on Highway 81 just outside Maple Wood for that purpose. The day I took the Bug to get an inspection, Skinny, my neighbor and friend, decided to come along to check it out. We got there but had to wait in line for an hour. As I approached the garage door, the inspector told me, "I need to check your brakes." I said, "Okay. What do you need me to do?" He said, "Back up and drive inside reaching a speed of at least ten miles per hour and slam your brakes on." I did as I was told. He said, "Your brakes are fine. Now, I need to check the lights, brake lights, blinkers, windshield wipers, and horn."

Standing beside my open window, he told me which one he wanted me to turn on. He kept giving me hard looks as I was putting wires together on each of his commands, but he said nothing. When it came to the horn, I couldn't find the right wires and kept turning on the other ones. By then, Skinny and I were laughing, but the inspector was getting irritated and kept saying, "Horn! Blow the damn horn!" Finally, as I put two wires together and the wipers came on, Skinny stuck his head out of the passenger's window and yelled, "*Beep*." It sounded just like the Bug's horn, and the inspector said, "Okay, the horn works."

After that inspection, I told Samantha, and Skinny told his wife, but we never told anybody else. For a long time, the four of us had many laughs over the incident. Later, I put nametags on all the wires to make sure we always connected the right ones.

The front passenger seat was broken down, and Samantha complained constantly about her back hurting when she sat in it. I had to drink more Blue Ribbons before I could tackle that job. I finished a six-pack and ripped that seat out in no time. To give Samantha a comfortable ride, I bought her a beautiful, aluminum folding lawn chair for which I paid a dollar at the Dollar Store where she was working. I was proud of myself as I placed it in the car; it fit perfectly.

The first time Samantha got in it, she gave me a huge smile and a big thank you. I gave her my best knowing grin. Slowly taking off down the dirt road was great; Samantha was happy, so I was happy. But getting out on the highway and taking off quickly to get into traffic was a different story. The chair folded up with Samantha in it. She and the chair went over backward; her legs shot up. She started screaming something about neutering me as her legs and arms thrashed about. Not wanting to think about something like that, I jammed the brakes on hard, and bad got worse—she flew forward still in the chair. Her head hit the dash, and she dropped like a rock to the floor with the chair on top of her.

She was screaming some more about cutting off my only manhood and flushing it down the toilet. I pulled off the road, got out, ran around to the passenger door, and helped her up hoping she would forget about her threats. She may have been pregnant, but she gave me a mean right to the gut. She pulled that new chair out and threw it into the woods. She got into the rear seat with arms crossed and saying, "Take me home!"

After that day, I was Driving Miss Samantha.

CHAPTER 120

A United Front

It became obvious that Mama and Samantha could not live under the same roof. Samantha had agreed to move to Maple Wood even knowing Mama blamed her for my father's death. I don't know how she stayed in that home for a year. Almost daily, she would complain to me about how badly Mama treated her.

One day, I came in and found her crying uncontrollably. I sat beside her and asked, "What happened, honey?" though I knew it had to have been Mama. She said, "Your Mama called me a goddamn Yankee carpetbagger." In anger, I started to go talk with Mama, but sweet Samantha stopped me saying, "Honey, it's not worth it. She'll never change her mind." I said, "You're right."

The next day, Samantha and I spoke to Mama about it and everything else. Words and anger rose quickly. She was a stubborn woman, and I again knew she would never change her mind. She still blamed Samantha for his death, and that was her way of getting even. I had only once before seen that prejudiced side of Mama.

I was working a lot of overtime in the production area, so Samantha had quit her job and was staying home every day with Mama. After that incident, I knew we had to move out. The day that we moved, Mama cried and hung onto Bella. I looked at her; to me, she was faking it. I had seen her do that before, and I had not believed it then either.

We rented a sparingly furnished house close to the high school in downtown Maple Wood. It had two bedrooms and a heater built into a wall in the hallway. We put Bella in the second bedroom in her crib. Because the wall heater did not heat her bedroom, we bought a small electric heater for her. In the middle of the first night, we were awakened by Bella screaming at the top of her lungs. Running into her room, I was excepting to do battle with some awful monster that was trying to kill her. Poor Bella was standing in her crib staring at that red-eyed monster—the heater. I have always felt so bad about that scare in her young life. After that, we put her in our bedroom but kept the heater out of her sight.

CHAPTER 121

Tensions

We lived in that house for a few months and started talking about having a house built. When my father had bought this land, he put the lot the house was on in his name. The lot I had dug for the supposed fallout shelter was in my sister's name. The biggest surprise was that he had put the two remaining lots in my name. I did not know that until after his death.

One of Mama's neighbors told us about another neighbor who had just bought a new trailer and had traded in his old one as a deposit. We spoke with him, and he gladly showed us the trailer. It was ten feet wide and seventy feet long. It had two bedrooms, one bathroom, a kitchen and dining room combination, and a living room that pulled out from the body of the trailer. There was carpet throughout, and it was in very good shape. I am not sure if we loved the unit or we loved the idea of owning our own home, but we were excited.

I had just received a 25¢-an-hour raise and was then making $2.30 an hour with a lot of overtime. The next day, we spoke with the trailer company and came to an agreement–they would move the trailer to my lot and set it up for free since the lot was only about a hundred yards away. Our first home cost less than $3,000, and our payment, with no down payment, was under $100 a month. I obtained two fifty-gallon drums from my company to hold kerosene. I built a stand about six feet tall for the drums right behind the trailer; gravity would draw the kerosene into the heater.

By that time, Bella was climbing out of her crib regularly and climbing into bed with us. Early one morning, we were awakened by our front door slamming. I had lived in that neighborhood for years and had never seen or heard any suspicious activity. Nobody locked doors, so keeping with that tradition, we were not locking ours. I got out of bed and checked Bella's room; she was not in her crib. I look out her window and saw Mama walking back toward her house carrying Bella on her hip. I was relieved, but Samantha was very upset and pointed out to me that Mama should not be coming into our home and taking Bella without our permission. Thinking about it, I agreed with her. I dressed and walked over to Mama's house to have a word about it.

Tensions between Mama and Samantha were still very high, and I did not want to bring them back to a boil. That morning as I went into Mama's house, she was walking around the house still carrying Bella. It was easy to see that both were very happy. She had already made drip coffee, so pouring a cup, I sat at the table as she cooked half a pound of bacon, fried some leftover grits in the bacon grease, and cooked eggs after adding a little lard to the mix in the old, cast iron skillet. She sat at the table with Bella on her lap. I smiled as she ate grits as fast as Mama could feed her them. While sitting, eating, and talking, I gently brought up the subject of her coming over to get Bella. It worked, and in the end, she said from then on, she would let us know the night before when she planned to come over for Bella. Thanking her, I gave a big sigh of relief and an even bigger one when I spoke with Samantha and told her of the arrangement. With a smile, she thanked me.

The next morning, I woke up and walked past Bella's room on the way to the bathroom. I saw that she was already awake and playing quietly in her crib. As I was finishing in the bathroom, I heard the front door slam. Anger filled my body as I heard Samantha angrily yell out my name. Walking quickly to Bella's room, I saw that she was not in her crib, but her dirty diaper was lying on the mattress. My anger was rising almost to the boiling point as I looked out her window and saw the surprise of my life—Bella, naked as a jaybird, was running as fast as her little legs could carry her toward Mama's house alone. My anger turned to a smile and then laughter as I walked back to the bedroom.

Samantha was beside herself when she saw me laughing, but she quickly changed her attitude when I told her what I had seen. She was concerned that Bella could open the door and go outside by herself. I agreed. I dressed and walked to Mama's just to make sure Bella had made it to her house. As I walked into the house, Mama became defensive. With a laugh, I told her what I had seen and told her we would be locking the doors at night.

The next day, I drove into the woods to cut down pine trees for a fence. I loaded them into the VW with them hanging out the windows on both sides. After digging holes and putting the posts in, I bought hardware wire I strung between the posts. I built a gate out of the same posts and wire. The next day, we let Bella play in the fenced area. Checking on her, we saw that she seemed to be content just digging in the dirt. About an hour later, I happened to look out and could not see her. Going outside, I saw her walking down the street butt-naked toward Aunt Lana's house, Skinny's wife. Her clothes were strewn about the yard.

I caught up with her and brought her back to the yard. I dressed her and watched as she promptly unlocked the gate and headed out again. I returned to the hardware store for a childproof gate lock. He laughed and said, "I have just the thing for you." He produced a lockset I had never seen before. I installed it with the hope she could not get out. It seemed to work for a while, but she continued to take off her clothes whenever she played in the yard.

One day, a neighbor who lived alone, told Samantha that when she was sleeping, she was awakened by someone trying to break into her house through her bathroom window. She told Samantha that because she lived alone, she normally locked the doors and windows at night. On that night, the person was making enough noise trying to pry the bathroom window open that it woke her up. She immediately called the sheriff's office: "I'm alone, and somebody's breaking into my house. He's halfway through the bathroom window." The deputy said, "When he gets all the way in, call us back," and hung up. She told Samantha that she was startled, but taking the phone with her, she yelled, "I have the sheriff's department on the phone! They're on their way." Whoever it was immediately climbed out and left.

She told Samantha, "You should always keep your doors and windows locked while Johnny's working the graveyard shift." Samantha told her she had already started locking our doors at night and told her about Bella getting out. They had a good laugh about that.

One night a few weeks later while I was working the eleven-to-seven shift, somebody tried to break into our house around 3:00 a.m. and woke Samantha up. With the information, from our neighbor, Samantha called our friend Aunt Lana. Within a few minutes, Aunt Lana's husband, Skinny, was knocking on Samantha's door telling her he was there. When she opened the door, she smiled because Skinny was there in his boxers carrying a double-barreled, loaded shotgun. He told Samantha he had not seen anybody while running to her door.

The next morning when she told me about the incident, she said somebody had grabbed one of the bedroom windows and shook it real hard as if trying to pull it out of the wall. Next, the person went around to the door, pulled real hard on it, and shook it as he had the window. It was summer, and the trailer windows were all open, but because they were jalousie-style windows, a person would have to rip the entire window off to gain access.

The next day, I told Mama about somebody trying to break in. She got mad and said that at night when I worked the graveyard shift, she would stay with Samantha and protect them. I knew it would be useless to argue with her.

That night as I left for work around ten thirty, Mama walked over from her house carrying an empty Coke bottle. When I got home the next morning, I asked Samantha, "How did it go last night?" She told me that when she went to bed shortly after I had left for work, Mama had curled up on the floor next to the front door holding the Coke bottle. Sometime around 3:00 a.m., they were awakened by someone shaking a bedroom windows as he had done the night before. Whoever it was grabbed the door handle and did the same thing as if trying to force the door open.

Samantha said, "With all the noise, Bella started to cry." With awe in her voice, Samantha told me that Mama woke up, unlocked the front door, and pushing it open hard enough to make a loud bang against the outside of the trailer, had yelled, "You son of a bitch! I'll get you!" She went out with the Coke bottle raised. Samantha called Skinny, who arrived in minutes again in his briefs carrying that shotgun.

About ten minutes later, Mama walked back a little out of breath but still carrying that Coke bottle. She told Samantha and Skinny, "I could have caught that son of a bitch, but my legs are too short. I chased him all the way over to the trailer park, where I lost him. I think he's some drunken sailor." That trailer park she talked about was the same one my father had moved us into in the 1950s. Mama was sixty-five years old at the time.

CHAPTER 122

Chief

The next day, I searched the *Pensacola Journal* newspaper and saw a three-year-old German shepherd for sale. I called, and the seller said the price was $25. He told me that he had bought the dog to protect his wife when he was away; the dog liked woman but not men. I told him that would be perfect; I said my wife and I would be over in an hour.

Samantha and I drove to Pensacola. The dog was in a fenced front yard. He started growling as we got out of the car. I couldn't believe it—he looked so much like Cap that I immediately fell in love with him. I would have paid $100. A man came out and yelled at the dog, raising his hand as if to strike him. The dog cowered, still growling, and didn't move while keeping his eyes on the man. I understood why the dog didn't like males.

A woman came out and called the dog, which got up, ran to her, and sat. I took an instant dislike to that man, and I didn't want this to take long, so I took out $25 cash and said, "I'll take him." He said, "Okay," and took the money. He called the dog over and put a rope around his neck. He handed me the rope. Opening the gate, I walked the dog to our car with no trouble and opened the passenger door. He got into the back seat. He was huge; all he would do was stand, not lie down or sit as we drove home. His head was hanging over both of us. He leaned against Samantha, who was scared to death, while keeping his eyes on me, but he never showed any hostility.

Getting home, I led him into the yard. He walked around the area and raised his leg on the single tree. "Marking his territory," I told Samantha. We got him some water, which he drank quickly. He lay in the dirt. I walked over to see if I could pet him. He got up and walked away. I asked Samantha to pet him. At first, she didn't want to, but I reminded her of what the owner had said and how we had seen his wife call him over to her. With reservations, she said, "Chief, come here, boy." He went right to her, and she petted him. We saw he loved her attention.

We waited until the next day to introduce him to Bella. We knew the previous owner had kids, but we waited anyway. He took an immediate liking to her, and Bella hugged him and started walking around the yard holding his chain collar. He followed her everywhere.

It was two weeks before I again worked the eleven-to-seven shift. It took me talking and feeding him every day for those two weeks before he trusted me to put my hands around him and give him a hug as he licked my face.

On my first night back on the graveyard shift, the prowler returned. He shook the bedroom window and the door just as he had previously. That time, with Chief standing in the hallway on the inside growling, Samantha opened the door and screamed, "Get him, boy!" Chief raced out the door. She called Aunt Lana. Within minutes, Skinny, in his briefs and carrying his faithful shotgun, arrived, and that time, Aunt Lana was with him. They knocked on the door, and Samantha went outside carrying Bella, who had been awakened by the noise. She told them she had let Chief out when the man shook the window and door.

While standing there talking, they heard noises coming from a short distance away in the woods. All three walked in that direction with Skinny keeping the shotgun up and ready. When they arrived, they found Chief had treed a man. He had climbed a small pine tree, and his butt was about six feet off the ground. Chief would growl, jump, and bite his ass, and the man would yell, "Ouch." Samantha told the man that she would call the dog off if he left and never came back. He said, "I'll never come back if you call that dog off." Skinny told him, "If I see you again, I'm going to shoot you." For emphasis, he poked him with the barrel of the shotgun. The man said, "Please, guys, just call the dog off and I'll leave."

Taking Chief by his collar, Samantha told the man, "Now git!" He climbed down and ran off. Yes, that sweet, young mother had said, "Now git!" to protect her child. Oh yeah and if you didn't notice, she was talking like a rebel. All three laughed all the way back to the trailer. We never had another prowler for as long as we lived there.

One day while I was working the day shift, Samantha had let Bella out in the yard to play. By then, she never worried because Chief always stayed right beside her. About an hour later, she received a frantic phone call from Steve, a young sailor to whom I had sold the Charger. He was a renter living in Aunt Lana's trailer right down the street. He told her that a naked Bella was walking down the street with Chief. He said that he had gone out and walked to her saying, "Bella, honey, come here." Steve said something that made Samantha laugh even though it wasn't funny. Bella had her arm over Chief's back; she looked at him and said, "Det'im, boy!" Chief growled and charged Steve. He said he ran back to his trailer and just as he closed the door, Chief hit it and dented it. Samantha ran down the dirt road and found Bella still walking with Chief; she brought them home.

She had kept both in the house until I came home. She told me the story and said I had to fix the gate lock. Going out, I looked around and found a hole dug under the wire fence; Bella and Chief had crawled out. Laughing, I told Samantha that Chief had dug a hole and that was how they had gotten out.

After that, we kept a close eye on them and learned a big surprise. It was Bella who was digging the holes with Chief helping her. I finally had to put boards down into the dirt all along the fence to stop them from digging their way out.

CHAPTER 123

Chloe

Early on a Wednesday morning in December 1969, Samantha woke me up saying her water had just broken and she was in labor. After leaving Bella with Mama, I drove her to the Maple Wood hospital. She was sitting on the back seat of my VW telling me to hurry.

When we arrived, a nurse asked if I would like to go through delivery with her. With surprise in my voice, I said, "Thank you! I sure do." Nothing else was asked of me as she showed me where to change. She said, "Hurry! It won't be long." After putting on hospital garb, I was ushered into the birthing ward.

The doctor was sitting on a three-legged stool like a milking stool and had a metal bucket on the floor between his legs. He talked me through the entire delivery. At first, I stood beside Samantha holding her hand, but the doctor said, "Johnny, it's time." I stood behind him. The birth was the most beautiful thing I had ever seen. At one point, I yelled at the doctor, "Stop it! You're hurting her," meaning Chloe. As her head showed, the doctor used very large tongs to grasp the baby. They looked like those used to move blocks of ice around in an icehouse. He started pulling and twisting so much that I thought for sure he would break her neck.

I had seen a calf and a colt born in Louisiana. Remembering how their front feet were grasped and pulled hard to help with the berthing, I never expected that a doctor would help a woman having a baby by pulling on her head like that. After she was born and while the doctor was taking care of Samantha, a nurse cleaned and wrapped Chloe up in a birthing blanket as she called it. She smiled and asked me, "Do you want to hold your baby girl?" With no hesitation and with my heart swelling with pride, I held her and marveled at how beautiful she was. I could not stop admiring her full head of blond hair. With my eyes running over with tears, I kissed her gently on the forehead, the only open spot out from under the blanket. For just a moment, her eyes opened, and looking deep into them, I made her a promise. "Chloe, I'll always love and protect you from the evils of this world. I will never harm you. I know that with my guidance, you will grow up to be a loving mother yourself." I have always thought she smiled and closed her eyes. I placed her on Samantha. We cried together, love pouring from us for our new baby.

A couple of hours later, I drove to Mama's house to let her know we had another girl. For only the second time in my life, the first being when my father died, I saw her get very emotional as her eyes filled with tears. I picked Bella up and told her, "Honey, you have a brand-new baby sister." She started clapping and saying, "Baby, baby, baby." She looked around as if one was going to walk through the front door. Smiling, I hugged her and said, "Your Mama will come home soon and bring her." She started saying, "Mama, Mama, Mama," and looking all around for her. To get her mind off Mama and baby, I walked to our trailer and let her play with Chief, which she loved to do, and it worked.

I brought Samantha and Chloe home in only two days. She looked to me as if she had already gained a couple of pounds—the baby that is. Mama held her and again became very emotional. We let Bella sit on Mama's couch and hold her baby sister. I never knew how much love a child could show; it was written all over her face and in her words as she talked to her. All she wanted to do was hold the baby. I had never shown such love at an early age toward my sister, and I was completely awed by the sentiment.

After that, life got back to normal. Slowly, without my realizing it, the months passed, and my drinking and anger returned. In early summer 1970, I had gotten another 25¢-an-hour raise; I was making $2.55 an hour and still working overtime. Because we had two children, I felt the VW was not adequate and safe enough for the four of us. We sold the old VW for $500 and used that as a down payment on a used 1969 Ford Galaxy four door through the credit union at work for about $3,000. The payments, as were the payments for the trailer, were under $100 a month.

CHAPTER 124

Mindless Matter

Work at the chemical plant was okay. I did not mind it, and I liked the people I worked with, but I hated the rotating shift work. Every week, our shifts changed, and it was causing my health and frame of mind to slowly worsen.

As months passed, my drinking and anger rose up to bite me hard, and in my soggy brain, I felt it had to be pointed somewhere. It is said that you hurt the ones you love. I started to withdraw even more but with bursts of anger. Many times, Samantha begged me to talk to her, but I refused; I kept my feelings buried so nobody would see them. The shield I had put up so long before was still working. My anger was coming out sideways, but I didn't know it until it was too late.

One day after I had been out drinking all night after getting off work at eleven, Samantha was waiting for me. She wanted to talk. I came in drunk and woke Bella and Chloe up. Shit hit the fan. Only once before had I seen her so mad. She gave me an ultimatum. "Quit drinking, act like a responsible adult who has a family, or else." In my drunken stupor, I looked at her and asked, "What are you going to fucking do, leave?" She never said another word. She went in with the two babies, dressed them, and took them into the kitchen for breakfast. I went to bed and slept all day. I didn't get up until it was time to go to work that night.

Samantha had not spoken a word to me, so I got dressed. Walking out the door, I slammed it hard. Driving to work that night, I kept asking myself, *What's her problem?* I was sipping a pint of my blackberry brandy, so reaching work, I sat in the parking lot until I finished it. That night was a long shift. At 7:00 a.m., they offered me an overtime shift, but I refused. On the way home as I sipped brandy, I thought, *I wonder what she's going to say to me. Will she apologize?*

I sat in the car in the driveway and finished the brandy. I saw Chief lying in the front yard. I didn't see Bella, so I went inside calling for Samantha with anger in my voice. There was no answer. Looking throughout the trailer, I couldn't find them. I peeked through the bedroom window toward Mama's house but couldn't see anybody. I was angry as I walked over. Samantha was sitting on Mama's couch crying. Mama had the girls; Chloe was on her hip and Bella was standing on a chair beside her as she was cooking. I walked over, sat, and putting my arm around her asked, "What's wrong, honey?" She said she had gotten a call from her mother saying that her grandfather was very sick and was not expected to live. He had been living with them for many years. For her, losing him was more like losing a father.

I didn't know what to say or do. I had never had to comfort somebody like that before, only myself. I sat there holding her in my arms until her sobbing stopped. We decided that she would fly home with the girls. The next day, I drove her to the airport.

After dropping her off, I drove to my watering hole sipping brandy as I went. I drank myself into a stupor that night and never went home. In fact, I didn't go home or to work for several days, calling in sick each day; I slept in my car. Eventually running low on money, I had to go home.

For two more days, I sat in the trailer in the dark and drank every bit of alcohol and brandy I had. I was blaming Samantha for all my troubles; she was at the root of my anger. In my drunken state, I remembered what Player had taught me so many years ago— "Johnny, never let a woman wrap her legs around you. She's trying to trap you into marriage by getting pregnant."

Alcohol can affect people in different ways. It wasn't that way with Samantha and me, but as you can see, it was me. It turned my problems into so much anger that in a twisted way, I started blaming Samantha for everything. It wasn't me, so it had to be Samantha.

I finally went back to work. I withdrew so much that I wouldn't talk to the guys unless they said something about work. I was so angry at Samantha, and I cursed her many times. I got off work at eleven that night and continued to drink.

Over the next couple of weeks, I never called Samantha. Feeling like a free man, I was drinking every day and night. At one point, Mama was crying and said, "Johnny, you are just like Daddy." She meant my father. "I should have killed him years ago." I laughed and said, "Why don't you just kill me then?" My sister, who was still living with her, got into the conversation. "Johnny, you have two beautiful babies to think of." My anger was boiling over. I looked at the two of them and said, "Get out of my goddamn house!" It wasn't until my sister turned on me with such a tirade that I realized I was in Mama's house.

I went straight home. I sat in the dark. I was so angry that I didn't drink; I just wallowed in self-pity. I am not sure how long I sat there, but I remember seeing daylight pouring through the windows. I was shaking so much that I thought I was dying. I was experiencing the DTs for the first time. I started crying calling out for Mama and Samantha. That long day was one I have never known again. Though I started that day, it took several long days and nights for me to dry out. I continued to work, but it was very tough.

Reader, I hope you can see what alcohol can do to a person. Never a thought crossed my mindless matter of a brain of what Samantha and her family were going through. It was all about me and *What am I going to tell this young woman who's trapped me?*

CHAPTER 125

The Pressure Was on Me

A few days later, I called Samantha. I said, "Hi, honey," but she said nothing for a long time. For the first time in my life, I knew what it felt like to have loved and then lose that love. I knew that if I wanted my family back, I had to change and change fast, or all would be lost. The pressure was on me. I knew I had to make some hard choices.

Over the next two weeks, Samantha and I talked every day. I begged her to come home. I told her how much I loved her, missed her, and needed her. During that period, I never had a drink. In the end, I agreed that I would do whatever it took to change my life and begin acting like a normal husband and father. Samantha returned to Maple Wood, and I did try real hard. I quit gambling, and my drinking slowed down considerably. I tried to spend more quality time with her and the girls.

In late summer 1970, Samantha decided to go to nursing school to become an RN. She started school in Maple Wood, and Mama watched the girls. I was very proud of her as she learned everything so fast and became the top student in her class. She took a nationwide test and scored in the top 97 percent and was able to receive a scholarship.

Things were going well for us except for my job. The work was still okay, but the changing shift work was something I had never gotten used to, and it was affecting my entire life. I talked with human resources weekly about finding me a single shift to work on—I did not care which one. Every week, they said, "We're working on getting you something on the day shift, so don't quit, just wait."

In January 1971, I was so depressed that I was losing weight, and I slowly started drinking again. I couldn't eat or sleep, and my temper was flaring up at the drop of a hat. My whole life felt like it was in turmoil, and I didn't know what to do about it. I had a family and responsibilities, so I kept on working and making my complaints only to the front office. I did tell Samantha I was having trouble with the shift work, but I did not want to impede her progress at school, so I kept most of my depression to myself as I continued to drink. Samantha begged me to talk to her, but I continued to dismiss her concerns.

One night in early March, I went in to work the eleven-to-seven shift. Standing by the time clock to punch in, I was so depressed that instead of punching in, I walked into the foreman's office and said, "I'm sorry, but I quit right now." Of course, he tried to talk me into working my shift and talk to the front office the next day, but I was steadfast. "I can't. I haven't slept in three days and have eaten only once. I just can't do it anymore." I had become very friendly with that foreman. He knew the problems I had and how I was trying to get onto only one shift. We shook hands. He said he was sorry to lose me. "You're the only one on my crew who can run every piece of equipment here." I said, "I'm sorry too." I left. I got home and told Samantha. She was not mad as I thought she would be; she reassured me we would make out okay.

For the first few days, I mostly slept while Samantha kept going to her classes and Mama watched the girls. I started looking for another job. There were not many; I applied at only two places, but those jobs were taken by people with more experience.

As a last resort, I went to the highway patrol headquarters in Pensacola to see if I could apply. The officer told me I was too late. He said a new class had just begun on the first of the month. Samantha and I discussed it, but we had no idea what I could do. The pressure was on. I had to find a job and fast. Samantha's father called from Massachusetts saying that a company was hiring truck drivers; he suggested we go up there, get a job, and live. After much discussion, we decided to move back to Massachusetts.

CHAPTER 126

A New Job

After planning with Mama's neighbor to rent our trailer for us, I made amends with Mama, who was very upset, rented a U-Haul trailer, and packed it. Thinking it might be quicker, I went through Atlanta on my way to I-95 North. That was a big mistake; it took me four hours to get through.

Along the way, we were stopped by the state police, who said that because of high winds, we had to leave the Massachusetts Turnpike; there was a chance our trailer could have been blown over. The trooper followed us to the next exit. I did not know the area; having Samantha, the two kids, and Chief along made me nervous as I tried to navigate backroads at night. It took us two more days of traveling, and money became a problem. But it was not as bad as my personal problems. Instead of sleeping in a motel, we stayed in the car. Late at night, Samantha tried to get me to talk to her, but as I had done so many times in the past, I refused and denied that anything was wrong. Looking back on those times, I weep deeply inside of myself because I see how much quality time I missed with Samantha and my two girls those early days.

We arrived in Sandy Town, and I quickly learned that the trucking company Samantha's father had told us was hiring truck divers turned out to be the New England Tractor Trailer School, which taught students how to drive trucks. I was angry but did not say anything to him. I knew that the whole situation was my fault. I was feeling it was just one more time that I was letting somebody down. But that time, it was my wife and family.

I applied at the construction company I had worked for, but they were not hiring. After a week and a half, I still had not found a job. Samantha's mother told us we had to do something for money because she did not have enough to feed us also.

The next day, a Monday, Samantha and I went to the town hall and spoke with the welfare agent. We explained the situation to her and how I was looking for a job. Sitting in her chair, leaning back with arms crossed over her chest, she looked at us and said, "Pack up your junk and your kids and go back to Florida." She dismissed us.

Leaving her office, Samantha was mad and said, "I think that she could have at least given us some guidance other that moving." Back at Samantha's parents' house, we told her mother how it had gone with welfare. She was angry because we still had no money for her.

I continued to look for a job. On Wednesday night, Samantha wrote a letter to the State Welfare Department in Boston telling them of our meeting with the department and asking for some help. The letter was addressed to the Boston office, and we mailed it. Three days later the agent we had spoken to called and asked Samantha to come back to the office. We got there and were quickly ushered into her office. We saw Samantha's letter opened on her desk. She was all smiles as she said happily, "I've decided to help you, and in fact, I have a check for you." She handed Samantha a check made out to both of us in the amount of $75. She said, "You both will be receiving a check for that amount every month." Samantha and I looked at each other and figured out what had happened. Samantha's letter had been rerouted to her instead of to Boston. I said, "Since we talked to you the last time, I've found a job and will start work on Monday." With surprise in her voice she said, "Then you both must sign this check, so I can deposit it." Thinking nothing about it, we signed the check.

Two days prior to that, Samantha's father had told me that a neighbor who had worked for the Sandy Town Water Department for about thirty years had just retired and his job had become available. At that time, the water department worked out of the old police station on Dike Road, about a five-minute walk from Samantha's parents' house. That morning, I walked there and spoke with the foreman. He told me I would have to go to the town hall and speak with Ed Kessler, the director. I drove to the town hall and spoke with Eddie. He told me, "In most cases, town jobs go to townspeople. That's the way it's always been." But he and I an immediate liking to each other and he liked the idea that I was young and had just come from out of state; that meant I was not involved in town politics. He hired me on the spot; I would start out as a laborer at $2.05 an hour. I went home and gave the good news to everybody, especially Samantha's mother.

The job was more of a normal job; I would work from 7:00 a.m. to 3:30 p.m. My being from the south was a novelty for my fellow workers, but I fit right in with the work having had a background as a boiler man in the navy. It seemed that everywhere I went, drinking was always a part of life, so of course my drinking continued.

CHAPTER 127

A Fresh Start

By June 1971, we were able to save enough money to rent a place. It was a fresh start. We looked for a house to rent. We found one close by. It was available for $125 month. Because money was tight, and overtime was not as often as it had been previously for me, Samantha took a job as a secretary for a lumber company. She started to work in the mornings before I did, so I was able to drive her every morning. Samantha's mother agreed to watch grandchildren, for a price.

Life was starting to look up until I contacted the credit union in Florida concerning the Boat, as my coworkers affectionately called my Ford Galaxy. I was two months in arrears, and because I was living out of state, they wanted me to talk with a company about making up the payment or having the car repossessed. I called the company in Watertown, Massachusetts and made an appointment to meet with the manager the following Saturday. I pointedly asked him, "Are you taking the car?" He said, "No. The credit union wants to see if we can work something out, so you can pay off the car." Feeling good about the meeting, I agreed to go.

I got there and walked into his office. He said, "Where's the car parked? I need to check it out. I need the keys to make sure it's in good shape." I gave him the keys. He put them in his desk drawer, picked up a phone, and said, "Got it." He told me, "Okay, the car's, now repossessed. You can leave." I said, "I thought we were going to talk about a payment plan, so I could pay the back payments." He laughed and said, "Son, I lied. The car is now in my possession. You can go home." I asked him if I could get my personal items out of the car. He said, "No. The car's already gone." He laughed at the bewilderment on my face and said, "My associate has a set of master keys and has already taken the car away." I looked at this man, but all I saw was my father's face saying, "Well, you failed again just like I knew you would."

With despair in my voice, I said, "I don't even know where I am or how to get home." He said, "Take a cab." Shoulders drooping, I replied, "I don't have a penny in my pocket." With disgust in his voice, the man took a $5 bill out of his pocket, threw it on the desk, and said,

"Take a bus. Now get the fuck out of my office!" Looking at him, all I saw was my father's face laughing at me and saying, "Well, plowboy, I always said you'd never amount to anything." With a deep sigh of defeat, shoulders slumping, I picked up the $5 bill and walked out.

With no knowledge of where a bus station was, I started walking aimlessly. I went into a liquor store and bought some cheap whiskey. I sat on the curb and drank it out of a brown paper bag. For a couple of hours, I just wandered and felt about as low as I had ever felt. In the afternoon, I started asking strangers how to get out of town. It was well after midnight by the time I hitchhiked back to Sandy Town. We had no phone, and I'd be damned if I would call Samantha's parents.

Samantha had long since put the kids to bed and was worriedly waiting up for me. I relived what had happened and how I had to hitchhike back. She sniffed me and asked, "What about the whiskey?"

With a big sigh, she tried again to get me to talk. I refused. The more she asked, the angrier I became. I saw the hurt in her eyes. I just could not release anything even though I knew it was eating me up. That night as we went to bed and she lay there crying, I knew it was not because of losing the car but because I would not let her in. I was keeping that wall up to keep everybody out. I just would not talk to her about anything.

I was still living close enough to walk to work every morning, but Samantha worked in the Sandy Town business center and needed a ride. The problem was solved by Monday morning when Al, a neighbor across the street, volunteered to drive her to work by leaving a little early to go to work himself. We had become friends with him and his wife, Sherry. They had a young girl the same age as Bella, so sometimes, we would babysit her, and sometimes, they would babysit our two girls.

Sometimes on the weekends, Sherry's sister would babysit her daughter and Samantha's mother would babysit our girls so the four of us could go out to bars for a night of fun, including times I took them to the Hill Billy Ranch in Park Square. At the time, I did not realize how bad a judgment that was. Every time after going there, I would have terrible arguments with Samantha with her getting the worst of the yelling. Over and over, she would ask, "Johnny, please open up and talk to me. I can't help you if you don't." Tight lipped, I always refused.

CHAPTER 128

The Plymouth

After a couple of months, it became obvious that we needed a car. We did not have the money to buy one from a used-car dealership, so I asked my coworkers if they knew anybody we could buy a cheap car from. Jack, our backhoe operator, told me that his father, had an old car he would probably sell me for cheap.

The next day, I met him at his father's house. I was shown a car that I recognized. Back in the late 1950s and early 1960s, my aunt Rosie had the same color car. It was a '55 Plymouth with automatic shift on the dash. The car needed a jump to get started, but once running, the engine sounded strong. Ron told me that the car had trouble stopping also. I bought the car for $75. I bought a new battery and replaced the brake lines. The car was totally original and ran beautifully. I had the owner's manual, and I learned that the Plymouth ran better in cold weather than in hot, which was great because summer was ending, and I knew winter would come howling in.

I was able to drive Samantha to work again, but soon afterward, she decided she did not want to work at the lumber company anymore. Sherry, our friend across the street, had stated that she wanted a job. Samantha talked to her boss and got Sherry an interview; she got the job.

Samantha watched her daughter during the daytime for a small fee, and I started driving Sherry to work every morning. She was a pretty girl with very long, red hair—I would say down to her butt. It wasn't too long before Samantha started finding long, red hair all over the front seat and started asking if I was having an affair with her. I assured her I was not, but I knew she was in a jealous way; nothing I could say changed her mind. As my drinking continued, I started blaming Samantha for not believing me just as my father and others had done. I continued transferring my suppressed anger onto her.

One day while driving Sherry to work, she started sitting close to me. She turned toward me with her left arm on the back of the seat. She started touching my arm and shoulder.

I pushed her hand away, but she tried to put it back. I kept shrugging it off. Reaching the lumber company, I told her, "I don't think my driving you should continue." She smiled. Putting her hand back on my arm, she said, "Johnny, we have been talking about it, and we'd like to swap with you and Samantha. I've dreamed about fucking you, Johnny." Shaking my head, I said, "There's no way in hell I'll allow him to sleep with Samantha." She tried to change my mind, but in disgust, I said, "Get out of the car." With a smile, she said, "Please, Johnny, will you think about it?" I drove off tires spinning.

That afternoon, I told Samantha what she had told me. We never spoke to them again. In the mornings as I was leaving for work, I would see him driving her to work. She always smiled at me.

CHAPTER 129

One, Two, Three

The house we rented in Sandy Town was very small, so during the day, we chained Chief in the yard. Feeling safe about it, we allowed Bella and Chloe to play out there. They mostly sat and dug in the dirt with Chief watching over them. He never allowed any of the local kids or dogs to get near them. There was no leash law at that time. Every day, the neighborhood kids would walk by and tease him. Sometimes, they would pretend to grab one of the girls. I think the girls thought it was a game, so they would naturally giggle and scream. Chief would growl and bark at them, and Samantha spent a lot of time chasing the kids away.

One day, Samantha heard kids saying, "One, two ..." She ran to the door just as two kids holding a small dog by all four legs said, "Three!" and threw the dog at Chief. She yelled at the kids as they ran away and went to rescue the poor dog, which Chief had by the throat.

A couple of days later, she heard some kids counting again. She reached the door and saw two kids holding a third kid by his hands and feet ready to throw him to Chief. She was able to stop them just in time. After that, we kept him in the house except to go out for peeing and pooping.

CHAPTER 130

Old Dreams Return

In October, because of our neighbors, we started looking for another house to rent and found one on Bay Street in the Green Harbor section of Sandy Town. It was what locals called a winter rental, meaning for the winter, rent was very cheap, but in the spring through summer, the rent was higher, and it usually rented by the week. We were able to rent the house for $150 a month until the end of April.

It wasn't long before Samantha decided she wanted to get another job. Having gone through nurses' training, she took a position as a nurse's aide at a hospital in Plymouth working the eleven-to-seven shift. She started driving the old Plymouth back and forth to work. It did not take her long before she made friends with Lisa, an RN on her shift who lived a short distance from us. She asked Samantha if she wanted to commute with her, and Samantha gladly accepted.

One day, we heard a loud commotion and then a terrible stink coming from under the house. I went out and saw Chief eating a dead skunk. I tried to take it away from him, but he growled and bared his teeth. Considering what he had gone through to kill that skunk, he could have it. He ate every bit of it, hide and all. We washed that dog with everything people gave us to get rid of the stink, but nothing worked. We had to keep him on an enclosed porch out front until it finally wore off with bathing every other day.

There was only one heater in the living room for the entire house. That winter was very cold and snowy, but that old Plymouth ran as good as the book said it would. With Samantha working nights, I was home alone watching the girls. My drinking increased again. As time passed, I would sit in the living room in the dark, drinking and crying. My old dreams returned. I kept seeing my father. Sometimes, I would lash out at him with a fist. Sometimes, my questioning myself must have gotten loud because a few times, one or both girls would come downstairs from the bedroom asking, "Who are you talking to, Daddy?" Those times made things only worse for me as my depression deepened. I thought of how I was letting my kids down after promising them I would take care of them.

That winter was long for me, but Samantha was around people who did not have my troubles, so she could at least live some sort of a normal life. I don't know why she stayed with me.

In April 1972, we had to move out, so I talked to the owner of the florist's shop where we had lived for a short time before moving to Florida in 1968. She said we could rent a one-room apartment downstairs for $150 a month plus utilities. By then, the town had changed all individual departments and put them together forming the DPW, the Department of Public Works. We were living next door to the police department, and the DPW was directly behind us. I could walk to work in two minutes.

CHAPTER 131

A Life Change

At that time, I was making $2.30 per hour working with the water department. Before my wife and I were married, we had discussed having children. We wanted to have four children—two boys and two girls, so we talked about having two more children, but money had become an obstacle.

A McDonald's restaurant had recently opened. I applied for a job and was hired as a cook working nights. In those days, we cooked everything to order, and I quickly became a dependable employee, so I received a lot of work time. Nobody worked more than forty hours a week, so there was never any overtime, but sometimes, I did work up to the maximum hours. Working both jobs—almost eighty hours a week—and having a little more money, we bought a '67 Ford station wagon from two mechanics at the highway department for $550. The car engine had caught on fire, but they had rebuilt it. We then had the old Plymouth and the Ford station wagon.

It wasn't too long before one of the managers told me I had become a good worker and asked me if I would be interested in joining the auxiliary police. He said that the duty was volunteer work mostly on Sundays, holidays, and whenever else needed. He said I would get a uniform with an auxiliary police patch and drive an old police cruiser made over into an auxiliary police cruiser. I immediately said I would volunteer.

Within a few days, I had an interview with the auxiliary police chief and was appointed. I started the next week and loved it; it made me feel special. On Sundays, I would park the cruiser next to a church, put the blue lights on, and stand beside it. The parishioners were polite and greeted me with respect. I would step out into the street and stop traffic for them to cross. I loved the way they would look at me as if I were important. Sometimes at night, I would patrol school areas; I patrolled graveyards especially on Halloween. I would drive from area to area, and when I saw something that I thought the regular police should investigate, I would call it in on my radio. Sometimes, a cruiser would not be dispatched, but other times, one was; that depended on the nature of the call and on how busy the regular police were.

On occasion, older cops would tell me, "You're not a cop. You shouldn't be out here doing this. Go back to watching the schools!" On other occasions, I was thanked, and on a few occasions, somebody was arrested. I was never fazed by any negativity shown me by the regular police. I loved my job, and I did the best I could. It was a life change for me.

After a few weeks, the auxiliary police chief called me into his office. He said he was getting good reports on me and said that some paid details were offered to auxiliary officers when they were not filled by regular police officers. He said that most of the time, it would be in bars at night. He told me I would have to wear a gun, which I would check out at the police station when going on duty. I would be paid the same as a regular police officer for a minimum of four hours. In those days no special training was need. You showed up, they handed you a gun and radio and you went to your assignment. He explained that I would be paid cash at the end of the night and would claim it on my taxes at the end of the year. He asked if I would be interested in working some details, and of course, I told him yes.

The next week, he asked if I would work a detail that Friday night at a bar called The Ranch, a place I knew had a bad reputation for fights, but I said yes because I needed the money and I knew I would love the excitement.

That Friday night, I saw people in the bar whom I knew as I worked my first paid detail with a regular police officer named Donnie Jones. Some came over and talked with me, but others completely ignored me. Everything went very smoothly, and Officer Jones was very professional. At the end of the night, he shook hands with me and said, "It was good working with you, Johnny." I left the bar feeling great about myself and couldn't wait to tell Samantha about my night. Officer Jones and I became friends, and we have been for the past forty plus years.

That night, I could not go right to sleep. I thought about how my life had changed so abruptly; I felt doing something good for the town had finally brought some good to me. Then my thoughts wandered back to the first time I had put on a belt and a badge so many years ago and my aspirations back then. With a smile, I allowed my mind to remember those times even though they had ended badly. That also had turned out to be a life-changing experience for me.

CHAPTER 132

Dora

One day while I was working with the water department, we were laying a main water line on a road and I was directing traffic around the jobsite. At one point, the police chief, drove up, stopped, and asked, "Hey Johnny, you do this pretty good. Have you ever considered becoming a police officer?" With a laugh, I replied, "Does it pay better than the water department?" He said, "Yes it does." I responded, "Well, I just thought about it then. Yes." The chief laughed and said, "After work, stop by my office and I'll give you an application."

That afternoon, I walked through the backyard of the police station to get home, and I saw the chief leaning against a cruiser with his arms folded just watching me as I walked by. I said, "Hi, Chief." He yelled, "Hey Johnny, I thought you were coming by my office to get an application." Laughing, I said, "I thought you were kidding." He shook his head and told me to follow him. He gave me the civil service application.

That night, I told Samantha, and she asked me what I was going to do with it. "Fill it out," I said, which I did that night and mailed it the next day. With no babysitter available, Samantha had to quit her job at the hospital, but she started working again for the florist shop. She was not paid, but that kept our rent at $150, or so the owner said.

A short time later, my sister Dora, left Florida and moved in with us. She was not working and said she would babysit the girls. Samantha went to work for a nursing home in Plymouth, Massachusetts, as a nurse's aide on the eleven-to-seven shift while I worked for the water department days and McDonald's at night. On the weekends, I volunteered for the auxiliary police. Heavy drinking continued at home, but that time, it was also with my sister. Sometimes when I could get a break at McDonald's I would go to my car and sip brandy. Though I was drinking heavily, I did not loosen up and talk; I kept all my wounds bottled up. I thought alcohol would help, but I now know that it only covered up everything and made my life more miserable. I became even more withdrawn.

My sister started to get on my nerves; she was buying marijuana from one of the landlord's sons. At first, I didn't mind her smoking an occasional joint, but only outside—never inside. As time passed, she started smoking and drinking more and more. Every time I walked in, the smoke was so thick that I could almost cut it with a knife. I repeatedly told her to stop or at least to go outside when she smoked. At first, she complied, but probably because of cold weather, it did not take long before she was back smoking inside. On one occasion, I was so mad that I flushed her weed and beer down the toilet and told her I would turn her in to the police if she didn't stop.

She became enraged, started screaming, and got completely out of control. She punched me and yelled, "You didn't protect me from our father when we were growing up, and you're still not protecting me! You want to turn me in to the police?" Looking at her with disgust, I said, "Dora, you know we were both just trying to survive." She said, "It wasn't you who had to put his dick in your mouth." With intense anger, I said, "Where do you think he was putting his dick when he had me bent over in the backyard and you stood and watched?" She was startled. I said, "Yeah, I saw you standing in your window many times watching as he fucked me up the ass and you have the gall to stand here and tell me I didn't protect you when I couldn't even protect myself? How dare you! Dora, you're my sister, and I love you, but I want you to move out." She was angry and said, "I'll look for a job tomorrow." I said, "Fine" and walked away. She never smoked inside again.

About a week later, she announced that she had an interview in Old Town, Massachusetts. The next day when I got home, she said she had applied for and received a job starting Friday and would be moving out at the end of the week. She said she would be making about $500 plus tips a week. With a heavy heart, I asked, "What kind of a job is it?" In a mocking attitude, she said, "Masseuse. And I'll be wearing this!" She showed me a one-piece garment that had two thin straps that would barely cover her nipples, and it had one thin lower strap that would barely if at all cover her womanhood.

That night, I pleaded with her not to take the job, to look for something in Sandy Town, but it was to no avail. Friday morning, she called a cab and left. She did not come back that night, and having no way to contact her, Samantha and I worried that something may have happened.

About two weeks later, she called and said she was living in Old Town and would not be back. She would not give me a phone number. About a month later, she called and in a soft, purring voice said she was still a masseuse and was stripping in a place called The Pink Pussy.

She talked about different props she used in the massage parlor. Speaking highly of herself, she talked about how a lot of the men enjoyed her and asked for her specifically. She said they really liked the long feather she used on them. She asked, "Would you like it if I used it on you, Johnny?" I was shocked. Before I could answer, she said, "The manager of the parlor recently died. Would you be interested in coming to Old Town to take his place? I've already talked to the owners, and they agreed that you could come. They'll pay you a thousand a week to start until you get to know the business. Then, they'll increase your pay." She begged me to quit my "Silly little town and burger-flipping jobs" and come work with her. If she had not been my sister, I would have used stronger language in telling her no. After that conversation, I did not hear from her for almost two years.

CHAPTER 133

Sandy Town Hills

During that time, I was making extra money on the axillary police, and money was coming in, so we were able to save some and started looking for a house to buy. Working for the water I had gotten to know a lot of people in town. One person I met was a Realtor. I told him about how much we could afford and what we had for a down payment.

He started showing us houses, mostly a little above our price range, day after day. The one advantage I had was I knew the sections of town I didn't want to live in, but he showed us everything. One day, he showed us a house in the Beach section and I would not even get out of the car. He got angry and said, "What the hell, Johnny? What's wrong with this house?" I said, "I told you I don't want a house in this area." He pointed at the house saying, "Look how beautiful it is." I said, "Yes it's beautiful." It was a good-looking with a lot of fresh paint. The landscaping was also very nice.

With a big sigh, I got out of the car and said, "Follow me." He got out, and we walked up to the door just as the owner came out smiling to greet us. I said hi to her and told Ken, "Watch this." I walked to the big bay window and punched a finger right through the wood. I said, "The water level is about twelve inches below, and the entire area here is so damp that wood rots very quickly." I apologized to the woman as she was yelling obscenities at us. I walked back and got in the car.

I told Samantha, "I told him so." Returning to the car he said, "I have only one more house to show you, but you're not going to like it." I said, "Let's go see it now." He replied, "It's nine at night, and I don't have the keys." Samantha said, "Get them, and let's go see it." He sighed and said, "Okay, but this is the last one I have, and you won't like it."

He drove to his office for the keys and drove to the house. As we pulled into the driveway, he said, "I told you that you wouldn't like it." Without getting out of the car, I said, "We'll take it. Let's go in." He said, "We can't. The electricity is turned off." Samantha said, "Bring your flashlight and let's go."

We went in. It was a very small house. There was a kitchen with a small bathroom off it. The dining room and living room were small. Up a steep flight of stairs were a half dormer and two eight-by-ten-foot bedrooms. The ceiling was less than six feet high. Samantha and I laughed when I tried to stand up but couldn't. Samantha said, "See? Being short does come in handy sometimes."

Ken said, "I said you wouldn't like it." I said, "We love it, and I love the area—all sand and no highwater table." I walked to the basement, which had a dirt floor. Samantha and I saw the place's potential. It was on just under half an acre of land. With surprise in his voice, he said, "I'll start the paperwork tomorrow."

With his help and a small mortgage with the owner, we passed papers with the bank very quickly. Our first real home, which was twenty by twenty-four feet with a small dormer on back, cost us $96 a month. We were living in prestigious Sandy Town Hills.

CHAPTER 134

A True Friend

That spring, I took the grueling, eight-hour civil service test for the police department. I asked them afterward if I would be able to find out my score, and they told me no.

A few months later, I was notified by the civil service that I needed to take a physical test. While drinking with some friends out behind the highway barn on a Friday afternoon, I brought up the subject of the physical. I told them my concern was my heavy smoking; I would have to run a mile in a certain time. Art, a DPW worker, said, "Why don't you start running now just to get in some shape?" Thinking about it, I said, "Yeah, that's a good idea if I can keep it up." He said, "Don't worry about that, Johnny. I'll be right there with you every step of the way." Laughing, I said, "Yeah, okay," and we continued to drink.

The next morning at 6:00 a.m. sharp, I heard banging on my door. I got up half asleep and only in my undershorts. Art was at the door. I opened it and asked, "What's up?" He said, "Get dressed. We're starting your running today." I was hesitant, but he kept pushing until I agreed.

We drove a short distance to a school and jogged around its field twice, about a quarter mile each lap. That first day was tough, and I was breathing very heavily. I threw up a few times, but he kept pushing me as he ran alongside me also throwing up and breathing heavily.

We planned to meet the next morning at the school at the same time. After those first times, we would meet after work at 4:00 p.m. and before going to work at 6:00 a.m. We would run with him pushing me every step. It was physical punishment for us.

One day while we were running, I asked, "Why are you doing this for me?" He asked, "Do you really want to become a cop?" I said yes. He said, "Then we're going to make this happen." We kept on running.

It had been a long time since I had felt close to or trusted anybody. Over the next couple of months, we ran every day, with Art right beside and pushing me anytime I faltered. My drinking after work stopped for that time, but my smoking did not.

On the day of my physical, I sat in my car outside the YMCA where the test was being held, closed my eyes, and pictured my father's angry face. I smiled and said, "You were wrong. I am going to amount to something."

I went in and took the test. I felt the best I had been in a long time. When I did the running on a track above the gym floor, another recruit ran alongside me. After about ten minutes, he stopped, but I kept running. I heard my name being called by recruits standing on the gym floor below— "Run, Johnny! Run!" I smiled as I thought of Art running alongside me over the past months. I remembered what Coach had told me that day. I started running faster with a smile on my face. I finished the run in the required time.

That afternoon, I told Samantha the good news and called Art to give him the good news as well. With no fanfare, he said, "I knew you could do it." I laughed and said, "Thanks, Art. I'll never forget you."

A year later after having gone through the police academy, I was on the midnight-to-eight shift. One night, I went on a domestic-violence call. I went in and saw a female I knew with multiple bruises and cuts on her face and arms. She was holding a bath towel to her face to stop the blood. She was crying hysterically; I could not make out what she was trying to say. I asked her to sit at the kitchen table, which she did, and I asked her to calm down. Within a moment or so, she started talking, and I could understand what she was saying. I asked her who had done that to her, and she pointed toward the living room and said, "My husband."

I asked my partner to help her. I walked into the living room and saw my friend Art sitting on the couch with a beer in his hand. With a great sadness in my heart, I asked, "Art, did you do this?" With a smile, he said, "Yeah, Johnny, I did. The bitch deserved it. She's been fucking the neighbor." I advised him of his rights. My first arrest as a police officer was that of a true friend. After that night, I never saw him again. I heard he had moved out of town.

CHAPTER 135

Provisional Position

In the spring, twelve provisional positions became available in the police department. I applied, and because I had been working as an auxiliary and had taken the police test through the civil service, I was appointed and sworn in. I quit working at McDonald's; I was working days at the water department and evenings and nights on the six-to-two shift at the police department. My drinking got worse; I had more coworkers to drink with after my shift was over. Some nights, we drank until daylight. Then I would go to work with the water department.

I continued trying to drown all my old feelings and thoughts. Samantha and I had moved into our new house, and she repeatedly tried to get me to talk, let out my thoughts and feelings, but I still refused. The more she asked, the angrier I got. Looking back on those times, I know now that talking would have been the best thing for me, but I was not yet ready for that. Many nights, we would go to bed with her crying, but I would just lie there and sometimes ask in an angry voice, "Why are you crying?" It made me only madder at her. More and more, she became the brunt of my anger.

I was shutting down, and the drinking was making it worse. Though life had changed for us for the better, I started thinking of all the years my father had told me how I would never amount to anything. In my twisted mind, I was starting to believe him as I slipped deeper into that abyss of broken souls. I didn't realize that the answer to my problems was lying right beside me and she would help; all I had to do was ask.

CHAPTER 136

Lies and More Lies

After working both full-time jobs for about six months, the head of the DPW called me into his office and said I had to make a choice about whom I wanted to work for. He was known by many people in town as a drunk. Many times, because of his position, he was given a ride home when he should have been arrested for DUI. As we spoke that day, I smelled alcohol on his breath. I knew he hated the police department based on what he had told me previously. Because I was working for the police department, I knew he would hate me. With disgust in my voice, I said, "I choose the police department. One of these days, you'll regret this." He said, "Get the fuck out of my office!"

I worked the six-to-two shift through the summer and into the first of the next year. Then through the Civil Service Department, the town hired six full-time police officers. Six provisional officers, including me, were terminated.

I checked with the water department to see if I could go back to work there, but they had already replaced me with an old townie. For two months, I was unemployed. Drinking even more, I lay around feeling sorry for myself; I wanted my life to end. I knew that my father's prophecies had come true. I blamed everything on myself and had no idea what to do. I knew I loved my girls and Samantha, but I felt a complete failure.

One day, a friend told me that a lumber company in Sandy Town was hiring. The next day, I drove there and spoke with Louise, the assistant manager, whom I had met while working for the water department. She ushered me into the manager's office, and I had a short interview. When I was leaving, she said, "See you soon, Johnny," with a big wink. Thinking she might put in a good word for me lifted my spirits.

The next day, the manager called and offered me the job for $2.50 an hour with the promise that I would receive a 25¢-an-hour raise after a month and again at the end of the summer. The job required that I work forty-eight hours, Monday through Saturday. I was paid overtime each week for the extra eight hours. I worked in the yard loading lumber and delivering lumber and other large items. I liked the job because it was outside and was manual labor. I worked with a foreman and two other laborers all of whom liked to drink. It seemed my entire life was encompassed by alcohol no matter where I went, and I fell right into the role that life was dishing out.

The first month passed, and I did not get the raise. The manager kept putting it off about that saying, "I'll talk to the front office." Summer turned into fall, and again, I did not get the promised raise. Samantha had not been asking me to talk, so I believed she had given up on me. I was feeling that I had dodged another bullet and believed it was behind me, but she started asking again. My anger came out sideways, and I shoved it onto her. Looking back, I know she saw my turmoil, but I still refused to talk and sunk deeper into my thoughts.

After lies and more lies, in the fall, instead of giving me the promised raise, they let me go because, the manager said, "Business is slowing down." I knew business normally slowed down in the fall and winter, but I had expected them to keep their promise.

CHAPTER 137

A Dream Fulfilled

I was out of work for about a month or two when the town called for the new civil service list for the police department. When it came down, I was second on the list—a dream fulfilled. In November, I was sworn in, appointed as a full-time police officer, and enjoyed starting out on the midnight-to-eight shift. For two months, I was placed with an experienced officer.

Because of a new law, I and the other officers just hired attended the police academy in January 1975. At the end of my first week at the academy, I had a real epiphany. Going home Friday night, I sat with a beer and went deep into thought. For the first time in many years, I thought of my past dream of becoming a police officer and couldn't believe it had happened. I started to cry. Samantha put her arms around me. I believe I cried harder than I had ever cried. As I sat there, many other repressed thoughts came up.

All Samantha said was, "Johnny, please talk to me." I saw the love and desire to become closer to me in her eyes, and it shook me to my core. In a choking voice, I started to talk. At first, it was not much about my life before her but what I was feeling then. I knew that it was not what she wanted to hear, but for me, it was the start on a long road to recovery. In the end, she held my face in her gentle hands and looking into my eyes said, "I love you, Officer Johnny." As you can imagine, I really lost it and started crying even harder.

CHAPTER 138

A New Life

After graduating from the police academy, I was assigned to the midnight-to-eight shift permanently. Having previously worked that shift, I eagerly looked forward to this next chapter of my life. I learned the duties of my new job quickly. Because I had been talking with Samantha up to a point, she and I were able to sit down and openly discuss our relationship. I was not yet able to give her the complete story of my childhood, so some of her questions still went unanswered though she continued to beg me asking, "Please, Johnny, talk to me. Let me in. I can't help if you won't."

I started seeing her in a new way, but I was still holding back. By working day to day as a police officer, I was finding that the only people who truly understood what I was experiencing were other police officers. As a group, we didn't talk about work with anybody else—only with each other.

I got home one morning after a particularly hard night; three children had died in a house fire. Lying in bed, I started shaking badly. Looking over at Samantha, I asked, "Are you shaking the bed?" With a questioning look, she replied, "No. Why?" I told her what had happened that night. We had a long talk, and it was decided that my work would always be available to her. In my heart, I knew that because I was not yet ready to talk about my past, she at least wanted us to start this new life on an even keel with everything out in the open. She understood there were some things I couldn't or wouldn't talk about, but slowly, we achieved a little more openness.

After that night and for many years to follow, those body shakes became a normal way of life for me. Becoming a Police Officer was not an easy job.

At that time, several members of the force were attending Northeastern University. In early spring that year, Samantha and I discussed my attending college. I told her about my high school days and how hard school had been for me, but she smiled and said, "I know you can do it."

To test the waters, I took a class that spring. To my great surprise, I enjoyed it. In the fall, I enrolled full time. Shortly after that, we found out Samantha was pregnant with our third child.

CHAPTER 139

Johnny Jr.

One night in the spring of 1976 while I was working the midnight shift, the desk sergeant called me on the radio telling me to report to the station. I got there, and he said one of my daughters had called for the ambulance because Samantha had gone into labor. He said he did not want to put it over the radio and I thanked him for that. Arriving home, a short time later, I found her already in the ambulance ready to leave for the hospital. After she left, I changed clothes and told the girls I would call them later. Samantha's sister watched the girls as I drove to the hospital.

Because I had been through the birthing of Chloe, the hospital, the same one that had not let me into the delivery room when Bella was born, allowed me in during the birth. About two hours later, Johnny Jr. was born. I held Samantha's hand through the birth. As before, I was amazed at this tiny, pink, squirming, and crying baby knowing that he was the result of our love for each other. As I held him, my heart was beating so fast that I thought it would surely burst out of my chest. I gave him a long kiss on the forehead. As I did, his eyes opened, and as he looked at me, I smiled and said, "Son, I promise you that I'll always stand beside you with love and protection to guide you through life to the best of my ability." His eyes closed, and I swear I saw a smile on his tiny lips as if he had understood every word I had spoken just as his sisters had done.

I called the girls, and they were thrilled that they would have a brother. As I lay in bed that night, I looked toward the heavens and said, "You see, Daddy? I'll show you that I have indeed become something."

The next day, I brought the biggest teddy bear—about four feet tall—I could find. I also found one of those fake license plates with his name that I attached to it. I walked through the hospital on air. I couldn't wait to see him. *I have a son!*

A few days later, Samantha was in a wheelchair holding him as his big sister, Bella, was walking beside them on our way out of the hospital and home. Her love for him was showing through that huge smile on her face. I took them to see Samantha's parents. His other sister, Chloe, held him, and she too was all smiles with love.

CHAPTER 140

Ricky

That September as I started my second year of school, we found out Samantha was again pregnant. Once again, on a cold and snowy night in 1977 while I was working the midnight shift, the desk sergeant called me to the station and told me to hurry because the ambulance had already been dispatched. Arriving at my house, I found that Samantha and the ambulance had already left for the hospital.

Again, Samantha's sister watched the girls. Making sure everyone was settled in, I changed fast and headed out. I reached the hospital just as Samantha was being ushered into the delivery room. I was able to stand beside her and hold her hand as Ricky was born. Moments later, Samantha, still in pain, asked, "Johnny, do we now have enough children?" Smiling, I said, "We have the two of us, two beautiful girls, and two wonderful boys, exactly what we talked about before we married. Yes, honey, we have everything we wished for." I gently kissed her tears away saying, "I love you more than life, and I promise we'll raise our children with love, respect, and compassion."

A short time later, I held Ricky for the first time. He was a handful; he wasn't crying or squirming, but he looked so strong and content swaddled in his blanket. As I kissed him, I said, "Ricky, I promise you that you will always know only love from me. Regardless of what life brings, I'll always stand beside you with hope and understanding. I promise to guide you when you need me, and I will always be there for you."

We brought him home a couple of days later and brought him to Samantha's parents. Everybody marveled at how big he was. Smiling, my chest pushed out so far that I thought my buttons would pop, I said, "That's my son. He takes after his daddy." Everybody laughed, including the girls. I thought I heard Johnny Jr. make a little noise too.

CHAPTER 141

Diligent Work Brings Results

I was attending school full time, working the midnight shift, and picking up an occasional overtime shift; that was very demanding on our whole family. I was tired and always dealing with work; there were many times when I was less than the loving and understanding husband and father I wanted and had promised to be. Drinking was still a problem, but looking back, I give Samantha so much credit for keeping our house together for six years as I diligently worked toward a bachelor's degree in law enforcement, which I received in 1980. With a smile, I told my peers that I had earned only half my degree; Samantha had earned the other half.

One cold night while on routine patrol, my partner and I were following a car zigzagging all over the road. After following it for a while, I put my blues and siren on. After a short while, the driver pulled over. It was my old boss, the head of the DPW. He asked, "Hey, fucking officer Johnny, why're you stopping me?" I asked him for his license and registration. He said, "For what? You know who the fuck I am in this town. I own it!" After a few minutes, he was still refusing to produce the papers. I asked him to step out of the car. He refused. I opened the driver's door and pulled him out. I smelled alcohol on his breath. By then, he was screaming bloody murder about "fucking cops." I cuffed him and said he was under arrest for DUI, refusing to produce the papers I had requested, and resisting arrest. I read him his Miranda rights and placed him in the rear of my cruiser.

All the way back to the station, he yelled about how I would regret this. He threatened to take my career away from me. He said he had people who would kill me with a snap of his fingers. I never said a word to him until his booking at the police station. Before I left to go back out on patrol, I walked to his cell, looked him in the eyes, and said, "Have a good night, sir." He yelled and screamed about how my days were numbered. After that night, I did not see or hear from him again. Case closed.

CHAPTER 142

Trusting in Me

In 1981, I had a chance to change shifts, and I chose the eight-to-four shift during the day. My first few days on that shift were very different. Coming off the midnight shift was an adventure itself. Most of the people I had dealt with were drunk, on drugs, wanted for some crime, or committing a crime. After my first day, I went home to talk with Samantha. She was happy that I was talking to her and that I would be working a normal shift. After about an hour of discussion, I came away with a new outlook. With her help and guidance starting the next day, my whole work and home outlook changed.

Patrolling the south end of Sandy Town with a confidence I had never known, I quickly started to make many friends in the community. Every morning right after going on duty, I would have coffee and a corn muffin at a diner. It did not take long before I started receiving information concerning drugs, B&Es (breaking and entering) and gambling by various groups and individuals. I turned the information over to a detective, but over the year, I did not see any results from my information. I started keeping all the information at home hoping that at some time, it would be used by somebody.

One afternoon just as the next shift was coming on duty, I was talking to an officer about a house and asked him if he knew about any drug activity there. He laughed and said, "You should talk to Sergeant Day. You two probably have tons of information between you." Wanting to keep my informants and information confidential, I approached Sergeant Day about a week later. As I talked with him, I sensed he too was leery about disclosing information.

But one afternoon after I had talked with him several times, he gave me a box of papers and folders with handwritten notes. With a smile, he said, "This is what I have on various crimes in Sandy Town." I was floored but graciously took the box saying, "I'll look them over and keep them confidential." He said, "I know you will. I trust you." Knowing that he trusted me boosted my confidence.

Two nights later, we got together at his house. I had brought my box of information, and we started comparing notes. Between us, we had a lot of information about some of the same locations and persons. For several nights, we pored through our information but did not know what to do with it. I had told him I had turned some of my information over to a detective, but over the past year, nothing had been done with it. After several talks, we decided to approach the captain. He got excited about what we had put together and told us to continue with what we were doing and to keep everything quiet—meaning just between the three of us.

After weeks of compiling our information, the sergeant and I had enough to obtain search warrants for several motor vehicles, homes, and businesses for drugs and stolen items including firearms and gambling paraphernalia that based on our information were connected to someone connected to the local mafia.

On the day of the raid, the whole day shift was kept over, and most of the police on the four-to-midnight shift were used. Extra officers were called in for overtime though they did not know why they were working. Specific officers from the state police were brought in as well as some of our own detectives.

That night at the end of the raids, we had seized a good number of drugs, money, betting material, and stolen items, and people had been arrested. By the next day, word had spread quickly throughout town. When I walked into my diner for coffee and a corn muffin that morning, everybody stood, clapped, and cheered. I stood there like a kid who had been caught with his hand in the cookie jar, but I was smiling. I told everyone, "Folks, we couldn't have done anything without your help. All of you know what you contributed to this investigation. It shows how much police need the help of citizens to do their job, and I hope you continue to help in the future." I heard more clapping and cheering.

After that, more and more people started giving me information. I started keeping files on people in and out of town. At times, it came in so fast that I could hardly keep up with it. I started keeping a little black book so to speak like those you see in movies. I wasn't a detective, but I was acting like one.

CHAPTER 143

A Dream Achieved

Not long after that, the captain appointed me as the juvenile officer, but the chief would not allow me to wear civilian clothes. I did not care because I was thrilled with the promotion. A short time later, the chief retired, and the captain was promoted to chief.

I had a good working relationship with the new chief. One day I asked him for permission to ride the police Harley-Davidson on patrol. I had been riding bikes since my scoter in junior high. In 1971 I had bought and rode a 1971 Triumph 750cc moto cycle for several years. He approved my request, and for the next year, I proudly rode the bike and wrote many tickets.

One day while I was on patrol, the station radioed me to report to the chief's office. That was unusual, so old thoughts of my father immediately started me thinking, *what have I done wrong now? I thought I was doing everything right.* I went to the station and reported to the chief. He must have seen the apprehensive look on my face because he laughed and said, "Don't worry. I'm promoting you to detective, but you can't ride that bike anymore, okay?"

I was speechless. Over the past few years, I had been able to solve many crimes and had arrested many people. Most of them had been involved in drugs and B&Es; one of them had committed twenty-five B&Es. During that time, I had made it plain to everyone that I wanted to make detective, so I had achieved my dream.

After thanking him, I confided in him that over the past year, I had collected a lot of information on drugs and related crimes. He said that when I started cultivating informants, it would spread out just like a tree throughout the town. I laughed and said, "I already have a bush started then, and it's growing." He laughed and said, "Keep up the good work, Johnny." I said, "Yes sir, I will." By that time, I had more than a hundred informants in that little black book of mine.

That night, Samantha and I talked. She cried out of happiness when I told her of the promotion; she said, "I knew you could do it!" I said, "For a long while, I've wanted to become a detective, but at first, I didn't have the confidence that I could do it. But with your help and encouragement, I made it. Thank you."

Over the next year, I put my heart and soul into my job and loved every minute of it. I was working the four-to-midnight shift. When Samantha said she wanted us to join a Friday-night couples bowling league, I refused at first, but she gently kept after me about it. One day, I asked the captain about it, and he approved my working eight to four during the day on Fridays.

The couples league did a world of good for me personally and for my relationship with Samantha. I made many friends, and I eventually became president of the league.

I still would not talk about my life before meeting Samantha; she gently always asked but never pushed me about it. I guess she knew that one day when the time was right, I would talk to her.

CHAPTER 144

Better Side to Life

I was sitting at my desk in the detective's division going over an affidavit in support of a search warrant. After having made a controlled buy, I had good and fresh information through informants and concerned citizens about a house occupied by a couple who were selling cocaine, marijuana, and pills that had the street name black beauties. I had information that the couple had a newborn and the house was also a party house for teenagers.

I had been told that the floor downstairs had been taken up exposing the floor joists except for a small section in the back. The downstairs plumbing was not in working order. An open stairway led upstairs to only a subfloor. The upstairs plumbing was not in use except for one drainpipe. This open pipe contained a large funnel that girls and boys would urinate into. A metal bucket was used for human waste, which was then dumped into an open cesspool in the backyard. There were no walls, only bare studs throughout the house. Through my informants, I knew the day and time these dealers received their drugs.

The next day, I told my chief about the upcoming drug raid that night. I drove to our courthouse and received the appropriate search warrant. At 6:00 p.m., accompanied by officers from my department and two detectives from nearby towns, I executed the warrant.

I entered the house through the front door and saw it was in the condition the informants had told me it was. The small floored section in the back on the first floor contained a queen-sized bed, a nightstand with a lamp, and another table with two chairs, the only furniture in the house. On the table, I saw a brick-sized white substance known on the street as a small house; I believed it was cocaine. I also observed a large zip lock bag containing a dark herbal substance I believed to be marijuana. I saw several liquor bottles, some half full. Drug paraphernalia for packaging and selling drugs were also on the table.

A male and female were sitting at the table cutting, mixing, and packaging the drugs for sale. Lying on the bed behind them was a naked baby. After field testing the cocaine, I arrested the couple, seized the evidence, and called child services for the baby.

After the arrest, I was back in my office with my feet on my desk. I thought about the raid and the baby mixed up in that mess. He was so young and innocent. As tears filled my eyes, my thoughts returned to those long-ago times when my father had put me through abuse that no child should be put through. Then with a smile, I thought that due to my intervention, the baby might have a real chance to grow up in a normal family. I chuckled and said aloud, "Thanks, Samantha. Because of you, I think I have started that growth you keep talking about."

That night, I told Samantha about the baby and about my thoughts afterward. I said, "Thank you." She said, "See? I told you there was a better side to life." I replied, "Yes, you're right, honey. Maybe this would be a good time for us to have that talk, okay?"

I saw tears welling up in her eyes as I started divulging secrets I had kept hidden for so long. I wasn't ready to expose all, but I did tell her more than I had before. We talked for a couple of hours with me doing most of the talking and her asking only a few questions—mostly just listening.

That night, I think we slept the best we had in a long time.

CHAPTER 145

Self-Awareness

Over the next several years, after making sergeant, I worked as a detective and loved the job more than any other I had ever had. I worked closely with now Lieutenant Day, other detectives in nearby towns, and the state police. I had over a hundred confidential informants, and I tried hard to rid my town of as many drug dealers as possible.

During that time, Samantha and I joined a group, taught by a College Professor; our weekly meetings covered psychic development and self-awareness. At first, I had no idea how this would work out because I did not want to talk. But over time with Samantha, the Professor and the other members, all women, I started talking more than I ever had. Though I still would not talk about my more-serious secrets, I can now say it was a wonderful experience.

Sadly, in 1991, my world came crashing down. I was retired by the town after receiving an injury while executing two search warrants. For the next year, I fell back into a great depression. I drank almost every day, and I did not want to talk to anybody including Samantha. Each time she would approach me, I saw pain in her eyes because she was not able to help me with what I was experiencing.

The next summer, thinking about my experience of riding the department's Harley-Davidson, I decided to buy a bike. I found one for sale within my budget in New Hampshire. My son Ricky came with me as I drove there and bought the bike, a navy-blue, '81 Gold Wing.

On the way home, we stopped at a store to get a sandwich and drink, and I bought a scratch ticket and won $100. Ricky and I were in the truck eating when he said something that changed my thinking and my world: "Dad, you know all of us love you and respect the job that you did, but now, that's in the past. You need to move on. Look at this beautiful bike you just bought, and now, you won a hundred bucks. If that doesn't tell you something, nothing ever will."

I smiled and looked at my fourteen-year-old son. *Is he for real?* I was so proud of him. I said,

"Ricky, you talk way above you age just like your mother does. She's taught you well." He laughed and said, "You both have, Dad." With a big sigh, I gave him a hug. "Thank you, son. I really needed that. I love you." He hugged me and said, "I love you too, Dad."

That night, I thought of what Ricky had said. With a smile, I remembered that when he was born, I had promised to guide him when he needed me. That day was my turn to need him, and I was grateful that the past had come back to me in a positive way.

CHAPTER 146

NEDA

After that night, with Ricky 's help, my life started to mean something again as my love for my family improved. Samantha and I joined a motorcycle club and started traveling with its members. Sometimes, we traveled out of state for a week, and we even went to Canada several times.

One trip stands out in my mind. In 1994, we took a trip out west with three friends. We were gone for three weeks and covered more than 6,000 miles on our motorcycles. Late one afternoon, it was getting dark, and we pulled into our motel somewhere in South Dakota. We had not eaten since that morning, and there was no restaurant nearby. Across the road was a small country store, so we walked over to buy something for supper. As I entered, a young black boy about seven or so walked in behind me. He walked up to me, smiled, and started walking beside me.

He started asking questions about my motorcycle and if I had ever had trouble with my chain coming off. As we walked along, he grabbed items, mostly junk food, and stuck them under his torn, ragged shirt. I stopped and talked to him about stealing. After a few minutes, he said, "Okay" and returned all the items to exactly where he had picked them up from. I was amazed; I told him I was proud of him. I told him that good things happened to people who did good things. He smiled and said, "I know." I was blown away. Samantha had heard the whole conversation; she was smiling at me.

I bought a few extra things, mostly junk food. Samantha and I turned to the kid and said, "Here's something nice for you because of what you did." He smiled and said, "Thank you." Before I could say a word, he asked, "Could you help me with my bike?" I said, "Sure. What's wrong with it?" He said, "The chain's off." I said, "Let's look at it."

Samantha, the kid, and I walked outside, and he pointed to a small bike leaning against a post. It was old and rusty—no fenders or chain guard. The chain was hanging well below the sprocket. I laughed and said, "I had this same problem with my bike when I was about your age." I turned the bike upside down and got the chain back on with only one turn of the pedals. He hopped on and said, "Thank you, Johnny." I did not remember telling him my name, but I said, "You need to ask your daddy to tighten the rear sprocket up so the chain will stay on." He gazed at me and said, "I don't have a daddy." He rode off. Samantha and I stood watching him go. He seemed to just disappear. We were stunned. Memories flooded me as I remembered the day the chain came off my bike and the black man helped me. Could it be true? Does history truly repeat itself?

Samantha and I still talk about that story. The incident was so surreal that we wonder if it really happened. The most astonishing part of the story is that within moments of riding away, he just disappeared. We asked our friends if they had seen where he had gone. No one could say. I had told Samantha my story about the chain coming off my bike and the large black man who helped me. I had also told her about the Cushman scooter and how the chain had kept coming off that as well. That night, we talked for a long time about how my incidents and that young boys mirrored each other, especially with him asking me about my motorcycle's chain ever coming off. We still consider the incident wonderful and amazing.

In early 1992, I reached out to another retired officer who was operating a private investigation firm. With my background, I was hired immediately. Over the next few months, I went back to doing what I loved to do—investigations and surveillance. Samantha was hired to transcribe reports, and on occasion when a male and female were needed on a case, she worked as an investigator. My resolve was slowly dissolving, and our relationship was jumping forward faster than ever. Talking was coming easy for me, but still not about everything; there were some things I was still not ready to expose.

Later that year, someone in our motorcycle club who knew I was working as a private detective said that a retired state policeman who also owned a detective agency was looking for another detective. After an interview, I was hired and started working out of State Street in downtown Boston. For a few months, we continued in that manner, and then, he opened an office in the suburbs. He hired Samantha as his office manager and used her as a detective as needed. Samantha and I worked together at that office.

The following summer, we decided to open our own business, so we obtained our private investigation licenses. Our business was named—North East Detective Agency. Our business took off faster than we had expected, and Samantha and I were kept very busy sometimes working in separate areas of the state at the same time and sometimes traveling out of state separately.

CHAPTER 147

Mama

During that time, my sister Dora called me often. I heard the pain in her voice as we talked sometimes for long periods. Many times, I begged her to go into rehab, but she always said, "No, that shit don't work." Mama had sold her house in Florida and was living with Dora in Old Town. On occasion, I would talk to her trying to find out what was going on, but she never had much to say except, "I wub you, Johnny." It still always sounded false to me.

During those conversations, all the old feelings I was trying so hard to suppress would come rushing back. Because they made me feel old and broken, I had no interest in seeing either one, and in fact on some occasions, Dora, in a drunken and drug-induced frame of mind, made it clear I was not wanted in her house.

One night, I was awakened by the insistent ringing of the phone. I opened my eyes and looking at the clock saw that it was 3:00 a.m. I sleepily asked, "Who is this?" In a very heavy and slurred voice, I heard my sister scream, "You better come get this fucking bitch before I kill her!" The line went dead. Samantha asked, "Johnny, who is it?" I said, "It's Dora." I repeated what she had said. I turned the light on beside the bed and dialed Dora, but it only rang, rang, and rang. I waited about ten minutes and called again. No answer.

I got up and starting to get dressed. Samantha asked, "Honey, what are you going to do?" With a big sigh and a pain that was starting to hurt deep in my belly, I said, "Go up there. What else can I do?" Samantha got up and started dressing. She said, "I'm going with you." I woke the boys and said, "Mom and I have to go to Auntie Dora's to see Granny." They were now thirteen and we felt safe leaving them. After giving them a kiss and saying, "I love you," I set an alarm clock on their dresser to wake them for school. Samantha walked in, and for a few moments, I stood there, my arm tightly around her shoulder. We looked at them resting peacefully and thought how blessed we were to have such a loving family. I gave her a long kiss and said, "I love you and I always have."

By three thirty, Samantha and I were on the road to Old Town, on the other side of Boston about an hour away from us at that time of the morning. After hearing her on the telephone and having been around Dora in the past when she was high on drugs and alcohol, I decided to bring my handgun with me. On several occasions, she had verbally threatened to kill me or have me killed by some "Really bad dudes I know in Old Town" as she had put it.

We arrived at her apartment at 4:40 a.m. We entered the outer door and went into the hallway. Dora's apartment was on the left. My mind was racing. Over the years, some meetings between my sister and me had been just short of becoming physical. Many times, I tried to talk my mother into moving out of her apartment and coming to live with Samantha and me. She always refused saying, "She needs me to be with her." I checked the door, but it was locked. I knocked several times. No answer. I banged on it hard. After about five minutes, the door to the apartment across the hall cracked open and somebody in a small voice said, "There's been a lot of yelling, screaming, and banging in there. It's quiet now. You might be too late." The door closed quietly. I continued banging on the door.

After a few minutes, the door was yanked open. Lana, Dora's live-in girlfriend, stood in front of us. Looking down, she said, "You should be careful. She's very dangerous tonight." I asked, "Does she have any weapons?" Without answering, she turned and in a lumbering way started waddling upstairs. Samantha started to follow, but I gently pushed her behind me saying, "Honey, let me go first." The stairway was pitch-black, but I saw light coming from a room off the landing at the top. I drew my gun and followed Lana, keeping a sharp eye out.

At the top of the stairway, Lana moved to my right into the dining and living room area. Heavy smoke filled the air; it was marijuana. I saw Mama and Dora sitting at the kitchen table; Dora was drinking from a large bottle of vodka. She turned to me. Staring into her eyes was like looking into a deep, black hole filled with emptiness. Her facial muscles changed; they made her face look all screwed up. Her hatred for me was so thick that I had a hard time speaking. I said, "Hi, sis. What's going on tonight?" I saw despair and fear on Mama's face. Dora asked me, "What are you going to do, fucking shoot me?" During the tense moments, I had forgotten about the gun. I put it in my pocket and with sadness said, "No Dora, I'm not going to shoot you. I love you." She stood and walked by me and into the hallway saying, "Fuck you, asshole."

I sat in the chair she had vacated. Samantha walked around me and sat. While keeping an eye on Dora but looking at Mama, I saw that she was wearing the same old nightgown and red housecoat Samantha and I had bought her years ago. They hung on her as if she were a hook in the closet. Both of her hands were folded in her lap. I picked one up. In amazement, I saw every nook and cranny on her fingers, knuckles, and the back of her hand. There were all sizes of black and blue marks, some fresh and some old, covering up plain old age marks. It looked so small and frail, but I knew in times past that hand had been able to hold a long switch that she had made me go cut after I had done something silly. She especially hated it if she caught me "taking the Lord's name in vain" as she would put it. With a burst of bravado, she would say, "Go out in the woods and cut me a long jump butt!" I would laugh and go find the smallest one I could, but she would keep after me until finally I would bring one that was longer than her five-foot frame. A smile crossed my lips as I remembered how I would jump all around and tease her by saying, "Nah nah! You can't get me." Her frustration would only entice me more until I finally ran off laughing with my friends.

My smile quickly disappeared. I asked, "Mama, what's going on?" With a blank look on her face, her head bowed, and in a tired voice, she said, "I don't know, Johnny." With tears welling up, I looked at the woman who had raised me. She was my Mama, the only one I ever knew. She was about ninety years old now, and she looked terrible. Her arms were so skinny that my thumb and forefinger could easily encompass them. Her eyes were so sunken into her skull that it was hard to tell what color they were. What little hair she had was totally gray. Her cheekbones protruded out so far that they looked like growths on her face. I could tell she did not have her false teeth in because her lips were sunken into her mouth. Skin hung on her body like an old rag draped over her.

For a moment, my eyes crinkled in another halfway smile as I saw a large, thick, black hair on her chin; somehow, one had survived. As a child, I would sometimes peek at her as she would pluck them. On some occasions, I would sneak up behind her, grab a hair or two, and pull real hard, often pulling one out, and yell, "I got this one!" as I ran away. She would always try to slap my hand, but she was never fast enough as she would say, "Ninny, you stop that." Mama always liked to talk as if she were talking to a baby.

Dora had not let me in the apartment in a year, so I was not prepared for what I was seeing. I saw bruises new and old all over her body. Some appeared round and black in the middle. My heart started to beat faster as I realized what I was looking at—cigarette burns. Glancing behind me, I saw Lana peeking around the doorway from the living room. Her face too was all screwed up, and I saw hatred all over it. I thought, *this woman is my sister's lover, and I have never spoken ill words to or about her.* In fact, I didn't believe we had said more than a dozen words to each other. I had met her only a few times, once when she and Dora had come to our home in Sandy Town a couple of years earlier and had brought Mama for Thanksgiving. *What hatred for me is she entitled to?*

CHAPTER 148

My Sister's Revenge

I turned to Dora, who was in the darkened hallway taking a long pull of vodka from the bottle. Her bloodshot eyes seemed to glow in the dark. A chill ran down my spine not of fear but of anger. In a drunken gait, she walked toward me and bumped me hard on my head with her shoulder. She continued into the kitchen. "Dora, don't hit me!" I said. She set the vodka bottle on the counter and walked back past me. She hit me in the back of my head with her arm and walked into the hallway. I again said, "Dora, that's enough. Stop hitting me!"

With determination written all over her face, she walked to me again and swung a fist at my face, which I blocked. As she stumbled toward the kitchen counter, I said, "Dora I mean it. Stop hitting me. Come, sit down. Let's talk!" I turned to Samantha and said, "Call 911" just as she was already picking up the phone. Dora picked up the vodka bottle and smashed it on the counter, sending glass and vodka flying everywhere. Holding it by the neck over her head, she charged me and tried to jab the ragged, sharp edges into my face as she screamed, "You fucking pig! I hate you!"

As Dora crashed into me, I grabbed her wrists. Her momentum carried us into the glass table, which shattered under our weight, and we fell. I lay there with Dora on top of me still trying to push the broken bottle into my face. Mama, still seated in her chair, said in a soft and gentle voice, "Now both of you kids stop fighting."

Still holding Dora's wrists, I got to my feet and pulled her up as she made unintelligible noises. She started kicking me in the legs and the genitals. I heard Samantha in a loud, crying voice giving someone the address. Mama was making loud clicking sounds as drool ran down her chin and she was shaking her head slowly from side to side. Lana walked out from behind the doorway with arms raised, fists clenched, and pure evil and hate all over her face. I knew I had to end this before somebody was hurt.

I gave Dora a push, and she fell backward, landing on her butt and hitting her head on the doorjamb but still clutching the broken bottle. Lana knelt beside her saying, "Please don't hurt her." In a quiet and controlled voice, I said, "She's my sister. I'm not going to hurt her." I asked Samantha, "Are they coming?" She said, "Yes, they're on the way." I asked, "Will you be okay?" She said, "I'll be fine." I said, "I'll wait outside." I headed out.

I climbed into our van and rolled the window down. I thought about the incident. I knew she hated me for not having protected her when we were young, but I wasn't sure what she meant by "Fucking pig." Was it because I was a cop, or was it because she hated all men? I thought maybe it was both. The emotion of the moment overcame me. As the pain in my belly increased, I grabbed it and leaned forward. I started to cry from deep inside with the knowledge that we had lost so much of ourselves over the years. I didn't blame Dora for her actions that night, but I wished she would understand that I too was a child just trying to survive back then. When the police and ambulance arrived, I stayed in my van praying that my tormented sister and Mama would be okay.

In about twenty minutes, an officer approached my van. He said, "You did the right thing coming outside and waiting." I replied, "I know, officer. I've been in your shoes before and have given people the same advice." He asked, "You a cop?" I said, "I used to be. I'm retired."

He said I should take my mother out of that apartment; he said he would call for another ambulance and have her taken to the hospital. He also said something that made me shudder; he told me I should bring charges against Dora for elder abuse. I shook my head. I said, "She's had a hard life. I can't bring charges against her, but I will take our mother with us tonight to a hospital."

CHAPTER 149

Mama's Death

We took Mama to the hospital in which three of our kids had been born. The emergency room took her right in and decided to keep her overnight. The doctor who admitted her also told me I should bring charges against my sister for elder abuse. I talked with him for quite a while to explain the situation. In the end, he still said, "You should bring charges against her." I said, "I can't, but I'm going to take care of Mama."

She was kept in the hospital for about two weeks. Every day, we visited her and had good conversations. During one, she told Samantha and me that Dora had tried to get her to have sex with her and Lana. She asked, "What do two girls do with one another?" We just told her we didn't know.

Mama's condition was such that we couldn't give her the care she needed; we had to place her in a nursing home. Samantha felt bad because at one time, Mama had asked Samantha, "Please don't ever let Dora put me in a nursing home." Samantha had promised her that she would not.

We would visit her as often as possible. At first, all she talked about was seeing her Mama and talking to her. At one point, my cousin, his wife, and their daughter came from Louisiana to visit with her. After that visit, she never spoke again.

One day in 1995, Samantha and I had an investigation in Florida. We flew out and had to stay for a week. When we returned, we learned that Mama had suffered a stroke and was in the hospital. They were acting very strange.

I went to the hospital and was told that Dora had taken her out. They said Dora had told them that she was Mama's only living family member and had instructed them to not give out any information to anyone looking for her. I was so angry. I called Dora day and night for two weeks but never got an answer. Samantha and I drove to her apartment, but after banging on the door for what seemed hours, we left.

A week later, Samantha and I had another case in Florida. After being there for a few days, our son Ricky called. I asked, "Did Dora call?" He said, "No, Dad, but your cousin's wife called." I asked, "Did she say what she wanted?" Ricky said, "No, she just said to call her when you get a chance."

I called her a week later. She said, "Johnny, we waited as long as we could. We buried your Mama today." I am not sure exactly how the conversation went after that, but my anger was above boiling. I asked, "Why didn't you tell Ricky she had died?" She said, "I thought you knew." I couldn't talk to her anymore. I hung up.

A few days later, Dora called. Obviously drunk and high, she asked, "So I guess we can't talk anymore, huh?" I said, "Dora, I never want to speak or see you again."

In 1998, Samantha and I had been working so much that we took a much-needed vacation. We went to Louisiana to see Mama's grave. We stayed with my cousin and his wife; they took us to the grave. We had the biggest surprise of all. Dora had died, and Lana had shipped her body to Louisiana; my cousin had had her buried with Mama.

I had so many thoughts. Kneeling beside the grave, I let my tears flow and said, "Mama, Dora, rest in peace. I love both of you."

That night was long. My cousin's wife and I talked. She said that Lana had sent her a box. "I didn't know what to do with it, so I was going to throw it away. Do you want it?" I asked what was in it, and she said, "Some old papers and pictures." I said, "Yeah, I want it."

I looked in and saw a baby picture of Dora and one of me. There were other pictures, including some of my birth mother and my father, a birth certificate for my brother, and other important papers about me and my birth mother and her disappearance.

I couldn't believe what I was holding. I had wanted information on my birth mother ever since I was a kid, and there were some about when she had disappeared. After looking at the contents, my anger rose, and I had to leave. It was obvious that she had seen the contents and was going to throw them away; I wondered how she could have contemplated doing that. I had never known those papers or pictures existed.

Samantha and I left early the next morning to south Florida for a month.

CHAPTER 150

Retirement Times Four

Our business was so busy that for the next four years, we took a one-month vacation in winter in south Florida. In 2002, we had had enough of the gangs, rapes, murders, drugs, and workers' comp cases that we closed our business. Our children had moved out by then and were living on their own.

Owning a big house with four bedrooms became a hindrance instead of a necessity, so we sold it and downsized to a fifty-five-and-over retirement community. I retired as a PI and worked as a security officer at a state university campus nearby. Still not satisfied, I quit and went to work for a courier company driving from Massachusetts, to Pennsylvania daily. Then, I quit the courier company and returned to the state university.

One night while working the four-to-midnight shift at the university, a deep sorrow came over me, and I thought of Samantha and our life together. I became so guilt ridden that I called her. I must have sounded as if I had lost my mind, but as usual, she was calm and collected. I heard the wanting in her voice, the same I had heard for years. I promised her that when I got home, I would tell her what she wanted to know.

I pulled out blank paper and started writing down my memories. I got home, and we talked about incidents I had never revealed to her before. At first, it was very hard because other than my best friend, Grant, I had never told anybody about my life. That was a beginning.

Over the next few years, I spoke more and more to Samantha. I was also still writing about my life. As I would get to certain areas, I would discuss them with Samantha first. The one area she was firm about wanting to know was if my father had sexually abused me. At first, I continued to deny it; I felt it was too personal, and I didn't want to share it. Even after all those years, I still thought the abuse had been the result of something I had done; it had been my fault. Finally, I answered all her questions and told her everything she wanted to know.

I then started using a computer to write. I also searched for my birth mother through the internet but with no success.

I told Samantha I wanted to write a book about my life, and she supported me in that. At first, I tried to write it as a fictional account based on true incidents, but the more I wrote, the more I realized I could not turn my life into fiction. Samantha and I talked it over, and she convinced me to just write it. At that point, I had written pages and pages of jumbled thoughts and remembered facts, but nothing was in order.

During my search for my birth mother, I found a person with her name. I eventually called her, and after talking with her for about an hour, I cried with Samantha, who cried with me.

Samantha and I drove to meet her and two of her sisters. She told me that her father was my birth mother's brother and that she and her sisters were my cousins. Her father had named her after my mother. I told her about all my jumbled written memories, and she also said I should continue writing but to put it in book form. She said that after we had hung up that day, she felt sad because she was sure I thought I had finally found my birth mother and had called her only to find out she wasn't.

For many years, Samantha and I had talked about going to south Florida for the winters. Since we had gone to the western part of Florida, we looked forward to going back. In 2010, we went to Pine Island, Florida, and fell in love with the people and the area. We stayed for a month in our camper.

The following year, we stayed for two months on Pine Island, but that time, we left our camper in storage at the RV park. The following winter, we stayed there for three months and left our camper on a site. The follow year, we started going to Florida for the entire winter.

Samantha and I have now become a part of the RV park's snow bird population; we spend about seven to eight months in Florida. We joined the Pine Island Writers Group. Its writers and published authors have welcomed us as if we too were published authors. Through positive comments, guidance, and encouragement and with Samantha's support, I have now chosen to add a new and exciting chapter to my life. I have become an author starting with my memoir.

EPILOGUE

I have spent most of my life not afraid of death; I just didn't like the idea of being dead. What I could have been doing was preparing for it because it will come all too fast. For the most part, I would have welcomed it, and in fact, I wished for it most times.

I thought of the many times I spent alone deep in thought and wondering why I kept on living, but I could never answer that question. For many years as a child and for many more years, I had pondered it. Often, I thought I was taking on the world as an adult, but I wasn't. My father had never allowed me to play as all children need to do. I never had my right of passage into manhood. I was still a child trapped inside a man's body with childish thoughts, acts, and fears.

From early on, I believed what my father had told me over and over— "You never do anything right, and you'll never amount to anything." I had felt that my life had no purpose and that I had nothing to live for. There is a quote from Maya Angelou that I firmly believe in; "There is no greater agony than bearing an untold story inside you!" I believe if you don't let it out, it will eat you alive.

I wonder how I made it to this day. My memories charge me at breakneck speed. As I brace for the pain and sadness to overwhelm me, I am amazed that both, which I lived with for so long, are absent. Then, I remember I had always been afraid to release my anger because I feared the pain would overpower me.

However, with Samantha's help, the good memories have slowly replaced the bad ones. Absolute, unconditional love has now consumed my life. My wife, children, twelve grandchildren, and the many friends I have made over the years have filled my heart. I have become the good me I had searched for but had withheld from the world and from myself for so long. I realize that this life is a preparation for the next and that a soul should not leave this world without loving and being loved.

I know others have endured lives much worse than mine, but I hope after reading this book, they too can go into the world, help others, and find peace and love along the way. There is so much to live for, and I believe God put all beings on earth for a purpose. I don't know what mine is, and I may never know, but when I die, Cap and I will stand together in front of him, and he will smile on us knowing that we did whatever it was he put us here for.

I cannot believe that one heart can hold so much love. The fact that my father never experienced this is nothing more than a sad punctuation mark that was printed the day I let go of him. Samantha told me to write a letter that listed everything he ever did or said that made me feel less than I knew I was. Pen in hand, I wrote sixteen pages and addressed everything I could remember.

I wrote three more pages that described my successes in detail, and I told him I was all he said I would never be. I let him know that everything he had done to hurt me only ensured my children would never suffer as I had. I believe that was part of God's plan for him. I told him that Samantha and I had built a loving and secure home for our children and ourselves. I wrote that each time one of our children was born, love was multiplied to the point of total capacity. Yet as soon as the next one came along, that capacity grew, and thus so did my heart.

I assured him that I had not lied when I leaned into his coffin, kissed him, and said, "I love you." I explained to him I loved who he was meant to be.

Samantha and I took the letter outside, built a fire, and burned it. As I watched the ashes and smoke rise, I asked God to allow Daddy to know that I was finally letting him go.

Looking to the heavens, I said, "Bent, Daddy, but not broken!"

ABOUT THE AUTHOR

J. C. King grew up in the deep South and served in the Navy during the Vietnam War. He earned a bachelor's degree in law enforcement from Northeastern University. In 1974, he joined a police force and became a sergeant of detectives, retiring in 1991. He went on to become a licensed private investigator, certified clinical/forensic hypnotherapist with the national Guild of Hypnosis and a nondenominational minister with the Congregational Church of Practical Theology. After retiring again in 2002, he became a security officer for a local university before retiring yet again. He spends his winters in Bokeelia, Florida, boating, fishing, relaxing, and writing.

[illegible]

[illegible]

Printed in the United States
By Bookmasters